T0344504

Improving Security, Privacy, and Trust in Cloud Computing

Pawan Kumar Goel
Raj Kumar Goel Institute of Technology, India

Hari Mohan Pandey
Bournemouth University, UK

Amit Singhal
Raj Kumar Goel Institute of Technology, India

Sanyam Agarwal
ACE Group of Colleges, India

A volume in the Advances in
Information Security, Privacy, and
Ethics (AISPE) Book Series

Published in the United States of America by
    IGI Global
    Engineering Science Reference (an imprint of IGI Global)
    701 E. Chocolate Avenue
    Hershey PA, USA 17033
    Tel: 717-533-8845
    Fax: 717-533-8661
    E-mail: cust@igi-global.com
    Web site: http://www.igi-global.com

Library of Congress Cataloging-in-Publication Data

CIP Data in progress

Title: Improved Security, Privacy, and Trust in Cloud Computing

ISBN: 9798369314319

This book is published in the IGI Global book series Advances in Information Security, Privacy, and Ethics (AISPE) (ISSN: 1948-9730; eISSN: 1948-9749)

British Cataloguing in Publication Data
A Cataloguing in Publication record for this book is available from the British Library.

For electronic access to this publication, please contact: eresources@igi-global.com.

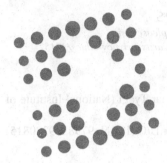

Advances in Information Security, Privacy, and Ethics (AISPE) Book Series

ISSN:1948-9730
EISSN:1948-9749

Editor-in-Chief: Manish Gupta, State University of New York, USA

MISSION

As digital technologies become more pervasive in everyday life and the Internet is utilized in ever increasing ways by both private and public entities, concern over digital threats becomes more prevalent.

The **Advances in Information Security, Privacy, & Ethics (AISPE) Book Series** provides cutting-edge research on the protection and misuse of information and technology across various industries and settings. Comprised of scholarly research on topics such as identity management, cryptography, system security, authentication, and data protection, this book series is ideal for reference by IT professionals, academicians, and upper-level students.

COVERAGE

- Information Security Standards
- Electronic Mail Security
- Global Privacy Concerns
- Privacy-Enhancing Technologies
- Data Storage of Minors
- Access Control
- CIA Triad of Information Security
- IT Risk
- Privacy Issues of Social Networking
- Computer ethics

IGI Global is currently accepting manuscripts for publication within this series. To submit a proposal for a volume in this series, please contact our Acquisition Editors at Acquisitions@igi-global.com or visit: http://www.igi-global.com/publish/.

Titles in this Series

For a list of additional titles in this series, please visit:
www.igi-global.com/book-series/advances-information-security-privacy-ethics/37157

Emerging Technologies and Security in Cloud Computing
D. Lakshmi (VIT Bhopal University, India) and Amit Kumar Tyagi (National Institute of Fashion Technology, New Delhi, India)
Information Science Reference • copyright 2024 • 400pp • H/C (ISBN: 9798369320815) • US $315.00 (our price)

Risk Detection and Cyber Security for the Success of Contemporary Computing
Raghvendra Kumar (GIET University, India) and Prasant Kumar Pattnaik (KIIT Univeristy, India)
Information Science Reference • copyright 2023 • 480pp • H/C (ISBN: 9781668493175) • US $225.00 (our price)

Privacy Preservation and Secured Data Storage in Cloud Computing
Lakshmi D. (VIT Bhopal University, India) and Amit Kumar Tyagi (National Institute of Fashion Technology, New Delhi, India)
Engineering Science Reference • copyright 2023 • 516pp • H/C (ISBN: 9798369305935) • US $265.00 (our price)

Contemporary Challenges for Cyber Security and Data Privacy
Nuno Mateus-Coelho (Lusófona University, Portugal) and Maria Manuela Cruz-Cunha (Polytechnic Institute of Cávado and Ave, Portugal)
Information Science Reference • copyright 2023 • 308pp • H/C (ISBN: 9798369315286) • US $275.00 (our price)

For an entire list of titles in this series, please visit:
www.igi-global.com/book-series/advances-information-security-privacy-ethics/37157

701 East Chocolate Avenue, Hershey, PA 17033, USA
Tel: 717-533-8845 x100 • Fax: 717-533-8661
E-Mail: cust@igi-global.com • www.igi-global.com

This book is dedicated to those who embrace the challenges of the digital frontier with a commitment to integrity, innovation, and the well-being of individuals and organizations alike.

To the pioneers pushing the boundaries of technology, may your vision and resilience continue to shape the future of cloud computing, ensuring it becomes a beacon of security, privacy, and trust for generations to come.

To the guardians of privacy, who champion the rights of individuals in the digital age, may your efforts inspire a culture of respect for personal data and the fundamental principles of autonomy.

To the stewards of trust, who build bridges between users, providers, and stakeholders, may your dedication to transparency and accountability pave the way for robust and enduring partnerships in the evolving landscape of cloud services.

To the families and loved ones who provide unwavering support, understanding, and encouragement, this work stands as a tribute to your enduring patience and belief in the pursuit of knowledge.

May this book contribute to a collective understanding of the intricate dance between technology and humanity, fostering a world where the cloud serves as a catalyst for progress, safeguarded by the principles of security, privacy, and trust.

Table of Contents

Preface.. xv

Acknowledgment xvii

Introduction.. xix

Chapter 1
Securing Cloud Infrastructure in IaaS and PaaS Environments 1

*Ashok Kumar Nanda, Department of Computer Science and
    Engineering, B.V. Raju Institute of Technology, India*
*Abhishek Sharma, Department of Computer Science Engineering, Shri
    Vaishnav Vidyapeeth Vishwavidyalaya, India*
*P. John Augustine, Department of Information Technology, Sri Eshwar
    College of Engineering, India*
*B. Rex Cyril, Department of Computer Science, St. Joseph's College
    (Autonomous), India*
*Venneti Kiran, Department of Computer Science and Engineering
    (AIML), Aditya College of Engineering, Surampalem, India*
*Boopathi Sampath, Mechanical Engineering, Mythayammal
    Engineering College (Autonomous), India*

Chapter 2
Impact of Artificial Intelligence and Machine Learning in Cloud Security 34

I. Eugene Berna, Bannari Amman Institute of Technology, India
K. Vijay, Rajalakshmi Engineering College, India
*S. Gnanavel, Department of Computing Technologies, SRM Institute of
    Science and Technology-Kattankulathur, India*
J. Jeyalakshmi, Amrita VishwaVidhyapeetham, India

Chapter 3
An Intelligent Data Retrieving Technique and Safety Measures for
Sustainable Cloud Computing 59
    Keshav Kumar, Haldia Institute of Technology, India
    Krishan Kundan Kumar, Haldia Institute of Technology, India
    Ritam Chatterjee, Haldia Institute of Technology, India
    Ritam Kundu, Haldia Institute of Technology, India
    Santanu Koley, Haldia Institute of Technology, India
    Pinaki Pratim Acharjya, Haldia Institute of Technology, India

Chapter 4
Enhancing Cloud Security: The Role of Artificial Intelligence and Machine
Learning 85
    Tarun Kumar Vashishth, IIMT University, India
    Vikas Sharma, IIMT University, India
    Kewal Krishan Sharma, IIMT University, India
    Bhupendra Kumar, IIMT University, India
    Sachin Chaudhary, IIMT University, India
    Rajneesh Panwar, IIMT University, India

Chapter 5
Role-Based access Control (RBAC) and Attribute-Based Access Control
(ABAC) 113
    Javed Akhtar Khan, Gyan Ganga College of Technology, India

Chapter 6
Application of Artificial Intelligence in Cybersecurity 127
    Geetika Munjal, Amity Univesity, Noida, India
    Biswarup Paul, Amity Univesity, Noida, India
    Manoj Kumar, University of Wollongong, UAE

Chapter 7
Accountable Malicious Entity Detection Using Re-Encryption Mechanism to
Share Data 147
    S. T. Veena, Mepco Schlenk Engineering College, India
    N. R. Somnath Babu, Mepco Schlenk Engineering Collge, India
    P. Santosh, Mepco Schlenk Engineering Collge, India

Chapter 8
Balancing Innovation and Security in the Cloud: Navigating the Risks and
Rewards of the Digital Age..164
    S. Boopathi, Mechanical Engineering, Muthayammal Engineering
       College (Autonomous), India

Chapter 9
Data Storage and Transmission Security in the Cloud: The Artificial
Intelligence (AI) Edge...194
    Ankita Nayak, KIIT University, India
    Atmika Patnaik, King's College, India
    Ipseeta Satpathy, KIIT University, India
    B. C. M. Patnaik, KIIT University, India

Chapter 10
Privacy and Surveillance in Digital Era: A Case for India 213
    Vikram Singh, Ch. Devi Lal University, Sirsa, India
    Sanyogita Singh, Panjab University, India

Chapter 11
A Model for Trust Decision, Data Analysis, and Evaluation to Identify
Quality Web Services...239
    Shobhana Kashyap, National Institute of Technology, Jalandhar, India
    Avtar Singh, National Institute of Technology, Jalandhar, India

Compilation of References 266

About the Contributors 293

Index...297

Detailed Table of Contents

Preface xv

Acknowledgment xvii

Introduction xix

Chapter 1
Securing Cloud Infrastructure in IaaS and PaaS Environments 1

    Ashok Kumar Nanda, Department of Computer Science and
        Engineering, B.V. Raju Institute of Technology, India
    Abhishek Sharma, Department of Computer Science Engineering, Shri
        Vaishnav Vidyapeeth Vishwavidyalaya, India
    P. John Augustine, Department of Information Technology, Sri Eshwar
        College of Engineering, India
    B. Rex Cyril, Department of Computer Science, St. Joseph's College
        (Autonomous), India
    Venneti Kiran, Department of Computer Science and Engineering
        (AIML), Aditya College of Engineering, Surampalem, India
    Boopathi Sampath, Mechanical Engineering, Mythayammal
        Engineering College (Autonomous), India

Cloud computing has revolutionized IT infrastructure deployment and management, but it also presents security and resilience challenges. The study delves into the principles and strategies of cloud security to safeguard cloud environments and guarantee business continuity. It explains the concepts of infrastructure as a service (IaaS) and platform as a service (PaaS), their benefits and challenges, and the complex web of security principles within the cloud, including the shared responsibility model, best practices, and identity and access management. The guide explores cloud threats, focusing on common threats and emerging trends. It covers data security, network security measures, and security monitoring. It emphasizes integrating security into DevOps, securing CI/CD pipelines, and infrastructure as code (IaC) security. It covers disaster recovery, business continuity, cloud backup strategies, high availability, and cloud-based solutions, enabling organizations to effectively manage cloud security and resilience.

Chapter 2
Impact of Artificial Intelligence and Machine Learning in Cloud Security 34

    I. Eugene Berna, Bannari Amman Institute of Technology, India
    K. Vijay, Rajalakshmi Engineering College, India
    S. Gnanavel, Department of Computing Technologies, SRM Institute of
       Science and Technology-Kattankulathur, India
    J. Jeyalakshmi, Amrita VishwaVidhyapeetham, India

The rapid advancement of artificial intelligence (AI) and machine learning (ML) technologies has had a significant impact on cloud security, as it has in many other sectors. This abstract examines how AI and ML are affecting cloud security, highlighting their major contributions, difficulties, and potential. Traditional approaches to cloud security provide improved threat detection, real-time monitoring, and adaptive defense mechanisms. These technologies are adept at processing enormous volumes of data, allowing them to spot trends, anomalies, and potential dangers that more traditional security measures would miss. In order to quickly identify and take appropriate action in response to unauthorised access, data breaches, and other malicious activities, AI-driven systems can quickly analyse user behaviour, network behaviour, and system logs. It introduces complexity in the form of adversarial assaults, model interpretability, and data privacy issues. For users to trust AI-driven security systems and to comprehend their decision-making processes, openness of these systems is essential.

Chapter 3
An Intelligent Data Retrieving Technique and Safety Measures for
Sustainable Cloud Computing 59

    Keshav Kumar, Haldia Institute of Technology, India
    Krishan Kundan Kumar, Haldia Institute of Technology, India
    Ritam Chatterjee, Haldia Institute of Technology, India
    Ritam Kundu, Haldia Institute of Technology, India
    Santanu Koley, Haldia Institute of Technology, India
    Pinaki Pratim Acharjya, Haldia Institute of Technology, India

Data refers to raw facts and figures. After processing data, the information is created. Information like facts or statistics that can be recorded, stored, and analysed can be in various forms such as text, numbers, images, audio, or video. The amount of data generated every day in the data-driven world of today makes it nearly difficult to keep it all locally. Cloud services are being used by so many people and businesses to store these massive and hefty volumes of data on cloud servers. Additionally, as the need for cloud computing grows, so does the need for data recovery methods and services. The ability to recover data and information from the backup server when the primary server is down is the primary goal of recovery services and technologies. A secondary server to hold backups for the primary cloud server will be more expensive to add than the primary server itself, which is already quite expensive and time-consuming to build. The goal of this chapter is to provide realistic, cost-effective solutions to this urgent problem.

Chapter 4

Enhancing Cloud Security: The Role of Artificial Intelligence and Machine

Learning 85

Tarun Kumar Vashishth, IIMT University, India
Vikas Sharma, IIMT University, India
Kewal Krishan Sharma, IIMT University, India
Bhupendra Kumar, IIMT University, India
Sachin Chaudhary, IIMT University, India
Rajneesh Panwar, IIMT University, India

Cloud computing has revolutionized the way organizations store, process, and manage data, offering flexibility and scalability. However, the rise in cyber threats poses significant challenges to maintaining robust cloud security. This chapter delves into the pivotal role that Artificial Intelligence (AI) and Machine Learning (ML) play in enhancing cloud security. By harnessing the capabilities of AI and ML, organizations can proactively detect, mitigate, and respond to evolving cyber threats, ultimately fortifying their cloud infrastructure. AI-driven techniques empower security systems to recognize patterns, anomalies, and potential threats within vast datasets. ML algorithms can learn from historical attack data, enabling the prediction of future threats and the development of more effective defense mechanisms. Moreover, AI-enhanced authentication and access control mechanisms bolster identity management, reducing the risk of unauthorized access and data breaches.

Chapter 5

Role-Based access Control (RBAC) and Attribute-Based Access Control

(ABAC) 113

Javed Akhtar Khan, Gyan Ganga College of Technology, India

This chapter explores the profound impact of artificial intelligence (AI) and machine learning (ML) on the realm of cloud security. As organizations increasingly migrate their operations and data to cloud environments, ensuring robust security measures becomes paramount. The integration of AI and ML technologies introduces novel ways to enhance threat detection, prevention, and response in the cloud. This chapter delves into various aspects of this synergy, discussing the benefits, challenges, and future prospects of utilizing AI and ML for safeguarding cloud infrastructures. This chapter also presents the benefits, challenges, and future directions. This abstract underscores the transformative potential of AI and ML in fortifying cloud infrastructures and safeguarding sensitive information in the digital age.

Chapter 6

Application of Artificial Intelligence in Cybersecurity 127

Geetika Munjal, Amity Univesity, Noida, India

Biswarup Paul, Amity Univesity, Noida, India

Manoj Kumar, University of Wollongong, UAE

Cybersecurity is the knowledge and practice of defending computers, mobile devices, servers, electronic devices, networks, and precious data from malicious attacks. Traditional security methods have advantages in various ways, but they may sometimes seem to be ineffective due to lack of intelligence and vitality to meet the current diverse needs of the network industry thus latest techniques need to be developed to handle these threats. The developments in Artificial intelligent (AI) techniques have simplified life by providing efficient solutions in different domains including cyber security. This chapter has reviewed existing tools of cyber security, highlighting different ways artificial intelligence can be applied in providing Cybersecurity solutions. AI-based security systems make decisions for helping people, it is particularly worrying that these systems do not currently have any moral code thus current chapter also highlights the need to ethical code in providing AI solution for cyber security.

Chapter 7

Accountable Malicious Entity Detection Using Re-Encryption Mechanism to Share Data..147

S. T. Veena, Mepco Schlenk Engineering College, India

N. R. Somnath Babu, Mepco Schlenk Engineering Collge, India

P. Santosh, Mepco Schlenk Engineering Collge, India

Recently data sharing through the cloud is widely used and becoming a trend. But protecting data confidentiality and integrity is essential. Data confidentiality and integrity are maintained using cryptography. However, since it cannot ensure that the data hasn't been altered, there is still a trust issue. The proxy re-encryption (PRE) technique was presented as a solution to this. It includes encrypting the data twice, allowing one to determine whether or not it has been altered. The PRE system is also prone to attacks that forge re-encryption keys. Here the data is encrypted twice so that the data can be checked whether it is modified or not. But the PRE system is prone to the abuse of re-encryption keys. Therefore, accountable proxy re-encryption (APRE) is proposed. Here, if the data is altered by proxy, the system will detect whether proxy is malicious or the delegator is trying to frame proxy as malicious. Also, the authors extend the algorithm and implemented base64 encoding and decoding. This prevents many passive cyber attacks.

Chapter 8
Balancing Innovation and Security in the Cloud: Navigating the Risks and
Rewards of the Digital Age...164
    S. Boopathi, Mechanical Engineering, Muthayammal Engineering
        College (Autonomous), India

This chapter delves into the intricate relationship between innovation and security in the digital age. It highlights the challenges of the digital age and the transformative impact of cloud computing, emphasizing its role in driving innovation. The chapter also delves into cloud service and deployment models, discussing the benefits and challenges of cloud security. It also discusses the role of innovation in driving progress through case studies and addressing challenges organizations face. The chapter also discusses risk assessment and mitigation in the cloud, compliance, regulatory challenges, legal and ethical considerations, and best practices. It also explores emerging technologies like AI and machine learning, Zero Trust security, and future directions.

Chapter 9
Data Storage and Transmission Security in the Cloud: The Artificial
Intelligence (AI) Edge..194
    Ankita Nayak, KIIT University, India
    Atmika Patnaik, King's College, India
    Ipseeta Satpathy, KIIT University, India
    B. C. M. Patnaik, KIIT University, India

Cloud computing has profoundly changed the face of data management for enterprises, providing increased scalability, ease of access, and cost savings. Nonetheless, this change has highlighted the crucial need for strengthened security measures to protect sensitive data from the ever-changing spectrum of cyber threats. Following the cloud's rise as a storehouse for large datasets, the quest for sophisticated security solutions has gained traction. This motivation has resulted in the incorporation of artificial intelligence (AI) into the cloud security architecture. As cloud storage becomes increasingly popular, organizations are becoming more concerned about data security. Sensitive data is transmitted, ranging from messages and images to financial and health information. As technology advances, there is a growing threat to customer data in the cloud, making greater cloud security more important than ever. This study aims to give a comprehensive insight into the role of AI in data storage and transmission security in the cloud.

Chapter 10
Privacy and Surveillance in Digital Era: A Case for India 213
    Vikram Singh, Ch. Devi Lal University, Sirsa, India
    Sanyogita Singh, Panjab University, India

With a majority of the human population on the internet, online activity has become the order of the day. And that is why the internet is where criminals of every hue and color join forces and innovate in innovative ways. Not all "lands" have laws to deal with cybersecurity and privacy. Criminals across the globe have exploited the gap between technology and laws. The Indian Constitution recognizes privacy as a fundamental right, albeit with certain restrictions. Governments, in the name of providing secure cyberspace, infringe upon the privacy rights of citizens. And surveillance in India is chiefly governed by the Indian Telegraph Act u/s 5, which permits the government and its agencies to surveil provided a qualifying prerequisite preexists. Various surveillance apparatuses have been established by the GoI. Allegedly, the surveillance regime poses a grave threat and a chilling effect on privacy and freedom of expression rights as enshrined in the Indian Constitution. This chapter discusses cybersecurity, privacy, and surveillance regimes in Indian cyberspace.

Chapter 11
A Model for Trust Decision, Data Analysis, and Evaluation to Identify
Quality Web Services..239
Shobhana Kashyap, National Institute of Technology, Jalandhar, India
Avtar Singh, National Institute of Technology, Jalandhar, India

Cloud computing has emerged as a powerful paradigm for delivering web services, and includes scalability, flexibility, and cost efficiency. Due to functional overlap and diversity, web services form a major challenge for selecting adequate services to develop user-provider trust. To address the issue, this study presented a machine learning based trusted model to assist users in selecting trustworthy web services. In the initial stage, using K-Means clustering method the services are selected based on three clusters such as high, medium, and low trust. Next, the trust score is generated by evaluating performance parameters to identify the best services. Experiments conducted with QWS datasets demonstrate that the proposed approach efficiently predicts adequate services with a minimum error rate and high accuracy gain. This technique achieves a 99.32%, 99.36% and 99.48% accuracy rates for the low, medium, and high trust prediction, respectively. The result shows that it is more effective than existing approaches and builds a strong trust relation between users and providers.

Compilation of References 266

About the Contributors 293

Index...297

Preface

In the dynamic landscape of contemporary computing, the migration to cloud platforms has ushered in unprecedented opportunities for innovation, efficiency, and collaboration. The vast potential of cloud computing, however, comes hand in hand with intricate challenges, most notably in the realms of security, privacy, and trust. As organizations increasingly entrust their critical data and operations to the cloud, it becomes imperative to address and enhance the foundational elements that underpin the integrity and reliability of these digital ecosystems.

This book, *Improving Security, Privacy, and Trust in Cloud Computing*, delves into the multifaceted dimensions of cloud computing, exploring the intricacies of safeguarding data, preserving privacy, and fostering trust in cloud-based environments. Through a comprehensive examination of current practices, emerging technologies, and future trends, this volume serves as a valuable resource for practitioners, researchers, and decision-makers navigating the intricate intersection of cloud computing and security.

The journey begins with a thorough exploration of the evolving landscape of cloud computing, setting the stage for a nuanced understanding of the challenges and opportunities it presents. We navigate the intricate web of security concerns, from data breaches to identity theft, and examine how cutting-edge encryption, authentication, and access control mechanisms can fortify the cloud against cyber threats.

The importance of privacy in the digital age cannot be overstated, and within these pages, we dissect the nuanced interplay between cloud computing and individual privacy rights. With a critical eye on regulations and ethical considerations, we explore strategies to strike a delicate balance between leveraging the power of cloud services and protecting the sensitive information they harbor.

Trust forms the bedrock of any successful cloud ecosystem, and we delve into the mechanisms that can be employed to cultivate and sustain trust in the digital realm. From robust service-level agreements to transparent auditing frameworks, this book provides insights into how organizations can build and maintain trust with their stakeholders in the cloud era.

As we embark on this exploration, it is our sincere hope that the insights and knowledge shared within these pages will contribute to the ongoing dialogue surrounding security, privacy, and trust in cloud computing. By fostering a deeper understanding of the challenges and solutions, we aim to empower individuals and organizations to harness the full potential of cloud computing while navigating the complexities of the digital landscape responsibly and securely.

Pawan Kumar Goel
Raj Kumar Goel Institute of Technology, India

Hari Mohan Pandey
Bournemouth University, UK

Amit Singhal
Raj Kumar Goel Institute of Technology, India

Sanyam Agarwal
ACE Group of Colleges, India

Acknowledgment

The creation of this book, "Improving Security, Privacy, and Trust in Cloud Computing," has been a collaborative journey that would not have been possible without the support, expertise, and encouragement of numerous individuals and institutions. As we reflect on the completion of this project, we extend our heartfelt gratitude to those who have played a pivotal role in bringing this endeavor to fruition.

First and foremost, we express our sincere appreciation to our families for their unwavering support and understanding throughout the countless hours dedicated to research, writing, and revision. Their encouragement has been a source of inspiration, and their patience has been a constant reminder of the importance of balance in our lives.

We extend our gratitude to our colleagues and peers whose insightful discussions, constructive feedback, and shared experiences have enriched the content of this book. The exchange of ideas and perspectives has been invaluable, shaping the depth and breadth of our exploration into the intricate domains of cloud security, privacy, and trust.

A special acknowledgment goes to the dedicated professionals in the field of cloud computing who generously shared their expertise and experiences. Their real-world insights and practical knowledge have added a layer of authenticity to our discussions, ensuring that the content remains relevant and applicable to the challenges faced by organizations and individuals in the rapidly evolving landscape of cloud technology.

We express our thanks to the editorial and production teams whose diligence and expertise have transformed our manuscript into a polished and well-presented work. Their commitment to excellence and attention to detail have been instrumental in delivering a final product that meets the highest standards.

Our gratitude extends to the academic and research institutions that have provided the intellectual environment and resources necessary for the development of this book. The pursuit of knowledge is a collective endeavor, and we are fortunate to be part of communities that foster innovation, curiosity, and academic rigor.

Finally, we extend our thanks to the readers who embark on this journey with us. Your interest in the topics covered within these pages is a testament to the relevance and importance of addressing the multifaceted challenges of security, privacy, and trust in cloud computing.

In conclusion, the completion of this book is a testament to the collaborative efforts of many, and we are deeply grateful for the support and contributions of each individual and institution involved. May this work contribute to the ongoing discourse and advancements in the field, ultimately fostering a more secure, private, and trustworthy cloud computing landscape for all.

Editorial Advisory Board

Sanyam Aggarwal, *ACE College of Engg. & Mgmt., Agra, India*

Pawan Kumar Goel, *Raj Kumar Goel Institute of Technology, Ghaziabad, India*

Hari Mohan Pandey, *Bournemouth University, United Kingdom*

Amit Singhal, *Raj Kumar Goel Institute of Technology, Ghaziabad, India*

Introduction

In an era where the cloud is the linchpin of our digital infrastructure, the confluence of technology and trust has never been more vital. As we navigate the vast landscape of cloud computing, its potential to revolutionize the way we store, process, and share information is undeniable. Yet, with great innovation comes great responsibility, and the imperative to fortify the pillars of security, privacy, and trust has never been more pressing.

Improving Security, Privacy, and Trust in Cloud Computing is a timely and comprehensive exploration of the critical considerations that underscore the marriage of cloud technology and the imperatives of a secure, private, and trustworthy digital environment. In these pages, the authors bring together a wealth of knowledge, expertise, and insights, providing a roadmap for both seasoned professionals and those new to the evolving complexities of cloud security.

The landscape of cloud computing is continually evolving, and this book serves as a beacon, guiding us through the shifting tides of challenges and opportunities. The authors eloquently articulate the nuanced interplay between security and innovation, emphasizing the need for robust frameworks that not only protect against cyber threats but also empower organizations to leverage the transformative potential of the cloud.

Privacy, often regarded as the cornerstone of personal freedom in the digital age, takes center stage in this exploration. The book navigates the intricate terrain of data protection, regulatory compliance, and ethical considerations, offering pragmatic approaches to ensuring that individuals' privacy rights are preserved even in the cloud's expansive domain.

Trust, the linchpin that binds users, providers, and stakeholders, is dissected and analyzed in granular detail. The authors unravel the intricacies of building and sustaining trust in an environment where data traverses virtual boundaries, emphasizing the importance of transparency, accountability, and collaboration.

As we stand at the crossroads of technological innovation and societal impact, this book serves as a guidepost, offering a forward-looking perspective on the evolving landscape of cloud security. The authors skillfully bridge the gap between theory and practice, providing real-world examples, case studies, and practical insights that empower readers to not only understand the challenges but to actively engage in fortifying the cloud against emerging threats.

We commend the authors for their dedication to demystifying the complexities of cloud security, privacy, and trust. This book is a testament to their commitment to advancing the discourse on these critical issues and providing a valuable resource for anyone seeking to navigate the ever-changing landscape of cloud computing responsibly and effectively.

May this book serve as a beacon, illuminating the path toward a future where cloud computing is synonymous with security, privacy, and trust.

Pawan Kumar Goel
Raj Kumar Goel Institute of Technology, India

Hari Mohan Pandey
Bournemouth University, UK

Amit Singhal
Raj Kumar Goel Institute of Technology, India

Sanyam Agarwal
ACE Group of Colleges, India

Chapter 1
Securing Cloud Infrastructure in IaaS and PaaS Environments

Ashok Kumar Nanda
Department of Computer Science and Engineering, B.V. Raju Institute of Technology, India

Abhishek Sharma
Department of Computer Science Engineering, Shri Vaishnav Vidyapeeth Vishwavidyalaya, India

P. John Augustine
Department of Information Technology, Sri Eshwar College of Engineering, India

B. Rex Cyril
Department of Computer Science, St. Joseph's College (Autonomous), India

Venneti Kiran
Department of Computer Science and Engineering (AIML), Aditya College of Engineering, Surampalem, India

Boopathi Sampath
Mechanical Engineering, Mythayammal Engineering College (Autonomous), India

ABSTRACT

Cloud computing has revolutionized IT infrastructure deployment and management, but it also presents security and resilience challenges. The study delves into the principles and strategies of cloud security to safeguard cloud environments and guarantee business continuity. It explains the concepts of infrastructure as a service (IaaS) and platform as a service (PaaS), their benefits and challenges, and the complex web of security principles within the cloud, including the shared responsibility model, best practices, and identity and access management. The guide explores cloud threats, focusing on common threats and emerging trends. It covers data security, network security measures, and security monitoring. It emphasizes integrating security into DevOps, securing CI/CD pipelines, and infrastructure as code (IaC) security. It covers disaster recovery, business continuity, cloud backup strategies, high availability, and cloud-based solutions, enabling organizations to effectively manage cloud security and resilience.

DOI: 10.4018/979-8-3693-1431-9.ch001

1. INTRODUCTION

Cloud computing, a key player in digital transformation, has revolutionized IT resource management through Infrastructure as a Service (IaaS) and Platform as a Service (PaaS) offerings. However, this has raised concerns about security, as organizations must navigate the potential risks associated with these cloud environments. Securing cloud infrastructure in IaaS and PaaS environments is no longer a peripheral consideration but an essential aspect of modern business operations. This book chapter provides a comprehensive guide to navigating the security challenges and opportunities associated with cloud migration, focusing on the shared responsibility model between cloud service providers and customers, enabling organizations to effectively utilize cloud computing(Saini et al., 2022).

Cloud security is a multifaceted discipline that demands a deep understanding of cloud service models, a vigilant approach to threat detection, and a proactive strategy for risk mitigation. In this book, we will explore the foundational principles of cloud security, delve into the evolving threat landscape, and dissect the best practices that organizations must adopt to protect their cloud assets. Whether you are a seasoned cloud practitioner or a newcomer to the cloud space, the insights and strategies presented here will equip you with the knowledge and tools needed to safeguard your digital assets in the cloud. The cloud, with its inherent benefits of flexibility, scalability, and cost-efficiency, has revolutionized the way organizations operate. This book explores the shared responsibility model for cloud security, focusing on Identity and Access Management (IAM), data security, network security, security monitoring, and incident response. It emphasizes the need for a transformation in security practices, ensuring the security of cloud resources for both providers and customers(Isharufe et al., 2020).

Moreover, we will discuss compliance and auditing in cloud environments, emphasizing the importance of adhering to regulatory requirements and standards. We will delve into secure DevOps and automation practices, recognizing that security must be integrated into every aspect of the development and deployment pipeline. This book explores disaster recovery and business continuity in the cloud to ensure organizations remain resilient. It also looks at future trends and challenges in cloud security, emphasizing the importance of understanding these dynamics to stay ahead of the curve in the constantly evolving cloud landscape(Bhajantri & Mujawar, 2019).

By the end of this book, you will be equipped with the knowledge and tools to confidently navigate the complex terrain of securing cloud infrastructure in IaaS and PaaS environments. With a strong foundation in cloud security principles and practical guidance, you'll be well-prepared to harness the full potential of the cloud while mitigating the associated risks. In the realm of modern technology, cloud computing stands as a towering innovation, reshaping the way businesses and individuals' access, store, and utilize digital resources(Parast et al., 2022). At its core, cloud computing represents a dynamic shift away from traditional computing paradigms. It offers unparalleled scalability, flexibility, and efficiency, enabling organizations to transform their IT infrastructure and adapt to the ever-evolving digital landscape. Cloud computing, in its essence, is a paradigm where data, applications, and computing resources are no longer tethered to local hardware but are instead delivered as services over the internet. The shift in technology liberates users from physical infrastructure constraints, promoting agility, cost-effectiveness, and accessibility, enabling businesses to innovate, individuals to collaborate, and industries to evolve(Mukhopadhyay et al., 2020).

The advent of cloud computing has democratized access to advanced computing capabilities, making it a powerful equalizer. Small startups can now access the same computing muscle as large corporations, and individuals can harness vast computational resources without the need for specialized hardware. It enables innovation by providing an easily accessible platform for development, data analysis, artificial intelligence, and much more(Alghofaili et al., 2021). This introduction serves as a gateway to the vast landscape of cloud computing. We will embark on a journey through the layers of cloud services, from Infrastructure as a Service (IaaS) to Software as a Service (SaaS). We will unravel the principles of cloud architecture, the models of service delivery, and the benefits and challenges that come with this transformative technology. Whether you are a seasoned IT professional or someone new to the cloud, this exploration will equip you with the foundational knowledge needed to understand, navigate, and leverage the potential of cloud computing(Achar, 2021).

This document delves into the various aspects of cloud computing, including service models, deployment options, security, compliance, and governance. It also discusses disruptive innovations and the future of cloud computing in a rapidly evolving digital landscape. The goal is to equip readers with the knowledge to make informed decisions about cloud adoption, strategy, and utilization. Cloud computing is not just a technology, but a fundamental shift in our digital world, and this document serves as a guide to embracing its transformative potential(George & Sagayarajan, 2023). In an era defined by the digital revolution, organizations worldwide have embarked on a transformative journey into the cloud. Cloud computing has ushered in a new paradigm, offering unprecedented levels of agility, scalability, and cost-efficiency. It has empowered businesses to thrive in a fast-paced, globally interconnected world, but as with any advancement, it brings a unique set of challenges, chief among them being the paramount issue of cloud security. The importance of cloud security cannot be overstated. As businesses increasingly entrust their most sensitive data, applications, and workloads to cloud environments, the need for robust and comprehensive security measures has become a pressing concern. The cloud's shared responsibility model, which divides security responsibilities between cloud service providers and their customers, underscores the need for a diligent and well-informed approach to safeguarding digital assets(Jyoti et al., 2020; Shahid et al., 2020).

This document delves into the complex world of cloud security, its importance, and the ever-evolving threats and vulnerabilities. The stakes are high as data breaches, compliance violations, and cyberattacks continue to emerge. The reliance on the cloud for business-critical operations and the growing digital attack surface have elevated security to a paramount concern. The document covers various aspects of cloud security, including identity and access management, data protection, network security, incident response, and compliance. It serves as a comprehensive guide for organizations and individuals embracing cloud security(Gozman & Willcocks, 2019; RM et al., 2020).

The cloud is a transformative shift in organizational operations, collaboration, and innovation, with security at its core. It ensures the benefits of the cloud, such as flexibility, efficiency, and innovation, without compromising confidentiality, integrity, and information availability. The journey to understand and implement cloud security is dynamic and evolving, and this document provides guidance on this crucial landscape.

2. FUNDAMENTALS OF IAAS AND PAAS

2.1 Infrastructure as a Service (IaaS)

Infrastructure as a Service (IaaS) is a cloud computing service model that provides virtualized computing resources over the internet. With IaaS, organizations can access and manage fundamental IT infrastructure components, such as virtual machines, storage, and networking, without the need to invest in and maintain physical hardware. IaaS platforms provide on-demand scalability, allowing users to provision and de-provision resources as needed. This shift from on-premises to cloud provides greater flexibility, cost-efficiency, and agility for businesses. Customers retain control over operating system, middleware, and applications(George & Sagayarajan, 2023).

2.2 Platform as a Service (PaaS)

Platform as a Service (PaaS) is another cloud service model that builds on the foundation of IaaS. PaaS provides a higher level of abstraction, offering a platform and environment for application development, deployment, and management. PaaS (Platform as a Service) allows developers to focus on code writing and maintenance without worrying about infrastructure or operational tasks. It includes development tools, databases, application hosting, and runtime environments, facilitating collaborative development, version control, and automated scaling(Isharufe et al., 2020).

2.3 Benefits and Challenges of IaaS and PaaS

Both IaaS and PaaS offer numerous benefits to organizations(Alghofaili et al., 2021; Mukhopadhyay et al., 2020; Parast et al., 2022):

- **Scalability:** IaaS and PaaS platforms allow businesses to scale resources up or down based on demand, which is cost-effective and ensures optimal performance.
- **Cost Savings:** By eliminating the need for extensive on-premises infrastructure, organizations can reduce capital expenditures and operational costs.
- **Flexibility:** IaaS and PaaS support a wide range of applications and workloads, making them adaptable to various business needs.
- **Speed and Agility:** These cloud service models enable rapid provisioning and deployment of resources and applications.
- **Simplicity:** PaaS, in particular, simplifies development and deployment, reducing the complexity of managing infrastructure.

However, there are also challenges to consider:

- **Security and Compliance:** Cloud security is a significant concern, and ensuring data protection and compliance can be complex.
- **Dependency on Providers:** Organizations depend on cloud service providers, which can introduce vendor lock-in and availability concerns.
- **Integration:** Migrating existing applications and data to the cloud can be challenging and requires careful planning.
- **Cost Management:** While cloud services can reduce costs, they can also lead to unexpected expenses if not carefully managed.

Understanding the fundamental aspects of IaaS and PaaS is crucial for making informed decisions about cloud services adoption and optimization within an organization. Both models offer transformative capabilities, but they also present unique considerations and challenges.

3. SECURITY PRINCIPLES IN THE CLOUD

3.1 Shared Responsibility Model

The Shared Responsibility Model is a crucial concept in cloud security, dividing security responsibilities between cloud service providers (CSPs) and cloud customers. CSPs are responsible for securing cloud infrastructure and services, while customers are responsible for securing data, applications, and configurations placed on the cloud. The summary provides a detailed breakdown of the responsibilities(Gozman & Willcocks, 2019; Rayhan & Rayhan, 2023; RM et al., 2020).

- **CSP Responsibilities:** The cloud provider is responsible for the security "of" the cloud, including the underlying infrastructure, physical security, and the security of the cloud services they offer. This encompasses network security, server and data center protection, and ensuring the availability and reliability of the services.
- **Customer Responsibilities:** Cloud customers are responsible for the security "in" the cloud. This includes securing their data, applications, operating systems, configurations, and access control. Customers are also accountable for compliance with relevant regulations and best practices. They must implement security measures, identity and access management, encryption, and monitoring to protect their assets in the cloud.

The Shared Responsibility Model emphasizes that cloud security is a collaborative effort, emphasizing the importance of understanding the division of responsibilities for effective risk mitigation.

3.2 Security Best Practices

The text emphasizes the importance of implementing robust security practices to safeguard cloud environments, outlining several practices for cloud security(Kavitha et al., 2023; Rahamathunnisa, Subhashini, et al., 2023; Srinivas et al., 2023).

- **Access Control:** Employ strict access control policies to ensure that only authorized users and systems have access to cloud resources. Utilize role-based access control (RBAC) and implement strong authentication methods, like multi-factor authentication (MFA).
- **Data Encryption:** Encrypt data both in transit and at rest. Use encryption protocols and ensure proper key management to safeguard sensitive information from unauthorized access.

- **Security Monitoring:** Implement continuous monitoring and logging to detect and respond to security incidents. Utilize intrusion detection and prevention systems (IDPS) to identify and mitigate threats in real time.
- **Regular Auditing and Compliance:** Regularly audit and assess your cloud environment for security compliance with industry standards and regulatory requirements. Keep records of audits and assessments.
- **Patch Management:** Keep software, operating systems, and applications up to date with security patches. Vulnerabilities in outdated software can be exploited by attackers.
- **Incident Response Plan:** Develop a comprehensive incident response plan that outlines procedures for responding to security breaches or incidents. Test and refine the plan regularly.
- **Backup and Disaster Recovery:** Implement robust backup and disaster recovery solutions to ensure data integrity and availability in case of unexpected data loss or system failures.
- **Security Training and Awareness:** Educate your staff about security best practices and ensure they are aware of the risks associated with cloud usage. Human error is a common factor in security incidents.
- **Security Automation:** Leverage automation tools to enforce security policies, monitor for anomalies, and respond to security events in real time.
- **Cloud Security Tools:** Utilize cloud-specific security tools and services offered by CSPs to enhance security. These can include cloud-native firewalls, identity and access management (IAM) tools, and security analytics platforms.

The Shared Responsibility Model and the implementation of security best practices are essential for maintaining a secure cloud environment, as security in the cloud is an ongoing process requiring vigilance, adaptability, and a commitment to staying updated.

3.3 Compliance and Regulations in the Cloud

Compliance and regulations are crucial in cloud security, defining legal and industry-specific requirements for organizations handling sensitive data. Cloud service providers (CSPs) provide services and tools to help customers meet these requirements(Anitha et al., 2023; Karthik et al., 2023; Kavitha et al., 2023; Maguluri et al., 2023).

- **Data Protection Regulations:** Many industries are subject to specific data protection regulations. For example, healthcare organizations must adhere to the Health Insurance Portability and Accountability Act (HIPAA), while financial institutions must comply with the Payment Card Industry Data Security Standard (PCI DSS). When using the cloud for data storage and processing, organizations need to ensure that the CSP's services meet these regulatory requirements.

- **International Data Transfer:** If your organization operates in multiple countries, you may need to consider regulations regarding international data transfer, such as the European Union's General Data Protection Regulation (GDPR). Ensure that your cloud provider has mechanisms in place for compliant international data transfer.

- **Data Residency and Sovereignty:** Some countries have laws that require certain data to be stored within their borders. Understand data residency and sovereignty regulations, and choose a CSP with data centers located in compliance with these requirements.

- **Compliance Certifications:** Look for CSPs that have achieved industry-specific compliance certifications. Many providers undergo audits and attain certifications to demonstrate their commitment to security and compliance. For example, Amazon Web Services (AWS) has compliance certifications such as SOC 2, ISO 27001, and FedRAMP.

- **Audit Trails and Logging:** Cloud providers often offer robust logging and auditing capabilities. These tools help organizations maintain records that can be crucial for regulatory compliance and incident response.

- **Legal and Liability Considerations:** Work closely with your legal department to understand the legal implications of using a cloud service and any potential liability issues. Draft clear contractual agreements with CSPs that address security, privacy, and compliance concerns.

- **Security Assessments and Audits:** Regularly assess and audit your cloud infrastructure and data storage to ensure compliance with relevant regulations. This can involve both internal and external audits or assessments.

- **Privacy Policies and Consent:** If you collect and process personal data, you must have clear privacy policies and obtain user consent where necessary. Transparency in how data is collected, stored, and used is a crucial element of compliance.

- **Incident Response Planning:** Regulations often require organizations to have a well-defined incident response plan in place. This plan should include procedures for reporting security incidents to regulatory authorities and affected individuals.

- **Training and Awareness:** Ensure that your staff is educated about compliance requirements, and provide ongoing training to stay up-to-date with changes in regulations.

Figure 1. Threat landscape in the cloud

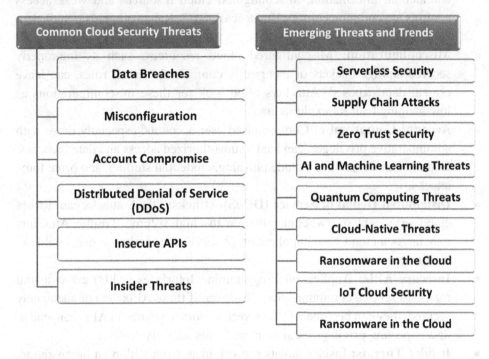

- **Regulatory Changes:** Stay informed about changes in regulations that may affect your cloud operations. Regulations are subject to updates, and compliance requirements may evolve over time.

Organizations using cloud services must adhere to compliance and regulations to avoid legal consequences and damage to their reputation. It's crucial to collaborate with legal experts and choose providers that understand and support these regulatory obligations.

4. THREAT LANDSCAPE IN THE CLOUD

The figure 1 depicts the threat landscape in the cloud and explained below.

4.1 Common Cloud Security Threats

- **Data Breaches:** Data breaches remain a top concern in the cloud. Attackers may gain unauthorized access to sensitive data, leading to the exposure of personally identifiable information (PII), intellectual property, or other confidential information. Misconfigured cloud resources and weak access controls are common culprits(Hema et al., 2023; Rahamathunnisa, Sudhakar, et al., 2023).

- **Misconfiguration:** Misconfigured cloud resources, such as improperly secured storage buckets or incorrectly configured firewall rules, can leave critical data exposed. Attackers often look for these misconfigurations as low-hanging fruit for exploitation.

- **Account Compromise:** Compromised user accounts, especially those with administrative privileges, can lead to unauthorized access and data breaches. Common attack vectors include phishing, credential stuffing, and brute force attacks.

- **Distributed Denial of Service (DDoS) Attacks:** DDoS attacks can disrupt cloud services by overwhelming them with a high volume of traffic. Attackers may target a cloud-based application or service, rendering it inaccessible to legitimate users.

- **Insecure APIs:** Application Programming Interfaces (APIs) are essential for cloud service communication. However, if these APIs are not adequately secured, they can become an attack vector. Vulnerabilities in APIs can lead to data exposure, privilege escalation, and other security issues.

- **Insider Threats:** Insider threats can originate from within an organization. Employees or contractors may misuse their access privileges to steal data, sabotage systems, or engage in other malicious activities.

4.2 Emerging Threats and Trends

- **Serverless Security:** As serverless computing gains popularity, new security challenges emerge. Ensuring the security of serverless functions and event-driven architectures is a growing concern. Organizations need to consider issues like function privilege escalation and data exposure in serverless environments(Syamala et al., 2023; Venkateswaran, Vidhya, et al., 2023).

- **Supply Chain Attacks:** Attackers are increasingly targeting the software supply chain, introducing vulnerabilities into the development and deployment pipeline. This can result in the distribution of compromised software packages and libraries, leading to security incidents.

- **Zero Trust Security:** The adoption of the Zero Trust security model is on the rise. This approach assumes that threats may already be inside the network or cloud environment and requires continuous verification of identity, devices, and services to mitigate risks.

- **AI and Machine Learning Threats:** As organizations employ AI and machine learning in the cloud, attackers may attempt to manipulate or poison machine learning models and datasets. Ensuring the integrity and security of these technologies is a growing concern.

- **Quantum Computing Threats:** While quantum computing is still in its infancy, it has the potential to break widely used encryption methods. Organizations are starting to consider post-quantum encryption strategies to protect data in the long term.
- **Cloud-Native Threats:** Cloud-native technologies, such as containers and orchestration platforms like Kubernetes, introduce unique security challenges. Threat actors may exploit vulnerabilities in container images, orchestrators, or configurations.
- **Ransomware in the Cloud:** Ransomware attacks targeting cloud data and infrastructure are becoming more common. Attackers may encrypt cloud resources and demand ransoms for decryption keys.
- **IoT Cloud Security:** As the Internet of Things (IoT) continues to grow, securing the cloud infrastructure that handles IoT data becomes crucial. Device vulnerabilities and weak cloud integration can pose significant threats.

Organizations must comprehend common and emerging threats and trends to develop robust cloud security strategies. This includes proactive threat detection, mitigation, and security awareness. Staying updated with the evolving threat landscape is crucial for adapting security measures to new challenges.

5. IDENTITY AND ACCESS MANAGEMENT (IAM)

5.1 IAM in Cloud Environments

Identity and Access Management (IAM) is a crucial aspect of cloud security, ensuring proper management of user identities and permissions within a cloud environment, while also enforcing security policies and compliance requirements to ensure appropriate access to resources, data, and services(Agrawal et al., 2024; Satav et al., 2024). The Information and Analytics Management (IAM) in cloud environments are explained below:

- **User Identity Management:** This involves creating, managing, and deleting user accounts. It includes assigning unique identifiers (usernames or email addresses) and maintaining user profiles. Often, IAM systems integrate with external directories such as Active Directory or LDAP for user management.
- **Authentication:** Ensuring that users and systems are who they claim to be is a core IAM function. This typically involves using various authentication

methods, including passwords, multi-factor authentication (MFA), and biometrics.

- **Authorization:** Once authenticated, IAM systems control what resources and services users or systems can access. This is where access control policies, permissions, and roles come into play.
- **Access Control:** IAM tools provide mechanisms to grant or deny access to resources and services. This includes fine-grained control over permissions, specifying who can read, write, update, or delete data, and under what conditions.
- **Audit and Compliance:** IAM systems often maintain logs and records of access and authentication activities. These logs are essential for security audits, compliance reporting, and investigating security incidents.
- **Single Sign-On (SSO):** IAM can implement SSO solutions that enable users to access multiple services and applications with a single set of credentials, enhancing user convenience and security.

5.2 Role-Based Access Control (RBAC)

Role-Based Access Control (RBAC) is a widely used method in Information Access Management (IAM) systems to control access permissions. It assigns users or entities roles based on their job functions or responsibilities, defining their actions within the system(Rahamathunnisa, Sudhakar, et al., 2023; Srinivas et al., 2023).

- **Roles:** Roles are defined based on job functions or responsibilities, and each role is associated with a set of permissions. For example, an organization might have roles like "System Administrator," "Developer," or "Marketing Manager."
- **Permissions:** Permissions are specific actions or operations that a user or entity can perform. These may include reading, writing, deleting, or configuring resources and data.
- **Role Assignment:** Users or entities are assigned to roles based on their job requirements. For example, a system administrator would be assigned the "System Administrator" role, which grants permissions to manage system-level resources.
- **Least Privilege:** RBAC adheres to the principle of "least privilege," meaning that users or entities are given the minimum access necessary to perform their job tasks. This minimizes the potential for unauthorized or unintended actions.

- **Scalability:** RBAC is scalable and flexible. As organizational roles evolve or new roles are introduced, IAM administrators can adjust role assignments and permissions accordingly.
- **Access Revocation:** When a user's role or job function changes, IAM administrators can easily modify their role assignments to ensure access privileges align with their new responsibilities.

RBAC streamlines access control in complex environments, enhancing security by minimizing over-privileged accounts, and is a crucial part of IAM in cloud environments, ensuring scalability, flexibility, and security.

5.3 Implementing Strong Authentication

Strong authentication is crucial for enhancing security in cloud and other computing environments, providing an extra layer of security beyond traditional passwords, making it harder for unauthorized individuals or entities to access sensitive systems and data(Dhanya et al., 2023; Pramila et al., 2023; Ramudu et al., 2023).

- **Multi-Factor Authentication (MFA):** MFA is a fundamental component of strong authentication. It requires users to provide two or more factors for verification. Factors include something you know (e.g., a password or PIN), something you have (e.g., a smartphone or smart card), and something you are (e.g., biometric data like fingerprints or retina scans). Implement MFA for all user accounts in your cloud environment, requiring at least two different factors for authentication.
- **Use Strong Password Policies:** Encourage users to create strong and unique passwords. Strong passwords should be lengthy, include a combination of upper and lower-case letters, numbers, and special characters, and should not be easily guessable. Enforce regular password changes and educate users about password security best practices.
- **Single Sign-On (SSO):** SSO solutions can enhance security by allowing users to authenticate once and then access multiple services or applications with a single set of credentials. Implement an SSO system that supports MFA for even stronger authentication.
- **Biometric Authentication:** Where possible, leverage biometric authentication methods like fingerprint or facial recognition. Biometrics provide a high level of security and user convenience.
- **Certificate-Based Authentication:** Certificate-based authentication involves issuing digital certificates to users or devices. Users and devices must present

a valid certificate to access resources. This method is highly secure and is often used for machine-to-machine communication.

- **Hardware Tokens and Smart Cards:** Implement hardware tokens or smart cards as one of the authentication factors. Users must possess the physical token or card to gain access.
- **Contextual Authentication:** Implement contextual authentication, where the authentication process takes into account the user's context, such as their location, device, and behavior patterns. If the context appears suspicious, additional authentication factors can be required.
- **Session Management:** Implement session management controls to ensure that authenticated sessions are not hijacked. Implement session timeouts and provide the ability for users to log out.
- **Secure Communication:** Ensure that all authentication processes and the exchange of authentication data occur over secure channels using encryption.
- **Regular Auditing and Monitoring:** Regularly audit and monitor authentication logs and activities. Be vigilant for any suspicious activities and take immediate action in the event of unauthorized access attempts.
- **User Education:** Educate users on the importance of strong authentication and the risks associated with weak authentication practices. Provide guidance on creating and managing strong passwords.
- **Compliance:** Ensure that your strong authentication implementation aligns with industry-specific compliance regulations and requirements, such as HIPAA, GDPR, or PCI DSS, as applicable.
- **Continuous Improvement:** Regularly assess your authentication mechanisms and consider adopting the latest security technologies and methods as they evolve.

Strong authentication methods significantly reduce unauthorized access to your cloud environment and protect sensitive data from potential breaches, making them a crucial part of a comprehensive cloud security strategy.

6. DATA SECURITY IN THE CLOUD

Cloud data security is crucial for protecting sensitive information, encompassing the encryption, classification, handling, and data loss prevention (DLP) to ensure data protection (Figure 2).

Figure 2. Data security in the cloud

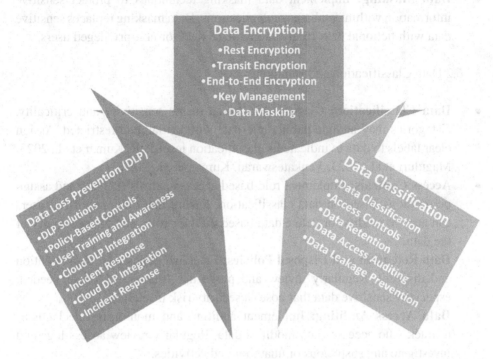

6.1 Data Encryption

- **Data at Rest Encryption:** Implement encryption for data stored in the cloud, ensuring that data is protected even when it is not actively being accessed. Most cloud providers offer encryption features for data at rest. Use encryption keys and manage them securely(Agrawal et al., 2023; Rahamathunnisa, Subhashini, et al., 2023; Srinivas et al., 2023).
- **Data in Transit Encryption:** Ensure that data transmitted to and from the cloud is encrypted using secure protocols such as HTTPS or SSL/TLS. Encryption during transit safeguards data as it traverses the internet or internal networks.
- **End-to-End Encryption:** When appropriate, use end-to-end encryption to protect data from the point of creation to the point of consumption. This ensures that data remains encrypted and confidential throughout its lifecycle.
- **Key Management:** Proper key management is crucial for data encryption. Securely manage encryption keys to prevent unauthorized access to encrypted data. Utilize hardware security modules (HSMs) for added protection.

- **Data Masking:** Implement data masking techniques to protect sensitive information within databases or applications. Data masking replaces sensitive data with fictional or partially anonymized data for non-privileged users.

6.2 Data Classification and Handling

- **Data Classification:** Classify data based on its sensitivity and criticality. Categories may include public, internal, confidential, and restricted. Assign clear labels to data to indicate its classification level(P. R. Kumar et al., 2023; Maguluri et al., 2023; Venkateswaran, Kumar, et al., 2023).
- **Access Controls:** Implement role-based access controls (RBAC) and assign permissions based on data classification. Ensure that only authorized users can access, modify, or delete data based on their roles and the sensitivity of the data.
- **Data Retention and Disposal Policies:** Establish policies for data retention and disposal. Regularly review and purge data that is no longer needed, especially sensitive data that poses a security risk if retained.
- **Data Access Auditing:** Implement auditing and monitoring mechanisms to track who accesses and modifies data. Regularly review access logs and investigate any suspicious or unauthorized activities.
- **Data Leakage Prevention:** Implement controls to prevent unintentional data leakage. This includes preventing data from being sent outside the organization by email, cloud storage, or other means.

6.3 Data Loss Prevention (DLP)

- **DLP Solutions:** Deploy DLP solutions that can monitor, detect, and prevent the unauthorized transfer of sensitive data. These solutions use content inspection and contextual analysis to enforce security policies(Agrawal et al., 2023; Rahamathunnisa, Subhashini, et al., 2023).
- **Policy-Based Controls:** Define and enforce DLP policies that specify what types of data are sensitive and how they should be handled. Policies can be configured to block, quarantine, or alert on data leakage incidents.
- **User Training and Awareness:** Educate users about DLP policies, data handling best practices, and the importance of protecting sensitive information. Make them aware of the risks of data leakage.
- **Cloud DLP Integration:** If using cloud services, consider integrating DLP solutions that can monitor and protect data within the cloud environment. This is especially important if sensitive data is stored or processed in the cloud.

- **Incident Response:** Develop an incident response plan for DLP incidents. This plan should outline steps to take when a data leakage incident occurs, including notification, containment, investigation, and remediation.

Implementing a comprehensive approach to cloud data protection, including encryption, data classification, and Data Logging (DLP), can help organizations reduce data breaches and maintain the confidentiality and integrity of their sensitive information.

7. CLOUD NETWORK SECURITY

Cloud network security is crucial for protecting data and resources from threats and unauthorized access(Awaysheh et al., 2021; R. Kumar & Goyal, 2019). The components include Virtual Private Clouds (VPCs), Firewalls and Security Groups, and Intrusion Detection and Prevention Systems (IDPS) as shown in Figure 3.

Figure 3. Components of cloud network security system for protecting data and resources

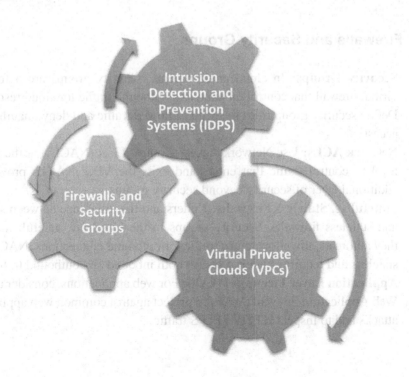

7.1 Virtual Private Clouds (VPCs)

- **VPC Configuration:** Create and configure Virtual Private Clouds (VPCs) to isolate your cloud resources from the public internet. VPCs act as private network environments within the cloud, allowing you to control traffic flow and access.
- **Subnet Segmentation:** Within your VPC, create subnets to further segment and organize your network. For example, you can have public subnets for resources accessible from the internet and private subnets for internal resources.
- **Private Connectivity:** Use Virtual Private Network (VPN) or Direct Connect services to establish secure and private connections between your on-premises network and your cloud VPC, ensuring data remains secure during transit.
- **VPC Peering:** When operating multiple VPCs, consider VPC peering to allow secure communication between them. This enables different VPCs to interact while maintaining network separation.
- **Network Access Control Lists (NACLs):** Configure NACLs to control inbound and outbound traffic at the subnet level. NACLs act as stateless firewalls, allowing you to define rules for network traffic.

7.2 Firewalls and Security Groups

- **Security Groups:** In cloud environments, security groups are a form of virtual firewall that control inbound and outbound traffic for cloud resources. Define security group rules to specify allowed traffic and deny unauthorized access.
- **Network ACLs:** Use Network Access Control Lists (NACLs) at the subnet level to control traffic that enters and exits the VPC. NACLs provide an additional layer of security beyond security groups.
- **Stateful vs. Stateless Firewalls:** Understand the difference between stateful and stateless firewalls. Security groups in the cloud are stateful, meaning they automatically allow return traffic for outbound connections. NACLs are stateless and require explicit rules for both inbound and outbound traffic.
- **Application Layer Firewalls (WAF):** For web applications, consider using a Web Application Firewall (WAF) to protect against common web application attacks and to inspect HTTP/HTTPS traffic.

7.3 Intrusion Detection and Prevention Systems (IDPS)

- **IDPS Deployment:** Deploy Intrusion Detection and Prevention Systems (IDPS) to monitor network traffic for signs of malicious activities or security threats. These systems analyze network packets and can take automated actions to block or contain threats.
- **Signature-Based and Anomaly-Based Detection:** IDPS solutions often use signature-based detection (identifying known patterns of attacks) and anomaly-based detection (detecting deviations from normal network behavior) to identify threats.
- **Custom Rules:** Create custom rules within the IDPS to detect specific threats or vulnerabilities relevant to your environment.
- **Alerting and Incident Response:** Configure alerting mechanisms so that security incidents are promptly reported to your incident response team. Define response procedures for different types of security alerts.
- **Regular Updates and Tuning:** Keep your IDPS signatures and rules up-to-date and fine-tune them as necessary to reduce false positives and increase detection accuracy.

Cloud network security is a dynamic field that requires continuous monitoring and adaptation to address emerging threats. Implementing VPCs, firewalls, and IDPS solutions can provide a robust defense against unauthorized access, malicious activities, and network-based threats.

8. SECURITY MONITORING AND INCIDENT RESPONSE

Key considerations for security monitoring, incident response, and cloud forensics and investigations are crucial for maintaining the security and integrity of cloud environments(Al-Issa et al., 2019; Awaysheh et al., 2021; R. Kumar & Goyal, 2019).

8.1 Cloud Security Monitoring

- **Logging and Auditing:** Enable comprehensive logging and auditing of cloud resources and services. Cloud providers offer tools to capture and store logs, which are essential for security monitoring.
- **Cloud-Native Security Services:** Leverage cloud-native security services and tools provided by your cloud service provider. These services often include security information and event management (SIEM) capabilities.

19

- **Third-Party Security Solutions:** Consider integrating third-party security solutions for advanced monitoring, threat detection, and log analysis. These solutions can offer more extensive and tailored security monitoring capabilities.

- **Real-Time Monitoring:** Implement real-time monitoring to detect and respond to security incidents as they occur. Automated alerts and notifications can trigger immediate actions.

- **Security Information and Event Management (SIEM):** Use SIEM solutions to aggregate and analyze logs from various sources within your cloud environment, allowing for correlation of events and improved threat detection.

8.2 Incident Detection and Response

- **Incident Response Plan:** Develop a comprehensive incident response plan that outlines procedures for identifying, mitigating, and recovering from security incidents. Ensure that the plan is regularly updated and tested.

- **Incident Classification:** Classify incidents based on their severity and potential impact. Differentiate between security incidents and non-security-related events.

- **Security Orchestration and Automation:** Implement security orchestration and automation tools to streamline incident response processes. Automation can assist with threat containment and remediation.

- **Incident Triage:** Establish an incident triage process to assess the criticality and scope of each incident. Prioritize incidents based on their potential impact and urgency.

- **Containment and Eradication:** Develop procedures for containing and eradicating security threats. This may involve isolating affected systems, applying patches, or resetting compromised accounts.

8.3 Forensics and Investigations

- **Digital Forensics Tools:** Use digital forensics tools and techniques to investigate security incidents and determine the root cause. Preserve evidence for potential legal or regulatory requirements.

- **Chain of Custody:** Maintain a chain of custody for evidence collected during forensic investigations. This ensures the integrity and admissibility of the evidence in legal proceedings.

- **Incident Reporting:** Comply with incident reporting requirements as mandated by relevant regulations and internal policies. Notify appropriate authorities, stakeholders, and affected parties when necessary.
- **Lessons Learned:** Conduct post-incident reviews and lessons learned sessions to improve incident response and prevention strategies. Share findings across the organization to enhance security awareness.
- **Legal and Regulatory Compliance:** Ensure that your forensic investigations and incident response activities align with legal and regulatory requirements, especially when dealing with incidents involving data breaches.
- **Collaboration:** Collaborate with internal and external parties, such as law enforcement agencies, cybersecurity experts, and legal counsel, during forensic investigations and incident response efforts.

Maintaining the security and compliance of your cloud environment requires effective monitoring, incident detection, response, forensics, and investigations, along with continuous improvement and a proactive approach to address evolving threats and vulnerabilities.

9. COMPLIANCE AND AUDITING

Cloud compliance and auditing are crucial for ensuring industry regulations and security standards are met, including key aspects of regulatory compliance, cloud auditing and logging, and preparing for audits and assessments(Agrawal et al., 2024; Satav et al., 2024; Srinivas et al., 2023).

9.1 Regulatory Compliance in the Cloud

- **Understand Applicable Regulations:** Identify the specific regulatory requirements that pertain to your industry and organization. Regulations such as GDPR, HIPAA, PCI DSS, or SOC 2 may apply to different cloud use cases.
- **Cloud Service Provider (CSP) Compliance:** Assess the compliance certifications and attestations of your cloud service provider (CSP). Many CSPs undergo audits to demonstrate their adherence to various regulations.
- **Data Encryption:** Ensure that sensitive data is encrypted both in transit and at rest, which is a common requirement in many data protection regulations.
- **Data Retention and Deletion:** Implement data retention and deletion policies to comply with regulations that require data to be retained for a specific period and then securely destroyed.

- **Access Control and Authentication:** Enforce strong access controls, user authentication, and role-based access control (RBAC) to limit access to sensitive data and systems.

9.2 Cloud Auditing and Logging

- **Logging and Auditing:** Configure cloud resources and services to generate comprehensive logs. Ensure that logs capture security-relevant events, access activities, and changes to configurations.
- **Centralized Log Storage:** Store logs centrally in a secure and tamper-evident location, separate from the cloud environment being monitored. This prevents potential tampering or deletion of logs.
- **Log Retention and Encryption:** Define log retention policies that align with regulatory requirements. Encrypt log data to protect it from unauthorized access.
- **Log Analysis and Alerting:** Use log analysis tools and SIEM solutions to review logs for suspicious activities and generate alerts for potential security incidents.

9.3 Preparing for Audits and Assessments

- **Compliance Frameworks:** Familiarize yourself with industry-specific compliance frameworks that apply to your organization. These frameworks provide detailed guidelines and control objectives.
- **Self-Assessment:** Conduct self-assessments to evaluate your cloud environment's compliance with relevant regulations. Identify areas of non-compliance and prioritize remediation efforts.
- **External Auditors:** Engage external auditors who specialize in cloud compliance. They can provide independent assessments and certifications required by certain regulations.
- **Documentation:** Maintain comprehensive documentation of security policies, procedures, and controls. Document the steps taken to ensure compliance and regularly update these documents.
- **Internal Audits:** Conduct internal audits and assessments to verify that your cloud environment aligns with security and compliance policies.
- **Penetration Testing:** Consider performing penetration testing to identify vulnerabilities and assess the effectiveness of your security measures. Remediate any security weaknesses discovered.

Figure 4. Secure DevOps and automation

Integrating Security into DevOps

Continuous Integration and Continuous Deployment (CI/CD) Security

Infrastructure as Code (IaC) Security

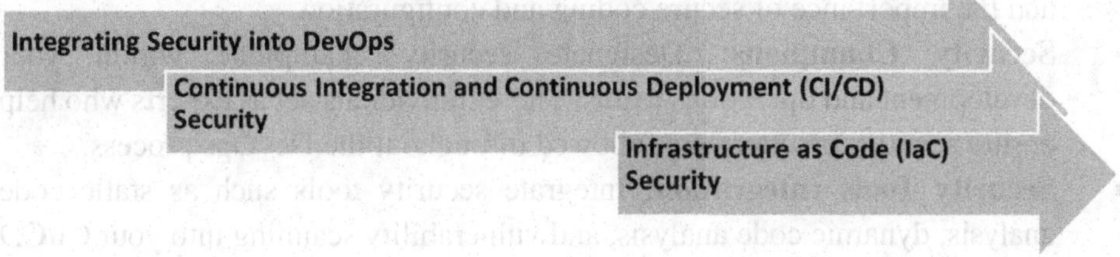

- **Security Awareness Training:** Train your staff on compliance requirements and security best practices to ensure that they are aware of their responsibilities in maintaining compliance.
- **Incident Response Plan:** Develop and document an incident response plan that outlines procedures for reporting and responding to security incidents, as compliance often requires prompt incident notification.
- **Regular Reviews and Updates:** Continuously monitor and review your compliance posture, making updates as necessary to align with changing regulatory requirements and evolving cloud services.

Maintaining regulatory compliance in the cloud requires continuous efforts, including technical controls, policy adherence, and regular audits. Adhering to established compliance frameworks and best practices demonstrates an organization's commitment to data security and regulatory obligations.

10. SECURE DEVOPS AND AUTOMATION

Secure DevOps and automation are crucial in modern software development and cloud environments(Boopathi, 2023; Gnanaprakasam et al., 2023; P. R. Kumar et al., 2023). The integrating security into DevOps, addressing security in CI/CD pipelines, and ensuring Infrastructure as Code security as shown in Figure 4.

10.1 Integrating Security into DevOps

- **Shift Left Security:** Embrace the "shift left" approach, which means integrating security at the earliest stages of the software development and deployment lifecycle. Developers should be involved in security practices from the start.

- **Security Training:** Provide security training to development and operations teams, ensuring that they understand security best practices, threat models, and the importance of secure coding and configuration.
- **Security Champions:** Designate security champions within your development and operations teams. These individuals act as experts who help ensure security practices are followed throughout the DevOps process.
- **Security Tools Integration:** Integrate security tools such as static code analysis, dynamic code analysis, and vulnerability scanning into your CI/CD pipelines to automatically detect and remediate security issues.

10.2 Continuous Integration and Continuous Deployment (CI/CD) Security

- **Automated Testing:** Implement automated security testing as part of your CI/CD pipeline. This includes static application security testing (SAST), dynamic application security testing (DAST), and container image scanning.
- **Code Review:** Conduct peer code reviews to identify and fix security issues early in the development process. Code reviews should include security-specific checks.
- **Container Security:** Secure container images by scanning them for vulnerabilities and enforcing best practices for container configuration.
- **Secret Management:** Safely manage and store sensitive credentials and secrets, such as API keys and passwords, using dedicated secret management tools.
- **Immutable Infrastructure:** Consider adopting the concept of immutable infrastructure, where infrastructure changes are made by replacing instances rather than modifying existing ones. This reduces the attack surface and simplifies security management.

10.3 Infrastructure as Code (IaC) Security

- **IaC Best Practices:** Develop Infrastructure as Code (IaC) templates that adhere to security best practices. Apply security controls within your IaC templates to enforce security configurations.
- **Static Analysis of IaC:** Use static analysis tools to scan IaC templates for security issues and misconfigurations before deployment.
- **Version Control:** Store IaC templates in version control systems to track changes and maintain a history of infrastructure modifications.

Figure 5. Disaster recovery and business continuity planning

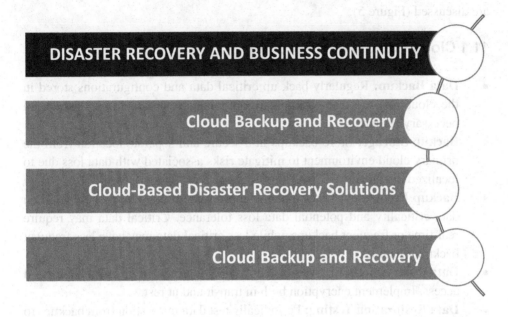

- **Automated Deployment and Testing:** Automate the deployment of infrastructure and apply automated tests to validate the security of the deployed resources.
- **Continuous Monitoring:** Implement continuous security monitoring of your cloud infrastructure to detect and respond to security threats and changes in real-time.
- **Backup and Recovery:** Regularly back up IaC templates and configuration settings to ensure quick recovery in case of unexpected changes or breaches.

Implementing security in DevOps and automating security practices in CI/CD pipelines and IaC is crucial for achieving speed and security in software development and cloud deployment. By following best practices, organizations can reduce security vulnerabilities and ensure security is an integral part of the DevOps lifecycle.

11. DISASTER RECOVERY AND BUSINESS CONTINUITY

Disaster recovery and business continuity planning are crucial for ensuring the resilience of cloud-based operations(Boopathi, 2023; Ingle et al., 2023; Maheswari et al., 2023; Ramudu et al., 2023; Veeranjaneyulu et al., 2023). The cloud backup, recovery, high availability, redundancy, and cloud-based disaster recovery solutions are discussed (Figure 5).

11.1 Cloud Backup and Recovery

- **Data Backup:** Regularly back up critical data and configurations stored in the cloud. Ensure that backups are automated, consistent, and include all necessary resources.
- **Backup Storage:** Store backups in a secure and separate location from the primary cloud environment to mitigate risks associated with data loss due to localized disasters.
- **Backup Frequency:** Determine the appropriate backup frequency based on data criticality and potential data loss tolerance. Critical data may require real-time or frequent backups, while less critical data may have less frequent backup schedules.
- **Data Encryption:** Encrypt backup data to protect it from unauthorized access. Implement encryption both in transit and at rest.
- **Data Restoration Testing:** Periodically test data restoration from backups to ensure that the process is efficient and effective. Testing verifies the integrity of backups and the ability to recover data in case of an incident.

11.2 High Availability and Redundancy

- **Multi-Region Deployment:** Consider deploying cloud resources and services in multiple geographic regions to achieve high availability. This approach helps mitigate the impact of regional outages.
- **Load Balancers:** Implement load balancers to distribute traffic evenly across multiple instances or services, ensuring that a single point of failure does not disrupt operations.
- **Auto-Scaling:** Use auto-scaling to automatically adjust resource capacity based on traffic or demand, maintaining performance during peak periods and providing redundancy in case of failures.
- **Failover Mechanisms:** Configure failover mechanisms to redirect traffic to healthy resources in the event of system failures. This minimizes downtime and service interruptions.
- **Redundant Data Storage:** Utilize redundant data storage solutions, such as RAID configurations, object storage replication, or database replication, to prevent data loss due to hardware failures.

11.3 Cloud-Based Disaster Recovery Solutions

- **Disaster Recovery as a Service (DRaaS):** Consider using DRaaS solutions that provide cloud-based disaster recovery capabilities. DRaaS can replicate and failover your workloads in the cloud, minimizing downtime and data loss.

- **Data Center Failover:** If your organization operates its own data centers, establish a cloud-based disaster recovery solution to provide redundancy and failover capabilities in case of data center outages.

- **Business Continuity Plans:** Develop and maintain business continuity plans that outline procedures for maintaining essential business operations during and after a disaster. Test these plans regularly to ensure their effectiveness.

- **Incident Response Plan:** Include a well-defined incident response plan as part of your business continuity efforts. This plan should address various scenarios, including cyberattacks, data breaches, and natural disasters.

- **Communication and Notification:** Establish clear communication and notification processes to inform employees, customers, and stakeholders about the status of operations during and after a disaster.

- **Regular Testing and Drills:** Conduct regular disaster recovery and business continuity testing and drills to validate the effectiveness of your plans and procedures.

Disaster recovery and business continuity in the cloud are crucial for minimizing disruptions and ensuring an organization's ability to operate effectively, and successful planning, preparation, and testing are key to achieving these goals.

12. CONCLUSION

Cloud environments are crucial for organizations as they increasingly rely on infrastructure and services. Strategies for cloud security include infrastructure, access control, data protection, and disaster recovery. A proactive approach is essential to protect data, applications, and resources against evolving threats. A shared responsibility model is essential, as organizations must tailor security measures to meet specific needs and compliance requirements. Integrating security into software development and deployment ensures early identification and rectifying of vulnerabilities, demonstrating a commitment to regulatory standards. Compliance frameworks provide a structured approach to meet industry-specific requirements, while regular audits and assessments validate the effectiveness of security measures and compliance adherence.

Cloud backup, recovery, and disaster recovery are essential for business continuity in the cloud. Organizations must be prepared for unexpected incidents like technical failures, natural disasters, or cyberattacks. Cloud solutions minimize downtime and data loss. In today's dynamic threat landscape, cloud security requires vigilance, adaptation, and a holistic approach. Integrating security into every layer and process helps organizations harness cloud potential, protect digital assets, and maintain business continuity.

REFERENCES

Achar, S. (2021). An Overview of Environmental Scalability and Security in Hybrid Cloud Infrastructure Designs. *Asia Pacific Journal of Energy and Environment*, *8*(2), 39–46. doi:10.18034/apjee.v8i2.650

Agrawal, A. V., Magulur, L. P., Priya, S. G., Kaur, A., Singh, G., & Boopathi, S. (2023). Smart Precision Agriculture Using IoT and WSN. In *Handbook of Research on Data Science and Cybersecurity Innovations in Industry 4.0 Technologies* (pp. 524–541). IGI Global. doi:10.4018/978-1-6684-8145-5.ch026

Agrawal, A. V., Shashibhushan, G., Pradeep, S., Padhi, S. N., Sugumar, D., & Boopathi, S. (2024). Synergizing Artificial Intelligence, 5G, and Cloud Computing for Efficient Energy Conversion Using Agricultural Waste. In Practice, Progress, and Proficiency in Sustainability (pp. 475–497). IGI Global. doi:10.4018/979-8-3693-1186-8.ch026

Al-Issa, Y., Ottom, M. A., Tamrawi, A., & ... (2019). eHealth cloud security challenges: A survey. *Journal of Healthcare Engineering*, 2019. PMID:31565209

Alghofaili, Y., Albattah, A., Alrajeh, N., Rassam, M. A., & Al-Rimy, B. A. S. (2021). Secure cloud infrastructure: A survey on issues, current solutions, and open challenges. *Applied Sciences (Basel, Switzerland)*, *11*(19), 9005. doi:10.3390/app11199005

Anitha, C., Komala, C., Vivekanand, C. V., Lalitha, S., & Boopathi, S. (2023). Artificial Intelligence driven security model for Internet of Medical Things (IoMT). *IEEE Explore*, 1–7.

Awaysheh, F. M., Aladwan, M. N., Alazab, M., Alawadi, S., Cabaleiro, J. C., & Pena, T. F. (2021). Security by design for big data frameworks over cloud computing. *IEEE Transactions on Engineering Management*, *69*(6), 3676–3693. doi:10.1109/TEM.2020.3045661

Bhajantri, L. B., & Mujawar, T. (2019). A survey of cloud computing security challenges, issues and their countermeasures. *2019 Third International Conference on I-SMAC (IoT in Social, Mobile, Analytics and Cloud)(I-SMAC)*, (pp. 376–380). ACM. 10.1109/I-SMAC47947.2019.9032545

Boopathi, S. (2023). Deep Learning Techniques Applied for Automatic Sentence Generation. In Promoting Diversity, Equity, and Inclusion in Language Learning Environments (pp. 255–273). IGI Global. doi:10.4018/978-1-6684-3632-5.ch016

Dhanya, D., Kumar, S. S., Thilagavathy, A., Prasad, D., & Boopathi, S. (2023). Data Analytics and Artificial Intelligence in the Circular Economy: Case Studies. In Intelligent Engineering Applications and Applied Sciences for Sustainability (pp. 40–58). IGI Global.

George, A. S., & Sagayarajan, S. (2023). Securing Cloud Application Infrastructure: Understanding the Penetration Testing Challenges of IaaS, PaaS, and SaaS Environments. *Partners Universal International Research Journal*, 2(1), 24–34.

Gnanaprakasam, C., Vankara, J., Sastry, A. S., Prajval, V., Gireesh, N., & Boopathi, S. (2023). Long-Range and Low-Power Automated Soil Irrigation System Using Internet of Things: An Experimental Study. In Contemporary Developments in Agricultural Cyber-Physical Systems (pp. 87–104). IGI Global.

Gozman, D., & Willcocks, L. (2019). The emerging Cloud Dilemma: Balancing innovation with cross-border privacy and outsourcing regulations. *Journal of Business Research*, 97, 235–256. doi:10.1016/j.jbusres.2018.06.006

Hema, N., Krishnamoorthy, N., Chavan, S. M., Kumar, N., Sabarimuthu, M., & Boopathi, S. (2023). A Study on an Internet of Things (IoT)-Enabled Smart Solar Grid System. In *Handbook of Research on Deep Learning Techniques for Cloud-Based Industrial IoT* (pp. 290–308). IGI Global. doi:10.4018/978-1-6684-8098-4.ch017

Ingle, R. B., Senthil, T. S., Swathi, S., Muralidharan, N., Mahendran, G., & Boopathi, S. (2023). Sustainability and Optimization of Green and Lean Manufacturing Processes Using Machine Learning Techniques. IGI Global. doi:10.4018/978-1-6684-8238-4.ch012

Isharufe, W., Jaafar, F., & Butakov, S. (2020). Study of security issues in platform-as-a-service (paas) cloud model. *2020 International Conference on Electrical, Communication, and Computer Engineering (ICECCE)*, (pp. 1–6). IEEE. 10.1109/ICECCE49384.2020.9179414

Jyoti, A., Shrimali, M., Tiwari, S., & Singh, H. P. (2020). Cloud computing using load balancing and service broker policy for IT service: A taxonomy and survey. *Journal of Ambient Intelligence and Humanized Computing*, *11*(11), 4785–4814. doi:10.100712652-020-01747-z

Karthik, S., Hemalatha, R., Aruna, R., Deivakani, M., Reddy, R. V. K., & Boopathi, S. (2023). Study on Healthcare Security System-Integrated Internet of Things (IoT). In Perspectives and Considerations on the Evolution of Smart Systems (pp. 342–362). IGI Global.

Kavitha, C. R., Varalatchoumy, M., Mithuna, H. R., Bharathi, K., Geethalakshmi, N. M., & Boopathi, S. (2023). Energy Monitoring and Control in the Smart Grid: Integrated Intelligent IoT and ANFIS. In M. Arshad (Ed.), (pp. 290–316). Advances in Bioinformatics and Biomedical Engineering. IGI Global. doi:10.4018/978-1-6684-6577-6.ch014

Kumar, P. R., Meenakshi, S., Shalini, S., Devi, S. R., & Boopathi, S. (2023). Soil Quality Prediction in Context Learning Approaches Using Deep Learning and Blockchain for Smart Agriculture. In R. Kumar, A. B. Abdul Hamid, & N. I. Binti Ya'akub (Eds.), (pp. 1–26). Advances in Computational Intelligence and Robotics. IGI Global. doi:10.4018/978-1-6684-9151-5.ch001

Kumar, R., & Goyal, R. (2019). On cloud security requirements, threats, vulnerabilities and countermeasures: A survey. *Computer Science Review*, *33*, 1–48. doi:10.1016/j.cosrev.2019.05.002

Maguluri, L. P., Arularasan, A. N., & Boopathi, S. (2023). Assessing Security Concerns for AI-Based Drones in Smart Cities. In R. Kumar, A. B. Abdul Hamid, & N. I. Binti Ya'akub (Eds.), (pp. 27–47). Advances in Computational Intelligence and Robotics. IGI Global. doi:10.4018/978-1-6684-9151-5.ch002

Maheswari, B. U., Imambi, S. S., Hasan, D., Meenakshi, S., Pratheep, V., & Boopathi, S. (2023). Internet of Things and Machine Learning-Integrated Smart Robotics. In Global Perspectives on Robotics and Autonomous Systems: Development and Applications (pp. 240–258). IGI Global. doi:10.4018/978-1-6684-7791-5.ch010

Mukhopadhyay, B., Bose, R., & Roy, S. (2020). A novel approach to load balancing and cloud computing security using SSL in IaaS environment. *International Journal (Toronto, Ont.)*, *9*(2).

Parast, F. K., Sindhav, C., Nikam, S., Yekta, H. I., Kent, K. B., & Hakak, S. (2022). Cloud computing security: A survey of service-based models. *Computers & Security*, *114*, 102580. doi:10.1016/j.cose.2021.102580

Pramila, P., Amudha, S., Saravanan, T., Sankar, S. R., Poongothai, E., & Boopathi, S. (2023). Design and Development of Robots for Medical Assistance: An Architectural Approach. In Contemporary Applications of Data Fusion for Advanced Healthcare Informatics (pp. 260–282). IGI Global.

Rahamathunnisa, U., Subhashini, P., Aancy, H. M., Meenakshi, S., Boopathi, S., & ... (2023). Solutions for Software Requirement Risks Using Artificial Intelligence Techniques. In *Handbook of Research on Data Science and Cybersecurity Innovations in Industry 4.0 Technologies* (pp. 45–64). IGI Global.

Rahamathunnisa, U., Sudhakar, K., Murugan, T. K., Thivaharan, S., Rajkumar, M., & Boopathi, S. (2023). Cloud Computing Principles for Optimizing Robot Task Offloading Processes. In *AI-Enabled Social Robotics in Human Care Services* (pp. 188–211). IGI Global. doi:10.4018/978-1-6684-8171-4.ch007

Ramudu, K., Mohan, V. M., Jyothirmai, D., Prasad, D., Agrawal, R., & Boopathi, S. (2023). Machine Learning and Artificial Intelligence in Disease Prediction: Applications, Challenges, Limitations, Case Studies, and Future Directions. In Contemporary Applications of Data Fusion for Advanced Healthcare Informatics (pp. 297–318). IGI Global.

Rayhan, R., & Rayhan, S. (2023). *AI and Human Rights: Balancing Innovation and Privacy in the Digital Age*. DOI.

RM, S. P., Bhattacharya, S., Maddikunta, P. K. R., Somayaji, S. R. K., Lakshmanna, K., Kaluri, R., Hussien, A., & Gadekallu, T. R. (2020). Load balancing of energy cloud using wind driven and firefly algorithms in internet of everything. *Journal of Parallel and Distributed Computing*, *142*, 16–26. doi:10.1016/j.jpdc.2020.02.010

Saini, D. K., Kumar, K., & Gupta, P. (2022). Security issues in IoT and cloud computing service models with suggested solutions. *Security and Communication Networks*, *2022*, 2022. doi:10.1155/2022/4943225

Satav, S. D., & Lamani, D. G, H. K., Kumar, N. M. G., Manikandan, S., & Sampath, B. (2024). Energy and Battery Management in the Era of Cloud Computing. In Practice, Progress, and Proficiency in Sustainability (pp. 141–166). IGI Global. doi:10.4018/979-8-3693-1186-8.ch009

Shahid, M. A., Islam, N., Alam, M. M., Su'ud, M. M., & Musa, S. (2020). A comprehensive study of load balancing approaches in the cloud computing environment and a novel fault tolerance approach. *IEEE Access : Practical Innovations, Open Solutions*, *8*, 130500–130526. doi:10.1109/ACCESS.2020.3009184

Srinivas, B., Maguluri, L. P., Naidu, K. V., Reddy, L. C. S., Deivakani, M., & Boopathi, S. (2023). Architecture and Framework for Interfacing Cloud-Enabled Robots. In *Handbook of Research on Data Science and Cybersecurity Innovations in Industry 4.0 Technologies* (pp. 542–560). IGI Global. doi:10.4018/978-1-6684-8145-5.ch027

Syamala, M., Komala, C., Pramila, P., Dash, S., Meenakshi, S., & Boopathi, S. (2023). Machine Learning-Integrated IoT-Based Smart Home Energy Management System. In *Handbook of Research on Deep Learning Techniques for Cloud-Based Industrial IoT* (pp. 219–235). IGI Global. doi:10.4018/978-1-6684-8098-4.ch013

Veeranjaneyulu, R., Boopathi, S., Narasimharao, J., Gupta, K. K., Reddy, R. V. K., & Ambika, R. (2023). Identification of Heart Diseases using Novel Machine Learning Method. *IEEE- Explore*, 1–6.

Venkateswaran, N., Kumar, S. S., Diwakar, G., Gnanasangeetha, D., & Boopathi, S. (2023). Synthetic Biology for Waste Water to Energy Conversion: IoT and AI Approaches. In M. Arshad (Ed.), (pp. 360–384). Advances in Bioinformatics and Biomedical Engineering. IGI Global. doi:10.4018/978-1-6684-6577-6.ch017

Venkateswaran, N., Vidhya, K., Ayyannan, M., Chavan, S. M., Sekar, K., & Boopathi, S. (2023). A Study on Smart Energy Management Framework Using Cloud Computing. In 5G, Artificial Intelligence, and Next Generation Internet of Things: Digital Innovation for Green and Sustainable Economies (pp. 189–212). IGI Global. doi:10.4018/978-1-6684-8634-4.ch009

ABBREVIATIONS

CI/CD: Continuous Integration and Continuous Deployment
DRaaS: Disaster Recovery as a Service
GDPR: General Data Protection Regulation
HIPAA: Health Insurance Portability and Accountability Act
IaaS: Infrastructure as a Service
IaC: Infrastructure as Code
IDPS: Intrusion Detection and Prevention Systems
MFA: Multi-Factor Authentication
NACLs: Network Access Control Lists
PaaS: Platform as a Service
PCI DSS: Payment Card Industry Data Security Standard
RAID: Redundant Array of Independent Disks
RBAC: Role-Based Access Control

SIEM: Security Information and Event Management
SOC 2: Service Organization Control 2
SSO: Single Sign-On
WAF: Web Application Firewall

Chapter 2
Impact of Artificial Intelligence and Machine Learning in Cloud Security

I. Eugene Berna
(iD) https://orcid.org/0000-0002-3066-6511
Bannari Amman Institute of Technology, India

K. Vijay
Rajalakshmi Engineering College, India

S. Gnanavel
(iD) https://orcid.org/0000-0003-2344-0482
Department of Computing Technologies, SRM Institute of Science and Technology-Kattankulathur, India

J. Jeyalakshmi
(iD) https://orcid.org/0000-0001-7545-6449
Amrita VishwaVidhyapeetham, India

ABSTRACT

The rapid advancement of artificial intelligence (AI) and machine learning (ML) technologies has had a significant impact on cloud security, as it has in many other sectors. This abstract examines how AI and ML are affecting cloud security, highlighting their major contributions, difficulties, and potential. Traditional approaches to cloud security provide improved threat detection, real-time monitoring, and adaptive defense mechanisms. These technologies are adept at processing enormous volumes of data, allowing them to spot trends, anomalies, and potential dangers that more traditional security measures would miss. In order to quickly identify and take appropriate action in response to unauthorised access, data

DOI: 10.4018/979-8-3693-1431-9.ch002

breaches, and other malicious activities, AI-driven systems can quickly analyse user behaviour, network behaviour, and system logs. It introduces complexity in the form of adversarial assaults, model interpretability, and data privacy issues. For users to trust AI-driven security systems and to comprehend their decision-making processes, openness of these systems is essential.

1. INTRODUCTION

An innovative tool called artificial intelligence (AI) has the potential to provide analytics and intelligence to defend against continuously evolving cyberattacks by quickly scanning millions of events and keeping an eye on a variety of cyberthreats in order to foresee issues and take appropriate action. As a result (K, 2023), there are numerous applications of AI that either assist human security personnel or completely automate them. There is an increasing trend towards using AI in cyber defence. Increased interest among academics in cybersecurity and AI has led to a plethora of studies addressing topics related to cyberidentification, cyberprotection, cyberdetection, cyberreaction, and cyberrecovery (Saini et al., 2023; Sudha & Akiladevi, 2022).

Cybersecurity policies, procedures, and technical measures are implemented to protect information and communication systems and the data they contain against compromise, unauthorised use or modification, and exploitation. Accelerating technical development and innovation, as well as the ever-evolving nature of cyber threats (K, 2023; Nassif et al., 2021), compound the difficulty of the challenge. In light of this hitherto unseen difficulty, AI-based cybersecurity tools have emerged to provide valuable assistance to security teams in efficiently mitigating threats and bolstering security. Due to the diversity of AI and cybersecurity, a standardised taxonomy is necessary for reviewing research on using AI to cybersecurity. Researchers and practitioners will benefit from having a shared knowledge of the technological processes and services that need to be enhanced using AI thanks to this standardised taxonomy shown in Figure 1.a.

Before AI and ML reach unfathomable levels of accuracy and efficiency, this special issue (Sarirete et al., 2022) is devoted to the study of them as aspects of data-driven innovation and digital transformation. An agenda and multidisciplinary research on AI and ML are required because of rising user expectations for technology and the benefits it provides to society (Lytras et al., 2021; Visvizi et al., 2020; Chui et al., 2020). The five main issues listed above should form the basis of any study proposal of this kind (Figure 1.b).

By DominikSowinsk state that, Cloud computing has been transformed by AI and machine learning (ML), which has improved performance, scalability, and

Figure 1. NIST cybersecurity framework

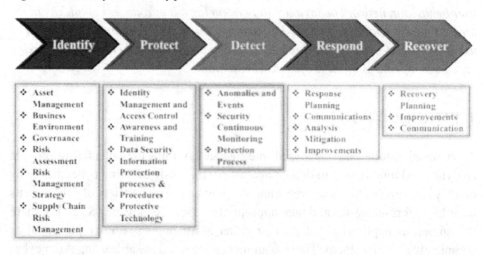

Figure 2. All facets of human behaviour are undergoing a digital transformation driven by AI

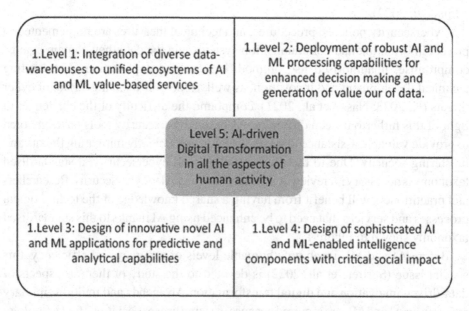

efficiency. Through automation, anomaly detection, and predictive analytics, they help to optimise operations. However, a wider spectrum of security threats is now associated with cloud computing because to the increasing accessibility and ubiquity of AI. The threat of adversarial assaults utilising AI has increased as access to AI tools has expanded. Aware adversaries are able to generate false or inaccurate information by using ML models for evasion, poisoning, or model inversion assaults. The number of possible enemies who are able to exploit these models and cloud settings grows as AI technologies become more commonplace.

1.1 New Tools, New Threats

One of the most concerning advances, though, is the use of AI by adversaries to find cloud weaknesses and produce malware. AI is a powerful weapon for cybercriminals because it can automate and expedite the discovery of vulnerabilities. They can use AI to analyse patterns, spot vulnerabilities, and take advantage of them more quickly than security professionals can react. AI may also produce sophisticated malware that evolves and learns to avoid detection, making it more challenging to stop.

These security issues are made more difficult by AI's lack of openness. The interpretation of AI systems, particularly deep learning models, is difficult, making it difficult to diagnose and address security concerns. Such occurrences are more likely now that a larger user base has access to AI. The benefit of AI's automation also brings with it a serious security risk: reliance. The effect of an AI system failure or security breach increases as more services rely on it. It is more difficult to pinpoint and fix this problem in the distributed cloud system without affecting service.

2. CLOUDCOMPUTING

Internet connectivity is used to access a variety of services using cloud computing. Included in this are server systems, database systems, networking infrastructure, and application infrastructure (Gutierrez & Lee, 2020; Halabi & Bellaiche, 2017; Kumar & Alphonse, 2018; Linguistics, 2017). By utilising cloud computing, it is no longer necessary to save data on an individual's computer or other device (Asharaf et al., 2023). Apps and information are accessible to digital users whenever they have Internet access.

2.1 Threat to Cloud Security

Figure 2 illustrates the serious problem of data security in the cloud, which is especially problematic given the sensitive nature of the data stored and processed there.1.a. Individuals and organisations should be aware of the various threats to cloud security and take precautions to counter them (Halabi & Bellaiche, 2018). These dangers include, among others:

Unauthorised access to private data kept in the cloud constitutes a data breach. Attackers may get unauthorised access to important data by taking advantage of

Figure 3. Threats to cloud security

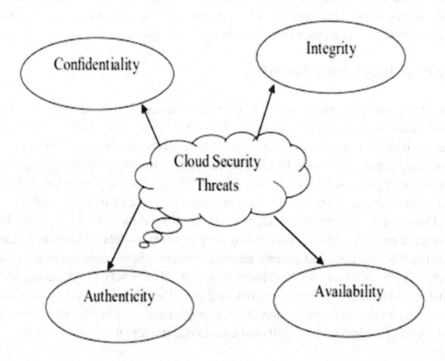

flaws in the cloud architecture, lax authentication, or improperly configured access controls. Inadequate Identity, Credential, and Access Management: Unauthorised access may result from improper management of user identities, credentials, and access rights (Dilek et al., 2015). Unauthorised users have a higher chance of accessing cloud resources if there are lax password regulations, shared credentials, and no multi-factor authentication.

CC will experience tremendous and widespread development. There are a number of risks that could cause protection and security issues. The analysis is based on the CIA feature and cloud hazards.

To protect the Cloud against potential threats and prevent harm, it is necessary to recognise and understand the types of assaults that can be launched. The assaults in cloud computing that get the most discussion The following are in Grusho et al. (2017), Gutierrez & Lee (2020), and Kumar et al. (2016):

a.   Attacks on **denial of service (DoS)** aim to reduce the users' access to services. Distributed denial of service allows multiple computers to perform a single attack (DDoS).

b.   When an attacker uses legitimate hosts on the network to hammer a victim with requests, this is known as a **zombieattack**. Such an attack prevents Cloud from acting as it is expected to, which affects Cloud services' availability.

c.   **Phishing attack**: involves tricking individuals into clicking on a fake link in order to get their personal information.

d.   The "Man in the Middle" attack happens when a third party intercepts or modifies the data being transmitted between two users. Cloud-based information exchanges are vulnerable to espionage.

3. SYSTEMATIC REVIEW ANALYSIS

Figure 3.a depicts in full the study's selection approach. After selecting and employing a search keyword in Scopus, 2395 studies were retrieved; these were then narrowed down using the inclusion and exclusion criteria (K, 2023). After excluding works not written in English, posters, reviews, surveys, editorials, books, chapters, workshop and symposium abstracts, duplicates, guidelines, and comparative studies, a total of 2029 publications remained. Twenty-two hundred and nine papers were read for their abstracts and titles. The review made it clear in the title and abstract if the study was irrelevant since it fell outside the scope of the review.

Figure 4. The method of selection and the number of studies at each stage of the SLR protocol

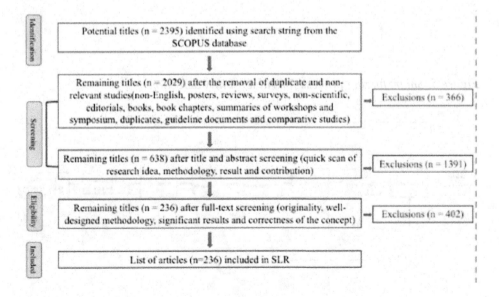

3.1 Automated Evaluation and Detection of Vulnerabilities

An automated vulnerability assessment is a methodical investigation into the state of a system's security using automated tools for locating, categorising, investigating, and ranking vulnerabilities. Automated solutions detect, categorise, and rank vulnerabilities using asset management systems, threat intelligence feeds, vendor vulnerability bulletins, and vulnerability repositories.

Automated vulnerability identification is a crucial step in locating weaknesses in servers, applications, and other assets of a company. Deep learning and transfer learning have been used by researchers to check the source code in order to detect software vulnerabilities (K, 2023; Leo et al., 2023; Fang et al., 2012). In order to aid developers in creating more secure code, researchers in these projects mine text for vulnerabilities using machine learning.

Researchers employ AI-based fuzzing to find security flaws in programmes and interfaces. One method is to inject malicious data into a programme or interface with the purpose of triggering errors like crashes, failed code assertions, illegal jumps or debug methods, and even memory leaks. An automated system for detecting attack possibilities, generating input, producing plausible test cases, and assessing crashes can be built using AI approaches, as shown in Figure 3.1.a. The clever fuzzing system uses techniques from logic and natural language processing to generate seeds, which it then uses to enhance code coverage via novel execution paths (Nassif et al., 2021; Sarirete et al., 2022).

Figure 5. Smart fuzzing process for vulnerability detection

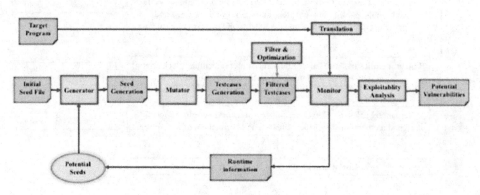

4. CLOUD COMPUTING SERVICES AND MODELS

The ability to provide services independently on demand, access to a vast network, sharing of resources, rapid scalability, and individualised support are all crucial. SaaS, PaaS, and IaaS are the three most common ways in which cloud services are made available to customers, and all three are included in NIST's definition of cloud computing (Halabi & Bellaiche, 2017). The NIST study also discusses the four cloud deployment models, each of which is characterised in terms of who has access to the cloud's resources. Figure 4.a depicts the four different types of clouds: public, private, community, and hybrid.

Figure 6. Characteristics, service delivery model, and deployment model of cloud computing

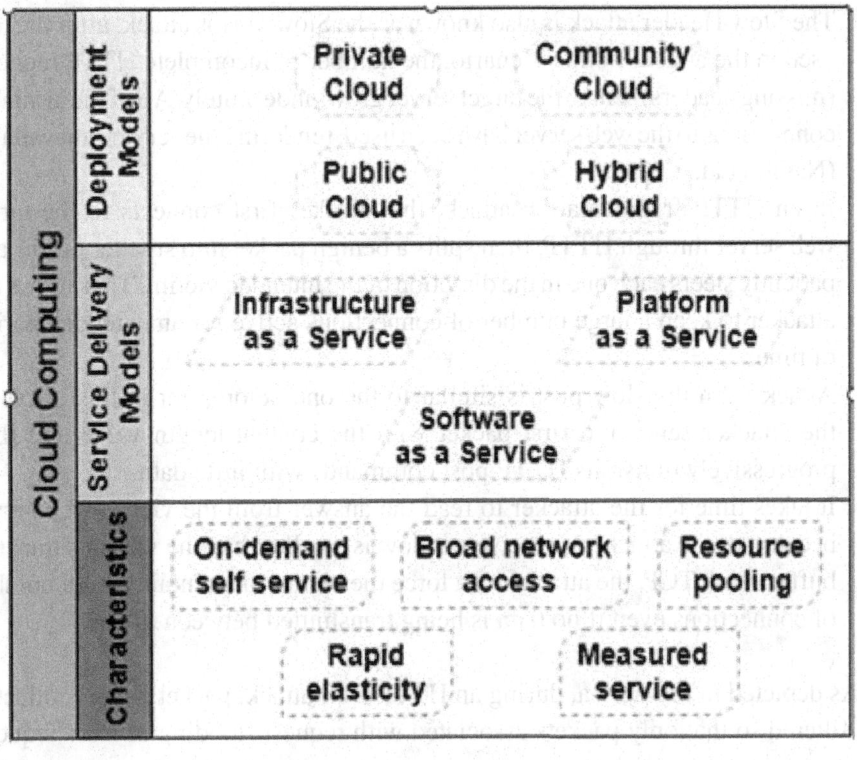

5. DENIAL-OF-SERVICE (DoS) ATTACKS

Low-rate traffic that appears to be genuine traffic and high-rate traffic that simulates the simultaneous access of many users to a system without malicious intent (flash crowd) may both be seen throughout a distributed denial-of-service (DoS) attack (Fang et al., 2012). Based on the protocol layer at which they are launched, DoS attacks are often categorised as follows:

a. **Network/transport-level DoS assault**: The attacker uses network and transport layer protocols to exert control over the targeted system. Protocols like TCP, UDP, ICMP, and DNS are frequently used for these tasks.

b. **Application-level DoS attacks:** Attacks at the application level are harder to detect since they have no distinguishing features and look like normal traffic rather than network or transport level attacks, despite using much less bandwidth. Application protocols including HTTP, DNS, and SIP are being used in these attacks due to their specific features.

In addition to application-level assaults, we need also mention HTTP flooding attacks, which fall into the following four categories.

a. The Slow Header attack is also known as the Slowworms attack, after the tool used in the attack. In this scenario, the number of incomplete HTTP requests (missing headers) sent to the target server grows indefinitely. All of the available connections to the web server have been used, rendering the service unavailable (Nassif et al., 2021).

b. In an HTTP fragmentation attack, the attacker first connects to the target web server through HTTP, then splits a benign packet into smaller pieces and patiently steers each one in the direction of the intended victim. This allows the attacker to keep a large number of connections active for an extended period of time.

c. Attack from the slow post is similar to the one before, but in this instance, the attacker sends the first packet with the content-length value and then progressively transmits HTTP post commands with little data.

d. It takes time for the attacker to read the answer from the victim web server because d) the attacker's receive window is smaller than the victim's transmit buffer. With TCP, the attacker can force the victim to maintain a high number of connections even if no data is being transmitted between them.

As depicted in Figure 5.a, during an HTTP DoS attack, packet data is collected and filtered so that only packets associated with request flooding or slow request/

Figure 7. Enhancing cloud computing analysis

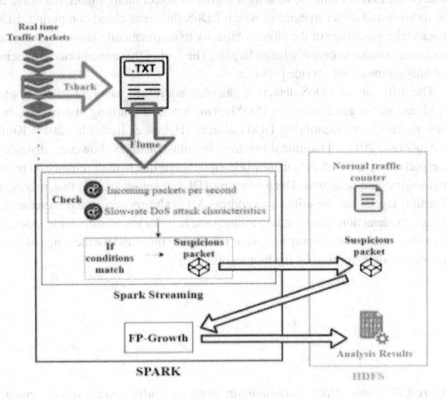

response attacks are examined. Attackers may use reflectors or botnets to mimic the effects of earlier strikes in order to boost the effectiveness of these Slow Rate DoS attacks (Kumar & Alphonse, 2018). It is crucial to note that the suggested solution can detect the onset of these attacks, allowing for quick detection and assisting the cloud administrator in taking action to mitigate the attack. In this instance, the implementation also permits, which is another crucial element.

6. ECONOMIC DENIAL OF SUSTAINABILITY ATTACK DETECTION SYSTEMS

DDoS attacks are prevalent, whereas EDoS attacks are relatively recent. But an EDoS assault might ruin a cloud service provider's reputation with their customers and perhaps lead to bankruptcy (Aldhyani & Alkahtani, 2022; Gutierrez & Lee, 2020). A distributed denial of service (DDoS) attack, on the other hand, can temporarily block access to a service for its intended audience. They are more advanced and modern than DDoS attacks, making it harder to detect them. Figure 6.a illustrates the indirect and direct manner in which EDoS threatens cloud computing. EDoS attacks take advantage of the cloud's capacity to automatically launch more virtual machines in order to overwhelm its targets. The cost of this unauthorised malicious use falls on the cloud service provider.

The difficulty of EDoS detection has been addressed using a variety of ways. SVM and self-organizing maps (SOM), two machine learning approaches, have been successful in identifying DDoS attacks (Halabi & Bellaiche, 2017; Kumar & Alphonse, 2018). Traditional machine learning methods, however, struggle to interpret massive EDoS data in network applications due to their reliance on feature engineering and selection. Deep learning (DL), a subset of ML that makes use of neural layers, can be utilised to address ML's shortcomings and increase data extraction, detection accuracy, and robustness. In order to solve difficult issues, DL algorithms make use of many nonlinear processing units and a wide range of neural network models inspired by the human brain.

Figure 8. Economic denial of sustainability threat to cloud computing service providers

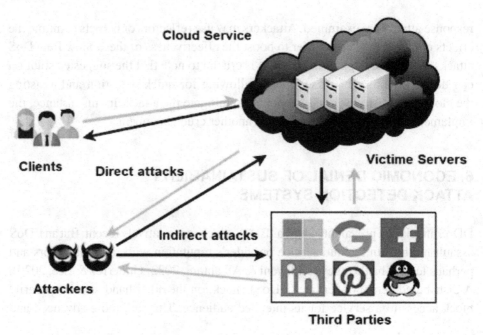

7. ARTIFICIAL INTELLIGENCE AND INTRUSION DETECTION

Artificial intelligence (AI) can be thought of as (i) the study of how humans think in order to design similarly intelligent machines, or (ii) the study of how to solve difficult problems that necessitate intelligence (such as making good decisions based on a large amount of data). The second definition is the one most relevant to the use of AI in cyber protection. The field of artificial intelligence (AI) seeks to create computer programmes that can simulate human intelligence by performing tasks like learning, reasoning, planning, etc. in an automated fashion (Chinnaiah & Niranjan, 2018; Fang et al., 2012; Leo et al., 2023).

The fundamental issue of mimicking intelligence has been subdivided into more narrowly focused subproblems, each of which has certain characteristics or abilities that an intelligent system ought to possess. The qualities listed below have received the greatest attention (Dilek et al., 2015; Halabi & Bellaiche, 2017; Kumar & Alphonse, 2018):

Figure 9. A typical IDPS

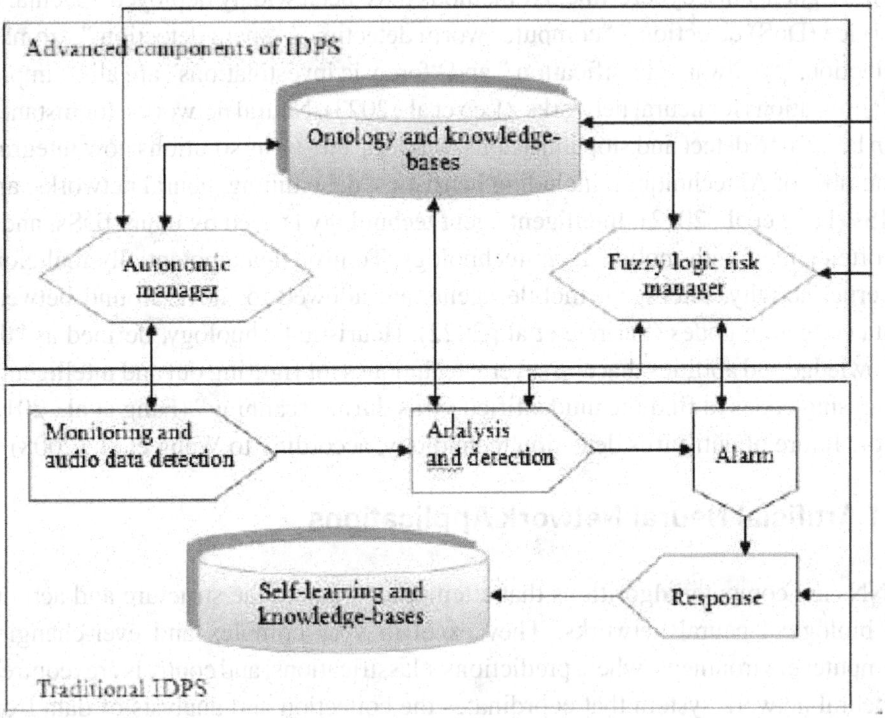

a)   Embodied agents, neural networks, and statistical AI methods that involve deduction, reasoning, and problem solving

b)   Learning (machine learning), planning (multi-agent planning and cooperation), and knowledge representation (ontologies), information retrieval (text mining, machine translation), natural language processing (navigation, localization, mapping, motion planning), motion and manipulation (localization, speech recognition, facial recognition), and perception (speech recognition, facial recognition) are just a few of the topics covered.

Although established procedures for protecting information while in transit over networks and the Internet, such as antivirus software, firewalls, encryption, and secure protocols, hackers can constantly come up with new ways to target network systems. An IDPS is a piece of hardware or software that is deployed within a network and has the ability to both identify possible intrusions and try to prevent them. Monitoring, detecting, analysing, and respondingto unauthorised actions are the four key security functions thatIDPSs serve shown in Figure 7.a.

8. AI APPLICATIONS TO THE DEFENCE OF CYBERCRIME

In the fight against cybercrime, AI methods have been widely deployed. "Denial of Service (DoS) detection," "computer worm detection," "spam detection," "zombie detection," "malware classification," and "forensic investigations" are all examples of applications for neural networks. (Leo et al., 2023). Neural networks, for instance, can be used to detect and stop intrusions. Modern anti-virus solutions now integrate a number of AI techniques, including heuristics, data mining, neural networks, and AISs (Fang et al., 2012). Intelligent agent technology is used by many IDSs, and it is often paired with mobile agent technology. To investigate potentially malicious internet activity, intelligent mobile agents are allowed to move around between data collection nodes (Sarirete et al., 2022). Heuristic technology, defined as "the knowledge and abilities that app several techniques for figuring out and intelligently analysing codes to find the unidentified virus during scanning" (Fang et al., 2012) is the future of anti-virus detection technology, according to Wang et al. (2008).

8.1 Artificial Neural Network Applications

ANNs are computer algorithms that attempt to simulate the structure and activity of biological neural networks. They excel in very complex and ever-changing computer environments where predictions, classifications, and controls are required. a neural network system that coordinates the collection and analysis of data from multiple sources, as well as the detection and reporting of abnormalities, alarms, and corrective measures. Experiments show that Neuro Net can successfully defend against distributed denial-of-service attacks that focus on TCP at low rates.

8.2 Agent Applications

Cooperatively responding to novel conditions, artificially intelligent agents are computer-generated teams that are both self-aware and computer-generated. They communicate with one another to share data. Intelligent agent technology is ideally suited for thwarting cyberattacks due to their adaptability to their deployment surroundings, mobility, and cooperative nature.

8.3 Artificial Immune System Applications

The purpose of AISs, like that of biological immune systems they ape, is to maintain stability in the face of disruption. In immune-based intrusion detection (), immunocytes undergo evolution (self-tolerance, cloning, variation, etc.) while antigens are detected simultaneously. To combat pathogens, the immune system creates antibodies, and changes in antibody concentration can be used to gauge how intense the infiltration is. As a result, AISs are crucial to the study of cyber security.

8.4 Advantages of AI Applications to IDPSs

There are many benefits that AI approaches bring to intrusion detection and prevention (see Table 1).

9. ATTRIBUTE BASED ENCRYPTION

According to Kamara and Lauter (2010), attribute-based encryption (ABE) is a type of public key cryptography that gives authorised users discrete and safe access to shared data. The user's secret key needs to be connected to an access policy in order for data encrypted using ABE features to be decrypted (Halabi & Bellaiche, 2017). Decryption is only feasible if the user's credentials are valid and adhere to the access rules. It offers revocation, collusion resistance, and scalability. It is helpful to divide ABE into "Key Policy Attribute Based Encryption" (KPABE) and "Cypher Policy Attribute Based Encryption" (CPABE), which are its constituent pieces. The access rules of KPABE are depicted in Figure 9.a and serve to safeguard both the ciphertext and the user's private keys. CPABE generates user ciphertext and secret keys based on the methods shown in Figure 9.b.

Table 1. Advantages in AI application

Technology	Advantages
Artificial Neural Networks	Information processing in parallel; learning through experience; handling complicated nonlinear functions in nonlinearity superiority to difficult, complicated differential equations; resilience to ambiguous and noisy data; flexibility and adaptability in terms of learning paradigms; Being an abstraction of biological brain networks, intuition.
Agents with intelligence	Mobility; helpfulness – they consistently try to complete tasks with conflicting goals; Objectivity - in achieving their goals; adaptability to the surroundings and the preferences of the user; Collaboration means being aware that a human user may make mistakes, provide ambiguous information, or omit crucial information; as a result, they shouldn't accept instructions without giving them some thought and double-checking any discrepancies with the user.
Synthetic Immune Systems	Dynamic structure; Distributed learning and parallelism - leveraging communications through data networks and parallelism in detection and elimination tasks; self-organization and self-adaptability, including the ability to automatically update incursion markers; Robustness; selecting the best available techniques to eliminate harmful behaviour; Diversity: Each detector node produces a set of non-self-detectors that is statistically distinct; Resource management Multiple layers of various structures are in responsible of keeping an eye on a particular site, so attackers cannot carry out their nefarious operations by getting past only one layer. Being independent of a single, easily replaceable component is known as disposability.

Figure 10. Key policy attribute-based encryption

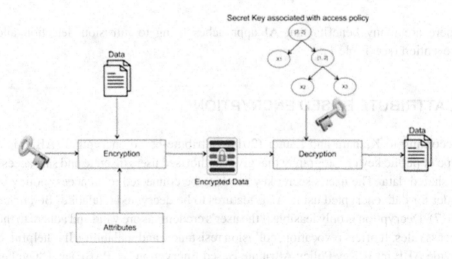

Figure 11. Ciphertext policy attribute-based encryption

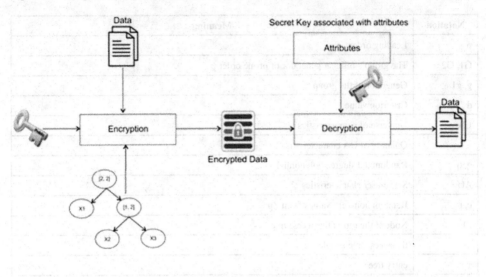

Certain parameters must be established before any data may be encrypted. The Authority, the data owner, and the data user are the three parties involved in data use. The authority generates a master secret key for data encryption and then provides it

Figure 12. Architecture of attribute-based encryption

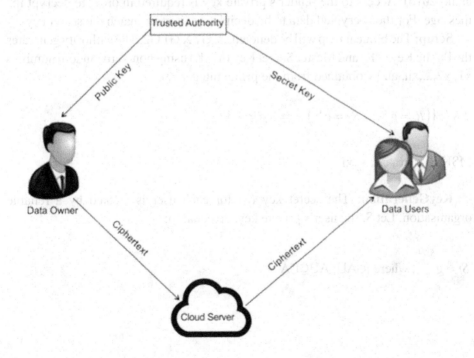

Table 2. Different notations used in various ABE algorithms

Notation	Meaning
p	Leading order
G1, G2	The group's bilinear generator of prime order p
g, g1	Generator of the group
d	Criterion value
UA	Universe of characteristics
n	Quantity of UA characteristics
q, q_x	Random d-1 degree polynomial
AU	Set of user characteristics
c, r	Random non-zero values from Zp
r0	Node at the top of the access tree
x	the access tree's node
τ	entry tree

with the data owner, as shown in Figure 9.c. Additionally, the authority constructs the user's secret key using the master secret key and the characteristics given in Table 9.1. A public key is delivered to the owner of data or metadata saved in the cloud prior to storage (Chinnaiah & Niranjan, 2018; Gutierrez & Lee, 2020; Kumar et al., 2016). Access to the sender's private key is required in order to decrypt the message. For the encrypted data to be deciphered, it must match the secret key.

Setup: The bilinear map will be denoted as: G1 X G1 G2. The authority generates the Public Key (PK) and Master Secret Key (MSK) using non-zero random numbers x1, x2,...,xn, and y obtained from the prime integer Zp.

$$PK = \left(\left(R_1 = g^{x_1}, ..., R_n = g^{x_n} \right), Y = \ell(g,g)^y \right)$$

$$MSK = (x_1, x_2, ..., x_n, y)$$

KeyGeneration: The secret key (S) for each user is created by a reliable organisation. Let S, the user's private key, be equal to:

$$Sj = g^{\frac{q(j)}{x_j}}, \text{ where } j \in AU; AU \subseteq UA$$

Encryption: The ciphertext is created using this algorithm. The message (M) is encrypted using PK, and the data owner uses a set of attributes () to identify themselves. A definition of the encrypted text E is:

$$E = \left(\omega, E' = MY^c = \ell(g,g)^{yc}, \{E_j = R_j^c\} j \in \omega \right)$$

Decryption: Using the secret key S, which was generated with the identity (AU), the data user decrypts the message from the ciphertext. The ciphertext is generated using the identity (). Only if |AUw|d is possible is the decryption. the message M as follows:

$M = E'/Y^c$

KPABE and CPABE are the two main classifications for ABE.

10. AI SECURITY CHALLENGES IN CLOUD

AI brings complicated security problems to cloud systems, which necessitates proactive measures and strategic planning. Best practises must be adopted as part of a company's digital transformation journey in order to guarantee the security of cloud services (Sowinski, 2023).

10.1 Privacy and Security Concerns

As artificial intelligence (AI) develops further, there are worries about how these new technologies may affect our security and privacy. For instance, if AI is used to track our online behaviour, it might be used to gather private information about our lives. Additionally, if AI is employed to develop self-driving automobiles, there may be dangers if these systems are compromised.

AI systems are also susceptible to sophisticated attacks. Some individuals mistakenly believe that AI solutions are impenetrable, but this is just untrue. Good attackers can fool and circumvent AI, but by assuming perfect security, businesses run the risk of becoming complacent and becoming exposed.

10.2 Data Is Very Siloed, Incomplete, or Unstructured

Both the deployment of artificial intelligence and its adaption are expanding quickly. Unstructured data is still a problem for AI, though. Unstructured data is data that is difficult to organise and interpret because it lacks a specified data model or structure. This can be in the form of text, pictures, or videos.

Unstructured data might be more challenging to deal with, but it can also hold a wealth of important information. When it comes to making decisions, unstructured data can frequently be more significant than organised data. This is due to the fact that unstructured data frequently offers more context and specificity than organised data.

The requirement to protect cloud services from malicious actors grows in importance as cloud services become more widely used. And while there are many techniques available to assist safeguard cloud environments, artificial intelligence (AI) is among the most promising (Sowinski, 2023). Threats that would otherwise go unnoticed can be recognised and countered with AI assistance. However, there are several difficulties with employing AI for security.

a. **Implement effective access control:** The security of your cloud environment depends on this. Follow the principle of least privilege by giving each user or programme only the minimal amount of access. For all users, multi-factor authentication ought to be required. To further limit access, think about utilising role-based access controls.

b. **Make use of encryption:** Sensitive data should be encrypted both in transit and at rest to prevent unauthorised access. Additionally, strong key management procedures should be used to guarantee that keys are changed frequently and kept in a safe place.

c. **Install intrusion detection and security monitoring systems:** Your cloud environment should be continuously monitored in order to spot potential risks and unusual behaviour. Implementing intrusion detection systems with AI-powered threat analysis can improve this monitoring. Particular advantages over agentless solutions are provided by agent-based technologies, which take use of the ability to interface directly with your environment and automate incident response.

d. **Regular penetration testing and vulnerability assessments:** Vulnerability assessments that are performed on a regular basis can reveal potential flaws in your cloud infrastructure. Combine them with penetration testing to mimic actual attacks and gauge your organization's resistance against them.

e. **Adopt a security plan that is cloud-native:** Accept the special security features and resources provided by your cloud service provider. Make sure you are adhering to your portion of the security requirement by understanding the shared responsibility paradigm. Use native cloud security tools from providers like Google Cloud Security Command Centre, AWS Security Hub, and Azure Security Centre.

10.3 AI's Advantages for Cloud Security

In terms of cloud security, artificial intelligence (AI) is becoming more and more significant (). AI can assist companies in better protecting this sensitive information when they shift their data and applications to the cloud.

a.   Less Need for Human Intervention

The use of AI in cloud security has numerous advantages. AI has the potential to uncover hazards that people would overlook and to shed light on the tactics used by attackers. AI can also be used to proactively respond to problems and automatically thwart attacks. Azure Sentinel, part of the Microsoft Azure cloud platform, is one illustration of this. Based on the kind of alert that sentinel issues, this solution allows incident responses to automatically start security remediation. This indicates that problems can be found and fixed by the system without the need for human interaction.

b.   Processing of Big Data

Big data is a term used to describe the enormous amount of data that businesses produce every day. Various sources of this information include clickstream data, transactions, and social media. Organisations have a number of difficulties when processing big data since it can be challenging to store and manage such vast amounts of data. Big data, however, also offers a number of benefits for businesses that can efficiently manage and make use of it. Big data can be utilised to enhance decision-making, find fresh business prospects, and streamline operational procedures.

c.   Using automated technologies to delegate

As automated technologies advance, artificial intelligence (AI) will increasingly hand off duties to them. This is done to give the AI more time to concentrate on more difficult jobs or those that call for human judgement. This trend has several advantages, including improved precision and efficiency. The possibility of losing a job as more and more jobs are transferred to automated technology is one of the concerns, though. Overall, there are both advantages and concerns associated with AI delegating to automated systems. We will be better equipped to control these risks and realise the full promise of this technology as we gain greater insight into the possibilities of AI.

d.   Event Recognition and Prevention:

The power of artificial intelligence to identify and prevent potential events increases in sophistication. A method called artificial intelligence (AI) event detection and blocking is used to keep an eye out for future events and stop them before they happen. There are numerous potentials uses for I event detection and blocking. It can be used to stop terrorist attacks, stop crime, and generally keep people secure. Additionally, it can be utilised to avoid accidents, safeguard confidential data, and stand up to natural calamities. The forecasting of hurricanes is a typical instance of this.

11. RESULTS AND DISCUSSION

11.1 Cloud Security Areas

These include data confidentiality, data privacy, DoS, and DDoS as well as vulnerability detection, intrusion detection, malware detection, privacy preservation, anomaly detection, and attack detection. The percentage, frequency, and quantity

Table 3. Field of cloud security discovered from gathered research articles

Cloud Security Applications	Research Papers	Percentage
Anomaly Detection	6	9%
Attack Detection	4	6%
Confidentiality of Data	3	5%
Data Privacy	9	14%
DoS	3	5%
DDoS	10	16%
ID	9	14%
Malware	6	10%
Privacy Preservation	6	10%
Security	5	8%
Vulnerability Detection	2	3%

Table 4. Cited works used in this research project

ID	Paper	Type	Year
A1	"Anomaly Detection System in Cloud Environment Using Fuzzy Clustering Based ANN"	Journal	2015
A2	"Machine Learning for Anomaly Detection and Categorization in Multi-Cloud Environments"	Conference	2017
A3	"A hybrid machine learning approach to network anomaly detection"	Journal	2007
A4	"Frequent Pattern Based User Behavior Anomaly Detection for Cloud System"	Conference	2014
A5	"Monitoring and detecting abnormal behavior in mobile Cloud infrastructure"	Conference	2012
A6	"Insider Threat Detection with Face Recognition and KNN User Classification"	Conference	2018

Table 5. Papers that examine the security implications of cloud anomaly detection

ID	Paper summary on Anomaly Detection
A1	Develops a system to improve the accuracy of detection systems at the hypervisor Cloud layer
A2	Demonstrates the feasibility of ML techniques for anomaly detection and categorizes attacks on Cloud
A3	Proposes an approach for detection and classification of attacks in network traffic
A4	Proposes a framework to operate anomaly detection for profiling user's behavior
A5	Presents a mobile Cloud infrastructure that monitors abnormal behavior and detects malware
A6	Proposes an authentication mechanism based in verifying facial features along with two factor authentications

of research articles in each subfield of cloud security are shown in Table 11.1.1. In Table 11.1.2, a few of the Reference papers are included.

Searching finding deviations from the norm in data is what anomaly detection is all about. Anomaly detection is essential because data outliers represent important and often key information that may be put to use in numerous contexts. A total of six papers address the topic of anomaly detection. However, we found that three of these studies specifically address the problem of identifying anomalous user conduct. The first three papers in Table 11.1.3 discuss cloud-based anomaly detection frameworks and systems. papers A4 and A5 also investigate anomalies, but their focus is on behavioural ones.

12. CONCLUSION

In conclusion, artificial intelligence (AI) and machine learning (ML) have had a profound impact on cloud security, bringing with them both advancements and concerns. Positively, AI and ML have considerably improved cloud security by making threat detection and response methods more effective. These tools can instantly analyse enormous volumes of data to spot patterns and anomalies that human operators might overlook. As a result (Dilek et al., 2015), possible security breaches are identified more quickly, false positives are decreased, and total incident response times are improved. The growth of predictive analytics in cloud security has also been aided by AI and ML. These solutions estimate security threats and vulnerabilities based on past data, enabling organisations to proactively correct flaws before unscrupulous parties may take advantage of them.

Furthermore, regular security processes like log analysis, authentication, and authorization can greatly benefit from automation thanks to AI and ML. This lessens the workload for security staff while also lowering the chance of human error in security operations. These improvements do, however, also present difficulties. A serious threat comes from adversarial attacks, in which perpetrators manipulate AI systems to make bad choices. Additionally, the intricacy of AI and ML models can make them vulnerable to flaws, which could make them a target for cybercriminals. Concerns exist regarding the ethical ramifications of AI and ML in cloud security as well. Important difficulties that must be addressed include privacy concerns, decision-making that is biased, and the lack of transparency in AI systems.

REFERENCES

Aldhyani, T. H., & Alkahtani, H. (2022). Artificial Intelligence Algorithm-Based Economic Denial of Sustainability Attack Detection Systems: Cloud Computing Environments. *Sensors (Basel)*, *22*(13), 4685. doi:10.339022134685 PMID:35808184

Asharaf, Z., Ganne, A., & Mazher, N. (2023). *Artificial Intelligence in Cloud Computing Security*. Research Gate.

Chinnaiah, M. R., & Niranjan, N. (2018, January). Fault tolerant software systems using software configurations for cloud computing. *Journal of Cloud Computing (Heidelberg, Germany)*, *7*(1), 3. doi:10.118613677-018-0104-9

Dilek, S., Cakır, H., & Aydın, M. (2015, January). Applications of Artificial Intelligence Techniques to Combating Cyber Crimes: A Review. *International Journal of Artificial Intelligence & Applications*, *6*(1), 21–39. doi:10.5121/ijaia.2015.6102

Fang, X., Koceja, N., Zhan, J., Dozier, G., & Dipankar, D. (2012). An artificial immune system for phishing detection. *Evolutionary Computation (CEC)*. IEEE. 10.1109/CEC.2012.6256518

Grusho, A., Zabezhailo, M., Zatsarinnyi, A., & Piskovskii, V. (2017). On some artificial intelligence methods and technologies for cloud-computing protection. *Mathematical Linguistics*, *51*(2), 62–74.

Gutierrez, J. N. P., & Lee, K. (2020). An Attack-based Filtering Scheme for Slow Rate Denial-of-Service Attack Detection in Cloud Environment. *J. Multim. Inf. Syst.*, *7*(2), 125–136. doi:10.33851/JMIS.2020.7.2.125

Halabi, T., & Bellaiche, M. (2017, April). Towards quantification and evaluation of security of cloud service providers. *J. Inf. Secur. Appl., 33,* 55–65. doi:10.1016/j.jisa.2017.01.007

Halabi, T., & Bellaiche, M. (2018, June). A broker-based framework for standardization and management of cloud security-SLAs. *Computers & Security, 75,* 59–71. doi:10.1016/j.cose.2018.01.019

Ramanpreet, K. (2023). Artificial intelligence for cybersecurity: Literature review and future research directions. *Information Fusion, 97,* 101804. doi:10.1016/j.inffus.2023.101804

Kumar, P., & Alphonse, P. J. A. (2018, April). Attribute based encryption in cloud computing: A survey, gap analysis, and future directions. *Journal of Network and Computer Applications, 108,* 37–52. doi:10.1016/j.jnca.2018.02.009

Kumar, R., Lal, S. P., & Sharma, A. (2016). Detecting denial of service attacks in the cloud. Proc. *IEEE 14th Int. Conf. Dependable, Autonomic Secure Comput., 14th Int. Conf. Pervas. Intell. Comput.* IEEE. 10.1109/DASC-PICom-DataCom-CyberSciTec.2016.70

Leo, O., Thomas, A., & Hussain, S. (2023). *Uses of Artificial Intelligence Techniques in Cyber security: A Narrative Overview.* IEEE.

Linguistics, M. (2017). Trust issues that create threats for cyber-attacks in cloud computing. Proc. *IEEE 17th Int. Conf. Parallel Distrib. Syst.* (pp. 900–905). IEEE. 10.1109/ICPADS.2011.156

Nassif, B., Talib, M. A., Nasir, Q., Albadani, H., & Dakalbab, F. M. (2021). Machine Learning for Cloud Security: A Systematic Review. *IEEE Access : Practical Innovations, Open Solutions, 9,* 20717–20735. doi:10.1109/ACCESS.2021.3054129

Samuel, P., Jayashree, K., Babu, R., & Vijay, K. (2023). Artificial Intelligence, Machine Learning, and IoT Architecture to Support Smart Governance. In K. Saini, A. Mummoorthy, R. Chandrika, & N. Gowri Ganesh (Eds.), *AI, IoT, and Blockchain Breakthroughs in E-Governance* (pp. 95–113). IGI Global. doi:10.4018/978-1-6684-7697-0.ch007

Sarirete, A., Balfagih, Z., Brahimi, T., Lytras, M. D., & Visvizi, A. (2022). Artificial intelligence and machine learning research: Towards digital transformation at a global scale. *Journal of Ambient Intelligence and Humanized Computing, 13*(7), 3319–3321. doi:10.100712652-021-03168-y

Sowinski, D. (2023). *Cloud security in the era of artificial intelligence.* Security Intelligence. https://securityintelligence.com/posts/cloud-security-in-the-era-of-artificial-intelligence/

Sudha, V., & Akiladevi, R. (2022). An integrated IoT blockchain security technique based on decentralized applications. Internet of Everything: Smart Sensing Technologies, 123-143.

Chapter 3
An Intelligent Data Retrieving Technique and Safety Measures for Sustainable Cloud Computing

Keshav Kumar
Haldia Institute of Technology, India

Ritam Kundu
Haldia Institute of Technology, India

Krishan Kundan Kumar
Haldia Institute of Technology, India

Santanu Koley
Haldia Institute of Technology, India

Ritam Chatterjee
Haldia Institute of Technology, India

Pinaki Pratim Acharjya
iD https://orcid.org/0000-0002-0305-2661
Haldia Institute of Technology, India

ABSTRACT

Data refers to raw facts and figures. After processing data, the information is created. Information like facts or statistics that can be recorded, stored, and analysed can be in various forms such as text, numbers, images, audio, or video. The amount of data generated every day in the data-driven world of today makes it nearly difficult to keep it all locally. Cloud services are being used by so many people and businesses to store these massive and hefty volumes of data on cloud servers. Additionally, as the need for cloud computing grows, so does the need for data recovery methods and services. The ability to recover data and information from the backup server when the primary server is down is the primary goal of recovery services and technologies. A secondary server to hold backups for the primary cloud server will be more expensive to add than the primary server itself, which is already quite expensive and time-consuming to build. The goal of this chapter is to provide realistic, cost-effective solutions to this urgent problem.

DOI: 10.4018/979-8-3693-1431-9.ch003

1. INTRODUCTION

Data refers to any information, facts, or statistics that can be recorded, stored, and analysed. It can be in various forms such as text, numbers, images, audio, or video. In the context of computing and technology, data often refers to digital information that is stored and processed by computer systems. This data can be structured or unstructured, and can be generated from a variety of sources such as sensors, software applications, or user input. Data is an essential component of many fields such as business, science, medicine, and engineering. It can be used to make informed decisions, discover patterns or trends, and gain insights into various phenomena. However, data alone is not useful until it is processed, analysed, and interpreted.

Electronic data production has reached an unprecedented scale, leading to a significant challenge for companies to store it. The traditional solution of using hard disk drives (HDDs) with terabytes of storage capacity is no longer sufficient to meet the data storage demands of IT companies. Even constructing an entire storage facility may not solve the problem, as the volume of data generated by companies continues to grow at an exponential rate.

To address this challenge, cloud computing was introduced. This innovative technology enables users to store their data on a remote cloud server rather than on their personal computers, freeing up valuable physical storage space. Accessing the data is as easy as logging into the cloud account, and cloud services are often more cost-effective than building a large-scale storage facility.

The widespread adoption of cloud computing has not been limited to businesses alone, as individuals also seek to leverage its benefits for data storage. However, this increased demand has also led to the risk of data loss. To mitigate this risk, cloud-based data recovery and backup procedures have been developed, providing additional layers of protection to ensure that valuable data is not lost due to unforeseen events such as hardware failure, cyber-attacks, or human error.

One significant advantage of cloud computing is its scalability. Businesses and organizations can easily scale their storage and computing resources up or down based on their changing needs, without having to invest in new hardware or infrastructure. This is especially useful for businesses with fluctuating demand, such as those in the retail or hospitality industry, where demand can vary based on seasonality or market trends. With cloud computing, businesses can quickly and easily adjust their storage and computing capacity, allowing them to be more agile and responsive to changing market conditions.

Another benefit of cloud computing is its accessibility. Cloud-based storage and computing resources can be accessed from anywhere with an internet connection, allowing businesses and individuals to work remotely or collaborate with others in different locations. This has become increasingly important in the wake of the

COVID-19 pandemic, as more businesses and organizations have shifted to remote work arrangements. With cloud computing, employees can access the same data and resources from their home offices as they would in the physical office, making remote work more seamless and efficient.

2. CLOUD COMPUTING

Cloud computing as a concept has its roots in the early days of computing. The idea of accessing remote computing resources was first proposed by J.C.R. Licklider, a computer scientist who worked on early developments in time-sharing and networking in the 1960s ("Britannica, The Editors of Encyclopaedia", 2023). He envisioned a future in which people could access computer power and applications from anywhere in the world, over a network of interconnected machines.

However, it was not until the 1990s that cloud computing started to take shape as we know it today. At that time, the internet was gaining widespread adoption, and companies began to realize the potential of hosting their applications and data online. This led to the development of Application Service Providers (ASPs), which offered businesses the ability to rent access to their software applications over the internet.

Figure 1. Cloud computing and its usages

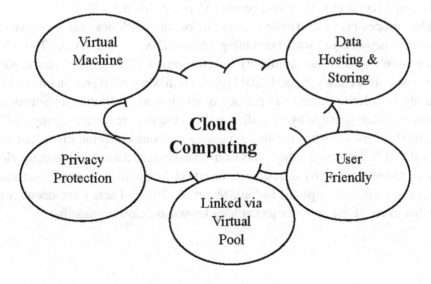

The term "cloud computing" was first used in 1996 by Compaq Computer, which used it to describe the delivery of computing services over the internet ("Solved Magazine. The history of cloud computing", 2023). In 2002, Amazon Web Services (AWS) launched its cloud computing platform, which offered on-demand access to computing resources such as storage, computing power, and database services.

The development of virtualization technology was a significant factor in the growth of cloud computing. Virtualization enables multiple virtual machines to run on a single physical machine, allowing for greater efficiency and utilization of computing resources. This technology paved the way for cloud providers to offer scalable and flexible computing services to their customers (Greeshmanth, R. C., et al., 2023).

Today, cloud computing has become an integral part of modern computing infrastructure, powering everything from online applications to scientific research projects (Daabseha, T. K. I. K., et al., 2023). With the rise of the internet of things (IoT) and the increasing volume of data being generated, cloud computing is expected to continue to play a critical role in enabling businesses and individuals to store, process, and analyse data (Ajeh, D. E., et, al., 2014). One of the most common and frequently used technologies in use today is cloud computing (Koley, S., et al., 2014). In essence, it gives customers access to a virtual machine or platform online where they can host or store their data and other documents. In addition to offering users and businesses with insufficient storage space a cheaper alternative to purchasing a storage device, one of the main reasons cloud computing (Koley, S., et, al., 2014) gained such rapid popularity was due to how simple it was to use. Its ease of use was a secondary factor. The only things a user really needs are an internet connection and a way to connect to the cloud server (Alarifi, A., et al., 2020).

Data processing is distributed among numerous machines that are connected through a network in cloud computing (Alzoubi, K., et al., 2020). This cloud architecture's systems are intimately linked together. Through virtualized pools, cloud computing (Koley, S., et al., 2014) power is maximised. It provides its services digitally in order to protect the privacy of its customers. Data management and access are made possible by virtualization's secure environment (Suganya, M., et al., 2023). Users' ability to use the computing environment is improved (Brezany, P., et al. 2017). To prevent other users from accessing the data of one user, the cloud service provider regularly refreshes its resources, including its servers, networks, storage, servers, and apps (El Haloui, M., et al., 2017). These components work together to create the complex technology known as "cloud computing."

3. NEED FOR CLOUD BACKUP

As was mentioned earlier in the introduction, an increasing number of people and businesses are adopting cloud services these days to host and store data, making the cloud server a top choice for data storage (Dang, L. M., et al., 2019). A serious fear of data loss also comes along with that obligation. Cloud servers now house a variety of sensitive data for numerous businesses and individuals (Hai, T., et al., 2023). What if a cloud server leaks data? What if a server in the cloud is breached? What if a cloud server malfunctions? What if a leak occurs while the data is being sent to the cloud server?

What would happen if an earthquake, tsunami, or other natural disaster caused a cloud server to be destroyed? A cloud server's data loss can happen in a number of different ways. Now, it is the duty of the cloud provider to reassure its clients regarding data security and protection (Hassan, H., et al., 2017). As a result, it becomes necessary to have a recovery strategy and backup to guarantee that, even in the event of a data breach or loss from the primary cloud server, the data can still be safely restored (Khan, N., et al., 2016). The resource pool architecture (Koley, S., et al., 2015) used in cloud server (Koley, S., et al., 2015) can store data efficiently.

In a nutshell the benefits of cloud computing can be summarised as

Figure 2. Need for cloud backup

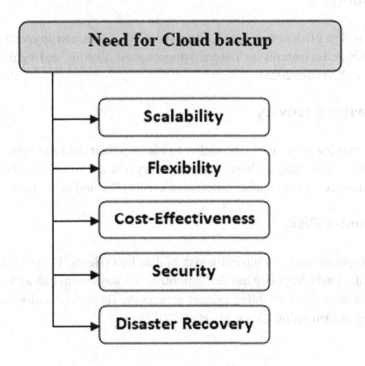

3.1 Scalability

One of the key advantages of cloud computing is its scalability. Cloud providers offer access to a vast pool of computing resources that can be scaled up or down based on the user's needs. This enables businesses to handle sudden spikes in demand without having to invest in additional hardware or infrastructure (Li, K. (2017).

3.2 Flexibility

Cloud computing offers the flexibility to access their data and applications from anywhere in the world, as long as they have an internet connection. This makes it ideal for remote working, collaboration, and access to critical data (Mahan, F., et al., 2021).

3.3 Cost-Effectiveness

Cloud computing is often more cost-effective than traditional computing models, as it eliminates the need for businesses to invest in expensive hardware and infrastructure. Additionally, cloud providers often offer pay-as-you-go pricing models, which enable businesses to pay only for the resources they use (Jaatun, M.G., et al., 2017).

3.4 Security

Cloud providers often have robust security measures in place to protect their users' data. This includes features such as encryption, access controls, and regular security audits (Wu, Y., et al., 2023).

3.5 Disaster Recovery

Cloud computing offers users the ability to back up their data and applications to remote servers, providing a robust disaster recovery solution in the event of a hardware failure, natural disaster, or other unforeseen events (Selvarajan, S., et al., 2023).

3.6 Minimize Risk

Cloud computing also minimizes the risk of data loss (Hewa, T., et al., 2022)..

Overall, cloud computing has revolutionized the way businesses and individual access and store data, enabling greater efficiency, flexibility, and scalability in computing infrastructure (IJena, M., et al., 2022).

4. EXISTING METHODS AND TECHNIQUES FOR CLOUD BACKUP

4.1 High Security Distribution and Rake Technology (HS-DRT)

The HS-DRT is a backup idea that makes use of high-speed encryption technology with a widely dispersed data transport method (Mittal, H., et al., 2022). It shows promise as an effective method for mobile clients like laptops, cell phones, and other devices, but it is unable to manage data duplication or the cheap cost of recovery implementation (Rawai, N. M., et al., 2013). It is made up of three parts: The datacentre, the supervisory server, and the various client nodes that the administrator has specified the first three main functions (Rigdon, E. E., et al., 2017).

PCs, cell phones, network-attached storage, and storage services make up the client nodes. They also have a secure network connection to the data centre and a supervisory server (Shakeabubakor, A. A., et al., 2015). The backup sequence and the recovery sequence are the two steps that this proposed system takes. In the backup sequence, it receives the data that needs to be backed up, and in the recovery sequence, the supervisory server (one of the HSDRT's components), which can happen often or in the event of a disaster, receives the data that needs to be recovered (Teh, S. et al., 2016). It initiates the recuperation process.

Like the rake reception operation, it gathers the encrypted fragmentations from various suitable clients (Williams, D. R., et al., 2013). At the second stage, the decryption will be finished once the fragmentations have been merged and descrambled in reverse order (Heilig, L., et al., 2014). By following these steps, the original data that needs to be backed up can be obtained by the supervisory server.

This model, however, has some drawbacks, making it difficult to be hailed as a perfect backup and recovery solution. Those limitations are:

- In order to make full use of the HS-DRT processor, it is essential to ensure that the web applications are configured correctly to utilize the engine (Hwang, K., et al., 2014).
- Second, when more duplicate copies of file data are present, the web application's performance will suffer on the related processor as a result (Khan, S., et al., 2015).

Advantages of using HS-DRT: HS-DRT is a scalable solution that can easily grow as your backup needs increase. User can add more servers and storage locations as needed, without affecting performance or reliability (Lal, P., et al., 2015).

Figure 3. High security distribution and rake technology
(Cloud, I., et al., 2014).

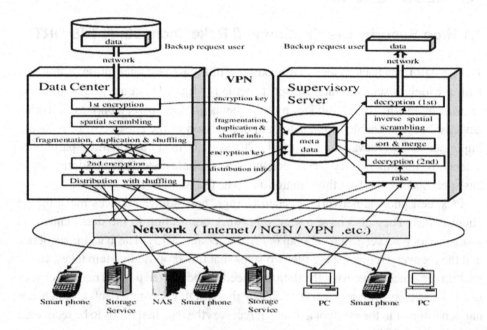

- HS-DRT provides advanced security features that protect data from unauthorized access and potential threats such as hacking, malware, and ransomware. HS-DRT uses multiple layers of encryption and authentication to ensure that data is secure (Mueller, H., et al., 2017).
- HS-DRT uses a distributed architecture to speed up backup and restore times. This means that backup data is split into smaller chunks and distributed across multiple servers, which allows for faster backup and restore times (Burda, D., et al., 2015).

Disadvantages of using HS-DRT: The cost of implementing HS-DRT can be high, especially for small businesses or individuals. The cost of specialized hardware, software, and maintenance can add up quickly.

- Needed high-speed as well as reliable internet connection to access the data and perform backups or recoveries.
- In HS-DRT we may face some security risks such as data breaches, unauthorized access, malware attacks, or compliance violations if the cloud provider doesn't have adequate security measures or policies.

- In HS-DRT the user may not have much visibility or control over how their data is stored and managed by the cloud provider.
- It increases the redundancy.

4.2 Parity Cloud Service (PCS)

The Parity Cloud Service (PCS) is a highly straightforward, user-friendly, and practical parity-based data recovery method. In PCS, the original data is divided into multiple fragments or data block, and additional parity blocks are generated based on these data blocks. Each parity blocks contain information about the original data blocks and are used to reconstruct the data if any of the data blocks are lost or corrupted. The parity blocks are stored in different locations than the data blocks, providing additional protection against data loss due to hardware failures, natural disasters, or other events.

Data can be recovered from a PCS with an extremely high probability and at a reasonable cost. To gain public trust in a personal data recovery service, it's vital to prioritize customer privacy and implement strong security measures such as encryption, multi-factor authentication, and secure data storage solutions. This approach can encourage users to confidently use the service without fear of compromising their sensitive data.

PCS can be used for a variety of applications, including backup and recovery, archiving, and disaster recovery. It can also be integrated with other cloud services, such as object storage or file systems, to provide a complete cloud backup solution.

A modern platform for privacy-protecting personal data recovery services is the Parity Cloud Service (PCS) (Adhikari, M., et al., 2017). Personal data recovery services should take four factors into account.

- Reliability.
- Efficiency in the economy.
- Convenience.
- Protection of privacy.

For data backup, PCS employs a novel method that creates virtual discs on the user's computer, creates parity groups across those virtual discs, and stores the parity data of the parity group in the cloud (Koley, S. et al., 2022; Koley, S. et al., 2022). The exclusive OR is employed by the PCS algorithms to generate parity information.

Advantages of using PCS: When compared to other techniques, it is extremely dependable.

67

Figure 4. Parity cloud service
(Hyungsoo, J., et al., 2017)

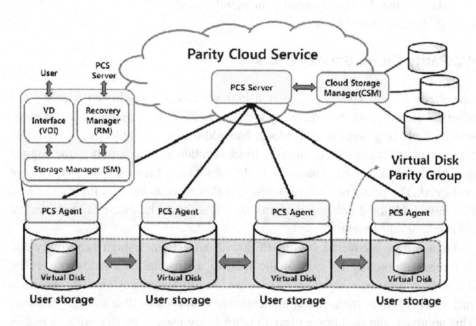

- PCS, uses parity recovery service to protect personal data from unauthorized access or disclosure.
- PCS requires a small storage space in the cloud for storing parity data, thus reducing cloud storage costs.

Disadvantages of using PCS: PCS is very complex to implement.

- It requires high internet connectivity for users to access user data.
- It stores user data on a third-party server which may pose security risks.

4.3 Cold and Hot Backup Service Replacement Strategy (CBSRS)

Copies of the actual database files make up physical backups. For instance, a physical backup might transfer database data from a local disc drive to a different safe place. Both hot and cold physical backups are possible.

Hot Backup: A hot backup is aback up performed on data while the database is actively online and accessible to users. It is a popular backup solution for multi-user system s as no downtime is required. Though it may not capture all the changes made by users during the backup process.

During a hot backup, users can make changes to the database. The database and the backup copy are synchronised using the changes that were logged in the log files created during the backup. When a full backup is required but a cold backup would require system downtime due to the service level, a hot backup is employed.

Cold Backup: The database and the backup copy are always synced since users cannot make changes to the database while it is being cold backed up. Only when the service level permits the necessary system downtime is a cold backup employed.

Physical backups can be made in a full or incremental fashion. It is advised to do regular cold complete physical backups. It generates a duplicate of the data, which may include the control file, transaction files (redo logs), archive files, and data files from a database. By offering a mechanism to retrieve original data, this backup type defends against loss and protects data from application error. Depending on how frequently user's data changes, perform this backup every week or every two weeks. It is advised to create cold complete backups so that users cannot make modifications while the backups are being made. Only modifications made since the last complete physical backup are captured. The premise is that only transaction log files produced after the last backup are stored, even though the files for databases vary. While the database is being used, incremental backup can be performed hot, but it decreases database performance.

Both cold backup and hot backup have distinctive qualities that make them particularly customized to satisfy consumers' requirements. In contrast to hot backup, which is frequently accessed through Oracle, the primary provider, and is highly expensive to maintain, cold backup for data is easily accessible at a reasonable cost. To ensure data integrity, which might be compromised if the backup happens while data and files are in flux, cold backup only works when the database is shut down and inaccessible to users. On the other hand, hot backup is a technique for accelerating work processes in multiuser systems and is intended to execute concurrently with the database actively online and visible to users. Data security is increased with cold backups, and the likelihood of data corruption is decreased. On the other hand, Hot backup is meant to save and restore practically all database entities and delivers quick data recovery.

When utilized separately, cold backups can only offer access to a particular timeframe when needed for data recovery. The database enters shutdown status and is unreachable during the backup process. Given that the database must be offline while the backup is taking place, this interferes with regular work schedules. Hot backups are expensive to maintain, thus operators must exercise particular caution while deploying them. The backed-up data cannot be used for point-level recovery if the hot backup in the process fails.

Figure 5. Cold and hot backup service

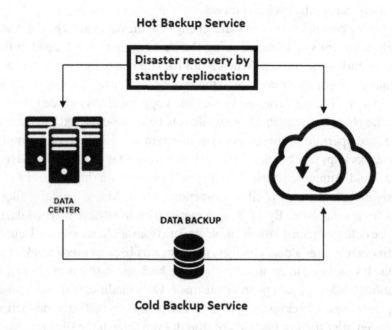

Advantages of using CBSRS: The advantages of using CBSRS are as follows.

- CBSRS ensures that data remains available even in the event of a service failure.
- CBSRS can help minimize downtime in the event of a service failure by quickly replacing it with backup service.
- CBSRS provides flexibility as it can be used with both cold and hot backup services, providing different levels of data availability and recovery time.

Disadvantage of using CBSRS: The disadvantages of using CBSRS are as follows.

- As data volume grows, so does the cost of implementation.
- CBSRS can be easily scaled up or down as business needs change. Additional backup services can be added as needed to meet growing demand or scaled back during periods of lower demand.
- CBSRS can be more cost-effective than other backup strategies, particularly for business with limited budgets. Cold backups require less storage and compute resources, while hot backups can be more efficient in terms of storage usage.

4.4 Linux Box

A Linux server is one that utilizes the free and open-source Linux operating system. It offers businesses a low-cost method of giving their customers information, apps, and services. Due to Linux's open-source nature, users have access to a vast community of supporters and resources. Linux (Ostroukh, A. V., et al., 2015) is used as the embedded operating system in a variety of devices, including network file systems, home appliances, and automobile entertainment systems. For routers, switches, DNS servers, home networking devices, and more, there are network operating systems. A crucial company concern is data backup.

Due to an increase in cyber threats, user error, and system flaws, user data is not secure. Backing up data ensures that important files and folders are not lost in the event of a security breach, an accidental deletion, or a system failure. Data backup is easy for individuals and small to medium-sized enterprises to perform, at least in part, using some kind of cloud architecture. However, data backup is complicated and frequently done, at least in part, on backup servers or external hard drives for large businesses where the amount of data is enormous (on the petabyte scale).

Linux Box generates a volume and ties it to an instance when the user needs to back up one. A volume is a virtual hard disc that is connected to a virtual machine (VM), which enhances performance and reduces latency. When a backup of the data in the VM is needed, volumes are typically attached. Data can be frequently backed up in the cloud using a Linux Box, lowering the possibility of data loss during emergencies. For small data sets, recovery time is slashed. It entails spending money on hardware and infrastructure. Uptime and recovery times are not guaranteed.

Figure 6. Linux box

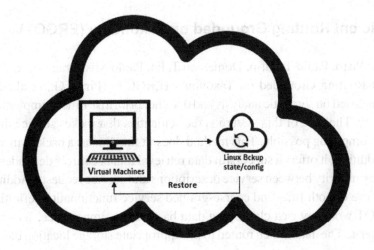

Advantages of using Linux Box: The advantages of using Linux Box are as follows.

- Linux is an open-source operating system, which means that it is freely available and can be customized to meet the needs of businesses. This can result in lower costs and greater flexibility when compared to proprietary software.
- Linux is known for its stability and reliability, which can be important in backup and disaster recovery scenarios. It also has a reputation for being less vulnerable to viruses and malware than other operating systems.
- Linux is compatible with a wide range of backup solutions, including both proprietary and open-source options. This can provide businesses with greater flexibility when choosing a backup solution.
- In comparison to other options, the implementation cost is very low.

Disadvantages of using Linux Box: The disadvantages of using Linux Box are as follows.

- Linux box requires higher bandwidth than any other model.
- While Linux has a large and active community, it may not have the same level of commercial support as other operating systems. This can make it more difficult for businesses to find help if they encounter issues with their backup solution.
- Linux can be more complex and difficult to learn for users who are used to other operating systems, such as Windows or MacOS. This can result in a steeper learning curve for IT staff responsible for managing the backup solution.
- Data privacy is an issue with this model.

4.5 Efficient Routing Grounded on Taxonomy (ERGOT)

Giuseppe Pirro, Paolo Trunfio, Domenico Talia, Paolo Missierand Carole Goble's Efficient Routing Grounded on Taxonomy (ERGOT) (Pirro, G., et al., 2008) is entirely focused on semantic analysis and does not prioritise time or implementation complexity. The core of this system is the semantics that makes service discovery in cloud computing possible. This method doesn't function as a backup mechanism and, in addition, it offers a successful data retrieval that is entirely dependent on the semantic similarity between service descriptions and service requests. Additionally, it makes use of both fine- and coarse-grained service functionality definitions.

ERGOT works by first classifying data based on its importance, sensitivity, or other criteria. The data is then routed to the appropriate storage location based on its classification. For example, critical data may be routed to multiple geographically diverse locations, while less critical data may be stored in a single location or in a less expensive storage tier. The taxonomy used in ERGOT can be customized to meet the specific needs of the organization. For example, the taxonomy may be based on the type of data, such as customer data, financial data, or employee data. The taxonomy may also be based on the level of sensitivity, such as public, confidential, or highly confidential.

ERGOT is a technique used in cloud backup that involves organizing data based on a taxonomy and routing the data to the appropriate storage location. ERGOT can improve the efficiency, security, and disaster recovery capabilities of cloud backup, making it an attractive option for organizations looking to enhance their backup and storage capabilities.

There are three components to this concept. Those are:

i) The utilization of a DHT (Distributed Hash Table) protocol facilitates the propagation of semantic service descriptions that are annotated with individual ontology concepts.

ii) With the help of a Semantic Overlay Network (SON), peers with similar semantically annotated service descriptions can be clustered together, and this network is built up gradually through service advertising via DHT.

iii) A metric to determine the degree of semantic similarity between various service descriptions.

Unlike traditional backup solutions, the ERGOT strategy offers efficient data retrieval that depends on the semantic resemblance among service requests and descriptions, and it combines two network paradigms to provide semantically-driven query replies in DHT-based systems. Although ERGOT faces challenges with semantic similarity search models, it overcomes these limitations by generating a SON over a DHT. The system's effectiveness in terms of search accuracy and network traffic was demonstrated after a thorough investigation of it under various network conditions. However, semantic similarity search models do not integrate well with DHT-based systems. They only run logarithmic performance-constrained exact-match searches.

Advantage of this approach: The advantages of using Efficient Routing Grounded on Taxonomy (ERGOT) are as follows.

• ERGOT reduces the amount of data that needs to be backed up by organizing it into taxonomy. This allows for more efficient use of storage resources and faster backup times.

Figure 7. Efficient routing grounded on taxonomy

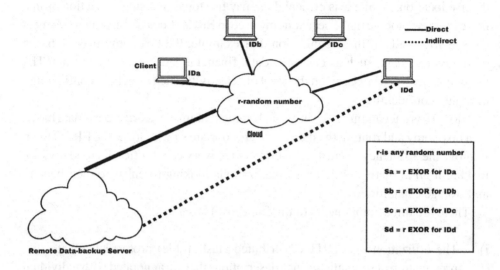

- ERGOT is highly scalable and can be used to protect large amounts of data in the cloud. It can easily handle growing data volumes and provide high availability of data across different geographical locations.
- This technique utilizes both high-level descriptions of service functionality as well as more detailed descriptions.
- ERGOT can provide better data privacy in cloud storage backup by encrypting the data fragments before they are stored in the cloud. This ensures that even if the data is accessed by unauthorized users, they cannot read or use it.

Disadvantage of this approach: The disadvantages of using Efficient Routing Grounded on Taxonomy (ERGOT) are as follows.

- However, the semantic similarity search paradigm does not work well with DHT-based systems' exact-match searches, which have logarithmic performance constraints.
- ERGOT requires a high degree of technical expertise and infrastructure to implement. The process of encoding and decoding data requires significant computational resources, which can be costly for small businesses or individuals.
- SONs must be connected to a limited number of peers since query efficiency improves with fewer peers that must be searched.

- ERGOT may not be compatible with all cloud storage platforms. This can limit the flexibility of businesses and individuals in choosing a suitable cloud storage solution.

5. PROPOSED TECHNIQUES FOR CLOUD BACKUP

We are proposing a novel method for cloud data backup that utilizes the tokenization and encryption capabilities of cloud service providers to enhance the security and privacy of user data. This approach involves converting data into digital tokens, which can be securely transferred and stored. The tokens can then be encrypted using advanced techniques such as AES or RSA encryption, adding an extra layer of protection to the backup process. This innovative solution has the potential to revolutionize the field of cloud data backup by providing users with greater confidence in the security of their data.

Once data is tokenized and encrypted, it can be securely stored on external devices such as hard disks or secure digital cards, which are often underutilized. To facilitate this storage process, members of the general public can contribute these devices and receive cryptocurrency as a token of appreciation for their valuable contribution. This innovative approach not only provides an extra layer of security for cloud data backup but also incentivizes individuals to participate in the storage process, ultimately reducing costs for cloud service providers. With this system, users can have peace of mind knowing that their data is being stored in a secure and cost-effective manner, while also contributing to the growth of the cryptocurrency market.

In order to be eligible for the cryptocurrency reward, users must store their data on their local machines and keep it available for retrieval by the cloud server. In the event that the cloud server experiences difficulties accessing its data, it can notify the file keeper and request their encrypted files. This innovative system not only provides users with a financial incentive to securely store their data, but it also offers an additional layer of protection for cloud servers in the event of data loss. By incentivizing secure data storage, this approach has the potential to revolutionize the field of cloud data backup and enhance the overall security of cloud storage systems.

With the increasing number of contributors joining the network, the usefulness of the cryptocurrency token is set to surge, thereby boosting the value of the currency. As a result, more people will be incentivized to contribute their underused storage resources, creating a mutually beneficial scenario for both the cloud company and its users. This innovative approach provides a secure and cost-effective way to store and access data in the cloud, which is a win-win situation for all parties involved.

5.1 Model Description

The proposed model for cloud data backup involves several key features.

- Firstly, the data is tokenized and distributed in a decentralized manner. This distribution is closely monitored and regulated by the central authority of the cloud service provider. By distributing the tokenized data in a decentralized manner, the likelihood of data breaches and theft is significantly reduced.

- Secondly, cloud companies can control the distribution of the tokenized data based on various factors, such as an individual's reputation, political and financial stability, internet connectivity, and government laws. Additionally, cloud companies can create a cryptographic currency token, which can be used to facilitate the exchange of data.

- To implement this model, cloud companies need to create an algorithm that can break user data into the smallest tokens and merge them using a powerful compression algorithm. The resulting file is then encrypted and sent to the contributor. To validate the transaction of data and distribute tokens, cloud companies can use the proof of work method.

- Moreover, cloud companies can store an encrypted ledger of the distribution of data within the contributor's memory. Every user of this cloud would be given a unique hash number that identifies the ledger holder. From there, cloud companies can retrieve the user's data.

- Finally, In the event of any unforeseen issues with a user's data on the server, our proposed model provides a robust and effective solution. Cloud companies can simply request the data collector to provide their file with the encrypted ledger, which facilitates the exchange of our cryptographic currency and enables the stored data to be made available online once again. This streamlined process ensures that any issues with user data can be resolved quickly and efficiently, with minimal disruption to the user's operations.

Overall, our proposed model offers a comprehensive and innovative solution to the challenges of cloud data backup. By leveraging the latest advancements in encryption and decentralization, we believe that our model represents a significant step forward in ensuring the privacy and security of user data in the cloud. Cloud companies that implement this model can offer their users a more reliable and secure backup process, which in turn can help to enhance their reputation and competitiveness in the marketplace.

Figure 8. Block diagram of proposed technique

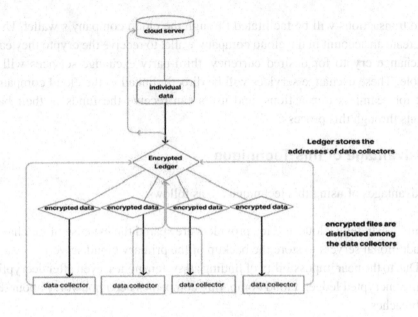

5.2 Tracking the Data Distribution

Each time a cloud computing company rents data to a user, the company will also store an encrypted ledger of the distribution, indicating how and where one's data has been distributed, within the contributor's memory. Each user of this cloud service will be given a hash number that identifies the ledger holder, enabling retrieval of the user's data. The system will be decentralized and immutable, like the crypto public ledger. The use of hashing and encryption will prevent data theft, and it will enable us to shortlist the file keepers to retrieve a specific individual user's data.

5.3 Retrieving User's Data

In the event that a cloud computing company experiences any issues with its users' data on the server, the company may request that the data collector provide the stored files along with the ledger to restore the user's data online. The request to share the data with the data collector will be sent 24 hours prior to the designated time for data retrieval. At that specific time, the company will initiate a process to retrieve the data. As an administrator, the data collector must grant permission to run the process. Once the process is complete, the system will return to its original state and the user's data will be restored online.

5.4 The Digital Transactions

Crypto transactions will be facilitated through the cloud company's wallet. Users must create an account in the cloud company wallet to receive the crypto they earn. To exchange crypto for desired currency, third-party exchange services will be available. These exchange services will be directly linked to the cloud company's wallet for seamless transactions, and users can receive the funds in their bank accounts through this process.

5.5 Advantage of this Technique

The advantages of using this technique are as follows:

- In this strategy, cloud service providers are spared the expense of purchasing additional servers to store the backup of the primary cloud server.
- Due to the near impossibility of finding all system nodes, even after decrypting the encrypted ledger, cloud computing companies need not worry about data breaches.
- This model is very cost efficient and almost self-financing.
- As this method is totally crowdsourced this model doesn't need regular employee.
- As in this model the data is totally decentralized, it'll not be affected by any natural or human-caused calamities.
- It is accurate to predict that an increase in the value of the crypto currency (reward) will exponentially increase the storage contributors and vice versa because the storage rental system is crypto-based.

5.6 Issues

- Though in this process data can easily be tampered with by the contributor, this model protects against data breach or theft. To prevent this, cloud companies must tokenize the data and then use the appropriate encryption.
- Cloud back up companies have to compress the tokens into a single file in that such a way by which user can decrypt and retrieve the data with ease and with proper information of parent of the tokens.
- This process is kind of time consuming as whenever the server needed to back up its data by these tokens, cloud companies have to wait for the contributor to upload their files to the server. (For solving this issue, cloud companies can encourage the contributor with giving them rewards on basis of how fast they upload the files to the server)

- As it is a crypto based rental system a drop in the crypto currency's (reward) value can make the company lose the trust of its storage contributors.
- To make the reward consistent cloud companies might have to invest in the currency.

The proposed idea of using a crowdsourced, decentralized model for cloud backup has several advantages, such as being cost-efficient, self-financing, and resilient to natural disasters. However, there are also potential issues to consider, such as the need for tokenization and encryption to prevent data tampering, the time-consuming process of waiting for contributors to upload files, and the risk of losing the trust of storage contributors due to fluctuations in the value of the reward currency. These issues can be addressed through careful planning and investments, making this model a promising option for cloud backup.

6. CONCLUSION

All of these options for cloud data backup demonstrate that none of the current models can solve the aforementioned issues. Each alternative method has advantages and disadvantages that vary based on the circumstance. All of these methods attempted to address various problems while keeping the implementation costs as low as feasible. However, there are certain methods where the price rises gradually as the amount of data increases. As an illustration, take the Cold and Hot back-up method, which executes backup and recovery based on the detection of failure triggers. The model we have outlined, addresses the bulk of the issue in the most efficient and cost-effective manner, something no other model has been able to achieve. Not only that, but our model is self-financing, which means that cloud companies do not need to invest frequently in them in order to keep them operating; rather, after some time, our model will start to create its own revenue and will no longer require their support of cloud company. Only thing that Cloud Company will need to ensure is that our model is implemented properly and because of this, we think that among the alternatives, our data backup solution is the best. Even if our data backup strategy addresses the majority of the problems in this area, there is still a tonne of room for innovation and development. We are sure that the work we put into this initiative will open up new opportunities for the academic community to work on this model.

REFERENCES

Adhikari, M., Koley, S., & Arab, J. (2017). Cloud Computing: A Multi-workflow Scheduling Algorithm with Dynamic Reusability. *Arabian Journal for Science and Engineering*, *43*(2), 645–660. doi:10.100713369-017-2739-0

Ajeh, D., Ellman, J., & Keogh, S. (2014). A cost modelling system for cloud computing. *In 2014 14th International Conference on Computational Science and Its Applications,* (pp. 74-84). IEEE.

Alarifi, A., Dubey, K., Amoon, M., Altameem, T., Abd El-Samie, F. E., Altameem, A., & Nasr, A. A. (2020). Energy efficient hybrid framework for green cloud computing. *IEEE Access: Practical Innovations, Open Solutions*, *8*, 115356–115369. doi:10.1109/ACCESS.2020.3002184

Alzoubi, K., Aljawarneh, N. M., Alsafadi, Y., Al-Radaideh, A. T., & Altahat, S. (2020). Role of Cloud Computing in Service Quality, Information Quality & Low Costs: An Empirical Study on Jordanian Customs. *International Journal of Academic Research in Business & Social Sciences*, *10*(6), 522–532. doi:10.6007/IJARBSS/v10-i6/7330

Brezany, P., Ludescher, T., & Feilhauer, T. (2017). Cloud-dew computing support for automatic data analysis in life sciences. *In 2017 40th International Convention on Information and Communication Technology, Electronics and Microelectronics (MIPRO),* (pp. 365-370). IEEE.

Burda, D., & Teutenberg, F. (2015). Understanding Service Quality and System Quality Success Factors in Cloud Archiving From an End-User Perspective. *Information Systems Management*, *32*(4), 266–284. doi:10.1080/10580530.2015.1079998

Cloud, I., Miyaho, N., Suzuki, S., Tokyo, Y. (2014). Study of a backup service concept using secure distributed networks. *IEICE Communication society-global newsletter*, *38*(3), 2

Daabseha, T. K. I. K., Raqqada, R. A., Albayaydahb, H. S., Alqarallahb, R. E., Alhtibata, A., Alzbouna, E., & Aldamena, H. K. (2023). Linking between cloud computing and productivity: The mediating role of information integration. *International Journal of Data and Network Science*, *7*, 1–8.

Dang, L. M., Piran, M. J., Han, D., Min, K., & Moon, H. (2019). A survey on internet of things and cloud computing for healthcare. *Electronics (Basel)*, *8*(7), 768. doi:10.3390/electronics8070768

El Haloui, M., & Kriouile, A. (2017). A Decision-Support Model Enabling a Proactive Vision of Cloud Computing Adoption. *Proc. of the 2nd International Conference of Cloud Computing Technologies and Applications–CloudTech*, (pp. 24-26). IEEE.

Greeshmanth, R. C., & Shah, M. A. (2023). Novel secure data protection scheme using Martino homomorphic encryption. *Journal of Cloud Computing (Heidelberg, Germany)*, *12*(1), 47. doi:10.118613677-023-00425-7

Hai, T., Zhou, J., Lu, Y., Jawawi, D., Wang, D., Onyema, E. M., & Biamba, C. (2023). Enhanced security using multiple paths routine scheme in cloud-MANETs. *Journal of Cloud Computing (Heidelberg, Germany)*, *12*(1), 68. doi:10.118613677-023-00443-5

Hassan, H., Nasir, M., Herry, M., Khairudin, N., & Adon, I. (2017). Factors influencing cloud computing adoption in small and medium enterprises. *Journal of Information and Communication Technology*, *16*(1), 21–41. doi:10.32890/jict2017.16.1.8216

Heilig, L., & Voß, S. (2014). A scientometric analysis of cloud computing literature. *IEEE Transactions on Cloud Computing*, *2*(3), 266–278. doi:10.1109/TCC.2014.2321168

Hewa, T., Braeken, A., Liyanage, M., & Ylianttila, M. (2022). Fog computing and blockchain-based security service architecture for 5g industrial iot-enabled cloud manufacturing. *IEEE Transactions on Industrial Informatics*, *18*(10), 7174–7185. doi:10.1109/TII.2022.3140792

Hwang, K., Shi, Y., & Bai, X. (2014). Scale-out vs. scale-up techniques for cloud performance and productivity. *In 2014 IEEE 6th International Conference on Cloud Computing Technology and Science,* (pp. 763-768). IEEE.

Hyungsoo, J., Yongsu, P., Chi-Won, S., & Sooyong, K. (2017). Parity-based personal data recovery service in cloud. *Cluster Computing*, *20*(3), 2655–2668. doi:10.100710586-017-0805-8

Jaatun, M.G., Lambrinoudakis, C., Rong, C. (2017). Special issue on security in cloud computing. *J Cloud Comp*, *17*.

Jena, M., Das, U., & Das, M. (2022). A Pragmatic Analysis of Security Concerns in Cloud, Fog, and Edge Environment. In Predictive Data Security using AI: Insights and Issues of Blockchain, IoT, and DevOps. Springer Nature Singapore.

Khan, N., & Al-Yasiri, A. (2016). Identifying cloud security threats to strengthen cloud computing adoption framework. *Procedia Computer Science*, *94*, 485–490. doi:10.1016/j.procs.2016.08.075

Khan, S., Al-Mogren, A. S., & AlAjmi, M. F. (2015). Using cloud computing to improve network operations and management. *In 2015 5th National Symposium on Information Technology: Towards New Smart World (NSITNSW)*, (pp. 1-6). IEEE.

Koley, S., & Acharjya, P. P. (2022). *Prevalence of Multi-Agent System Consensus in Cloud Computing*. Multi Agent Systems. doi:10.1007/978-981-19-0493-6_4

Koley, S., Acharjya, P. P., Keshari, P., & Mandal, K. K. (2022). *Predictive Analysis of Biomass with Green Mobile Cloud Computing for Environment Sustainability. Green Mobile Cloud Computing*. Springer. doi:10.1007/978-3-031-08038-8_12

Koley, S., & Ghosh, S. (2014). Cloud Computing with CDroid OS based on Fujitsu Server for Mobile Technology. *SKIT Research Journal.*, 4(2), 1–6.

Koley, S., Ghosh, S. (2014). CDroid in Fujitsu Server for Mobile Cloud. *Data Analytics and Business Intelligence: Emerging Paradigms*, 80.

Koley, S., & Ghosh, S. (2015). Cloud Computing with CDroid OS based on fujitsu Server for Mobile Technology. *Bilingual International Conference on Information Technology: Yesterday, Today, and Tomorrow*. Research Gate.

Koley, S., & Jain, R. (2015). Advanced Technique for best use of CDroid OS for Mobile Cloud and Sharing. *Bilingual International Conference on Information Technology: Yesterday, Today, and Tomorrow*. SSRN. 10.2139srn.2873585

Koley, S., & Singh, N. (2014). Cdroid: Used In Fujitsu Server For Mobile Cloud. *SSRN*, 2, 1–14. doi:10.2139srn.2873457

Lal, P., & Bharadwaj, S. S. (2015). Assessing the performance of cloud-based customer relationship management systems. *Skyline Business Journal, 11*(1), 89–101.

Li, K. (2017). Quantitative modeling and analytical calculation of elasticity in cloud computing. *IEEE Transactions on Cloud Computing, 8*(4), 1135–1148. doi:10.1109/TCC.2017.2665549

Licklider, J. C. R. Britannica, The Editors of Encyclopaedia. *Encyclopedia Britannica*, https://www.britannica.com/biography/J-C-R-Licklider [Accessed 01 June 2023].

Mahan, F., Rozehkhani, S. M., & Pedrycz, W. (2021). A novel resource productivity based on granular neural network in cloud computing. *Complexity, 2021*, 2021. doi:10.1155/2021/5556378

Mittal, H., Tripathi, A. K., Pandey, A. C., Venu, P., Menon, V. G., & Pal, R. (2022). A novel fuzzy clustering-based method for human activity recognition in cloud-based industrial IoT environment. *Wireless Networks*, *8*, 1–3. doi:10.100711276-022-03011-y

Mueller, H., Gogouvitis, S. V., Seitz, A., & Bruegge, B. (2017). Seamless computing for industrial systems spanning cloud and edge. *In 2017 International Conference on High Performance Computing & Simulation (HPCS)*, (pp. 209-216). IEEE. 10.1109/HPCS.2017.40

Ostroukh, A. V., & Salniy, A. G. (2015). Research of Performance Linux Kernel File Systems. *International Journal of Advanced Studies*, *5*(2), 12–17. doi:10.12731/2227-930X-2015-2-2

Pirro, G., Talia, D., Trunfio, P., Missier, P., & Goble, C. (2008). *ERGOT: Combining DHTs and SONs for Semantic-Based Service Discovery on the Grid.* (CoreGRID Technical Report Number TR-0177). CoreGRID.

Rawai, N. M., Fathi, M. S., Abedi, M., & Rambat, S. (2013). Cloud computing for green construction management, *Third International Conference on Intelligent System Design and Engineering Applications*, (pp. 432-435). IEEE.

Rigdon, E. E., Sarstedt, M., & Ringle, C. M. (2017). On comparing results from CB-SEM and PLS-SEM: Five perspectives and five recommendations. *Marketing: ZFP–Journal of Research and Management*, *39*(3), 4–16.

Selvarajan, S., Srivastava, G., Khadidos, A. O., Khadidos, A. O., Baza, M., Alshehri, A., & Lin, J. C.-W. (2023). An artificial intelligence lightweight blockchain security model for security and privacy in IIoT systems. *Journal of Cloud Computing (Heidelberg, Germany)*, *12*(1), 38. doi:10.118613677-023-00412-y PMID:36937654

Shakeabubakor, A. A., Sundararajan, E., & Hamdan, A. R. (2015). Cloud computing services and applications to improve productivity of university researchers. *International Journal of Information and Electronics Engineering*, *5*(2), 153. doi:10.7763/IJIEE.2015.V5.521

Suganya, M., & Sasipraba, T. (2023). Stochastic Gradient Descent long short-term memory based secure encryption algorithm for cloud data storage and retrieval in cloud computing environment. *Journal of Cloud Computing (Heidelberg, Germany)*, *12*(1), 74. doi:10.118613677-023-00442-6

Teh, S. K., Ho, S. B., Chan, G. Y., & Tan, C. H. (2016). A framework for cloud computing use to enhance job productivity. *In 2016 IEEE Symposium on Computer Applications & Industrial Electronics (ISCAIE)*, (pp. 73-78). IEEE. 10.1109/ISCAIE.2016.7575040

Williams, D. R., & Tang, Y. (2013). Impact of office productivity cloud computing on energy consumption and greenhousegas emissions. *Environmental Science & Technology*, *47*(9), 4333–4340. doi:10.1021/es3041362 PMID:23548097

Wu, Y., Wu, L., & Cai, H. (2023). Cloud-edge data encryption in the internet of vehicles using Zeckendorf representation. *Journal of Cloud Computing (Heidelberg, Germany)*, *12*(1), 39. doi:10.118613677-023-00417-7

Chapter 4
Enhancing Cloud Security:
The Role of Artificial Intelligence and Machine Learning

Tarun Kumar Vashishth
ⓘD https://orcid.org/0000-0001-9916-9575
IIMT University, India

Bhupendra Kumar
IIMT University, India

Sachin Chaudhary
ⓘD https://orcid.org/0000-0002-8415-0043
IIMT University, India

Vikas Sharma
ⓘD https://orcid.org/0000-0001-8173-4548
IIMT University, India

Rajneesh Panwar
IIMT University, India

Kewal Krishan Sharma
IIMT University, India

ABSTRACT

Cloud computing has revolutionized the way organizations store, process, and manage data, offering flexibility and scalability. However, the rise in cyber threats poses significant challenges to maintaining robust cloud security. This chapter delves into the pivotal role that Artificial Intelligence (AI) and Machine Learning (ML) play in enhancing cloud security. By harnessing the capabilities of AI and ML, organizations can proactively detect, mitigate, and respond to evolving cyber threats, ultimately fortifying their cloud infrastructure. AI-driven techniques empower security systems to recognize patterns, anomalies, and potential threats within vast datasets. ML algorithms can learn from historical attack data, enabling the prediction of future threats and the development of more effective defense mechanisms. Moreover, AI-enhanced authentication and access control mechanisms bolster identity management, reducing the risk of unauthorized access and data breaches.

DOI: 10.4018/979-8-3693-1431-9.ch004

INTRODUCTION

In an era defined by the relentless growth of digital data and the pervasive adoption of cloud computing, the paramount concern of organizations is ensuring the security and integrity of their data and systems. The allure of cloud technology, with its promises of scalability, accessibility, and cost-efficiency, has revolutionized the way businesses operate and manage their information. However, this convenience is not without its perils. The ever-evolving landscape of cyber threats poses a continuous challenge, demanding innovative solutions that can adapt and fortify the defences guarding the cloud.Traditional security mechanisms, though effective to a certain extent, have been rendered insufficient in the face of increasingly sophisticated threats. The solution, it appears, lies at the intersection of technology and intelligence. Artificial Intelligence (AI) and Machine Learning (ML), driven by their capacity to analyze vast datasets, identify patterns, and make real-time decisions, have emerged as the vanguards of cloud security.From the evolution of cyber threats to the limitations of conventional security measures, we embark on a journey to unravel the transformative potential of AI and ML in safeguarding cloud environments. By scrutinizing real-world applications and addressing the challenges that lie ahead, we aim to equip both cybersecurity professionals and business leaders with the knowledge and insights needed to fortify their digital assets in an era where data is the most valuable currency. Join us as we navigate the complex terrain of cloud security and unveil the future, where intelligence meets technology to guard the gateways of the cloud.

THE EVOLVING THREAT LANDSCAPE

In the realm of cyberspace, the threat landscape is in a perpetual state of evolution. This dynamic and ever-changing environment poses substantial challenges to organizations that rely on cloud computing to store and manage their data. Understanding the nature of this evolving threat landscape is crucial for comprehending the necessity of advanced security measures, particularly those driven by Artificial Intelligence (AI) and Machine Learning (ML).

1. **Increasingly Sophisticated Attack Techniques**: Attackers in the digital realm have not only grown in numbers but have also upped their game in terms of sophistication. Gone are the days when simple viruses and malware were the primary concerns. Today, cybercriminals employ intricate and multifaceted techniques to infiltrate cloud environments. These methods are designed to

circumvent traditional security measures, making them increasingly difficult to detect and prevent.

2. **Ransomware Attacks**: Ransomware attacks have garnered significant attention in recent years due to their devastating impact. In a typical ransomware attack, malicious actors encrypt an organization's data and demand a ransom for the decryption key. Such attacks not only result in immediate financial losses but can also lead to substantial downtime and data loss, severely affecting an organization's operations and reputation.

3. **Data Breaches**: Data breaches involve unauthorized access to sensitive information, which is then exfiltrated or exposed to unauthorized parties. The fallout from a data breach can be catastrophic, including financial penalties, loss of customer trust, and legal ramifications. The theft of personal and financial data has become a lucrative business for cybercriminals.

4. **Distributed Denial of Service (DDoS) Attacks**: DDoS attacks involve overwhelming a target system or network with a flood of traffic, rendering it inaccessible to legitimate users. These attacks have become not only more common but also more powerful and sophisticated, often involving the coordination of thousands of compromised devices. The motivation behind DDoS attacks varies, from financial extortion to ideological or political agendas.

5. **Reputation Damage**: Beyond the immediate financial implications, these cyber threats can tarnish an organization's reputation. News of a data breach or a successful ransomware attack can erode trust among customers, partners, and stakeholders. Rebuilding a damaged reputation can be a costly and time-consuming endeavour.

6. **IoT Devices and Interconnectivity**: The proliferation of Internet of Things (IoT) devices has further amplified the threat landscape. IoT devices, often with limited built-in security, can serve as entry points for attackers. Moreover, the increasing interconnectivity of systems means that vulnerabilities in one area of an organization's infrastructure can potentially impact the security of the entire network. This expanded attack surface makes it more challenging for security professionals to identify and mitigate potential risks.

The evolving threat landscape in cyberspace is characterized by the increasing sophistication of attack techniques, the prevalence of ransomware and data breaches, the persistence of DDoS attacks, and the potential for significant financial and reputational damage. Additionally, the proliferation of IoT devices and the interconnected nature of systems have expanded the scope of security concerns. To combat these evolving threats effectively, organizations must adopt advanced security measures, including those harnessing the power of AI and ML, to stay one step ahead of cyber adversaries.

Figure 1. Threats and its security measure

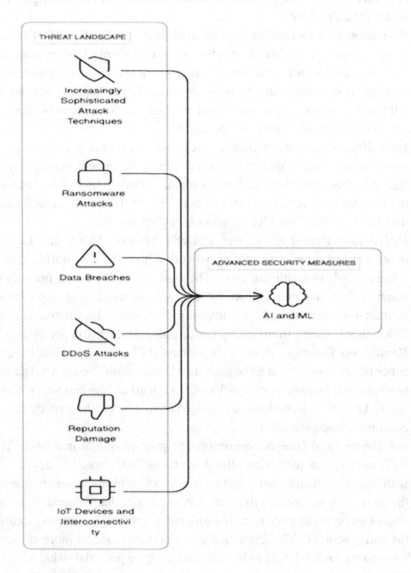

LITERATURE REVIEW

In (Subramanian & Tamilselvan, 2019), Subramanian, E. K., and Latha Tamilselvan present a novel cloud security solution harnessing machine learning (ML), particularly the Convolutional Neural Network (CNN), to pave the way for the next generation of cloud security with automated and responsive features.

In (Fernandes et al., 2014), Fernandes conducts a comprehensive literature review on cloud security issues, encompassing topics such as vulnerabilities, threats, and attacks, while also proposing a classification taxonomy for these aspects.

In (Muralidhara, 2017), Muralidhara, Pavan delves into the evolving domain of cloud computing security, emphasizing emerging threats and the countermeasures utilized to protect sensitive data and cloud-based applications.

In (Achar, 2022), Achar, Sandesh, provides insights into various aspects of AI-based cloud computing models, including their manifestations, roles, emerging trends, and associated challenges.

In (Nassif et al., 2021), Nassif discusses the diverse applications of machine learning techniques in proactively preventing or identifying security breaches and vulnerabilities within the Cloud environment.

In (Khorshed, 2011), Khorshed presents a dual contribution: a comprehensive survey on cloud computing, spotlighting adoption barriers and threat mitigation issues, followed by novel insights into leveraging machine learning for addressing common attack vectors.

In (Kumar et al., 2016), Kumar, Raneel, Sunil Pranit Lal, and Alok Sharma propose an approach for safeguarding virtual machines (VMs) from denial of service (DoS) attacks within a cloud environment.

In (Moreno-Vozmediano et al., 2019), Moreno-Vozmediano presents and assesses a novel predictive auto-scaling mechanism based on machine learning techniques for time series forecasting and queuing theory.

In (Dave et al., 2018), Dave et al. conduct a study that elucidates cloud security issues across various cloud-related domains, encompassing threats pertinent to cloud models and cloud networks.

In (Nenvani & Gupta, 2016), Nenvani, Geetanjali, and Huma Gupta delve into the security aspects of cloud computing architecture, particularly focusing on the Infrastructure as a Service (IaaS) layer. The paper comprehensively examines vulnerabilities within IaaS, specifically addressing issues related to virtualization, such as attacks on VM image sharing, VM isolation violation, insecure VM migration, and VM escape, while also proposing corresponding solutions.

In (Hesamifard et al., 2017), Hesamifard's et al. paper demonstrates the feasibility and practicality of training neural networks with encrypted data, enabling encrypted predictions and the secure return of these predictions in encrypted form.

In (He et al., 2017), He, Zhang, and Lee present a paper proposing a cloud-based DOS attack detection system leveraging machine learning techniques on the source side.

In (Butt et al., 2020), Butt and colleagues provide a comprehensive review analyzing security threats, issues, and solutions in cloud computing, focusing on the utilization of various machine learning algorithms, including supervised, unsupervised, semi-supervised, and reinforcement learning.

In (Salman et al., 2017), Salman and the research team investigate both the detection and categorization of anomalies, deviating from the common trend of solely focusing on detection in contemporary research.

THE SYNERGY OF AI AND ML IN CLOUD SECURITY

The synergy of Artificial Intelligence (AI) and Machine Learning (ML) in cloud security represents a powerful and transformative approach to addressing the complex challenges posed by the modern threat landscape. These technologies offer a range of advantages that collectively enhance the effectiveness and efficiency of cloud security measures:

1. Real-time Threat Detection:
   ◦ AI-driven systems have the capacity to process and analyze massive volumes of data in real-time. In cloud security, this capability is invaluable because it allows for the continuous monitoring of activities and events occurring within cloud environments.
   ◦ ML models, being data-driven, continuously learn and adapt to new information. This means that they can identify anomalies and potential threats as they emerge, often before they are formally recognized and documented as threats by security experts or databases.
   ◦ For example, if an AI system notices an unusual surge in login attempts from an unexpected location or device for a particular user account, it can flag this as a potential threat and take immediate action.
2. Pattern Recognition:
   ◦ ML algorithms are adept at identifying patterns and trends within data. In the context of cloud security, this capability can be harnessed to detect deviations from normal behavior.
   ◦ Unusual user behavior, such as a sudden increase in data access or an unusual data transfer pattern, can be flagged as potentially suspicious by ML models.
   ◦ Unauthorized access attempts, even if they do not trigger traditional security rules, can be detected by AI systems that recognize patterns of behavior consistent with past attacks.
3. Predictive Analysis:
   ◦ AI and ML can leverage historical data and ongoing observations to predict potential security breaches. By identifying patterns and trends

that indicate an imminent threat, these technologies allow organizations to take preemptive action.

- ○ For instance, if an AI system notices a series of unsuccessful login attempts followed by successful ones, it may predict that a brute-force attack is in progress and respond accordingly by increasing security measures.

4. Behavioral Analysis:
- ○ ML models can create detailed user and entity profiles based on historical data and ongoing behavior. These profiles allow for the detection of anomalous actions or deviations from established behavioral patterns.
- ○ For instance, if a user typically accesses specific resources and suddenly attempts to access sensitive data outside their typical scope, an AI-driven system can flag this as a potential insider threat or a compromised account.

5. Adaptive Response:
- ○ AI systems are not limited to detection; they can also take automated actions in response to security incidents. This capability is crucial for rapid threat mitigation.
- ○ When a potential threat is identified, an AI system can isolate compromised resources, revoke access, or apply other remediation measures in real-time. This reduces the reliance on human intervention, saving critical time and reducing the window of opportunity for attackers.

The synergy of AI and ML in cloud security provides organizations with a dynamic and proactive defense mechanism against the evolving threat landscape. These technologies excel at real-time monitoring, pattern recognition, predictive analysis, behavioral profiling, and automated incident response. By leveraging these capabilities, organizations can significantly enhance their ability to detect, respond to, and mitigate security threats in cloud environments, ultimately strengthening their overall security posture.

THE LIMITATIONS OF TRADITIONAL SECURITY MEASURES

Traditional security measures, such as firewalls, antivirus software, and intrusion detection systems, have played a crucial role in protecting cloud environments. However, they have their limitations:

Figure 2. Synergy of artificial intelligence (AI) and machine learning (ML) in cloud security

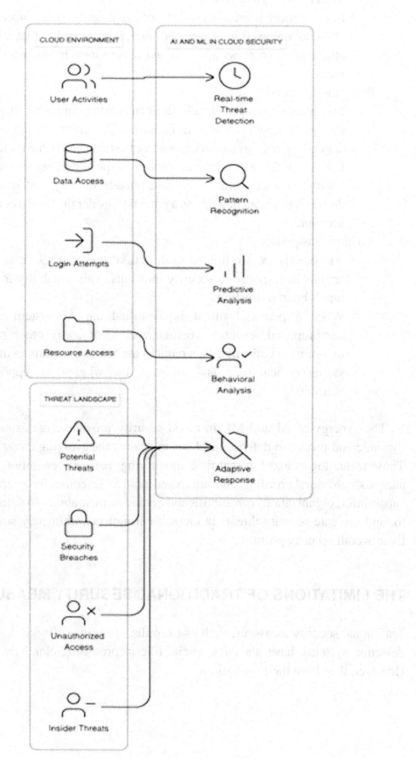

1. **Signature-Based Detection:** Signature-based detection is a cornerstone of many traditional security tools. This method involves identifying threats by comparing them to a database of known signatures or patterns of malicious code or behaviour. While effective in detecting known threats, it suffers from several limitations:
    - **Inability to Detect Zero-Day Attacks:** Signature-based systems cannot identify threats that have never been encountered before, commonly referred to as zero-day attacks. Since they rely on historical data, they can't recognize new and evolving threats.
    - **Signature Updates Delay:** Even when new threats are discovered, updating the signatures in security tools can be time-consuming. During this gap, systems remain vulnerable to the latest threats until patches or signatures are updated.
    - **Polymorphic Malware:** Modern malware can change its code or behaviour rapidly, making it difficult for signature-based systems to keep up.
2. **Manual Monitoring:** Traditional security measures often require human intervention for monitoring and incident response. While human expertise is invaluable, manual monitoring has its drawbacks:
    - **Time-Consuming:** Manually monitoring security logs and events is time-consuming. Security personnel must sift through vast amounts of data, which can lead to delays in threat detection and response.
    - **Error-Prone:** Humans can make mistakes, miss subtle signs of an attack, or misinterpret data, leading to false positives or negatives. Fatigue can also affect the accuracy of manual monitoring over time.
    - **Lack of Real-Time Awareness:** Manual monitoring may not provide real-time awareness of security incidents, which is crucial for mitigating threats promptly.
3. **Scalability:** Cloud environments are known for their dynamic nature, with resources being provisioned and de-provisioned rapidly. Traditional security measures face significant challenges in scaling to meet the demands of cloud environments:
    - **Resource Elasticity:** Cloud resources can be scaled up or down instantly based on demand. Traditional security tools might struggle to adapt to this elasticity, leading to potential security gaps during resource provisioning or de-provisioning.
    - **Complexity:** The complexity of cloud environments, with multiple services and interconnected components, can overwhelm traditional security systems, making it challenging to maintain a comprehensive security posture.

Figure 3. Traditional security measures

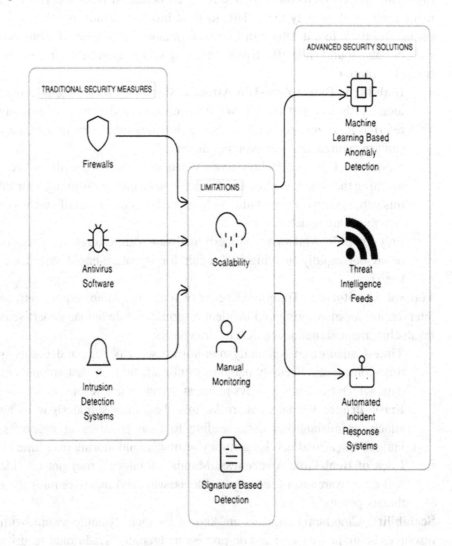

- ○ **Cost and Performance:** Scaling traditional security measures to match cloud infrastructure's scale can be costly and may impact system performance.

While traditional security measures like firewalls, antivirus software, and intrusion detection systems have been effective to some extent, they face limitations in dealing with the evolving threat landscape, the speed of cloud environments, and the need for real-time responses. To address these challenges, organizations often complement traditional security with more advanced and adaptive security solutions, such as machine learning-based anomaly detection, threat intelligence feeds, and automated incident response systems, to enhance their overall security posture in today's rapidly changing digital landscape.

THE PROMISE OF AI AND ML IN CLOUD SECURITY

Artificial Intelligence (AI) and Machine Learning (ML) have emerged as powerful tools in the realm of cloud security, offering a multitude of advantages to overcome the limitations of traditional security measures. Here, we'll explore in detail the promises that AI and ML bring to cloud security:

1. **Anomaly Detection**: AI and ML systems excel at anomaly detection, which involves identifying deviations from established patterns of normal behaviour. In the context of cloud security:
    - **Baseline Establishment**: Machine learning models can analyze vast datasets generated by cloud environments to create a baseline of "normal" behaviour. They learn from historical data and user interactions to understand what typical network traffic, system behaviour, and user activities look like.
    - **Detection of Unseen Threats**: Unlike signature-based detection, AI and ML can identify previously unseen threats or zero-day attacks. Any deviation from the established baseline, whether it's a new attack vector or an evolving threat, can trigger an alert.
    - **Reduced False Positives**: AI and ML-based anomaly detection tend to produce fewer false positives than rule-based systems, as they can adapt to the evolving nature of threats and the cloud environment.
2. **Predictive Analysis**: AI-driven predictive analysis involves using historical data and current trends to forecast potential security threats:
    - **Threat Prediction**: AI systems can analyze patterns in historical attack data and identify trends that might indicate potential threats. This allows organizations to take proactive measures to mitigate vulnerabilities before they are exploited.
    - **Vulnerability Assessment**: ML models can assess the security posture of cloud environments by identifying weak points or vulnerabilities. This information enables organizations to prioritize security efforts and patch or fortify vulnerable areas.
3. **Automation**: Automation is a significant benefit of AI and ML in cloud security:

- ○ **Threat Detection**: Machine learning models can automatically detect security threats in real-time, without the need for manual monitoring. This reduces response times and minimizes the risk of human error.
- ○ **Incident Response**: AI systems can orchestrate incident response workflows, such as isolating compromised resources, triggering alerts, and initiating remediation actions. This reduces the burden on security teams and ensures a swift and coordinated response.
- ○ **Patch Management**: ML can automate patch management by identifying which systems need updates and scheduling patches during non-critical periods to minimize disruptions.

4. **Scalability**: Cloud environments are dynamic, with resources scaling up or down as needed. AI and ML systems are well-suited to address the scalability requirements of cloud security:
   - ○ **Adaptability**: AI and ML models can adapt to changes in resource allocation, network traffic patterns, and the evolving threat landscape. They can scale seamlessly to provide continuous security coverage.
   - ○ **Efficiency**: These systems can handle the increasing volume of data generated in cloud environments efficiently. They can process and analyze data at scale, ensuring that no security events go unnoticed.

AI and ML technologies offer a promising solution to enhance cloud security by providing advanced anomaly detection, predictive analysis, automation, and scalability. These capabilities enable organizations to better protect their cloud assets, respond rapidly to emerging threats, and maintain a robust security posture in the dynamic and evolving world of cloud computing.

REAL-WORLD APPLICATIONS

AIand ML have been applied effectively in various real-world scenarios within the realm of cloud security. Let's delve into these applications in detail:

1. User Behaviour Analytics:
   - ○ **Overview**: User behaviour analytics (UBA) leverages AI to monitor and analyze user activities within a cloud environment. Its primary objective is to detect anomalous behaviour patterns that could signify unauthorized access or insider threats.
   - ○ **How it Works**: AI models, such as machine learning algorithms, continuously collect and analyze user activity data. They establish a baseline of normal behaviour for each user, including typical login times,

Figure 4. Artificial intelligence (AI) and machine learning (ML) in the realm of cloud security

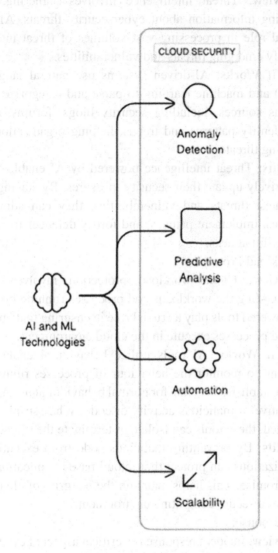

locations, and data access patterns. When deviations from this baseline occur, AI algorithms trigger alerts, indicating potential security threats.

○ **Benefits**: UBA helps organizations prevent data breaches by detecting suspicious activities early. It can identify compromised accounts, unauthorized access, or insiders with malicious intent. By promptly flagging these anomalies, organizations can take action to prevent security incidents.

2. Threat Intelligence:
   ○ **Overview**: Threat intelligence involves gathering, analyzing, and applying information about cybersecurity threats. AI and ML play a crucial role in processing vast volumes of threat intelligence data to identify emerging threats and vulnerabilities.
   ○ **How it Works**: AI-driven systems use natural language processing (NLP) and machine learning to parse and categorize threat data from various sources, including security blogs, forums, and feeds. They can identify patterns and trends, helping organizations stay ahead of evolving threats.
   ○ **Benefits**: Threat intelligence powered by AI enables organizations to proactively update their security measures. By staying informed about the latest threats and vulnerabilities, they can adjust their security policies, implement patches, and fortify defences to reduce the risk of successful attacks.

3. Cloud Workload Protection:
   ○ **Overview**: Cloud workload protection involves monitoring and safeguarding the workloads and processes running on cloud resources. AI-powered tools play a crucial role in ensuring that only legitimate and trusted processes execute in the cloud environment.
   ○ **How it Works**: AI tools utilize behavioural analysis and machine learning to monitor the behaviour of processes running in the cloud. They establish a baseline for normal behaviour and can detect deviations indicative of malicious activity or code. When suspicious behaviour is detected, these tools can isolate or terminate the offending processes.
   ○ **Benefits**: By preventing malicious code from executing in the cloud, organizations can protect their cloud-based applications and data from compromise. This helps maintain the integrity of cloud workloads and ensures a secure computing environment.

4. Incident Response:
   ○ **Overview**: Incident response is a critical aspect of cybersecurity. AI and ML can automate and enhance incident response processes, reducing response times and minimizing the impact of security incidents.
   ○ **How it Works**: Machine learning models can be trained to analyze security alerts generated by various security tools. They can prioritize alerts based on severity and the likelihood of a genuine threat. Automated responses can include isolating affected systems, initiating forensic analysis, or applying predefined security policies.
   ○ **Benefits**: Automation in incident response reduces the burden on security teams and accelerates the mitigation of threats. It ensures

Figure 5. AI and ML real time applications within the realm of cloud security

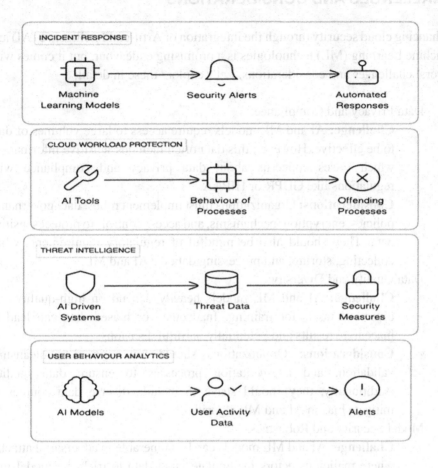

consistent and rapid actions are taken in response to security incidents, minimizing the potential damage or data loss.

AI and ML have brought transformative capabilities to cloud security, enabling organizations to proactively detect anomalies in user behaviour, stay ahead of emerging threats through threat intelligence, protect cloud workloads from malicious processes, and automate incident response for faster and more effective cybersecurity management in the cloud. These real-world applications enhance overall security and help organizations maintain a robust defence in today's complex digital landscape.

CHALLENGES AND CONSIDERATIONS

Enhancing cloud security through the integration of Artificial Intelligence (AI) and Machine Learning (ML) technologies is a promising endeavour, but it comes with several challenges and considerations. Let's explore these in detail:

1. Data Privacy and Compliance:
    ◦   **Challenge:** AI and ML models require access to large volumes of data to be effective. However, this data often includes sensitive information, which raises concerns about data privacy and compliance with regulations like GDPR or HIPAA.
    ◦   **Considerations:** Organizations must implement robust data governance policies, encryption mechanisms, and access controls to protect sensitive data. They should also be mindful of regulatory requirements when collecting, storing, and processing data for AI and ML.
2. Data Quality and Diversity:
    ◦   **Challenge:** AI and ML models heavily depend on high-quality and diverse datasets for training. Inadequate or biased data can lead to inaccurate results and potentially harmful decisions.
    ◦   **Considerations:** Organizations should invest in data cleansing, validation, and augmentation processes to ensure data quality. Additionally, they should strive to include diverse data sources to mitigate bias in AI and ML algorithms.
3. Model Security and Robustness:
    ◦   **Challenge:** AI and ML models can be vulnerable to adversarial attacks, where malicious actors manipulate input data to trick the model into making incorrect predictions.
    ◦   **Considerations:** Implement robust model validation techniques and deploy security mechanisms to detect and respond to adversarial attacks. Continuously monitor model performance and update models as new threats emerge.
4. Interoperability and Integration:
    ◦   **Challenge:** Integrating AI and ML solutions into existing cloud security architectures can be complex, as it requires seamless interoperability with existing security tools and workflows.
    ◦   **Considerations:** Ensure that AI and ML solutions can integrate with existing security infrastructure and provide APIs for easy communication. Comprehensive testing and validation are crucial to identify and address integration issues.
5. Resource Requirements:

- ○ **Challenge:** AI and ML algorithms can be computationally intensive, potentially straining cloud resources and increasing operational costs.
- ○ **Considerations:** Organizations must assess their resource needs and optimize AI and ML workloads for efficient resource utilization. This may involve selecting suitable cloud instances, leveraging distributed computing, or using serverless architectures.

6. Explainability and Transparency:
   - ○ **Challenge:** AI and ML models, particularly deep learning models, are often viewed as "black boxes" that provide results without clear explanations. This lack of transparency can be problematic in critical decision-making scenarios.
   - ○ **Considerations:** Explore AI and ML model interpretability techniques to make their decisions more understandable. Regulatory requirements may also mandate explainable AI in certain use cases.

7. Ethical Considerations:
   - ○ **Challenge:** AI and ML can perpetuate biases present in training data, leading to discriminatory outcomes or unethical decisions.
   - ○ **Considerations:** Implement fairness and ethics audits to identify and mitigate bias in AI and ML models. Develop clear guidelines and ethical frameworks for the use of AI in cloud security.

8. Training and Expertise:
   - ○ **Challenge:** Organizations may lack the in-house expertise needed to develop, deploy, and maintain AI and ML solutions for cloud security.
   - ○ **Considerations:** Invest in training and hiring experts in AI and ML. Alternatively, consider leveraging managed AI/ML services from cloud providers to reduce the expertise barrier.

9. Cost Management:
   - ○ **Challenge:** Implementing AI and ML solutions can lead to increased cloud infrastructure costs if not managed effectively.
   - ○ **Considerations:** Monitor resource usage closely, optimize AI and ML workloads, and conduct cost-benefit analyses to ensure that the benefits of enhanced security justify the expenses.

10. Continuous Monitoring and Adaptation:
    - ○ **Challenge:** The threat landscape and cloud environments are constantly evolving. AI and ML models need to adapt to new threats and changing conditions.
    - ○ **Considerations:** Establish processes for continuous monitoring of AI and ML models and update them regularly to remain effective against emerging threats. Implement feedback loops to improve models over time.

Figure 6. Challenges and considerations of AI & ML in cloud security

While AI and ML hold great promise for enhancing cloud security, organizations must navigate several challenges and considerations to ensure their successful implementation. Addressing data privacy, model security, integration, and ethical concerns while maintaining transparency and adaptability is crucial for leveraging the full potential of AI and ML in cloud security.

USE CASES OF AI AND ML IN CLOUD SECURITY

These use cases illustrate the practical application of AI and ML in enhancing cloud security. By leveraging these technologies, organizations can build more robust and adaptive security measures, proactively defend against threats, and respond rapidly to incidents, ultimately strengthening their cloud security posture.

Let's explore each of these use cases of Artificial Intelligence (AI) and Machine Learning (ML) in cloud security in detail:

1. Anomaly Detection:
    - **Unusual Activities:** AI-powered systems can continuously monitor and analyze activities within a cloud environment. They look for unusual login times, locations, access patterns, or data transfer volumes.
    - **Insider Threats:** Anomalies may indicate potential insider threats where employees or authorized users behave in unexpected ways, possibly compromising data or systems.
    - **Proactive Response:** When an anomaly is detected, the system can trigger alerts or take automated actions, such as blocking access or escalating the issue for further investigation.
    - **Example:** If a user who typically accesses cloud resources during office hours suddenly attempts to log in from a different continent in the middle of the night, the AI system can flag this as an anomaly and respond accordingly.
2. Threat Intelligence:

Figure 7. Use cases AI and ML in enhancing cloud security

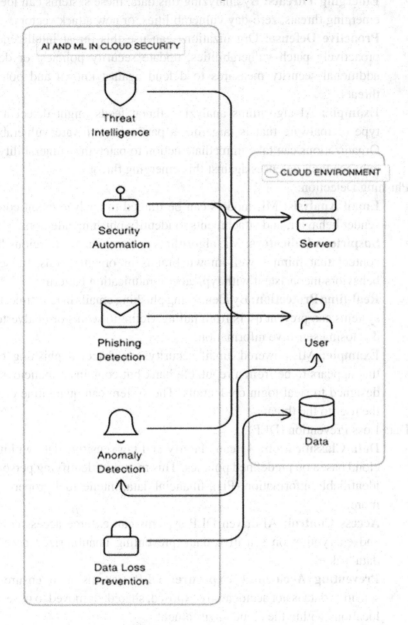

○ **Data Analysis:** AI and ML can process vast datasets of threat intelligence feeds from various sources, including cybersecurity databases, news reports, and security researchers.

- ○ **Emerging Threats:** By analyzing this data, these systems can identify emerging threats, zero-day vulnerabilities, or new attack vectors.
- ○ **Proactive Defense:** Organizations can use this threat intelligence to proactively patch vulnerabilities, update security policies, or deploy additional security measures to defend against known and potential threats.
- ○ **Example:** AI algorithms analyzing threat feeds might detect a new type of malware that is targeting a particular software vulnerability. Organizations can take immediate action to patch the vulnerability and enhance their defenses against this emerging threat.

3. Phishing Detection:
   - ○ **Email Analysis:** ML models can be trained to analyze email content, sender behavior, and attachments to identify phishing attempts.
   - ○ **Suspicious Indicators:** ML algorithms can recognize suspicious links, content that mimics well-known brands or organizations, or sender behaviors inconsistent with typical communication patterns.
   - ○ **Real-time Protection:** By identifying phishing emails in real-time, these systems can prevent users from falling victim to scams or inadvertently disclosing sensitive information.
   - ○ **Example:** ML-powered email security can detect a phishing email that appears to be from a reputable bank but contains a malicious link designed to steal login credentials. The system can quarantine or alert the user to the threat.

4. Data Loss Prevention (DLP):
   - ○ **Data Classification:** AI can classify and tag sensitive data within the cloud based on predefined policies. This includes identifying personally identifiable information (PII), financial data, intellectual property, and more.
   - ○ **Access Control:** AI-driven DLP systems can enforce access controls and encryption on sensitive data, preventing unauthorized access or data leakage.
   - ○ **Preventing Accidental Exposure:** DLP systems help ensure that sensitive data is not accidentally exposed, shared, or moved to unsecured locations within the cloud environment.
   - ○ **Example:** If an employee attempts to share a file containing customer credit card numbers in a public folder, the DLP system can automatically block the sharing action, ensuring that sensitive data is protected.

5. Security Automation:
   - ○ **Incident Response:** ML-driven automation can respond to security incidents in real-time. This includes isolating compromised systems,

changing access privileges, or even initiating incident response workflows.
- ◦ **Rapid Mitigation:** Automation reduces the time it takes to respond to security incidents, minimizing potential damage and reducing the window of opportunity for attackers.
- ◦ **Human Collaboration:** While automation can handle routine tasks, it can also escalate incidents to human security experts when necessary.
- ◦ **Example:** If an AI system detects unauthorized access to a critical server, it can immediately isolate the server from the network to prevent further compromise while simultaneously alerting security personnel for further investigation.

FUTURE SCOPE

1. Advanced Threat Detection and Response
   - ◦ Investigate how AI and ML can be employed to detect and respond to advanced threats like zero-day vulnerabilities and polymorphic malware in real-time.
   - ◦ Explore the development of predictive models that can anticipate potential security breaches and proactively protect cloud environments.
2. Explainable AI in Cloud Security
   - ◦ Research the integration of explainable AI techniques into cloud security models to improve transparency and trustworthiness in decision-making processes.
   - ◦ Evaluate the impact of explainability on the acceptance and adoption of AI-driven security solutions in the cloud.
3. Automated Incident Response
   - ◦ Investigate the potential of AI and ML in automating incident response processes in cloud environments, including incident classification, prioritization, and remediation.
   - ◦ Explore the challenges and ethical considerations associated with automating critical security decisions.
4. Federated Learning for Cloud Security
   - ◦ Explore the application of federated learning techniques to improve cloud security without compromising data privacy, especially in multi-cloud or hybrid cloud environments.

- Assess the scalability and effectiveness of federated learning models in mitigating cloud security threats.

5. Securing IoT Devices in the Cloud
   - Research how AI and ML can be utilized to secure Internet of Things (IoT) devices connected to cloud platforms, focusing on anomaly detection and threat prevention.
   - Investigate the challenges and potential solutions for managing the security of a massive number of IoT devices in the cloud.

6. Ethical Considerations and Bias Mitigation
   - Investigate the ethical implications of AI and ML in cloud security, including issues related to bias, fairness, and transparency.
   - Develop strategies and guidelines for responsible and ethical AI deployment in cloud security.

7. Quantum Computing and Post-Quantum Security
   - Explore the potential threats posed by quantum computing to traditional cryptographic techniques used in cloud security.
   - Research the development of quantum-resistant AI-driven security solutions to safeguard cloud data in a post-quantum era.

8. Integration of Human Expertise
   - Investigate how AI and ML can be used to enhance collaboration between human security experts and automated systems in cloud security.
   - Examine the role of human-machine partnerships in responding to evolving cloud security threats.

9. Regulatory Compliance and AI
   - Analyze the intersection of AI and ML in cloud security with various data protection and cybersecurity regulations (e.g., GDPR, CCPA).
   - Investigate methods for ensuring compliance while utilizing AI-driven security measures.

10. Scalability and Resource Optimization
    - Research techniques to optimize the resource utilization and scalability of AI and ML-based security solutions in the cloud, particularly for large-scale cloud infrastructures.
    - Develop strategies for efficient model training, deployment, and management in diverse cloud environments.

11. Continuous Learning and Adaptation
    - Explore methods to enable AI and ML models to continuously adapt and learn from evolving threats in real-time.
    - Investigate reinforcement learning and self-improving security systems in cloud environments.

12. Cross-Domain and Cross-Platform Security

Figure 8. Future scope of AI & ML in cloud security

- ○ Investigate how AI and ML can be used to bridge security gaps between different cloud providers, industries, and domains.
- ○ Research interoperability and standardization efforts to enhance security across heterogeneous cloud environments.
13. User-Centric Security
- ○ Explore the development of user-centric security solutions powered by AI and ML to personalize security measures based on user behaviour and preferences.
- ○ Assess the usability and acceptance of such systems by end-users in diverse cloud contexts.

CONCLUSION

1. **Enhancing Threat Detection and Response:**
   - ○ AI and ML excel in analyzing vast datasets in real-time. This capability is instrumental in identifying unusual patterns and anomalies in cloud traffic and user behaviour.
   - ○ ML models can detect and categorize known threats based on historical data, allowing for rapid responses to familiar attacks.
   - ○ AI-driven threat detection systems can spot novel threats by learning from their behaviour, thus staying ahead of attackers.
2. **Automation of Security Tasks:**
   - ○ AI and ML can automate routine security tasks, such as log analysis, patch management, and access control.
   - ○ This automation reduces the burden on human security teams, enabling them to focus on more complex tasks like threat hunting and strategic security planning.
3. **Proactive Threat Prevention:**
   - ○ Machine learning models can predict potential security issues by analyzing historical data and identifying patterns leading to breaches.

○   AI-driven systems can adapt and apply security policies dynamically in response to changing threat landscapes.

4. **Data Privacy:**

○   While leveraging AI and ML for security, organizations must ensure that sensitive data is handled with care. Privacy regulations like GDPR and CCPA impose strict requirements on data handling.

○   Techniques like differential privacy can be used to protect individuals' data while still allowing for effective security analysis.

5. **False Positives:**

○   AI and ML systems may produce false positives, flagging legitimate activities as potential threats. This can lead to alert fatigue and wasted resources.

○   Continuous refinement and training of machine learning models are essential to reduce false positives over time.

6. **Adversarial Attacks:**

○   Adversarial attacks involve manipulating AI or ML systems to produce incorrect results. In the context of cloud security, attackers may try to evade detection or trigger false alarms.

○   Implementing robust defences against adversarial attacks is crucial. Techniques like model hardening, adversarial training, and anomaly detection can help mitigate this risk.

7. **Evolution of Cloud Computing:**

○   Cloud computing is continually evolving with new services, architectures, and deployment models.

○   AI and ML must adapt to secure these evolving cloud environments. For example, serverless computing and containerization present unique security challenges that AI and ML can help address.

8. **Collaboration with Human Expertise:**

○   AI and ML are tools that should work in tandem with human security experts. Human expertise is critical for making judgment calls in complex situations and interpreting the context of security events.

○   Human-machine collaboration can lead to more effective and efficient incident response.

In conclusion, AI and ML are essential components of modern cloud security strategies. They provide the ability to detect and respond to threats at scale, automate security tasks, and proactively defend against emerging risks. However, it is imperative to use these technologies thoughtfully, considering data privacy, false positives, and the potential for adversarial attacks. As cloud computing continues to evolve, the role of AI and ML in securing it will also evolve, ensuring a safer and more resilient digital future.

REFERENCES

Achar, S. (2022). Adopting artificial intelligence and deep learning techniques in cloud computing for operational efficiency. *International Journal of Information and Communication Engineering*, *16*(12), 567–572.

Butt, U. A., Mehmood, M., Syed, B. H. S., Amin, R., Shaukat, M. W., Raza, S. M., Suh, D. Y., & Piran, M. J. (2020). A review of machine learning algorithms for cloud computing security. *Electronics (Basel)*, *9*(9), 1379. doi:10.3390/electronics9091379

Dave, D., Meruliya, N., Gajjar, T. D., Ghoda, G. T., Parekh, D. H., & Sridaran, R. (2018). Cloud security issues and challenges. In *Big Data Analytics: Proceedings of CSI 2015*, (pp. 499-514). Springer Singapore. 10.1007/978-981-10-6620-7_48

Fernandes, D. A. B., Soares, L. F. B., Gomes, J. V., Freire, M. M., & Inácio, P. R. M. (2014). Security issues in cloud environments: A survey. *International Journal of Information Security*, *13*(2), 113–170. doi:10.100710207-013-0208-7

Gulmezoglu, B., Eisenbarth, T., & Sunar, B. (2017). Cache-based application detection in the cloud using machine learning. In *Proceedings of the 2017 ACM on Asia Conference on Computer and Communications Security*, (pp. 288-300). ACM. 10.1145/3052973.3053036

He, Z., Zhang, T., & Lee, R. B. (2017). Machine learning based DDoS attack detection from source side in cloud. In *2017 IEEE 4th International Conference on Cyber Security and Cloud Computing (CSCloud)*, (pp. 114-120). IEEE. 10.1109/CSCloud.2017.58

Hesamifard, E., Takabi, H., Ghasemi, M., & Jones, C. (2017). Privacy-preserving machine learning in cloud. In *Proceedings of the 2017 on cloud computing security workshop*, (pp. 39-43). ACM. 10.1145/3140649.3140655

Khorshed, M. T. (2011). Trust issues that create threats for cyber attacks in cloud computing. In *2011 IEEE 17th international conference on parallel and distributed systems*, (pp. 900-905). IEEE. 10.1109/ICPADS.2011.156

Kumar, R., Lal, S. P., & Sharma, A. (2016). Detecting denial of service attacks in the cloud. In *2016 IEEE 14th Intl Conf on Dependable, Autonomic and Secure Computing, 14th Intl Conf on Pervasive Intelligence and Computing*, (pp. 309-316). IEEE. 10.1109/DASC-PICom-DataCom-CyberSciTec.2016.70

Moreno-Vozmediano, R., Montero, R. S., Huedo, E., & Llorente, I. M. (2019). Efficient resource provisioning for elastic cloud services based on machine learning techniques. *Journal of Cloud Computing (Heidelberg, Germany)*, *8*(1), 1–18. doi:10.118613677-019-0128-9

Muralidhara, P. (2017). The Evolution Of Cloud Computing Security: Addressing Emerging Threats. *International Journal Of Computer Science And Technology*, *1*(4), 1–33.

Nassif, A. B., Abu Talib, M., Nasir, Q., Albadani, H., & Dakalbab, F. M. (2021). Machine learning for cloud security: A systematic review. *IEEE Access : Practical Innovations, Open Solutions*, *9*, 20717–20735. doi:10.1109/ACCESS.2021.3054129

Nenvani, G., & Gupta, H. (2016). A survey on attack detection on cloud using supervised learning techniques. In *2016 Symposium on Colossal Data Analysis and Networking (CDAN)*, (pp. 1-5). IEEE. 10.1109/CDAN.2016.7570872

Pandey, U., Rajput, M., & Singh, R. (2023). Role of Machine Learning in Resource Usages and Security Challenges for Cloud Computing: Survey. In *2023 International Conference on Artificial Intelligence and Smart Communication (AISC)*, (pp. 525-530). IEEE. 10.1109/AISC56616.2023.10085687

Parameswarappa, P., Shah, T., & Lanke, G. R. (2023). A Machine Learning-Based Approach for Anomaly Detection for Secure Cloud Computing Environments. In *2023 International Conference on Intelligent Data Communication Technologies and Internet of Things (IDCIoT)*, (pp. 931-940). IEEE. 10.1109/IDCIoT56793.2023.10053518

Pavithra, B. (2023). Cloud Security Analysis using Machine Learning Algorithms. In *2023 Second International Conference on Augmented Intelligence and Sustainable Systems (ICAISS)*, (pp. 704-708). IEEE. 10.1109/ICAISS58487.2023.10250594

Salman, T., Bhamare, D., Erbad, A., Jain, R., & Samaka, M. (2017). Machine learning for anomaly detection and categorization in multi-cloud environments. In *2017 IEEE 4th international conference on cyber security and cloud computing (CSCloud)*, (pp. 97-103). IEEE. 10.1109/CSCloud.2017.15

Saxena, A., Asbe, C., & Vashishth, T. (2023). Leveraging a Novel Machine Learning Approach to Forecast Income and Immigration Dynamics. *Multidisciplinary Science Journal, 5.* . doi:10.31893/multiscience.2023ss0202

Sharma, V., Verma, V., & Sharma, A. (2019). Detection of DDoS attacks using machine learning in cloud computing. In Adv*ance d Informatics for Computing Research: Third International Conference, ICAICR 2019,* (pp. 260-273). Springer Singapore. 10.1007/978-981-15-0111-1_24

Sheet, M. F., & Saeed, M. J. (2022). Behavioral Features of Users as a Security Solution in Cloud Computing. In *2022 8th International Conference on Contemporary Information Technology and Mathematics (ICCITM)*, (pp. 25-29). IEEE. 10.1109/ICCITM56309.2022.10031680

Subramanian, E. K., & Tamilselvan, L. (2019). A focus on future cloud: Machine learning-based cloud security. *Service Oriented Computing and Applications, 13*(no. 3), 237–249. doi:10.100711761-019-00270-0

Vashishth, T. K., Kumar, B., Sharma, V., Chaudhary, S., Kumar, S., & Sharma, K. K. (2023). The Evolution of AI and Its Transformative Effects on Computing: A Comparative Analysis. In B. Mishra (Ed.), *Intelligent Engineering Applications and Applied Sciences for Sustainability* (pp. 425–442). IGI Global., doi:10.4018/979-8-3693-0044-2.ch022

Vashishth, T. K., Sharma, V., Chaudhary, S., Panwar, R., Sharma, S., & Kumar, P. (2023). Advanced Technologies and AI-Enabled IoT Applications in High-Tech Agriculture. In A. Khang (Ed.), *Handbook of Research on AI-Equipped IoT Applications in High-Tech Agriculture* (pp. 155–166). IGI Global., doi:10.4018/978-1-6684-9231-4.ch008

Vashishth, T. K., & Vikas, B. (2023). *Exploring the Role of Computer Vision in Human Emotion Recognition: A Systematic Review and Meta-Analysis. 2023 Second International Conference on Augmented Intelligence and Sustainable Systems (ICAISS)*, Trichy, India. 10.1109/ICAISS58487.2023.10250614

Wiranda, N., & Sadikin, F. (2021). Machine Learning for Security and Security for Machine Learning: A Literature Review. In *2021 4th International Conference on Information and Communications Technology (ICOIACT)*, (pp. 197-202). IEEE. 10.1109/ICOIACT53268.2021.9563985

KEY TERMS AND DEFINITIONS

Artificial Intelligence (AI): This refers to the development of computer systems that can perform tasks that typically require human intelligence, such as learning, problem-solving, decision-making, and natural language understanding.

Cloud Computing: Cloud computing is a technology paradigm that enables on-demand access to a shared pool of computing resources, such as servers, storage, and applications, over the internet, offering flexibility and scalability for users and organizations.

Internet of Things (IoT): The IoT is a concept that refers to the connection of everyday objects to the internet, allowing them to send and receive data. These objects can include devices like smartphones, thermostats, wearables, home appliances, and even vehicles. The idea behind IoT is to create a network where these objects can communicate with each other, collect and share data, and perform tasks more efficiently.

Machine Learning (ML): Machine learning is a field of artificial intelligence (AI) that involves developing algorithms and models that enable computers to learn and improve their performance on tasks from data, rather than being explicitly programmed. In essence, it's the science of enabling computers to make predictions, recognize patterns, and make decisions based on data and experience.

Natural Language Processing (NLP): This is a field of artificial intelligence that focuses on enabling computers to understand, interpret, and generate human language in a way that is both meaningful and contextually relevant.

Chapter 5
Role-Based access Control (RBAC) and Attribute-Based Access Control (ABAC)

Javed Akhtar Khan
Gyan Ganga College of Technology, India

ABSTRACT

This chapter explores the profound impact of artificial intelligence (AI) and machine learning (ML) on the realm of cloud security. As organizations increasingly migrate their operations and data to cloud environments, ensuring robust security measures becomes paramount. The integration of AI and ML technologies introduces novel ways to enhance threat detection, prevention, and response in the cloud. This chapter delves into various aspects of this synergy, discussing the benefits, challenges, and future prospects of utilizing AI and ML for safeguarding cloud infrastructures. This chapter also presents the benefits, challenges, and future directions. This abstract underscores the transformative potential of AI and ML in fortifying cloud infrastructures and safeguarding sensitive information in the digital age.

1. INTRODUCTION

In the rapidly evolving landscape of modern technology, the integration of Artificial Intelligence (AI) and Machine Learning (ML) has proven to be a catalytic force, reshaping industries and redefining conventional paradigms. One such domain that has witnessed a profound transformation is cloud security. As organizations increasingly migrate their operations and data to cloud environments, the need to ensure robust protection against a spectrum of evolving cyber threats has become an imperative

DOI: 10.4018/979-8-3693-1431-9.ch005

of paramount importance. In this context, the symbiotic relationship between AI, ML, and cloud security emerges as a potent solution, capable of revolutionizing the way we safeguard digital assets in an interconnected world.

n this exploration, we delve into the impact of AI and ML on cloud security, investigating their multifaceted roles in fortifying the integrity, availability, and confidentiality of data and applications. From advanced threat mitigation to automated incident response, the potential of these technologies is vast. As we embark on this journey through the intersection of AI/ML and cloud security, we uncover the transformative potential that promises a safer and more resilient digital landscape.

1.1 Cloud Security Landscape

The "Cloud Security Landscape" presents a panoramic view of the challenges, considerations, and evolving dynamics surrounding the protection of data, applications, and services in the cloud. The cloud, by its very nature, involves data traversal across diverse networks and geographical boundaries, necessitating a comprehensive reassessment of traditional security measures. It encompasses:

I.   **Shared Responsibility Model:** A fundamental pillar of cloud security, this model delineates the distribution of security responsibilities between cloud service providers and their clients.

II. **Threat Vectors and Attack Surfaces:** The expansive reach of cloud computing introduces novel threat vectors and widens the attack surfaces that malicious actors can exploit. This section dissects the potential entry points for threats and the techniques employed to exploit vulnerabilities.

III. **Data Confidentiality and Privacy:** Entrusting data to third-party cloud providers necessitates stringent measures to preserve confidentiality and privacy. Encryption, access controls, and data residency regulations play pivotal roles in safeguarding sensitive information.

IV. **Identity and Access Management (IAM):** As cloud environments host a multitude of users, devices, and applications, effective IAM is pivotal in ensuring authorized access and preventing unauthorized breaches.

V.   **Cloud-Native Security Tools:** Cloud-native security solutions are designed to protect cloud environments specifically, often offering features like cloud configuration scanning and native integration with cloud providers' security tools.

VI. **AI and ML in Cloud Security:** Artificial intelligence and machine learning are being used for threat detection, anomaly detection, and automated response in cloud security.

1.2 Role of AI and ML in Security

Artificial Intelligence (AI) and Machine Learning (ML) have emerged as pivotal tools in fortifying the security landscape. This section delves into the multifaceted roles that AI and ML play in bolstering security across various domains:

I.   **Threat Detection and Analysis:** AI and ML algorithms excel at sifting through colossal volumes of data to identify anomalies and potentially malicious activities. By learning from historical patterns and adapting to new threat vectors, these technologies enhance the early detection of cyber attacks, including advanced persistent threats (APTs), zero-day vulnerabilities, and insider threats.

II.   **Predictive Analytics:** ML algorithms can predict potential vulnerabilities and risks by analyzing historical data and recognizing patterns that precede security incidents.

III.   **Dynamic Access Control:** AI and ML technologies enable context-aware access control, where access privileges are dynamically adjusted based on user behavior, device attributes, and environmental factors.

IV.   **Fraud Prevention**: AI-powered fraud detection systems analyze transactional data to identify patterns indicative of fraudulent activities. ML models can adapt to evolving fraud tactics and reduce false positives, enhancing the accuracy of fraud prevention mechanisms.

V.   **Malware Detection:** ML algorithms can identify and classify new strains of malware based on their characteristics and behavior. This enables the development of more effective antivirus and anti-malware solutions.

2. AI AND ML FUNDAMENTALS

2.1 Overview of Artificial Intelligence

Artificial Intelligence (AI) is a multidisciplinary field of computer science focused on creating machines and software systems that can simulate human intelligence and perform tasks that typically require human intelligence. AI encompasses a wide range of techniques, algorithms, and approaches aimed at enabling computers to learn from data, reason through information, and adapt to new situations. Here's an overview of key concepts and areas within AI:

I.   **Machine Learning (ML):** A subset of AI, machine learning involves creating algorithms and models that enable computers to improve their performance on a task through learning from data. This learning process involves recognizing patterns, making predictions, and making decisions based on experience.

II. **Neural Networks:** Neural networks are a class of algorithms inspired by the structure and functioning of the human brain. Deep learning, a subfield of machine learning, focuses on using neural networks with multiple layers (deep neural networks) to automatically learn features from data. This has led to significant advancements in tasks such as image and speech recognition.

III. **Natural Language Processing (NLP):** NLP involves enabling computers to understand, interpret, and generate human language. This includes tasks like language translation, sentiment analysis, chatbots, and text generation.

IV. **Computer Vision:** This area focuses on enabling computers to interpret and understand visual information from the world. Computer vision algorithms can analyse and interpret images and videos, enabling applications such as facial recognition, object detection, and autonomous vehicles.

V.   **Robotics:** Robotics combines AI and engineering to create intelligent machines (robots) capable of performing tasks autonomously or semi-autonomously. This field has applications in industrial automation, healthcare, exploration, and more.

VI. **Reinforcement Learning:** This type of machine learning involves an agent learning how to make decisions in an environment to maximize a reward. It learns through trial and error, adjusting its actions based on the outcomes it experiences.

VII. **Expert Systems:** Expert systems are AI programs designed to mimic the decision-making abilities of a human expert in a specific domain. They use rules and knowledge bases to provide expert-level advice.

VIII.   **AI in the Cloud:** Cloud providers offer AI as a service, allowing organizations to access AI capabilities, tools, and resources without having to build their own infrastructure.

2.2 Basics of "Machine Learning" and We Can Also Say "Algorithmic Intelligence"

Machine learning is a field of artificial intelligence (AI) that focuses on the development of algorithms and models that enable computers to learn from and make predictions or decisions based on data. Instead of being explicitly programmed to perform specific tasks, machine learning systems use data to improve their performance over time. Machine learning can be categorized into different types:

Figure 1. Artificial intelligence

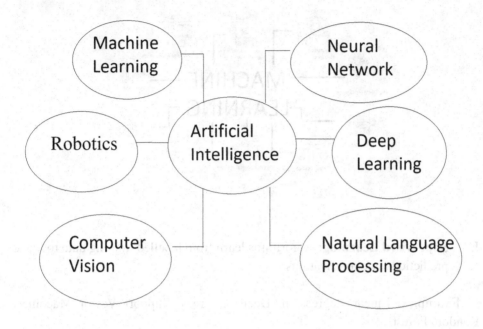

I.   **Supervised Learning:** In this type, the algorithm is trained on labelled data, where the correct output is provided. It learns to map input data to the correct output by identifying patterns and relationships in the training data.

II. **Unsupervised Learning:** Here, the algorithm is given unlabelled data and is tasked with finding patterns or structures within the data. It involves clustering similar data points together or reducing the dimensionality of the data.

III. **Reinforcement Learning:** In this approach, an algorithm learns to make decisions by interacting with an environment. It receives rewards or penalties based on its actions, allowing it to learn optimal strategies over time.

IV. **Deep Learning:** A subset of machine learning that uses neural networks with many layers to process and learn from complex data, such as images, text, and speech.

2.3 Types of Machine Learning Algorithms

Here are some common types of machine learning algorithms:

Figure 2. Machine learning

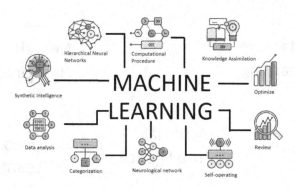

I. **Supervised Learning:** Algorithms learn from labelled training data to make predictions or classifications.

    Examples: Linear Regression, Decision Trees, Support Vector Machines, Random Forest.

II. **Unsupervised Learning:** Algorithms work with unlabelled data to find patterns, groupings, or relationships.

    Examples: Clustering (K-Means), Dimensionality Reduction (PCA), Anomaly Detection.

III. **Reinforcement Learning:** Algorithms learn by interacting with an environment to achieve a goal, receiving rewards for correct actions.

    Examples: Q-Learning, Deep Q-Networks (DQN), Policy Gradient methods.

IV. **Deep Learning:** A subset of machine learning using deep neural networks with multiple layers to learn representations from data.

    Examples: Convolutional Neural Networks (CNNs) for images, Recurrent Neural Networks (RNNs) for sequences.

V. **Neural Networks:** Algorithms inspired by the human brain's structure, consisting of interconnected nodes (neurons) that process and transmit information.

Figure 3. Types of machine learning

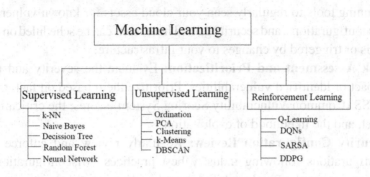

VI. **Decision Trees:** Hierarchical structures that make decisions based on a series of conditions or features.

VII. **K-Nearest Neighbours (KNN):** Instance-based learning method that classifies data points based on the majority class of their k-nearest neighbours.

VIII. **Naive Bayes:** Probabilistic algorithm based on Bayes' theorem, often used for text classification and spam filtering.

IX. **Random Forest:** Ensemble technique that combines multiple decision trees to improve accuracy and avoid overfitting.

X. **Support Vector Machines (SVM):** Algorithms that find the optimal hyperplane to classify data into different categories.

XI. **Principal Component Analysis (PCA):** Dimensionality reduction technique that transforms data into a lower-dimensional space while preserving variance.

3. PROACTIVE VULNERABILITY MANAGEMENT IN CLOUD SECURITY

Proactive Vulnerability Management in cloud security involves taking pre-emptive measures to identify, assess, and mitigate vulnerabilities within your cloud infrastructure and applications. Here's a more detailed overview of the key steps involved:

I. **Asset Inventory and Discovery:** Maintain an up-to-date inventory of all assets in your cloud environment, including virtual machines, databases, containers, and other resources. This visibility is essential for effective vulnerability management.

II. **Automated Vulnerability Scanning:** Use automated vulnerability scanning tools to regularly scan your cloud assets for known vulnerabilities, misconfigurations, and security gaps. These scans can be scheduled on a routine basis or triggered by changes to your infrastructure.

III. **Risk Assessment and Prioritization:** Evaluate the severity and potential impact of identified vulnerabilities. Prioritize them based on factors such as CVSS (Common Vulnerability Scoring System) scores, the criticality of the asset, and the likelihood of exploitation.

IV. **Security Configuration Review:** Regularly review and enforce security configurations following industry best practices. Misconfigurations are a common source of vulnerabilities, and addressing them can significantly enhance your cloud security posture.

V.   **Security Training and Awareness:** Train your team members on cloud security best practices, emphasizing the importance of identifying and reporting vulnerabilities. Foster a culture of security awareness across your organization.

Figure 4. Proactive Vulnerability Management in Cloud Security

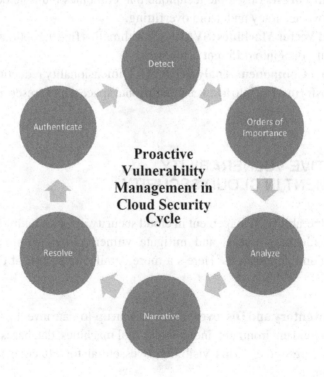

120

4. ADAPTIVE ACCESS CONTROL (AAC)

Adaptive access control in AI and ML for cloud security refers to the dynamic and context-aware management of user access to cloud resources. This approach leverages AI and ML techniques to continuously assess and adapt access permissions based on various factors, such as user behavior, device attributes, location, and the sensitivity of the data or resources being accessed. Here's an overview of how adaptive access control works in the context of cloud security:

I.   **Behavioral Analysis**: AI and ML can analyze user behavior patterns to establish a baseline of normal activities. AAC can trigger additional authentication steps or block access, safeguarding against compromised accounts or insider threats.

II. **Contextual Awareness:** AI and ML algorithms can consider contextual information, such as the user's location, device, time of day, and network behavior, to make more informed access control decisions. For example, if a user attempts to access sensitive data from an unfamiliar location, the system might require additional authentication steps.

III. **Anomaly Detection:** AI and ML can identify anomalies in user behavior that may indicate unauthorized access or data breaches.

IV. **Threat Intelligence Integration:** AI-powered AAC systems can be integrated with threat intelligence feeds to stay updated on emerging threats.

V.   **Real-time Risk Assessment**: AAC evaluates risk factors associated with specific access requests. It considers factors such as the sensitivity of the data being accessed, the user's role, and the user's location. This dynamic risk assessment ensures that access decisions are aligned with the current threat landscape.

4.1 Benefits of Adaptive Access Control in AI and ML in Cloud Security

I.   **Enhanced Security:** Adaptive access control responds to real-time threats and reduces the risk of unauthorized access, data breaches, and insider threats.

II. **User-Friendly:** It maintains a balance between security and user experience by only requiring additional authentication when necessary, reducing friction for legitimate users.

III. **Compliance:** Adaptive access control aids in meeting compliance requirements by providing fine-grained access control and robust auditing capabilities.

IV.   **Scalability:** AI and ML allow for the automated analysis of a large volume of access requests, making it suitable for cloud environments with diverse and dynamic user populations.

V.   **Proactive Threat Mitigation:** By identifying anomalies and risks early, adaptive access control helps organizations take proactive measures to mitigate potential security threats.

Adaptive Access Control in AI and ML is a dynamic and context-aware approach to managing user access to cloud resources. It enhances cloud security by continuously assessing user behavior and other contextual factors to make informed access control decisions while maintaining a positive user experience.

5. DATA PROTECTION AND PRIVACY

5.1 Data Classification and Encryption using AI

Data Classification and Encryption are vital components of data security and privacy. Artificial Intelligence (AI) can enhance these processes by automating and improving the accuracy of data classification and encryption techniques. Here's how AI can be applied to data classification and encryption:

5.1.1 Data Classification using AI

I.   **Content Analysis and Pattern Recognition:** AI-powered Natural Language Processing (NLP) and machine learning algorithms can analyse the content of documents, emails, images, and other data formats.

II.   **Contextual Understanding:** AI can learn from context, taking into account user roles, locations, and the purpose of data usage. This helps in accurately classifying data based on its relevance and context.

III. **Automated Tagging and Labelling:** AI can automatically assign classification labels or tags to data based on its content. These labels indicate the data's level of sensitivity or importance.

IV.   **Behavioural Analysis:** By studying user behaviour patterns, AI can identify how data is accessed, shared, and used. This behavioural analysis aids in classifying data based on its usage patterns.

5.1.2 Data Encryption using AI

I.   **Automated Key Management:** AI can assist in managing encryption keys, generating strong and unique keys, and rotating them at appropriate intervals.

II. **Dynamic Encryption:** AI can dynamically adjust encryption levels based on the data's sensitivity and context. For instance, AI might enforce stronger encryption for highly sensitive data or specific situations.

III. **Homomorphic Encryption:** AI can facilitate computations on encrypted data without requiring decryption, enabling privacy-preserving analysis and processing.

IV. **Quantum Encryption:** AI can contribute to the development and implementation of encryption methods that can withstand threats from quantum computing.

V.   **Anomaly Detection:** AI can identify unusual or unauthorized attempts to access encrypted data, enhancing security against potential breaches.

VI. **Cloud Security:** AI can assist in encrypting data in cloud environments, both at rest and in transit, while ensuring decryption occurs only when necessary.

The integration of AI into data classification and encryption processes offers several benefits, including improved accuracy, efficiency, and adaptability. However, it's important to carefully implement AI techniques to address potential biases, security vulnerabilities, and compliance requirements.

5.2 Privacy-Preserving Machine Learning Techniques

Here are some techniques that can be employed for privacy-preserving machine learning in the context of cloud computing:

I.   **Homomorphic Encryption:** Homomorphic encryption allows data to be encrypted and still used for computations. Cloud providers can perform calculations on encrypted data without ever needing to decrypt it, thus maintaining data privacy.

II. **Federated Learning:** Federated learning enables training models across distributed devices or servers. Instead of sharing raw data, only model updates are exchanged, minimizing data exposure and maintaining privacy.

III. **Differential Privacy:** Differential privacy involves adding noise to data before analysis to protect individual privacy. This ensures that results do not reveal sensitive information about specific data points.

IV. **Secure Multi-Party Computation (SMPC):** SMPC enables multiple parties to jointly compute functions on their private data while keeping their inputs

Figure 5. Data Protection and Privacy

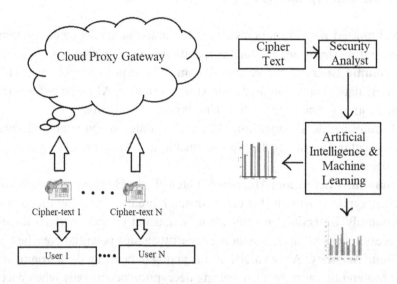

hidden from each other. It allows collaborative analysis while maintaining privacy.

6. CHALLENGES AND LIMITATIONS

Artificial Intelligence (AI) and Machine Learning (ML) have had a significant impact on various fields, including cloud security. While they offer promising solutions to enhance security measures, they also come with challenges and limitations that need to be addressed. Here's an overview of the impact, challenges, and limitations of AI and ML on cloud security:

6.1 Challenges

I.   AI and ML require large amounts of data to train and operate effectively. Handling sensitive data in cloud environments raises concerns about data privacy and compliance with regulations like GDPR.

II. Adversaries can manipulate AI and ML algorithms by providing inputs designed to mislead them. This can undermine the effectiveness of security systems.

III. If AI models are trained on biased data, they might make unfair or discriminatory decisions. This is particularly concerning in cloud security systems that affect user access and permissions.

IV.   Different cloud providers may offer different AI/ML tools and services, making it challenging to ensure interoperability and portability of security solutions across different cloud environments.

V.   Implementing AI and ML in cloud security can be complex. It requires expertise in both security and AI/ML, and integrating these technologies into existing security frameworks can be challenging.

6.2 Limitations

I.   AI and ML algorithms can produce false positives (identifying something as a threat when it isn't) or false negatives (failing to identify a genuine threat). Balancing this trade-off is challenging.

II.   Security threats evolve rapidly, and attackers can change tactics to evade AI-powered defenses. Keeping AI models updated to address new threats is an ongoing challenge.

III.   AI and ML algorithms can be computationally intensive, potentially leading to increased costs and resource consumption in cloud environments.

IV.   Integrating AI and ML into existing cloud security infrastructures requires expertise and careful planning, which can be a barrier for some organizations.

V.   AI and ML are not a replacement for human expertise in security. They should complement the work of security professionals, not replace them. A lack of skilled personnel who can understand and manage AI-driven security systems is a limitation.

7. FUTURE DIRECTIONS

AI and ML can enhance threat detection and prevention mechanisms in the cloud. Future directions include the development of advanced anomaly detection algorithms that can identify unusual behaviors and potential security breaches with higher accuracy. ML models will continuously learn from new data and adapt to emerging threats, improving the overall security posture of cloud environments.

By analyzing historical data and patterns, these technologies can forecast potential attack vectors, enabling organizations to proactively address vulnerabilities before they are exploited. Resource Optimization and Cost Management can help identify unused or underutilized resources, reducing attack surface and overall operational costs.

8. CONCLUSION

The integration of artificial intelligence (AI) and machine learning (ML) into cloud security represents a transformative and dynamic force that is reshaping how organizations protect their digital assets. As we peer into the future, it's clear that these technologies will play an increasingly pivotal role in safeguarding cloud environments against ever-evolving cyber threats.

Striking the right balance between automation and human oversight, ensuring the transparency and explainability of AI-driven decisions, and defending against adversarial attacks on AI models are among the complex issues that will need careful consideration.

REFERENCES

Achar, S. (2022). *Adopting Artificial Intelligence and Deep learning techniques in cloud computing*. Research Gate. https://www.researchgate.net/profile/Sandesh-Achar/publication/366205412_Adopting_Artificial_Intelligence_and_Deep_Learning_Techniques_in_Cloud_Computing_for_Operational_Efficiency/links/6397a7df11e9f00cda3de394/Adopting-Artificial-Intelligence-and-Deep-Learning-Techniques-in-Cloud-Computing-for-Operational-Efficiency.pdf

Ali, A. (2017). Unsupervised feature learning and automatic modulation classification using deep learning. *Physical Communication, 25*(1).

Bresniker, K. (2019). Grand Challenge. *Computer, 52*(12). https://ieeexplore.ieee.org/abstract/document/8909930

Harvard Press. (n.d.). *Privacy Preserving Machine Learning*. Harvard Press.

Chapter 6
Application of Artificial Intelligence in Cybersecurity

Geetika Munjal

(iD) https://orcid.org/0000-0001-5213-9993
Amity Univesity, Noida, India

Biswarup Paul
Amity Univesity, Noida, India

Manoj Kumar

(iD) https://orcid.org/0000-0001-5113-0639
University of Wollongong, UAE

ABSTRACT

Cybersecurity is the knowledge and practice of defending computers, mobile devices, servers, electronic devices, networks, and precious data from malicious attacks. Traditional security methods have advantages in various ways, but they may sometimes seem to be ineffective due to lack of intelligence and vitality to meet the current diverse needs of the network industry thus latest techniques need to be developed to handle these threats. The developments in Artificial intelligent (AI) techniques have simplified life by providing efficient solutions in different domains including cyber security. This chapter has reviewed existing tools of cyber security, highlighting different ways artificial intelligence can be applied in providing Cybersecurity solutions. AI-based security systems make decisions for helping people, it is particularly worrying that these systems do not currently have any moral code thus current chapter also highlights the need to ethical code in providing AI solution for cyber security.

DOI: 10.4018/979-8-3693-1431-9.ch006

1. INTRODUCTION

In the last two decades, information and communication sector has evolved a lot, bringing with it a seamless integration of technology with the day-to-day life. It provides a platform for communication, networking and digitization benefiting the entire world. This rise information technology has shifted the world paradigm with human using it to automate and semi automate various operations like businesses, healthcare, banking, finance, manufacturing, transportation, logistics, customer services, human resource, media, governments activities, defence, and various other fields. Thus, it can be said that cyberspace comprises of various infrastructures and systems built on and comprising of vital and sensitive data which serves the interests of governments, companies and general public. This development in cyberspace has not only brought immense opportunities but also unprecedented challenges. Arguably the biggest challenge in current digital world is keeping this space where different aspects of citizens lives are intertwined as secured and it can be termed as Cybersecurity. Cybersecurity can be explained as a set of technologies and channels used to safeguard computer software, hardware, applications, networks, programs against vulnerabilities via cyber criminals, malicious organizations, and hackers. It also prevents the unauthorized access to data belonging to both public and private sector. It is a complete assortment responsible for defending networks and data, applicable at network, host, data and application level (Buczak & Guven, 2015). A cyber-attack can be described as a malicious attempt to compromise, hinder, harm, gain unauthorized access and manipulate a computer system, network, digital device. Such an attack can be carried out by individuals, groups, or organizations with malicious intentions like stealing money, data or simply compromising vital systems and supply chains.

Artificial Intelligence (AI) is a field in computer science that includes complex mathematical models, analysing the data for correlations and patterns, and using these patterns to make predictions about future states and imitating human behaviour like thinking, planning, generating ideas, understanding speech and visuals . It can be a tool integrated in software that help us in making an attempt to get the essence of intelligence and developing intelligent machines that are able to assist us in complex tasks as well as automate them. AI is scaling up to our cognitive abilities and enhancing various fields like healthcare, technology, transport, education and most importantly cyber security (Saha et al., 2020). Due to their transformative abilities and flexible nature, artificial intelligence is being implemented in Cybersecurity to combat the challenges in the dynamic and ever changing cyberspace.

Today AI has been scaled up to our cognitive abilities and enhancing various fields like business healthcare, technology, transport, education and most importantly cyber security (Saha et al., 2020). Due to their transformative abilities and flexible nature, artificial intelligence is being implemented in Cybersecurity to combat the challenges in the dynamic and ever changing cyberspace.

This paper aims to present a review regarding the applications of artificial intelligence in the field of Cybersecurity and how it is enhancing the existing cyber-defence mechanisms. It presents research and analysis of existing literature, industry reports to highlight the challenges involved in today's digital world concerning Cybersecurity and its AI implementation. Overall the paper is divided in to 3 main sections of the paper. First section describes importance of Cybersecurity in the world, the conventional tools used in Cybersecurity and the limitations of them. The second section focuses on the various techniques and approaches of AI in Cybersecurity and how they impact the field. The third section highlights the limitations and ethical issues of using AI in Cybersecurity.

2. LITERATURE REVIEW

As computer networks are evolved with Internet of Things (IoT), which is the linkage of smart devices and home appliances with the internet, cybersecurity has become more essential because such systems are susceptible to many threats. Along with usefulness of internet it has also increased number of online treats, which can be credited to cybercriminals, hackers and even terrorist organization. Cyber-attacks have been ranked among the top five sources of global risk by the Global Risks Report of the World Economic Forum in 2019 (Taddeo et al., 2019). Figure 1 illustrates top Cybersecurity Threats,some forms of cybercrimes include cyber stalking, intellectual property theft, phishing, identity theft, email bombing, unauthorized access to data, system hack, server damage, spreading malware and computer viruses. Figure 1 illustrates top Cybersecurity threats.

According to reports and estimations, the damage from cyber attacks will add up to around $10.5 trillion yearly by 2025, which is a 300% rise if we compare it from 2015 data (Morgan, 2022). Damage costs include data damage and destruction, theft of monetary assets, intellectual property loss of productivity, personal and financial data, as well as disruption of supply chains, business affairs and reputational damage. It has been causing unprecedented damage to private and public businesses, increasing the IT budgets of enterprises of all sizes, as well as governments and educational institutions on a global scale. It is therefore imperative to have defences against such threats, making Cybersecurity a top priority to ensure a secure digital space. Cybersecurity mechanisms should be able to process large quantities data, be fast, robust and intelligent enough to learn and adapt to the variety of malware being generated. This is the prime reason why organizations of both public and private sector are resolving to integrating AI based techniques to efficiently monitor and

Figure 1. Top cybersecurity threats

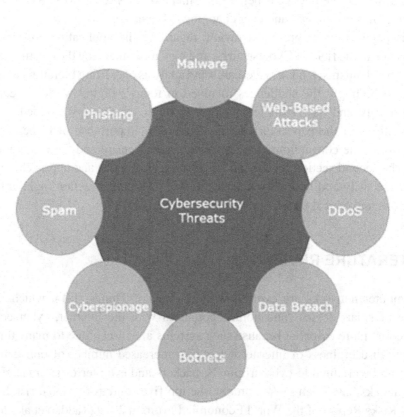

counter threats (Ansari et al., 2022). Artificial Intelligence help in defining patterns of any anomalous behaviour of any system or network. It can assist in internal threats such as unauthorized access or misuse of data. Estimates indicate that the market for AI in Cybersecurity will grow from US$1 billion in 2016 to a US$34.8 billion net worth. Table 2 illustrates market size trends and predictions for AI in Cybersecurity to give an idea of the amount of money invested in it. The compound annual growth rate is estimated to be around 27.8% during 2022-2023 due to vast increase Cybersecurity threats. The compound annual growth rate is estimated to be around 27.8% during 2022-2023 due to vast increase Cybersecurity threats.

3. CONVENTIONAL TOOLS IN CYBERSECURITY AND THEIR LIMITATIONS

When coming to development and application of AI ways in Cyber Security, we first need to understand the traditional tools in Cybersecurity, which are as follows:

3.1 Cyber Kill Chain and ISA

A cyber kill chain refers to the various phases that a cyber-attack follows. The first phase is the reconnaissance phase in which the attacker will try to detect the flaws or vulnerabilities throughout the system where an attack can be launched. As a gap is detected a malicious code is prepared which is transferred to the identified target in the delivery phase. Upon a successful deployment of the malware to the target, it installs the malicious code in the system to corrupt either the entire system or parts of it. This is the exploit phase. As the host system is now corrupted, it is under the directive of the attacker who then uses the new developed directives to carry out malicious activities. Usually, Cybersecurity experts deploy countermeasures depending upon the cyber kill chain (Yadav & Rao, 2015; Wirkuttis & Klein, 2017). A comprehensive approach in Cybersecurity to handle such grouping is Integrated Security Approach (ISA). This approach locates the section where the attack was targeted upon and gathers relevant information about the threat to generate an alarm or a warning usually before the exploit phase so that the threat can be dealt with using countermeasures to prevent further escalation or at least understand the nature and extent of damage if the breach has already taken place. Cybersecurity experts try to include remedial actions to revert back the system to its original state (Wirkuttis & Klein, 2017). To ensure proper handling of threats, the ISA needs to consider every phase of the cyber kill chain and act accordingly-prevention by giving out early warnings and alerts, detection by looking out for attacked sites and quick and suitable response to the attack.

3.2 Intrusion Detection Prevention System (IDPS)

A common tool for Cybersecurity is Intrusion Detection Prevention System (IDPS) which can be a software or hardware that responsible for working on a given data while processing and analysing it. It uses the two main methodologies: - i) Misuse detection that can scan patterns of an irregular system behaviour and detect some kind of malicious activity. ii) Anomaly detection that finds out any behaviour that can be characterized as an anomaly with respect to the normal system where the model was trained. These patterns are characterized based upon knowledge of previous threats that were experienced (Patel et al., 2012).

3.3 Limitations of Traditional Approaches in Cybersecurity

Rise of Sophisticated Attacks: In the recent years, security threats have become more variant and ever changing and even adapted to be able to bypass the safeguards kept place. While traditional methods to Cybersecurity problems are equipped to protect consumers against certain type of attacks, rise of sophisticated cyber attacks, such as Advanced Persistent Threats (APTs) (Li, 2018) has challenged traditional security approaches. Such an attack does not have previous records and act as soon as a flaw in the system is detected. In a survey of about 4000 midsized companies, it was found that amount of threats have increased about twice from the year 2021 to 2022 and that more than forty percent of the malware detected were never seen previously. Targeted and customized attacks have increased drastically ever since the covid-19 pandemic (Coro, 2022). The traditional approaches are thus shorthanded against such advanced threats. The prime objective of cyber security is to identify the indicators generated from a compromised system during the entirety of an ongoing attack. However this becomes a very difficult task as the system has to deal with bulk data being generated frequently in the expanding cyber world with so many devices getting connected. This also creates shortfall of Cybersecurity experts and subsequent high demand for the use of AI in Cybersecurity to facilitate the automation in a number of repetitive threat detection lessen the strain on Cybersecurity employees. Artificial intelligence is also capable enough to address these more proficiently as compared to other software-driven approaches.

Inferior Detection Rate and Reliability: Nature of cyber space is such that there is a lot of variation in the patterns of the network, thus patterns are identified and characterized inaccurately, this results in a low detection rate of the IDPS (Wirkuttis & Klein, 2017). The IDPS is also susceptible of wrongly identifying normal system behaviour as an anomaly and thus generating a false alarm. This causes much interruption in the usual proceedings and thus a security expert gets nvolved in finding the false detections instead of doing something more productive, leading to loss of time and resources. iii) Weak Processing Power and Low Automation: As the amount of data to be scanned is huge the IDPS are bounded to be slow is analysing the data (Apruzzese et al., 2023). This also makes them inefficient and unable to cope up with the variant nature of the digital canvas that is constantly expanding (Wirkuttis & Klein, 2017). Moreover, traditional measures also requires automation as there are cumbersome tasks like analysing large quantities of log data individually, readjustment of the system properties to cater to the changing network environment and resolving every individual warning messages.

4. AI APPROACHES TO CYBERSECURITY

4.1 Intelligent Agent Based Cybersecurity

These systems have Intelligent Agents that uses intelligent behaviours like sharing the knowledge gained among the entities, pro-activeness, and ability to categorize, quantify and respond so as to together find solutions to complex problems. The agents can be assumed as objects spread across the systems that are farsighted and able to communicate among themselves. Furthermore these agents are proactive and can notice any fluctuations or changes in the environment during any kind of Denial-of-Service (DoS) attack which is a cyber attack interferes in the normal functioning of the services by disabling certain resources. In this way these decentralized agents come together to safeguard the system from DoS attacks, while cooperating and exchanging information among each other (Yadav & Rao, 2015). The two main advantages of such agents are: i) The agents are decentralized and spread across the system, they are able to gather complete data from various parts of the system to properly analyse and identify the threats. ii) As these agents are 'intelligent' they can gather experiences from the past attacks and adapt accordingly so as to be better prepared for future attacks. Thus these agents are capable enough in the surveillance and assist in various stages of the cyber kill chain. In the recent years, cyber security experts have been grouping the intelligent agents to form a 'Cyber Police' to effectively combat against security threats in a decentralized fashion. Such police has shown promise to be able identify the potential target system as well as attacks as early as possible. Although it should be noted that prior legal and industrial permissions must be attained before defining such police force in the cyber environment as well as partnership with the ISPs and other different tools available to ensure efficient working (Guarino, 2013). Experts are also employing different kinds of agents, mainly detection and counterattack agents. The first group scouts the system for potential abnormal behaviours and the second group pursues countermeasures based on the decentralized data it was shared by the detection agents. If you notice, this approach sort of models the human immune system (Patil, 2016).

Expert systems based are computer programs having refines hybrid tools that are assembled to assist in decision making in complex problems from various fields such as healthcare, business, research, technology sciences, etc. An expert system has two main components- the knowledge base and the inference engine. The former can be said to be a database in which information belonging to a particular domain is the stored and the inference engine is from which answers can be derived(Patil, 2016) (Padron & Ojeda-Castro, 2017). In cyber security domain expert system can be applied with two approaches: i) Cased based reasoning (CBR) approach that considers the solutions of past experiences to tackle a new similar problem. The solutions are of course worked upon and enhanced as we encounter new problems in the system. ii) Rule based reasoning (RBR) that adheres to the guidelines declared by the expert system to first analyse then act according to the rules defined. This way they can help access in making decision regarding the threats in underlying system or whether they are infected in the first place. These AI based expert system have shown to be capable enough to be able to monitor large amounts of data across the different heterogeneous cyber landscapes on real time. Thus helping out the Cyber experts with the tedious task as well as generating early warning an alerts with accurate information about the nature o the threat (Patil, 2016; Tyugu, 2011).

4.2 Machine Learning in Cybersecurity

Machine learning (ML) is a subset of AI that is heavily associated with computational statistics and therefore is centred on prediction making. It involves using mathematical optimization and procedures to define methods, theory and applications for a particular field. It focuses on interpreting, categorizing, regression and decision making as per the data it was trained on (Patil, 2016). One of the ML approach is Artificial Neural Network (ANN) which are primarily used to prevent malicious intrusion by integrating with all the stages of the ISAs and is capable of working under every phase of the cyber kill chain. They monitor the system and act upon detecting any intrusion right before the delivery phase, thus accomplishing the intended purpose of Cyber. Not only this, just like a human brain, they are able to add to their arsenal knowledge from previous attacks which is a big advantage over traditional Cybersecurity techniques (Tyugu, 2011). ANNs are first trained with the data of normal network properties to recognize and formulate patterns. As it monitors the existing network any new data packet introduced to the system is quickly analysed and compared with the pre learned patterns to determine if it is malicious or not, mismatches will be deemed malicious and thus rejected by the IDPS. This way ANN facilitates anomaly based IDPS approach as well as address a major concern in IDPS system which is false alarm. As the datasets are meticulously handled and compared, the chances of a false detection of a threat or intrusion are decreased greatly, while traditional IDPS approaches are only successful against intrusions that are already known, the ANNs integrated approach is also able to defend against unknown attacks (Buczak & Guven, 2015). The special feature of ANNs is its high speed helping security professionals with automatic defining of the patterns into infected or not, using its past lessons. Today ANNs are integrated across several system such as firewall, network hubs, etc to combat against threats like DoS, intrusion, computer worms, spam, viruses and malwares and monitoring network traffic (Bitter et al., 2010).

Another ML technique is Support Vector Machines (SVM),which employs 'boundary concept' to segregate elements according to different class (Ghanem et al., 2017).In Cybersecurity, SVMs are primarily applied in intrusion detection system using four steps- The first one is Data Pre-processing where raw data is analysed and all trivial data found is taken out without any human assistance. SVMs can work on linearly, non linearly separable datasets by segregating the input vectors using a separation hyper plane. In case the datasets are not separable, it will use appropriate functions to map them in higher dimensional spaces so that they can be easily separated (Martínez Torres et al., 2019). The model mainly uses the concept of vectors and distances to train SVM model, performance of model is optimized so as to increase the accuracy of the model with the last stage being classification of the data according to the several attributes to determine the potential target class. SVMs have shown promise in determine potential threats and vulnerabilities for an intrusion using these steps, it can analyse Internet traffic patterns and separate them into their component classes thus help regulate traffic flow on internet (Abdiansah & Wardoyo, 2015).

A decision tree is also ML model which has a tree like structure with class labels such as leaves or nodes represent the object value which can be derived by the path from the root node to the leaf node (Raheja & Munjal, 2021). Decision tress is widely applied in achieving cybersecurity in number of ways including intrusion detection, where it is trained on past intrusions and learns to classify the incoming network traffic as ordinary or malicious form to cause an intrusion. As depicted in Figure 2 at each node, the attributes of the data that categorize the data elements into subsets as per the normalized information gain are selected. Decisions are made by the attribute with the highest normalized information (Xin et al., 2018). Decision tress is capable of automatically generating responsive safeguards which are trained to during its development (Abubakar et al., 2015). It also aids in anomaly detection because by constructing a decision tree from normal behaviour data, the model can detect deviations from the learned patterns to determine an anomalous behaviour of the system. It is also useful in classification of malware by understanding the file attributes and patterns of sample malicious files. Another application is misuse detection in which it compares the alleged misuse to the prescribed rules set before. The biggest advantage of this approach is its ability to implicitly extract attributes and their simpler interpretation. There are a few disadvantages of decision trees, which includes its limited capability to combat unknown intrusions, thus this approach requires regular updates with the newest intrusion and frequent training to combat against advanced treats. Another disadvantage is that while experts can effectively extract knowledge and rules from small trees by simply examining them, the process is much complicated when it comes to bigger trees. The deeper and wider a tree is, the less intuitive it becomes in extracting rules, hence decision tress

Figure 2. Structure of decision tree

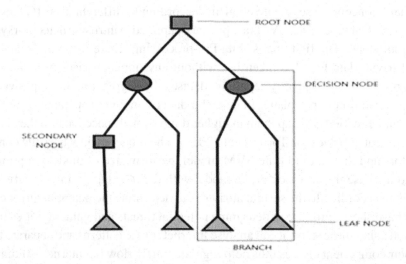

are mostlyapplied in smaller sections of larger security systems (Buczak & Guven, 2015; Raheja et al., 2021).

k- Nearest Neighbour k-NN is another ML method widely used to detect anomalies, the data is fed in to kNN model then it calculates the distance between elements across data points in the dataset and looks for the "k" closest data points (neighbours) in the feature space (Xin et al., 2018). This way the algorithms maps out the dataset and uses the distances to define patterns within it to train itself (Raheja & Munjal, 2021). Different studies show that this method can provide promising results, with good detection rate and low false alarm rate. The special feature of this algorithm is the use of a general formula for distance calculation that makes it a very convenient approach. KNN techniques have immensely aided intrusion detection systems due to the ability of fast understanding of new traffic patterns. They are thus equipped to combat against Zero day attacks which can infect the system before countermeasures are prepared (Pallaprolu et al., 2017). KNN models have been implemented to combat against Botnets which are networks of compromised computers or devices controlled by a malicious entity, used for various illicit activities like DDoS (Distributed Denial of Service) attacks, spam distribution, and data theft without owners' knowledge (Hoang & Nguyen, 2018). Security experts are also using this model for real-time threat detection and false-data injection. Since kNN calculates the distances among the instances of a dataset, thus its not very convenient to use it for larger datasets as they contains lots of different classes with numerous instances, hence they are used in smaller sections in Cybersecurity systems (Abubakar et al., 2015; Raheja et al., 2021).

In Cybersecurity, Genetic Algorithm (GA) is used to detect anomalies in IDPS systems, GA studies existing patterns to gain more insight and predictability on future patterns it will encounter. This way an IDPS integrated with GA can ensure quick identification for of new anomaly (Calderon, 2019). GA is also used to improve firewalls to aid network defence using network traffic pattern. GA can also aid in cryptography as it can decipher encryptions (Pallaprolu et al., 2017). This also helps generating numerous configurations to aid in vulnerability assessment for network and systems. The special trait of GA is its adaptive nature, it can adapt to the evolving and dynamic nature of cyber environment and thus combat against new emerging threats without an extensive human supervision. This model suffers from high computational complexity thus demand more time and resources also it requires extensive experimentation may not always adequate and are influenced by a number of factors (Padron & Ojeda-Castro, 2017; Kang & Kang, 2016).

4.3 Deep Learning in Cybersecurity

Deep learning (DL) uses more advanced algorithms that make use of only relevant data or the progress in the system while linking old and new data to form and identify patterns. DL is different from ML as it can handle large amounts of data (both supervised and unsupervised. DL methods are also able to interpret an image by using the vector of every pixel intensity value, edges, various shapes present in an image for which requires better hardware and more expertise (Calderon, 2019).

Deep Belief Network (DBN) is an unsupervised DL approach that comprises of a interrelated covert layers, arranged in a hierarchical fashion. In Cybersecurity, DBN are integrated with the IDPS where it analyses the data, estimates the number of hidden layers required during computation. During training the layers are treated individually, as the model starts training on the dataset of that layer to identify patterns and performs calculations to determine the future conditions. After training, the output of one layer is treated as the input to the next layer. DBN can determine possible intrusions with high degree of accuracy as well as detect any false positive warnings generated in the IDPS. Another characteristic feature of this model is its ability to 'self learn' because of which minimal human assistance is required and the model has room to improve upon itself (Calderon, 2019). Owing to its self-learning nature, DBN have also been effective against novel and advanced security treats thus they can be employed to identify potential vulnerabilities in web applications, by analysing user input patterns and web server logs (Kang & Kang, 2016). The Cybersecurity systems and networks are of dynamic nature involving large datasets thus DBN models are adapted to give better results (Berman et al., 2019).

Figure 3. Basic CNN architecture

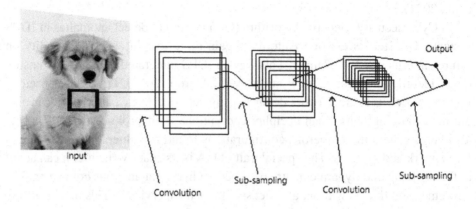

Another DL model is CNN that deals with data in the form of arrays so as to be able to handle structured grid like data and can represent its result in the form of two dimensional arrays (Calderon, 2019). It comprises of three layers, i) Convolution layer that is responsible in defining relationships among the data sets as per the weights (learnable parameters) of the input to produce a feature map, ii) pooling layer that interprets the feature map to extract relevant information and iii) Classification layer that is responsible for high level representation and classification of processed data. Detailed architecture is depicted in fig, where input is given in form of image and output attained inform of class label of that image.CNN are used for phishing attack by learning from features of a phishing mail or site and analyse the structure and visual elements to prevent potential phishing threats. Another application of CNN is in biometric authentication as it can deal with data in the form of 2D or 3D elements (Xin et al., 2018). CNNs are employed to break visual CAPTCHAs, which are used to prevent automated bots from accessing online services. CNNs process network traffic data and analyse packet headers or payload content to detect anomalies and signs of unauthorized access, intrusions, and cyber attacks (). The model is trained for dataset of known individuals to identify the vital patterns and carry out accurate authentication (Berman et al., 2019). Figure 3 illustrates the basic CNN architecture.

RNNs are advanced deep neural networks that use output of the hidden unit as input for the next additional input for next element, while processing one input at a time. It is best suited for tasks where the order and context of the data elements are essential for understanding and making predictions (Xin et al., 2018). RNN are capable of handling speech recognition, language translation and time series problems. RNNs are used widely in network traffic analysis by identifying unusual patterns or detect specific types of network attacks, such as DDoS attack. It provides real time analysis of network traffic data and log files to detect anomalies and potential cyber intrusions (Kim et al., 2016). RNNs being capable for time series analysis thus they are suitable for event logs and system metrics to study trends and anomalies. RNNs analyze system logs to identify sequences of events that could indicate security breaches or unauthorized activities. It can also help against phishing by analysing email content and detect phishing attempts based on the sequence of words or patterns used in phishing emails. RNNs also have the capability to study existing patterns and predict future patterns, thus being effective in dealing against new emerging intrusion with little or no past knowledge. RNN has thus proven to be an effective approach to address modern security challenges (Berman et al., 2019; Gasmi et al., 2018).

Generative Adversarial Neural Network (GAN) is a type of deep learning model in which two neural networks, one called the generator and the other called the discriminator are trained simultaneously in a competitive manner. The generator takes the input data and produces the output with same attributes of the original real data. The discriminator takes the output generated by the generator and real data and compares the two datasets. GANs are used in data augmentation by generating synthetic samples that closely resemble real data. Such augmentation of the dataset helps to improve the performance and robustness of machine learning models used in intrusion detection, malware classification, and other Cybersecurity tasks (Berman et al., 2019). GAN can generate a new and realistic data that resembles given training dataset. GANs have shown widely applicability in dealing with images and can be used in tasks like image generation and enhancement, hence it is useful in dealing with new Cybersecurity issues like deep fake video generation (Goodfellow et al., 2014). GANs can create visual representations of complex Cybersecurity data thus aiding analysts in identifying patterns, trends, and anomalies in large datasets. GANs can analyse email content or web pages to identify phishing attempts or suspicious social engineering tactics based on patterns in text and images, thus helping in phishing detection (Tasneem et al., 2022).

5. ROLE OF NLP IN CYBERSECURITY

Natural Language Processing or NLP is an amalgamation of mathematical algorithms, statistics and linguistics within the sphere of AI. It helps machines contextualize nuances and sentimental analysis of the text, instead of just blindly following the rules of a language so that the machine can learn and adapt to new commands and protocols automatically. It also helps machine in text classification and extracting useful pieces of information gained from learning. NLP is used in speech recognition, user behaviour monitoring, threat analysis, phishing detection and identifies software vulnerabilities.NLP greatly helps in automating the task of detection of possible targets by developing a language model in accordance with the existing code and performing a rundown of the entire code to scan and pluck out the bugs or flaws in the system. The operational time is also much faster as NLP breaks down the codes and understands the relationship of the various elements with help of machine and deep learning models. They are useful in dealing with attacks that are identified but not no remedy has been found and referred to as Zero-Day attacks since it does not require the execution of code and can automatically remove the malicious entities present (Tyugu, 2011).

6. LIMITATIONS OF AI IN CYBERSECURITY

Like every piece of technology developed, there are few limitations of using AI in Cybersecurity.

Piracy Risk: The biggest concern of incorporating AI is the potential piracy risk. Big corporations and governments are concerned that the AI tools handling Cybersecurity have complete accesses to a large amount of data that may also contain sensitive or confidential data. There is a big lack of trust between them and the third party AI tools that they have borrowed (Ansari et al., 2022).

Requirement of human supervision: Despite their accuracy, AI tools are also susceptible of making errors and generative false alarms themselves. This cause time wastage of security professions who need to analyse the entire system. As AI models are complex, this cause much more difficulty in finding what the error is or where the error actually took place. AI systems may automate Cybersecurity but they still are not completely autonomous themselves and need human supervision.

Lack of morals: There are also moral issues regarding AI as they replace humans in various fields. These systems do not have any moral code of conduct. There is also a lack of legal laws and regulations surrounding AI which can be taken unlawful advantage of by notorious entities of the society. Hence standard certification procedures must be developed and carried out.

High Cost: As we have seen earlier the research and development of AI is very large and requires large investments from organization without any certainty of success. It also requires expert professionals. Both of these are not affordable for developing or poor countries.

Inability to detect threats: Cyber environment is a dynamic space which is constantly evolving. In the recent years cyber threats have grown more sophisticated and customized than ever. As such even with several advantages of AI in Cybersecurity, many a times they are unable to detect and defend against attacks which can result in severe losses. Furthermore, if AI models are fed even a miniscule amount of wrong input, they will result in drastic errors (Ansari et al., 2022; Apruzzese et al., 2023).

7. ETHICAL ISSUES OF AI USAGE IN CYBER SECURITY

7.1 Cyber Criminals Are Using AI to Disrupt Cybersecurity

A growing concern is that hackers and malicious groups may use AI itself to disrupt Cybersecurity. They may develop tools that evade all defection and swiftly attacks their targets. Hackers are able to deceive AI based systems and may even target the AI powered safeguards, thus corrupting them. They can manipulate the data AI model has to train on thus making them defective. Attacks on AI are also hard to detect as they have complex internal processes. Criminals can also reverse engineer he internal processes to understand why exactly he attacks could be determined (Taddeo et al., 2019). A system may show normal behaviour with certain manipulations to the neural network and the bug will only be activated with a trigger, this way AI is tricked into believing everything is alright. And the system will be corrupted in such a manner that it will show only miniscule changes even after the trigger until a fatal attack is carried out when it is already too late. Criminals are using AI to coordinate launch automated attacks, develop malware viruses, automated phishing and money laundering, formulate methods to breach safeguard as well as carry out new threats like deep fakes and password hacking.

The complicated structure of Cybersecurity measures makes it very difficult to spot the small differences which end up being decisive and enough of the attackers to do their malicious activities. For example, wearing an AI image recognition system can be tricked to wrongly categorize its subjects by wearing specially crafted eyeglasses (Taddeo et al., 2019). It is therefore is very important to make a robust and well versed AI system to defend against such growing concerns.

7.2 Human-AI Interfaces

With the growing challenges to Cybersecurity, and AI system being integrate in it, there is immense need for coordination between and trust between human-AI interfaces. At any level problems arise when individual system components maximize their own goals without considering the system level objectives. Moreover, in an era where misinformation and manipulation is rampant, good decision making requires hybrid approaches that leverage and orchestrate the unique human and AI capabilities and perspectives. The important areas to consider and work upon are good human machine teaming, trust building and assistance.

The team up of human and machine needs to be such that humans are thorough and can easily explain the outcomes. The people working on such system should be able to identify goals, be active in decision making process and provide feedback that is worked upon with priority. Research is needed on how to minimize latency and negative consequences while providing stable output. In a diverse human-AI system environment, interactions must be managed with a goal to reduce human error, increase safety, and provide accountability (McDaniel et al., 2020).

8. CONCLUSION AND FUTURE THOUGHTS

This paper discussed how artificial intelligence is becoming an indispensable tool in Cybersecurity as the number of threats and their severity continue to grow. Traditional methods are not enough in this dynamic and fast changing cyber environment and how AI frameworks are being integrated in Cybersecurity. A lot of investment is done in this field and new techniques are being regularly formulated. Some of the approaches ML and DL approaches are discussed that act as tools to protect against threats. While AI is growing fast with a lot of potential, there still are a number of concerns surrounding their use in Cybersecurity which need to be addressed. The rapid advances in technology, new application domains, and the interplay between AI and Cybersecurity will continue to introduce new opportunities and challenges. As the IT sector is growing fast, so are cyber threats and thus more research and developments to be carried out to ensure a secure digital world.

Attention should also be given in fostering a reliable AI Cybersecurity System by investing in test beds and datasets to establish the AI community standards and metrics required to safely deploy future AI systems. Threat detection mechanisms must be tested and evaluated regularly. Possibilities include the creation and maintenance of realistic simulation environments and domain specific datasets. Test beds and datasets need to designed in such a way that the evaluation is in a in a structure, principled and sustainable manner. They should also have ground or reproducibility and be regularly reevaluated across various domains. Ample educational opportunities should be provided to include fresh minds in this domain. The pros and cons of AI should be educated to the young minds at the institution level where disciplines of computer science, data science, engineering, and statistics intersect. AI based courses should be included as part of the accreditation process.

Priority should be given to defining standards of AI implementation and that the suppliers must develop and train their models in house. The testing data and knowledge gained must be evaluated the system owners who will use the tools. This will foster good connections between the concerned parties as well as access data and models. In addition to the actual system working to detect threats, a clone system should run parallel as a control centre. The cone is not an exact duplicate of the original system neither an AI virtual simulation, rather a benchmark against which the behaviour of original system is evaluated. The divergence of actual and expected system behaviours help to address flaws and deficiencies early on, hence such parallel monitoring is encouraged.

REFERENCES

Abdiansah, A., & Wardoyo, R. (2015). Time complexity analysis of support vector machines (SVM) in LibSVM. *International Journal of Computer Applications*, *128*(3), 28–34. doi:10.5120/ijca2015906480

Abubakar, A. I., Chiroma, H., Muaz, S. A., & Ila, L. B. (2015). A review of the advances in cyber security benchmark datasets for evaluating data-driven based intrusion detection systems. *Procedia Computer Science*, *62*, 221–227. doi:10.1016/j.procs.2015.08.443

Ansari, M. F., Dash, B., Sharma, P., & Yathiraju, N. (2022). The Impact and Limitations of Artificial Intelligence in Cybersecurity: A Literature Review. *International Journal of Advanced Research in Computer and Communication Engineering*, *11*(9). doi:10.17148/IJARCCE.2022.11912

Apruzzese, G., Laskov, P., Montes de Oca, E., Mallouli, W., Brdalo Rapa, L., Grammatopoulos, A. V., & Di Franco, F. (2023). The role of machine learning in cybersecurity. *Digital Threats : Research and Practice*, *4*(1), 1–38. doi:10.1145/3545574

Berman, D. S., Buczak, A. L., Chavis, J. S., & Corbett, C. L. (2019). A survey of deep learning methods for cyber security. *Information (Basel)*, *10*(4), 122. doi:10.3390/info10040122

Bitter, C., Elizondo, D. A., & Watson, T. (2010, July). Application of artificial neural networks and related techniques to intrusion detection. In *The 2010 International Joint Conference on Neural Networks (IJCNN)* (pp. 1-8). IEEE. 10.1109/IJCNN.2010.5596532

Buczak, A. L., & Guven, E. (2015). A survey of data mining and machine learning methods for cyber security intrusion detection. *IEEE Communications Surveys and Tutorials*, *18*(2), 1153–1176. doi:10.1109/COMST.2015.2494502

Buczak, A. L., & Guven, E. (2015). A survey of data mining and machine learning methods for cyber security intrusion detection. *IEEE Communications Surveys and Tutorials*, *18*(2), 1153–1176. doi:10.1109/COMST.2015.2494502

Calderon, R. (2019). *The benefits of artificial intelligence in cybersecurity.*

Coro. (2022). *The Biggest Cyber Security Threats.* Coro. https://go.coro.net/cyberthreats2022

Gasmi, H., Bouras, A., & Laval, J. (2018). LSTM recurrent neural networks for cybersecurity named entity recognition. *ICSEA*, *11*, 2018.

Ghanem, K., Aparicio-Navarro, F. J., Kyriakopoulos, K. G., Lambotharan, S., & Chambers, J. A. (2017, December). Support vector machine for network intrusion and cyber-attack detection. In 2017 sensor signal processing for defence conference (SSPD) (pp. 1-5). IEEE. doi:10.1109/SSPD.2017.8233268

Goodfellow, I., Pouget-Abadie, J., Mirza, M., Xu, B., Warde-Farley, D., Ozair, S., & Bengio, Y. (2014). Generative adversarial nets. *Advances in Neural Information Processing Systems*, 27.

Guarino, A. (2013, June). Autonomous intelligent agents in cyber offence. In *2013 5th International Conference on Cyber Conflict (CYCON 2013)* (pp. 1-12). IEEE.

Hoang, X. D., & Nguyen, Q. C. (2018). Botnet detection based on machine learning techniques using DNS query data. *Future Internet*, *10*(5), 43. doi:10.3390/fi10050043

Kang, M. J., & Kang, J. W. (2016). Intrusion detection system using deep neural network for in-vehicle network security. *PLoS One*, *11*(6), e0155781. doi:10.1371/journal.pone.0155781 PMID:27271802

Kim, J., Kim, J., Thu, H. L. T., & Kim, H. (2016, February). Long short term memory recurrent neural network classifier for intrusion detection. In 2016 international conference on platform technology and service (PlatCon) (pp. 1-5). IEEE. doi:10.1109/PlatCon.2016.7456805

Li, J. H. (2018). Cyber security meets artificial intelligence: A survey. *Frontiers of Information Technology & Electronic Engineering*, *19*(12), 1462–1474. doi:10.1631/FITEE.1800573

Markets and Markets. (2019). *AI in cybersecurity market.* Markets and Markets www.marketsandmarkets.com

Martínez Torres, J., Iglesias Comesaña, C., & García-Nieto, P. J. (2019). Machine learning techniques applied to cybersecurity. *International Journal of Machine Learning and Cybernetics, 10*(10), 2823–2836. doi:10.100713042-018-00906-1

McDaniel, P., Launchbury, J., Martin, B., Wang, C., & Kautz, H. (2020). *Artificial intelligence and cyber security: opportunities and challenges technical workshop summary report.* Networking & Information Technology Research And Development Subcommittee And The Machine Learning & Artificial Intelligence Subcommittee Of The National Science & Technology Council.

Morgan, S. (2022, January 19). *2022 Cybersecurity Almanac: 100 Facts, Figures, Predictions And Statistics.* Cybersecurity Ventures. https://cybersecurityventures.com/cybersecurity-almanac-2022/

Padron, J. M., & Ojeda-Castro, A. (2017). Cyberwarfare: Artificial intelligence in the frontlines of combat. *International Journal of Information Research and Review, 4*(6), 4208–4212.

Pallaprolu, S. C., Sankineni, R., Thevar, M., Karabatis, G., & Wang, J. (2017, June). Zero-day attack identification in streaming data using semantics and Spark. In *2017 IEEE International Congress on Big Data (BigData Congress)* (pp. 121-128). IEEE. 10.1109/BigDataCongress.2017.25

Patel, A., Taghavi, M., Bakhtiyari, K., & Jr, J. (2012). An Intrusion Detection And Prevention System In Cloud Computing: A Systematic Review. *Journal of Network and Computer Applications, 36*(1), 25–41. doi:10.1016/j.jnca.2012.08.007

Patil, P. (2016). Artificial intelligence in cyber security. *International Journal of research computer application and robotics.*

Raheja, S., & Munjal, G. (2021). Classification of Microsoft office vulnerabilities: a step ahead for secure software development. *Bio-inspired Neurocomputing*, (pp. 381-402).

Raheja, S., Munjal, G., Jangra, J., & Garg, R. (2021). Rule-Based Approach for Botnet Behavior Analysis. *Intelligent Data Analytics for Terror Threat Prediction: Architectures, Methodologies, Techniques and Applications*, (pp. 161-179).

Saha, M., Sengupta, A., & Das, A. (2020). *Cyber Threats in Artificial Intelligence.*

Taddeo, M., McCutcheon, T., & Floridi, L. (2019). Trusting artificial intelligence in cybersecurity is a double-edged sword. *Nature Machine Intelligence, 1*(12), 557–560. doi:10.103842256-019-0109-1

Tasneem, S., Gupta, K. D., Roy, A., & Dasgupta, D. (2022, December). Generative Adversarial Networks (GAN) for Cyber Security: Challenges and Opportunities. In *Proceedings of the 2022 IEEE Symposium Series on Computational Intelligence*, (pp. 4-7). IEEE.

Tyugu, E. (2011, June). Artificial intelligence in cyber defense. In *2011 3rd International conference on cyber conflict* (pp. 1-11). IEEE.

Wirkuttis, N., & Klein, H. (2017). Artificial intelligence in cybersecurity. *Cyber, Intelligence, and Security*, *1*(1), 103–119.

Xin, Y., Kong, L., Liu, Z., Chen, Y., Li, Y., Zhu, H., Gao, M., Hou, H., & Wang, C. (2018). Machine learning and deep learning methods for cybersecurity. *IEEE Access : Practical Innovations, Open Solutions*, *6*, 35365–35381. doi:10.1109/ACCESS.2018.2836950

Yadav, T., & Rao, A. M. (2015). Technical aspects of cyber kill chain. In Security in Computing and Communications: Third International Symposium, SSCC 2015. Springer International Publishing.

Chapter 7
Accountable Malicious Entity Detection Using Re-Encryption Mechanism to Share Data

S. T. Veena
Mepco Schlenk Engineering College, India

N. R. Somnath Babu
Mepco Schlenk Engineering Collge, India

P. Santosh
Mepco Schlenk Engineering Collge, India

ABSTRACT

Recently data sharing through the cloud is widely used and becoming a trend. But protecting data confidentiality and integrity is essential. Data confidentiality and integrity are maintained using cryptography. However, since it cannot ensure that the data hasn't been altered, there is still a trust issue. The proxy re-encryption (PRE) technique was presented as a solution to this. It includes encrypting the data twice, allowing one to determine whether or not it has been altered. The PRE system is also prone to attacks that forge re-encryption keys. Here the data is encrypted twice so that the data can be checked whether it is modified or not. But the PRE system is prone to the abuse of re-encryption keys. Therefore, accountable proxy re-encryption (APRE) is proposed. Here, if the data is altered by proxy, the system will detect whether proxy is malicious or the delegator is trying to frame proxy as malicious. Also, the authors extend the algorithm and implemented base64 encoding and decoding. This prevents many passive cyber attacks.

DOI: 10.4018/979-8-3693-1431-9.ch007

1. INTRODUCTION

IN today's digital world, Data is a critical resource, and it is increasingly becoming more important in all aspects of our lives.Data sharing is also crucial in today's interconnected world. By sharing data, we can collaborate and work together to solve complex problems and make better decisions. Cloud storage is the greatest choice any time a user wishes to share a data.The confidentiality of the data is the fundamental worry while sharing data on the cloud. The confidentiality and integrity of the data cannot be ensured by the content owner. Encryption of data is a crucial fix for this problem. For this reason, a variety of encryption techniques are available. The data is encrypted by the content owner (or delegator), who also distributes the decryption key to data consumers. For this to work, the content owner must be connected online at all times. To tackle this issue (Blaze et al., 1998) proposed Proxy Re-Encryption (PRE). Applying PRE in cloud, initially the delegator, proxy, and delegatee share all their public key certificates for authentication. The data is encrypted by the content owner (or delegator) and uploaded to the cloud. Using a re-encryption key, the proxy re-encrypts the ciphertext. The shared data is first encrypted, and then the ciphertext is sent to the proxy. The content owner produces a re-encryption key in response to a content receiver's request and provides it to the proxy, who then re-encrypts the ciphertext and forwards it to the receiver.

But the proxy and content owner together has the ability to find the decryption key and can abuse the data. Also the data owner can frame a proxy as malicious.

So to ensure data security and to check if the delegator or proxy is malicious, (Guo et al., 2021) proposed Accountable Proxy Re-encryption(APRE). Here there will be a court module. Anyone can approach the court to verify it. The proxy with a delegatee can modify the data or the delegator can accuse the proxy is accountable. To identify it, the court module is used. The court module uses a judge algorithm. The algorithm gets the initial ciphertext and then it asks the proxy and the delegator to decrypt it. By observing the plaintext the court module will find whether the proxy or delegator is accountable.

The APRE scheme does not capture all the attacks. There will be many attacks over network, which will lead to Chosen Plain Text (CPA)/Chosen Cyber CCA. This can result in serious loss to the data owner. Hence, to extend the security further, our system used base64 encoding and decoding.

2. RELATED WORKS

Other than proxy re-encryption techniques (Sun et al., 2018) presented a revocable identity-based encryption scheme with cloud-aided ciphertext evolution. In order to protect against chosen ciphertext attacks and avoid the fabrication of genuine ciphertexts or signatures, they devised a method revocable identity-based encryption (RIBE) scheme utilising ciphertext evolution.

As a security paradigm, to overcome the fact that in a traditional PRE scheme, a semi-trusted proxy can convert all ciphertexts for a delegator to ciphertexts for a delegatee once the proxy obtains the relevant re-encryption key from the delegator (Zeng and Choo, 2018) suggested sender-specified Proxy Re-encryption (SS-PRE) technique, which permits the assignment of decryption privileges for particular ciphertexts. The scheme is mainly for access methods tools. With improved computing efficiency, SS-PRE is protected from many attacks.

In order to prevent the misuse of proxy re-encryption keys, (Liu et al., 2019) suggested an accountable proxy re-encryption technique for transferring encrypted content among various users. Performance testing has demonstrated the usefulness of this approach. Here, the keys are safely encrypted while transferring for safety.

Cloud computing Attribute-Based Encryption (ABE) method proposed by (Li et al., 2019) for lowering storage and processing costs for users and the Proxy Cloud Service Provider (PCSP). Under the presumption of decision q-parallel bilinear Diffie-Hellman exponent, the scheme is secured (BDHE).

The Variable and Multi-Keyword Searchable Attribute-Based Encryption (VMKS-ABE) technique for cloud storage was introduced by (Wang et al., 2019). It is resistant to adaptive keyword and selective plaintext assaults. It handles number of computational functions and it can reduce work load for end-users side.

The content is safely transferred. In a set of broadcast re-encrypted ciphertexts,(Wang et al., 2019) suggested a method for receivers privacy. When compared to previous broadcasting systems and current privacy-preserving schemes, our scheme takes less time to decrypt.

With the Information-Centric Networking (ICN) paradigm, (Li et al., 2019) suggested an effective Proxy Re-encryption (PRE) technique, lowering user-side overhead and providing flexible data exchange. The method is effective in terms of computational cost and complexity and safe against the adaptive replay able selected ciphertext attack (RCCA) in complete ICN encryption.

In order to secure communication between fog-to-things computing, (Khashan, 2020) presented a system that combines lightweight symmetric and asymmetric algorithms, with very efficient computational cost for re-encryption procedures carried out by fog nodes. Revocable Identity-Based Broadcast Proxy Re-encryption (RIB-BPRE), a security concept developed by (Ge et al., 2021) addresses the problem of key revocation. A proxy in RIB-BPRE has the ability to remove a group of delegates from the re-encryption key that have been chosen by the delegator. Performance analysis shows that the suggested plan is effective and workable. It analyses the security for the model. Accountability Proxy Re-encryption (APRE), which employs a judge algorithm to identify potential misuse of decryption keys, was developed by (Guo et al., 2021). Data integrity for data shared on proxy servers is guaranteed by the APRE scheme. It ensures integrity of data. To allow authorised users access to data, (Agyekum et al., 2022) devised proxy encryption using identity-based encryption. Using this technique, cached content is effectively delivered to Internet of Things devices.

3. PROPOSED MODEL

Data is the most valuable resource in our daily lives, and it is crucial to ensure its confidentiality and integrity. However, when data owners share their data through the cloud, there is often a trust issue, as they cannot determine whether the shared data has been altered. To address this concern, Guo et al. proposed the Accountable Proxy Re-Encryption (APRE) scheme [1]. A fresh approach was introduced by the APRE plan to address the trust problem, in which a judge can determine guilt based on a convincing piece of evidence presented. Therefore, if a proxy distributes a decryption device while conspiring with any delegatee, the judge algorithm can identify the malicious proxy, and the proxy runs the risk of being discovered and held liable. Nevertheless, this existing system is vulnerable to many network attacks that may capture ciphertext passed over the internet and attempt to decrypt it by collecting multiple ciphertexts. Thus, we propose a new system that can tackle such network attacks.

A public key is initially generated for the proxy, data owner, and consumer, and is subsequently shared to all parties for authentication. Following the creation of the content owner's secret key, the plaintext is then encrypted by the delegator using the consumer's public key to generate the first-level ciphertext. The content owner then creates a re-encryption key using their secret key, the proxy's public key, and their own public key. To avoid obtaining the secret key and to stop harmful proxy behavior, the re-encryption key must be designed properly.

During the data sharing stage, as shown in Figure 1, the delegator encrypts the plaintext with the public key of the consumer, resulting in the first-level ciphertext. Both the first-level ciphertext and the re-encryption key are transmitted to the proxy. The proxy then utilizes the re-encryption key and its secret key to re-encrypt the first-level ciphertext. When the consumer requests access to the file, the proxy provides the content receiver with the re-encrypted cipher. The receiver decrypts the re-encrypted cipher using their secret key and obtains the original plaintext.

The content owner creates the second-level ciphertext by encrypting the plaintext with their own public key during the accountability phase, as depicted in Figure 2. The owner then performs a second-level decryption of the second-level ciphertext.

Figure 1. Data sharing phase

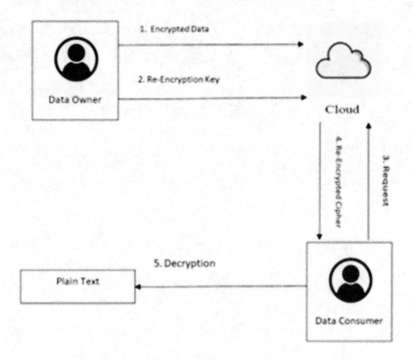

Figure 2. Accountability phase

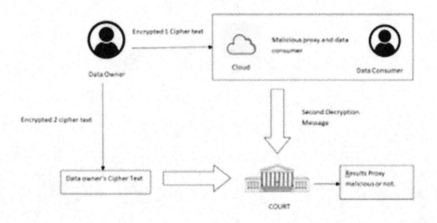

Figure 3. Flow chart

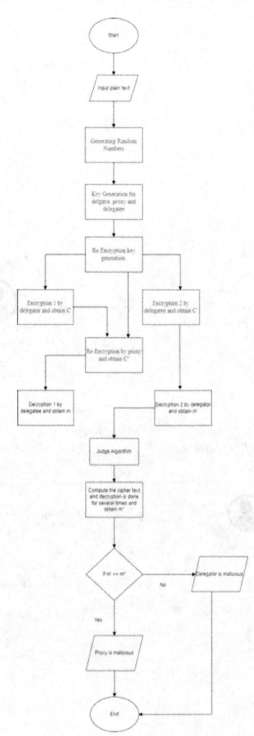

Following that, the judge algorithm creates a ciphertext that is once more decrypted at the secondary level. When the two second-level decrypted communications are compared, it can be inferred that the proxy is acting maliciously if they are similar. The flowchart of the proposed model is in Figure 3.

Re-encryption key abuse attacks are not prevented by an APRE scheme, but it does create a deterrent to the malicious party. In terms of the structure, our basic concept is to give the delegator and proxy various "decryption capabilities." That is, only one of them can achieve the desired decryption outcomes for specific erratic ciphertexts. We can identify if the proxy or the delegator is acting with bad intentions by using a decryption device to analyze specific ciphertexts. To make this work, we need to design the re-encryption key and the ciphertexts with a lot of attention to detail.

Nowadays there is lot of attacks happening over the network. Many passive attacks like sniffing are now possible. This will listen to the traffic silently and observe all the packets. This is very crucial in cryptography. When large numbers of ciphertexts are obtained by a attacker, then using many cryptanalysis tools the attacker can obtain the secret key. Once the secret is obtained by the attacker then there will be a huge loss. To prevent this many algorithms are used. One of the algorithms is base64 encoding and decoding. The base64 encoding and decoding is mainly used while the data is transferred over network or some communication channels. Base64 can be used to encode sensitive data, such as passwords or credit card numbers, before sending it over the network. This can prevent attackers from intercepting and stealing the data in transit. Base64 can be used to obfuscate code, making it more difficult for attackers to understand. While transmitting the re-encryption key and ciphertext to the cloud, attackers might steal it use it for obtaining secret key. This method will prevent this from attackers. Our scheme also gives protection against passive attacks that happen over network. Some of the attacks are man-in-the-middle attack, Eavesdropping, Spying, Packet sniffing, Footprinting, Traffic analysis.

4. PRELIMINARIES

Given that r is the generator of the group P, and that R and R_T are two cyclic groups with prime orders of P higher than or equal to 2, where P denotes the degree of security, a mapping function named e: $R \times R \rightarrow R_T$ is said to be bilinear when it meets the requirements listed below :

The first requirement, e: $R \times R \rightarrow R_T$ to be a bilinear map is that for any values of u, v, a, and b that belong to certain groups, $e(u^a, v^b)$ must be equal to $e(u,v)^{ab}$.

Another condition is that e must be non-degenerate, which means that if R is generated by r, then R_T must be generated by $e(r,r)$.

Lastly, e must be able to be computed efficiently, which is another condition for it to be considered a bilinear map.

5. DEFINITIONS AND SECURITY MODEL

We define a security parameter λ in our work to signify the degree of security. We present a PRE scheme made up of several algorithms, such as:

Initialize (λ): The public parameter value, which is choosen as random, is produced by this procedure after the security parameter is supplied.

ProxySet (value): The public and secret key pair for the proxy are created by this process and are designated as pk_p and sk_p, respectively.

KeyGeneration (value): The secret and public key pair for a user, represented as sk_x and pk_x, respectively, are generated by this process.

ReKeyGeneration (sk_x, pk_y, pk_p): Using the secret key sk_x, of the content owner, the public key pk_y of the consumer, and the public key pk_p of the proxy, this procedure creates a re-encryption key, denoted as $rk_{x \to y}$.

Encryption1 (pk_y, m): Using a content owner's public key pk_y and a message, this algorithm generates a ciphertext, designated as Z_y. This must not be re-encrypted

Encryption2 (pk_x, m): Using a content receiver's public key pk_x and a message, this algorithm generates another ciphertext, designated as Z_x. This ciphertext must be re-encrypted.

ReEncryption ($rk_{x \to y}, sk_p Z_x$): Using a re-encryption key $rk_{x \to y}$, the cloud server's secret key sk_p, and a ciphertext Z_x, this technique creates a re-encrypted ciphertext, indicated as Z_y.

Decryption1 (sk_y, Z_y): From a secret key sk_y and either a ciphertext Z_y or a ciphertext that has been re-encrypted Z_y as inputs, this technique generates a message.

Decryption2 (sk_x, Z_x): This procedure takes a secret key sk_x, ciphertext Z_x and creates a message.

$Judge^{D_{x,\mu}} \left(pk_x, pk_p \right)$: This technique identifies whether the proxy or the delegator created the decryption device by providing certain access and taking the public key pk_x, pk_p as inputs.

Base64 Encoding (Z_x): This algorithm encodes a ciphertext Z_x passed for re-encryption using Base64 encoding, converting it into binary and repeating 24-bit groups until the entire sequence of original data bytes is encoded.

Base 64 Decoding (D_x): This algorithm decodes an encoded ciphertext passed for re-encryption, discarding any extra padding characters used in the encoder.

The condition of correctness is that given any values of the proxy key pair (pk_p, sk_p) obtained from ProxySet(value), any user key pairs (pk_x, sk_x) and (pk_y, sk_y)

obtained from KeyGeneration(value), any re-encryption key $rk_{x \to y}$ obtained from ReKeyGeneration(sk_x, pk_y, pk_p), and any content from the plaintext space, the following conditions are satisfied:

Decryption1(sk_y), Encryption1(pk_y, m)=m;
Decryption2(sk_x), Encryption2(pk_x, m)=m;
Decryption1(sk_y), ReEncryption($rk_{x \to y}, sk_p$, Encryption2(pk_x, m)=m

6. CONSTRUCTION

An overview of the system and its underlying presumption is given in this section. Re-encryption keys are used in the system, and it's crucial to closely link them to the proxy in order to spot malicious activity. The judging algorithm will not be able to identify the proxy if it can generate an encryption key that is unrelated to itself. The re-encryption key must also stay private to prevent malicious delegations from framing the proxy. To act as a part of the cloud server's public key, the re-encryption key was developed. Only certain access to the decryption device can the creator of the device be identified and the guilty party ascertained. The ciphertext should be designed to reach different conclusions for the content owner and the proxy with a content receiver so that the judge can identify the author of the ciphertext by carefully examining the output of the decryption device.

Setup(λ): Assume λ is the parameter based on security and we have two groups R and RT of prime order p, where p is greater than or equal to 2 raised to the power of λ. We also have a bilinear map e:R×R→RT To initialize the system, we randomly select four elements from group R: g1, g2, h1, and h2. We then calculate L as the result of evaluating e on h1 and h2. These values represent the system parameters.

value= (g_1, g_2, h_1, h_2, L)

ProxySet(value): To generate the proxy key pair, select a random value z from the set of integers {0,1,2,...,p-1} and calculate $K=g_2$. Assign K as the public key pk_p and z as the secret key sk_p.

KeyGeneration(value): To generate the key pair, select two random values x_i and y_i from the set of integers {0,1,2,...,p-1}. Compute $X_i = h_1^{x_x}$ and $Y_i = g_1^{y_x}$. Set (X_i, Y_i) as the public key pk_i and (x_i, y_i) as the secret key sk_i.

ReKeyGeneration(sk_x, pk_y, pk_p): Given the secret key sk_i, the public key pk_y, and the public key pk_p, calculate the value $R = \left(h_2 Y_y K \right)^{1/x_x}$).

Assign R as the re-encryption key $rk_{x \to y}$.

Encryption1(pk_y,m). Given pk_y and m and choose $r \leftarrow K_p$ at random and calculate

$$z_a^{'} = L^r.m, z_b^{'} = g_1^r, z_c^{'} = L^r.e\left(h_x, Y_y\right)^r.$$

Calculate $Z_y^{'} = \left(z_a^{'}, z_b^{'}, z_c^{'}\right)$ and set as the first level ciphertext.

Encryption2($pk_x m$). Given pk_x and m and choose $r \leftarrow K_p$ at random and calculate

$$z_a = L^r.m$$

$$z_b = g_1^r$$

$$z_c = e(h_1,g_2)^r$$

$$z_d = X_x^r.$$

Calculate $Z_x = (z_a,z_b,z_c,z_d)$ set as the second level ciphertext.

ReEncryption($rk_{x\rightarrow y},sk_p,Z_x$). Given $rk_{x\rightarrow y}$, sk_p and Z_x, It calculates

$$z_a^{'} = z_a$$

$$z_b^{'} = z_b$$

$$z_c^{'} = e\left(z_d, R\right)/z_c^z.$$

Calculate $Z_y^{'} = \left(z_a^{'}, z_b^{'}, z_c^{'}\right)$ set as the re-encrypted ciphertext.

Decryption1(sk_y,Z_y). Given sk_y and Z_y, It calculates the message

$$m = z_a^{'}.e\left(h_1, z_b^{'}\right)^{y_y} / z_c^{'}.$$

Decryption2($sk_x Z_x$). Given sk_x and Z_x, It calculate the message

$$m = z_a / e\left(z_d, h_2\right)^{1/x_x}.$$

$Judge^{D_{i,\mu}}\left(pk_x, pk_n\right)$: It takes input the decryption device $D_{x,\mu}$ and kx, pkp and executes the following procedure.

Iterate the following experiment n = λ /μ times.

Randomly select $r,\ r' \in K_p$ and $m \in G_r$ and Calculate

$Z= z_a = m.L^r$.

$e\left(h_1, K\right)^{r-r'}, z_b = g_1^r,$

$zc = e\left(h_1, g_2\right)^{r'}, z_d = X_i^r)$

Apply the decryption to Z, and get the output m'. If m' is equal to m, print "Proxy". If not, return the message "Delegator is trying to frame proxy as malicious".

7. ALGORITHM

FUNCTION Encryption(*pk,m*):

    INPUT: A plaintext from the user and the public key of the delegate or delegator.

    OUTPUT: Ciphertext.

    Compute $Z_a = L^r.m$

    Compute $Z_b = g_1^r$

    If $pk == pk_y$

    Compute $Z_c = L^r.e(h_x, Y_y)^r$.

    Set $Z_y' = \left(z_a', z_b', z_c'\right)$.

    return Z_y'

    Else

    Compute $z_c = e(h_1, g_2)^r$.

    Compute $z_d = X_x^r$.

    Set $Z_x = (z_a,\ z_b,\ z_c,\ z_d)$.

    return Z_x

    FUNCTION ReEncryption($rk_{x \to y}, sk_p, Z_x$):

    INPUT: Re-encryption key, Secret key of the proxy and second level ciphertext.

    OUTPUT: Ciphertext, Z_y'.

    Compute $z_a' = z_a$.

    Compute $z_b' = z_b$.

Compute $z_c' = e(z_d, R) / z_c^z$.

Set $Z_y' = (z_a', z_b', z_c')$.

return Z_y'

FUNCTION Decryption(sk, Z):

INPUT: Secret key of the consumer or content owner and first level ciphertext or second level ciphertext.

OUTPUT: Plaintext, m.

If $sk == sk_y$

Compute $m = z_a' . e(h_1, z_b')^{y_y} / z_c'$.

return m

Else

Compute $m = z_a / e(z_d, h_2)^{1/x_x}$.

return m

FUNCTION $Judge^{D_{i,\mu}}(pk_x, pk_p)$:

INPUT: Public key of the content owner and public key of the proxy

OUTPUT: Plaintext, m'.

Compute $z_a = m.L^r . e(h_1, K)^{r-r'}$.

Compute $z_b = g_1^r$.

Compute $z_c = e(h_1, g_2)^{r'}$.

Compute $z_d = X_i^r$

Set Z= (z_a, z_b, z_c, z_d).

With Z run the decryption device several times and obtain m'.

If m' = m

Print "Proxy"

Else

Print "Delegator"

FUNCTION base64Encoding

1. **INPUT:** A string of text to encode.
2. **OUTPUT:** The resulting Base64 encoded string.
3. CONVERT the string to its ASCII representation.
4. DIVIDE the ASCII representation into groups of 3 bytes.
5. FOR EACH group of 3 bytes DO the following: a. CONVERT the bytes to a 24-bit integer. b. SPLIT the integer into 4 6-bit integers. c. MAP each 6-bit integer to its corresponding Base64 character.
6. APPEND the resulting Base64 characters to a new string.

7. IF the original string is not a multiple of 3 bytes, ADD padding with "=" characters until it is a multiple of 3 bytes.

FUNCTION base64Decoding

1. **INPUT:** A string of Base64 encoded text to decode.
2. **OUTPUT:** The resulting decoded string.
3. REMOVE any "=" padding characters from the end of the string.
4. CONVERT each Base64 character to its corresponding 6-bit integer.
5. COMBINE the 6-bit integers into groups of 4.
6. FOR EACH group of 4 integers DO the following: a. COMBINE the integers into a 24-bit integer. b. CONVERT the integer to 3 bytes.
7. CONCATENATE the resulting bytes into a new string.

8. RESULT AND DISCUSSION

The outputs from the decryption1 and decryption2 are obtained. The decryption1 gives the plain text to the data consumer. And the decryption2 produces an output when the cipher text from the encryption1 is given as input. The judge algorithm produces a cipher text which will be sent to decryption2 for several number of times. The output will be matched with the output of decryption2 obtained by the input of encryption1 cipher text.

This output shows the encryption module. The plain text to cipher text conversion is shown. The first encryption takes plaintext and data owner's public key as input and generates z_a, z_b, z_c. Together z_a, z_b, z_c combined to form the first level cipher text. The second encryption takes plaintext and data consumer's public key as input and generates z_a, z_b, z_c, z_d. Together the four values combined to form second level ciphertext. The output values generated is shown in Figure 4.

This output shows the decryption module. The decryption1 produces the plaintext for the data owner and the decryption2 value produces a value which will be used in judge algorithm.

Figure 6. Shows the scenario where the proxy is malicious. The judge algorithm will run for several times. After a certain number of times if the output matches, then the judge algorithm shows that proxy is malicious.

Figure 7. Shows the scenario where the delegator is trying to frame proxy is malicious. The judge algorithm will run for several times. After a certain number of times if the output not matches then the judge algorithm shows that delegator is framing proxy. It proves the proxy is innocent and the delegate is malicious.

Figure 4. Encryption process

```
Enter input string: Hai Hello
********************************************
Performing Encryption 1...
********************************************
Encryption 1 values:
c0 value is: 3128633909041335010135259125
c1 value is: 8
c2 value is: 2744000000


********************************************
Performing Encryption 2...
********************************************
Encryption 2 values:
c0 value is: 3128633909041335010135259125
c1 value is: 8
c2 value is: 3375
c3 value is: 30517578125
```

Figure 5. Decryption process

```
********************************************
Performing Decryption 1...
********************************************
The decrypted 1 plaintext is: Hai Hello
********************************************
Performing Decryption 2...
********************************************
The decrypted 2 plaintext is: 169599718466409725633462794.2
```

Figure 6. Proxy is malicious

```
The decrypted 2 plaintext is: 206537534854914610147139697929770015240068005093109043939046918730.3
The decrypted 2 plaintext is: 8310384204740763562996043409.6
The decrypted 2 plaintext is: 2044666645848905615125308136457662.4
The decrypted 2 plaintext is: 23127855866847474227842945722087713475390355400584632551725.5
The decrypted 2 plaintext is: 42150517317329521780243768576682357800898595300075654508255158609.5
The decrypted 2 plaintext is: 4790772270347572270934983226207756.6
The decrypted 2 plaintext is: 135254649862290507870017857195758402331.8
The decrypted 2 plaintext is: 169599718466409725633462794.2
*************************************
Proxy is malicious.
2023-04-13 13:58:34.873
*************************************
```

160

Figure 7. Delegator framing proxy as malicious

The decrypted 2 plaintext is: 1762431062146914706206470643715678655927.1
The decrypted 2 plaintext is: 7116245972112537163568233785601536740064888500179223120000116067005195374559.3
The decrypted 2 plaintext is: 39044617130932988551814725846920003172284695757433367517153319884133911152.0
The decrypted 2 plaintext is: 2003475779026297953422111955362375564306270591442291883111265831260418472251.5
The decrypted 2 plaintext is: 1639199326932840213993228466405122551320790222266672647.5
The decrypted 2 plaintext is: 9964291209879084222127144357259925701573571658857680952.8
The decrypted 2 plaintext is: 9970448397946700659926972640365330859904511204651161618361838.8
The decrypted 2 plaintext is: 9970448397946700659926972640365330859904511204651161618361838.8
The decrypted 2 plaintext is: 272254180132162954106284067044939906.5
•••

Delegator is framing proxy.
•••

Figure 8. Graph when proxy is malicious

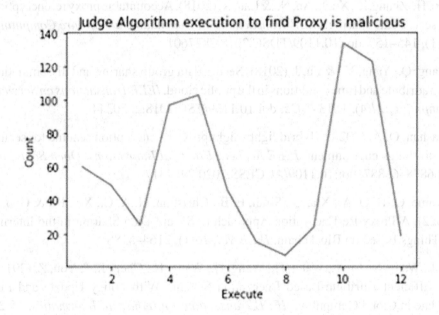

The graph shows the average execution of the judge algorithm to detect the proxy is malicious.

9. CONCLUSION

The main worry for consumers using cloud data sharing services is there is a trust issue. To overcome this issue, we developed the idea of Accountable PRE (APRE).

We originally formalised the idea of Accountable PRE (APRE), where the judge algorithm can identify the proxy that misuses its re-encryption key. Then, to stop cyber risks, we added base64 encoding/decoding. Additionally, it is decisional Diffie-Hellman (DBDH) secure and responsible under the premise of the Chosen Plaintext Attack (CPA). When compared to earlier analogous systems, ours provides superior performances.

REFERENCES

Ge, C., Liu, Z., Xia, J., & Fang, L. (2019). Revocable identity-based broadcast proxy re-encryption for data sharing in clouds. *IEEE Transactions on Dependable and Secure Computing, 18*(3), 1214–1226. doi:10.1109/TDSC.2019.2899300

Guo, H., Zhang, Z., Xu, J., An, N., & Lan, X. (2018). Accountable proxy re-encryption for secure data sharing. *IEEE Transactions on Dependable and Secure Computing, 18*(1), 145–159. doi:10.1109/TDSC.2018.2877601

Huang, Q., Yang, Y., & Fu, J. (2018). Secure data group sharing and dissemination with attribute and time conditions in the public cloud. *IEEE Transactions on Services Computing, 14*(4), 1013–1025. doi:10.1109/TSC.2018.2850344

Khashan, O. A. (2020). Hybrid lightweight proxy re-encryption scheme for secure fog-to-things environment. *IEEE Access : Practical Innovations, Open Solutions, 8*, 66878–66887. doi:10.1109/ACCESS.2020.2984317

Kwame, O.-B. O. A., Xia, Q., Sifah, E. B., Christian, N. A. C., Xia, H., & Gao, J. (2022). A Proxy Re-Encryption Approach to Secure Data Sharing in the Internet of Things Based on Blockchain. *IEEE Vol, 16*(1), 2164–5188.

Li, J., Wang, S., Li, Y., Wang, H., Wang, H., Wang, H., Chen, J., & You, Z. (2019). An Efficient Attribute-Based Encryption Scheme With Policy Update and File Update in Cloud Computing. *IEEE Transactions on Industrial Informatics, 15*(2), 1919–4770. doi:10.1109/TII.2019.2931156

Li, J., Wang, S., Li, Y., Wang, H., Wang, H., Wang, H., Chen, J., & You, Z. (2019). An efficient attribute-based encryption scheme with policy update and file update in cloud computing. *IEEE Transactions on Industrial Informatics, 15*(12), 6500–6509. doi:10.1109/TII.2019.2931156

Sun, Y., Susilo, W., Zhang, F., & Fu, A. (2018). CCA-secure revocable identity-based encryption with ciphertext evolution in the cloud. *IEEE Access : Practical Innovations, Open Solutions, 6*, 56977–56983. doi:10.1109/ACCESS.2018.2873019

Wang, S., Jia, S., & Zhang, Y. (2019). Verifiable and multi-keyword searchable attribute-based encryption scheme for cloud storage. *IEEE Access : Practical Innovations, Open Solutions*, 7, 50136–50147. doi:10.1109/ACCESS.2019.2910828

Zeng, P., & Choo, K.-K. R. (2018). A New Kind of Conditional Proxy Re-Encryption for Secure Cloud Storage. *IEEE Access : Practical Innovations, Open Solutions*, 6, 2169–3536. doi:10.1109/ACCESS.2018.2879479

Zahoman, LWu, LKe, JQu, WWang, WWang, H. (2019). Accountable Outsourcing Location-Based Services With Privacy Preservation. *IEEE Access Vol*, 7, 2169–3536.

Chapter 8

Balancing Innovation and Security in the Cloud:
Navigating the Risks and Rewards of the Digital Age

S. Boopathi
Mechanical Engineering, Muthayammal Engineering College (Autonomous), India

ABSTRACT

This chapter delves into the intricate relationship between innovation and security in the digital age. It highlights the challenges of the digital age and the transformative impact of cloud computing, emphasizing its role in driving innovation. The chapter also delves into cloud service and deployment models, discussing the benefits and challenges of cloud security. It also discusses the role of innovation in driving progress through case studies and addressing challenges organizations face. The chapter also discusses risk assessment and mitigation in the cloud, compliance, regulatory challenges, legal and ethical considerations, and best practices. It also explores emerging technologies like AI and machine learning, Zero Trust security, and future directions.

INTRODUCTION

The cloud has become a crucial tool in the digital age, offering flexibility, scalability, and accessibility for businesses to innovate and secure their operations. It has revolutionized data storage, processing, collaboration, and service delivery. However,

DOI: 10.4018/979-8-3693-1431-9.ch008

this digital transformation has also exposed organizations to new security risks. The challenge is to balance the potential for innovation with the need to protect sensitive information and critical assets from evolving threats. The cloud has revolutionized business operations by enabling rapid market entry of new products and services, process optimization, and revenue generation. However, it also poses risks like data breaches, cyberattacks, and regulatory compliance(Schneckenberg et al., 2021). This chapter delves into the complex relationship between innovation and security in the cloud environment, providing readers with the necessary knowledge and strategies to navigate this dynamic landscape.

This explores the fundamentals of cloud computing, its service and deployment models, and its impact on innovation and security. It examines real-world examples of organizations using cloud technology, their security challenges, and risk mitigation strategies. The text also discusses risk assessment, regulatory environment, and best practices for securing cloud assets. Through case studies and emerging trends, it aims to understand the current state of cloud innovation and security(Gozman & Willcocks, 2019). The decision to use the cloud in the digital age is not a simple choice between innovation and security, but a complex journey that requires careful consideration and informed decision-making. The digital age, also known as the Information Age or Fourth Industrial Revolution, has brought about unprecedented opportunities and challenges, with cloud computing being a central driver of this paradigm shift. This section explores the unique challenges presented by the digital age and how they intersect with the adoption of cloud technology, inviting readers to join us on this critical journey(RM et al., 2020).

The digital age has revolutionized innovation, with cloud computing playing a crucial role in enabling rapid development and market penetration. However, this rapid pace can also pose challenges, such as hasty deployments and inadequate security considerations. The digital age has led to an era of data abundance, with businesses and individuals collecting and storing vast amounts of data. This data has created complex data management and security challenges, necessitating the protection of sensitive data(Kunduru, 2023). As digital technologies advance, so do malicious actors' capabilities, making cybersecurity threats more sophisticated, frequent, and damaging. The cloud, as a prime target for cyberattacks, is a prime target for these threats, making it a constant battle to protect cloud-based systems and applications from these evolving threats.

The digital age has led to strict data protection and privacy regulations, impacting cloud-based operations. Organizations must comply with regional and global compliance requirements, while leveraging the benefits of the cloud. Ethical concerns about data privacy, ownership, and the ethical use of AI and machine learning in cloud-based applications are also a concern(Rayhan & Rayhan, 2023). Legal frameworks are evolving to address these challenges, adding complexity for cloud adopters. Navigating the challenges of the digital age requires a holistic understanding of the technological, organizational, and societal dynamics at play. In this context, cloud computing stands as both a solution and a challenge, offering the promise of innovation while demanding vigilant security measures. The next sections of this chapter will delve into the role of cloud technology in addressing and exacerbating these challenges, providing insights into how organizations can effectively balance innovation and security in the cloud(Shahid et al., 2020).

Cloud computing is a crucial pillar of the digital age, impacting every aspect of modern organizations. It allows organizations to rapidly scale their computing resources, accommodating fluctuating workloads and optimizing resource utilization. Cloud computing empowers innovation by allowing businesses to experiment, iterate, and scale their solutions without significant upfront investments in infrastructure. Its pay-as-you-go model helps organizations avoid the costly burden of maintaining and upgrading physical hardware(Jyoti et al., 2020). Outsourcing infrastructure and management responsibilities to cloud service providers allows organizations to direct their resources more efficiently, channeling funds into areas of innovation and security that directly impact their core mission(Hema et al., 2023).

Cloud services offer global accessibility, enabling remote work, collaboration, and service delivery to geographically dispersed customers. This global accessibility is crucial for modern organizations operating across borders and time zones. Cloud computing accelerates innovation by enabling rapid application development, experimentation with emerging technologies like artificial intelligence, and big data analytics. The cloud provides necessary infrastructure, reducing time and effort required for innovation(Venkateswaran, Vidhya, et al., 2023). Cloud services centralize data storage, promoting collaboration and innovation among team members. However, this also raises concerns about data security and privacy. Cloud providers invest heavily in security, offering robust solutions that can enhance an organization's overall security posture when implemented correctly. Addressing these challenges is crucial for a successful cloud adoption(Srinivas et al., 2023).

Cloud resources pool among multiple customers, enabling cost savings but also introducing security risks. The agility of cloud allows organizations to quickly adapt to market conditions and customer demands, facilitating rapid deployment of new features. However, security controls should not compromise speed(Satav, Lamani, et al., 2024). Cloud services often have built-in disaster recovery and business continuity features, ensuring organizations can recover from disruptions and maintain operations, enhancing security and resilience. Cloud computing is crucial in the digital age, enabling organizations to innovate rapidly and secure their operations in a data-driven world. However, a nuanced approach is needed to balance innovation and security in the cloud, a theme that will be further explored in subsequent sections(Syamala et al., 2023).

Objectives

This chapter provides a comprehensive understanding of cloud computing, its various service and deployment models, and its potential benefits for organizations. It explores how cloud technology allows for innovation, accelerates product and service development, and enhances competitiveness in the digital age. It also discusses cybersecurity threats and compliance regulations, emphasizing the need for securing cloud-based operations. The text emphasizes the tension between innovation and security in the cloud, emphasizing the importance of balancing these priorities. It offers practical strategies for organizations to effectively manage risks, legal and ethical considerations, and the development of security policies, governance, identity and access management, encryption, and data protection.

UNDERSTANDING CLOUD COMPUTING

Cloud computing is a crucial concept in the digital age, revolutionizing data storage, processing, and access. Understanding its service and deployment models is crucial for balancing innovation and security in the cloud, ensuring efficient data management(Agrawal et al., 2024; Rahamathunnisa, Sudhakar, et al., 2023; Srinivas et al., 2023; Syamala et al., 2023).

Cloud Service Models

Cloud computing offers a variety of service models, each tailored to specific business needs and objectives. These models represent the services provided by cloud providers to their customers. Understanding these models is crucial for making informed decisions about how to leverage cloud technology.

- **Infrastructure as a Service (IaaS):** IaaS is the foundational layer of cloud services, providing virtualized computing resources, such as virtual machines, storage, and networking. Users have control over the operating system and applications, enabling them to manage and customize their infrastructure. This service model is fundamental for organizations seeking flexibility and scalability without the burden of physical hardware management.
- **Platform as a Service (PaaS):** PaaS takes the cloud abstraction a step further by offering a platform for developing, testing, and deploying applications. It provides a managed environment with tools and services for developers to create and deploy applications, focusing on coding rather than infrastructure

management. PaaS accelerates application development and is conducive to innovation.

- **Software as a Service (SaaS):** SaaS delivers fully developed software applications to end-users over the internet. These applications, like email services and office suites, require no installation or maintenance. SaaS is a prime example of how the cloud enables rapid deployment and easy access, but it also raises security considerations regarding data privacy and protection.

Deployment Models

Deployment models refer to how cloud computing resources are physically located and managed. Different deployment models cater to diverse security and scalability requirements. Exploring these models is essential for tailoring cloud adoption to an organization's specific needs(Jyoti et al., 2020).

- **Public Cloud:** Public clouds are hosted by third-party cloud service providers and are open for use by the general public. They offer cost-effective, scalable solutions but can pose security concerns due to shared infrastructure. Balancing innovation and security in a public cloud environment is a common challenge.
- **Private Cloud:** Private clouds are dedicated to a single organization and can be hosted on-premises or by a third-party provider. They offer greater control and security but may require substantial investments. Understanding how to maintain security in a private cloud environment is a core consideration for organizations.
- **Hybrid Cloud:** Hybrid clouds combine elements of both public and private clouds, allowing data and applications to move between them as needed. They provide flexibility and security, making them a popular choice for organizations looking to balance innovation with data protection.
- **Community Cloud:** Community clouds are shared by multiple organizations with similar needs, such as those in the same industry. They offer shared resources while maintaining a degree of customization and security specific to the community's requirements.

This chapter explores the importance of understanding cloud service and deployment models to navigate the challenges and opportunities of cloud computing, while also discussing how organizations can effectively balance innovation and security within these contexts.

Benefits of Cloud Computing

- **Cost Efficiency:** Cloud computing eliminates the need for organizations to invest in and maintain physical infrastructure. This results in cost savings on hardware, maintenance, and power consumption. The pay-as-you-go model ensures that organizations only pay for the resources they use, making cloud computing a cost-effective solution(Kavitha et al., 2023; Venkateswaran, Kumar, et al., 2023).
- **Scalability and Flexibility:** Cloud services are highly scalable, allowing organizations to expand or reduce their computing resources as needed. This flexibility is especially valuable for businesses with fluctuating workloads or those seeking to quickly respond to market demands.
- **Global Accessibility:** Cloud services are accessible from anywhere with an internet connection. This global reach enables remote work, collaboration across geographical boundaries, and the ability to serve a worldwide customer base.
- **Rapid Deployment:** Cloud computing accelerates the deployment of applications and services. This is essential for organizations looking to innovate, experiment, and bring products to market faster. Development and testing cycles are shortened, allowing for more frequent updates.
- **Reliability and Redundancy:** Leading cloud providers offer high levels of service availability and redundancy. This reduces the risk of downtime due to hardware failures or disasters. Data is often replicated across multiple data centers, ensuring data durability.
- **Resource Pooling:** Cloud resources are often shared among multiple customers, leading to efficient resource pooling. This shared infrastructure can lead to cost savings, as organizations pay for shared resources rather than maintaining dedicated hardware.
- **Automatic Updates and Maintenance:** Cloud providers handle updates, maintenance, and security patches for the underlying infrastructure and services. This allows organizations to focus on application development and innovation without the burden of routine maintenance.

Challenges of Cloud Computing

- **Security Concerns:** Security is a paramount concern in the cloud. Data breaches, unauthorized access, and cyberattacks are ongoing risks. Ensuring data protection and compliance with regulations is a complex challenge(Koshariya, Kalaiyarasi, et al., 2023; Koshariya, Khatoon, et al., 2023; Venkateswaran, Vidhya, et al., 2023).

- **Data Privacy and Ownership:** Cloud providers may store data in various locations and jurisdictions, raising concerns about data privacy and ownership. Organizations must carefully consider data sovereignty and the legal implications of storing data in different regions.
- **Compliance and Regulations:** The complexity of global data protection regulations and industry-specific compliance requirements can be challenging to navigate. Organizations need to ensure that they adhere to these regulations, which may vary from one jurisdiction to another.
- **Limited Control:** Organizations that rely on public cloud services have limited control over the underlying infrastructure. This can be a challenge when customizing hardware or software to specific needs or maintaining compliance with industry-specific requirements.
- **Downtime and Connectivity Issues:** While cloud providers offer high availability, they are not immune to downtime. Network issues or outages can disrupt services, potentially leading to productivity and financial losses for organizations.
- **Data Transfer and Bandwidth Costs:** Moving large volumes of data to and from the cloud can incur significant data transfer and bandwidth costs, impacting an organization's overall cloud expenses.
- **Vendor Lock-In:** Migrating from one cloud provider to another can be complex and costly, as different providers use proprietary technologies and formats. Organizations may become locked into their chosen provider, reducing flexibility.

Organizations must comprehend the advantages and challenges of adopting cloud computing technology to ensure a balance between innovation and security.

INNOVATION IN THE CLOUD

This section explores the role of cloud computing in driving innovation across various industries (Figure 1), highlighting case studies of innovative solutions and discussing the challenges organizations face in pursuing innovation in the cloud(Mohanty et al., 2023; Rahamathunnisa, Subhashini, et al., 2023; Srinivas et al., 2023).

The Role of Cloud in Driving Innovation

The cloud revolutionizes business innovation by enabling the creation, testing, and delivery of new products, services, and experiences.

Figure 1. The cloud computing in driving innovation across various industries

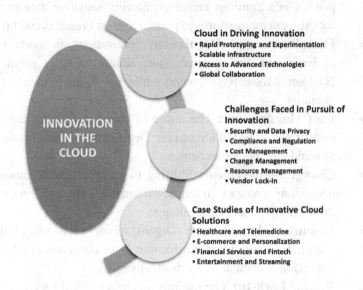

Cloud in Driving Innovation
• Rapid Prototyping and Experimentation
• Scalable Infrastructure
• Access to Advanced Technologies
• Global Collaboration

INNOVATION IN THE CLOUD

Challenges Faced in Pursuit of Innovation
• Security and Data Privacy
• Compliance and Regulation
• Cost Management
• Change Management
• Resource Management
• Vendor Lock-In

Case Studies of Innovative Cloud Solutions
• Healthcare and Telemedicine
• E-commerce and Personalization
• Financial Services and Fintech
• Entertainment and Streaming

- **Rapid Prototyping and Experimentation:** Cloud resources allow organizations to quickly test ideas and prototypes, reducing the time and cost required to bring innovative concepts to reality.
- **Scalable Infrastructure:** The cloud's scalability ensures that organizations can respond to increased demand without major investments in physical infrastructure. This agility is vital for innovations that require elastic resources.
- **Access to Advanced Technologies:** Cloud providers offer a wide array of advanced technologies, such as machine learning, artificial intelligence, and big data analytics. These tools enable organizations to develop innovative solutions that were previously out of reach.
- **Global Collaboration:** Cloud-based collaboration tools facilitate teamwork across the globe, fostering innovation through diverse perspectives and expertise.

Challenges Faced in Pursuit of Innovation

While the cloud is a powerful enabler of innovation, it also presents several challenges that organizations must address to reap the rewards(Anitha et al., 2023; Kavitha et al., 2023; Maguluri, Arularasan, et al., 2023; Srinivas et al., 2023). These challenges include:

- **Security and Data Privacy:** Balancing innovation with data security and privacy is a complex endeavor. Storing sensitive data in the cloud requires robust security measures to protect against breaches and unauthorized access.
- **Compliance and Regulation:** Innovations in certain industries, such as healthcare and finance, must adhere to strict regulatory frameworks. Navigating these requirements while innovating in the cloud demands careful planning.
- **Cost Management:** The allure of cloud innovation can lead to escalating costs if not managed effectively. Organizations must implement cost controls to avoid unexpected expenses.
- **Change Management:** Shifting to a cloud-centric innovation model may necessitate changes in organizational culture and processes. Adapting to these changes can be a challenge.
- **Resource Management:** Organizations must efficiently manage cloud resources to avoid underutilization or resource sprawl. Optimizing resource allocation is critical for cost-effectiveness.
- **Vendor Lock-In:** The use of proprietary cloud services can lead to vendor lock-in, limiting an organization's ability to transition to alternative solutions.

Balancing the pursuit of innovation with the challenges presented by cloud technology is a dynamic process. In this section, we explore how organizations are harnessing cloud-driven innovation, examining the transformational impact and the considerations required for success.

Case Studies of Innovative Cloud Solutions

This section provides real-world examples of cloud-driven innovation across various industries, including healthcare and e-commerce, to demonstrate how organizations have effectively utilized the cloud to drive innovation.

- **Healthcare and Telemedicine**: Explore how cloud-based telemedicine platforms have revolutionized patient care and diagnostics, providing timely and cost-effective access to medical expertise(Boopathi, 2023b; Karthik et al., 2023; Ramudu et al., 2023; Satav, Hasan, et al., 2024).
- **E-commerce and Personalization**: Discover how e-commerce giants utilize cloud-driven analytics and AI to provide personalized recommendations, enhancing the shopping experience.
- **Financial Services and Fintech**: Investigate how fintech startups leverage the cloud to create innovative financial services and platforms that challenge traditional banking models.

Figure 2. Importance of security in cloud computing

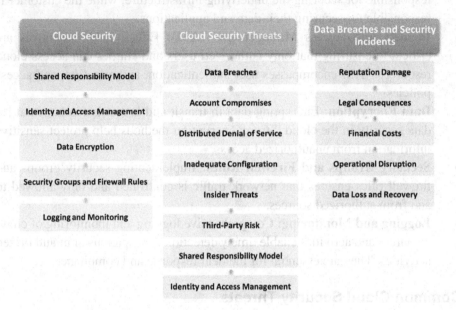

- **Entertainment and Streaming**: Uncover how media and entertainment companies use cloud resources to deliver high-quality streaming services and tailor content recommendations to viewers.

SECURITY IN THE CLOUD

This section explores the importance of security in cloud computing (Figure 2), highlighting common threats faced by users and the impact of data breaches and security incidents, emphasizing the need for comprehensive understanding of cloud security(Agrawal, Magulur, et al., 2023; Karthik et al., 2023; Kavitha et al., 2023; Rahamathunnisa, Subhashini, et al., 2023).

Cloud Security Fundamentals

Understanding the core principles and practices that underpin cloud security is crucial for establishing a robust foundation.

- **Shared Responsibility Model:** Cloud security is a shared responsibility between cloud service providers and their customers. The cloud provider is responsible for securing the underlying infrastructure, while the customer is responsible for securing their data and applications.

- **Identity and Access Management (IAM):** Effective IAM controls are critical to ensuring that only authorized users and entities can access cloud resources. IAM encompasses user authentication, authorization, and access policies.
- **Data Encryption:** Encrypting data in transit and at rest is fundamental for data security in the cloud. Strong encryption methods help protect sensitive information from unauthorized access.
- **Security Groups and Firewall Rules:** Implementing security groups and firewall rules ensures that network traffic is controlled and only allowed to and from authorized sources.
- **Logging and Monitoring:** Comprehensive logging and monitoring of cloud resources and activities enable timely detection of suspicious or unauthorized activities. They are essential for incident response and compliance.

Common Cloud Security Threats

Cloud computing presents distinct security threats and challenges that organizations must tackle.

- **Data Breaches:** Unauthorized access to sensitive data can lead to data breaches, resulting in loss of trust, legal consequences, and financial damage.
- **Account Compromises:** When user accounts are compromised, attackers may gain access to cloud resources and data. Proper user authentication and access control are critical to prevent this.
- **Distributed Denial of Service (DDoS) Attacks:** DDoS attacks can disrupt cloud services by overwhelming them with traffic. Cloud providers offer DDoS protection, but organizations must configure it correctly.
- **Inadequate Configuration:** Misconfigured cloud resources can expose data to the public internet, leading to security vulnerabilities. Regular security audits and configuration reviews are necessary.
- **Insider Threats:** Malicious insiders or negligent employees can pose significant security risks. Monitoring and access control measures can mitigate insider threats.
- **Third-Party Risk:** Cloud services often rely on third-party providers for components like authentication and payment processing. These providers can introduce security vulnerabilities, making third-party risk management crucial.

The Impact of Data Breaches and Security Incidents

Data breaches and security incidents can have severe repercussions on organizations in various ways(Arunprasad & Boopathi, 2019; Babu et al., 2022; Venkateswaran, Kumar, et al., 2023).

- **Reputation Damage:** Data breaches can erode customer trust and harm an organization's reputation, potentially leading to a loss of customers and business opportunities.
- **Legal Consequences:** Regulatory bodies may impose fines and legal actions on organizations that fail to protect sensitive data, especially in highly regulated industries.
- **Financial Costs:** Recovering from a data breach can be expensive, including costs for incident response, forensics, legal fees, and potential compensation to affected parties.
- **Operational Disruption:** Security incidents can disrupt business operations, leading to downtime and financial losses.
- **Data Loss and Recovery:** Data breaches may result in data loss or corruption. Recovery efforts can be challenging, and some data may be irretrievable.

BALANCING INNOVATION AND SECURITY

This section delves into the intricate task of balancing innovation with security in the digital age, providing strategies and real-world examples to illustrate successful balancing(Jyoti et al., 2020; RM et al., 2020).

The Tension Between Innovation and Security

The pursuit of innovation often poses security risks due to various dynamics as shown Figure 3.

- **Speed vs. Security:** Innovating quickly can outpace the implementation of security measures, leading to vulnerabilities. The need for rapid development often clashes with security's need for meticulous review and testing.
- **Openness vs. Control:** Encouraging openness and creativity in innovation may conflict with the need for stringent control and access restrictions to maintain security.

Figure 3. Tension between innovation and security

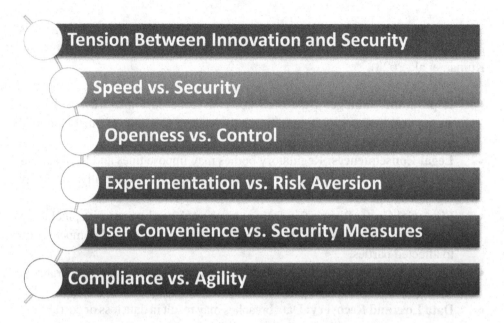

- **Experimentation vs. Risk Aversion:** Innovators seek to experiment and take calculated risks, while security measures aim to minimize risks and maintain a risk-averse stance.
- **User Convenience vs. Security Measures:** User-centric innovations may emphasize ease of use and accessibility, which can sometimes weaken security practices. Striking the right balance is critical to satisfy both objectives.
- **Compliance vs. Agility:** Compliance with regulations often involves strict security measures. However, these measures may slow down innovation due to the time and resources required for compliance.

Strategies for Achieving the Right Balance

Organizations can utilize various strategies to balance innovation and security(Rayhan & Rayhan, 2023).

- **Risk-Based Approach:** Implement a risk-based approach that assesses the potential risks of innovative projects. High-risk initiatives should undergo rigorous security scrutiny, while lower-risk projects can benefit from streamlined processes.

- **Security by Design:** Embed security considerations into the design and development of innovations from the outset. This approach promotes proactive security practices that are integral to the innovation process.
- **Education and Training:** Provide ongoing education and training to employees, emphasizing security best practices and awareness of potential threats. Well-informed staff can contribute to a culture of security(Agrawal, Pitchai, et al., 2023; Durairaj et al., 2023; Ingle et al., 2023).
- **Collaboration:** Foster collaboration between innovation and security teams. Bringing these teams together allows for the exchange of knowledge and the alignment of objectives.
- **Continuous Monitoring:** Implement continuous monitoring of systems and data to identify security issues as they emerge. This proactive stance can minimize the impact of security threats(Boopathi, 2021, 2023a; Maguluri, Ananth, et al., 2023; Sankar et al., 2023).
- **Adaptive Security:** Employ adaptive security measures that can respond to changes in the threat landscape and the evolving needs of the business.

Real-world Examples of Successful Balancing

The article provides examples of successful balancing of innovation and security, offering valuable insights through real-world examples(Harikaran et al., 2023; Karthik et al., 2023).

- **Secure Development Lifecycle (SDL):** Many organizations implement a secure development lifecycle that integrates security into every phase of the software development process. This proactive approach reduces security vulnerabilities while fostering innovation.
- **DevSecOps:** DevSecOps practices integrate security into the DevOps pipeline, enabling organizations to innovate rapidly while maintaining strong security. Automation and collaboration are key components of this approach.
- **Zero Trust Architecture:** The adoption of Zero Trust security principles assumes that no one, whether inside or outside the organization, can be trusted. This approach enhances security while accommodating innovation by securing access and data at a granular level.
- **Compliance and Innovation:** Organizations in regulated industries, such as healthcare and finance, balance compliance requirements with innovation by implementing strict security measures that meet regulatory demands while also encouraging new developments.

Figure 4. The process of risk assessment and migration

Identifying and Assessing Risks
- Risk Identification
- Risk Assessment
- Vulnerability Assessment
- Compliance and Legal Risks
- Business Continuity and Disaster Recovery

Developing a Cloud Security Strategy
- Policy and Governance
- Identity and Access Management (IAM)
- Encryption and Data Protection
- Security Awareness Training
- Security Tools and Technologies

Risk Mitigation and Management
- Control Implementation
- Incident Response Planning
- Monitoring and Evaluation
- Risk Transfer
- Documentation

Balancing innovation and security is a continuous process that necessitates adaptability and a comprehensive understanding of an organization's goals. By examining strategies and real-world examples, organizations can effectively promote innovation while ensuring robust security measures.

RISK ASSESSMENT AND MITIGATION

This section discusses the process of risk assessment (Figure 4), developing a robust cloud security strategy, and effectively mitigating and managing risks, which are crucial components of a robust security strategy (Maguluri, Arularasan, et al., 2023; Rahamathunnisa, Subhashini, et al., 2023).

Identifying and Assessing Risks

The initial step in establishing a strong cloud security posture involves identifying and assessing risks, which involve key aspects.

- **Risk Identification:** Begin by identifying potential risks associated with cloud adoption, including data breaches, compliance violations, insider threats, and more. This process should involve stakeholders from across the organization.

- **Risk Assessment:** After identifying risks, assess their potential impact and likelihood. This involves assigning risk levels and prioritizing them based on their potential consequences and probability.
- **Vulnerability Assessment:** Identify weaknesses or vulnerabilities in your cloud infrastructure and practices that could be exploited by threat actors.
- **Compliance and Legal Risks:** Evaluate risks related to compliance with industry-specific regulations and legal requirements, taking into account data protection laws, intellectual property, and privacy regulations.
- **Business Continuity and Disaster Recovery:** Assess risks related to business continuity and disaster recovery. Consider the potential impact of service disruptions or data loss on the organization.

Developing a Cloud Security Strategy

A well-defined cloud security strategy is crucial for addressing identified risks and protecting against potential threats, including(Reddy, Reddy, et al., 2023):

- **Policy and Governance:** Develop security policies and governance frameworks that align with organizational objectives and regulatory requirements. This should include defining roles and responsibilities, incident response plans, and access control policies.
- **Identity and Access Management (IAM):** Implement robust IAM practices to control access to cloud resources, ensuring that only authorized users and entities can interact with the cloud environment.
- **Encryption and Data Protection:** Utilize encryption to protect data at rest and in transit. Develop data protection strategies to safeguard sensitive information from unauthorized access.
- **Security Awareness Training:** Provide security awareness training to employees to promote a culture of security. Ensure that staff members are aware of best practices and potential threats.
- **Security Tools and Technologies:** Utilize security tools and technologies, such as intrusion detection systems, security information and event management (SIEM) solutions, and firewalls, to monitor, detect, and respond to security incidents.

Risk Mitigation and Management

Risk mitigation and management strategies are crucial for minimizing the impact of identified risks, considering various factors (Maguluri, Ananth, et al., 2023; Ugandar et al., 2023).

- **Control Implementation:** Implement controls and security measures to mitigate identified risks. This may involve deploying technologies, establishing security processes, and enhancing employee training.
- **Incident Response Planning:** Develop and regularly update incident response plans to effectively manage security incidents when they occur. These plans should define roles and responsibilities, communication procedures, and recovery processes.
- **Monitoring and Evaluation:** Continuously monitor the cloud environment for security incidents and vulnerabilities. Regularly evaluate and update the security strategy based on changing risks and threat landscapes.
- **Risk Transfer:** In some cases, organizations may choose to transfer certain risks through insurance or third-party arrangements. This can help mitigate the financial impact of security incidents.
- **Documentation and Compliance:** Maintain thorough documentation of security practices, audits, and compliance efforts. Ensure that the organization remains compliant with relevant regulations and standards.

The process of identifying, assessing, and mitigating cloud risks is continuous and iterative, necessitating organizations to adapt their security strategies as the threat landscape evolves and they innovate in the cloud.

COMPLIANCE AND REGULATIONS

This section delves into the influence of different regulatory frameworks on cloud security, the challenges of compliance, and the legal and ethical considerations in cloud operations.

Regulatory Frameworks Impacting Cloud Security

Organizations must understand various regulatory frameworks and industry-specific standards to ensure compliance and data protection in cloud security(Jyoti et al., 2020; Shahid et al., 2020).

- **General Data Protection Regulation (GDPR):** GDPR, applicable in the European Union, governs the processing of personal data and imposes stringent requirements for data protection and privacy.
- **Health Insurance Portability and Accountability Act (HIPAA):** HIPAA sets standards for the protection of health information and imposes specific requirements on healthcare organizations that use cloud services.

- **Payment Card Industry Data Security Standard (PCI DSS):** PCI DSS outlines security requirements for organizations that handle credit card payments and data, impacting cloud security for e-commerce businesses.
- **Sarbanes-Oxley Act (SOX):** SOX mandates financial reporting and auditing standards for public companies, with implications for data security and retention in the cloud.
- **California Consumer Privacy Act (CCPA):** CCPA regulates the data privacy rights of California residents, affecting cloud data handling for organizations operating in the state.

Compliance Challenges and Solutions

Organizations can overcome challenges in achieving cloud compliance by implementing strategies and solutions that help them meet regulatory requirements.

- **Data Classification and Protection:** Properly classify data and apply appropriate protection measures to ensure sensitive data is handled in compliance with regulations.
- **Audit and Reporting Tools:** Implement auditing and reporting tools to track user activity, configuration changes, and data access, facilitating compliance reporting and verification.
- **Secure Cloud Providers:** Choose cloud service providers that offer compliance-friendly services and tools to meet specific regulatory requirements.
- **Policy and Documentation:** Establish clear security policies and documentation to demonstrate compliance efforts. Keep records of security audits and assessments.
- **Security Awareness Training:** Provide training to employees and contractors on data protection, privacy, and regulatory requirements to ensure that compliance is understood and maintained.

Legal and Ethical Considerations

Legal and ethical considerations in cloud security extend beyond compliance regulations to encompass broader issues related to privacy and security(Maguluri, Arularasan, et al., 2023; Reddy, Reddy, et al., 2023; Ugandar et al., 2023).

- **Data Ownership:** Clarify data ownership and responsibility for data protection. Address legal considerations for data stored in the cloud, including data access and transfer.

- **Ethical Use of AI and Machine Learning:** Consider ethical implications of using AI and machine learning in cloud-based applications, particularly regarding data privacy, bias, and transparency.
- **Cross-Border Data Transfers:** Understand the legal and regulatory requirements for cross-border data transfers, as different jurisdictions may have distinct rules on data protection and sovereignty.
- **Data Retention and E-Discovery:** Ensure that cloud data retention policies align with legal requirements for e-discovery and the preservation of digital evidence.
- **Incident Response and Notification:** Develop clear incident response plans that comply with legal obligations for data breach notifications, including timelines and disclosure requirements.

To effectively manage cloud compliance and regulations, organizations must understand the specific requirements of regulatory frameworks and adapt security practices accordingly. Legal and ethical considerations must be integrated into their cloud security strategy to ensure data protection and ethical use of cloud technologies.

BEST PRACTICES FOR CLOUD SECURITY

This section emphasizes the significance of best practices in cloud security, including security policy and governance, effective identity and access management, and robust encryption and data protection measures for maintaining a secure cloud environment(Dotson, 2023).

Security Policy and Governance

- **Develop Comprehensive Security Policies:** Establish clear and comprehensive security policies that define security objectives, roles and responsibilities, incident response procedures, and compliance requirements.
- **Regularly Update Policies:** Security policies should be dynamic and regularly updated to adapt to evolving threats, technology changes, and regulatory updates.
- **Security Governance Framework:** Implement a governance framework that defines decision-making processes, accountability, and the enforcement of security policies throughout the organization.
- **Risk Management:** Conduct risk assessments and establish risk management processes to identify, assess, and mitigate security risks associated with cloud adoption.

- **Compliance Monitoring:** Continuously monitor and audit the cloud environment to ensure compliance with regulatory requirements and internal security policies.

Identity and Access Management (IAM)

- **Principle of Least Privilege:** Apply the principle of least privilege, which ensures that individuals and systems have access only to the minimum resources necessary to perform their tasks(Al-Issa et al., 2019).
- **Multi-Factor Authentication (MFA):** Implement MFA to enhance access security by requiring users to provide multiple forms of verification, such as passwords and biometrics.
- **Single Sign-On (SSO):** Use SSO solutions to simplify user access while centralizing control and ensuring secure authentication.
- **User Lifecycle Management:** Establish robust user lifecycle management processes, including onboarding, offboarding, and periodic access reviews to maintain the security of user accounts.
- **Role-Based Access Control (RBAC):** Assign roles and permissions based on job functions and responsibilities, ensuring that individuals have the appropriate level of access.

Encryption and Data Protection

- **Data Classification:** Classify data based on its sensitivity, and apply encryption and protection measures accordingly. Ensure that sensitive data is encrypted both at rest and in transit(Kumar & Goyal, 2019).
- **Key Management:** Implement strong key management practices to secure encryption keys, including key rotation and secure key storage.
- **Data Loss Prevention (DLP):** Use DLP solutions to monitor and control data flow, preventing unauthorized sharing of sensitive information.
- **Endpoint Security:** Secure endpoints and devices that access cloud resources with security measures such as endpoint encryption, antivirus, and intrusion detection.
- **Security in Transit:** Encrypt data in transit using secure protocols (e.g., HTTPS, SSL/TLS) to protect data as it traverses networks.
- **Data Backup and Recovery:** Establish data backup and recovery processes to ensure data can be restored in the event of data loss or security incidents.

Organizations can establish a robust cloud security posture by implementing best practices in security policy, governance, identity and access management, and

Figure 5. Emerging Technologies and Trends- best practices

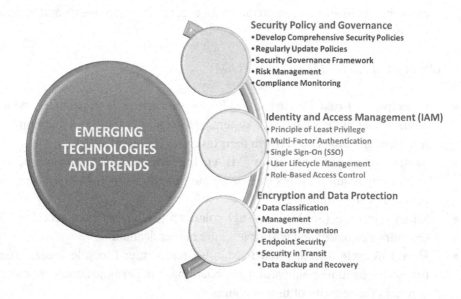

encryption and data protection, which safeguard sensitive data, mitigate risks, and ensure industry-specific regulations.

EMERGING TECHNOLOGIES AND TRENDS

This section emphasizes the significance of best practices in cloud security, including security policy and governance, effective identity and access management, and robust encryption and data protection measures for maintaining a secure cloud environment (Awaysheh et al., 2021; Kumar & Goyal, 2019). The figure 5 outlines best practices for utilizing emerging technologies and trends.

Security Policy and Governance

- **Develop Comprehensive Security Policies:** Establish clear and comprehensive security policies that define security objectives, roles and responsibilities, incident response procedures, and compliance requirements.
- **Regularly Update Policies:** Security policies should be dynamic and regularly updated to adapt to evolving threats, technology changes, and regulatory updates.

- **Security Governance Framework:** Implement a governance framework that defines decision-making processes, accountability, and the enforcement of security policies throughout the organization.
- **Risk Management:** Conduct risk assessments and establish risk management processes to identify, assess, and mitigate security risks associated with cloud adoption.
- **Compliance Monitoring:** Continuously monitor and audit the cloud environment to ensure compliance with regulatory requirements and internal security policies.

Identity and Access Management (IAM)

- **Principle of Least Privilege:** Apply the principle of least privilege, which ensures that individuals and systems have access only to the minimum resources necessary to perform their tasks.
- **Multi-Factor Authentication (MFA):** Implement MFA to enhance access security by requiring users to provide multiple forms of verification, such as passwords and biometrics.
- **Single Sign-On (SSO):** Use SSO solutions to simplify user access while centralizing control and ensuring secure authentication.
- **User Lifecycle Management:** Establish robust user lifecycle management processes, including onboarding, offboarding, and periodic access reviews to maintain the security of user accounts.
- **Role-Based Access Control (RBAC):** Assign roles and permissions based on job functions and responsibilities, ensuring that individuals have the appropriate level of access.

Encryption and Data Protection

- **Data Classification:** Classify data based on its sensitivity, and apply encryption and protection measures accordingly. Ensure that sensitive data is encrypted both at rest and in transit.
- **Key Management:** Implement strong key management practices to secure encryption keys, including key rotation and secure key storage.
- **Data Loss Prevention (DLP):** Use DLP solutions to monitor and control data flow, preventing unauthorized sharing of sensitive information.
- **Endpoint Security:** Secure endpoints and devices that access cloud resources with security measures such as endpoint encryption, antivirus, and intrusion detection.

- **Security in Transit:** Encrypt data in transit using secure protocols (e.g., HTTPS, SSL/TLS) to protect data as it traverses networks.
- **Data Backup and Recovery:** Establish data backup and recovery processes to ensure data can be restored in the event of data loss or security incidents.

Organizations can establish a robust cloud security posture by implementing best practices in security policy, governance, identity and access management, and encryption and data protection, which safeguard sensitive data, mitigate risks, and ensure industry-specific regulations.

CASE STUDIES

This section explores real-world case studies that provide valuable insights into successful cloud security implementations and lessons learned from these scenarios.

Case Study One: Secure Cloud Migration for a Healthcare Provider

- *Scenario:* A large healthcare provider faced the challenge of migrating sensitive patient data to the cloud while complying with stringent HIPAA regulations(Pramila et al., 2023; Reddy, Gaurav, et al., 2023; Sengeni et al., 2023).
- *Lessons Learned:* The case study highlights the importance of thorough data classification and encryption. It also emphasizes the need for cloud providers with healthcare-specific compliance capabilities. Compliance with regulatory frameworks can be achieved through a combination of technical and policy-based controls.

Case Study Two: Zero Trust Implementation for a Financial Institution

- *Scenario:* A financial institution decided to adopt a Zero Trust security model to enhance its overall security posture and protect against increasingly sophisticated cyber threats(Boopathi & Kanike, 2023; Maheswari et al., 2023; Syamala et al., 2023).
- *Lessons Learned:* This case study demonstrates the value of continuous user authentication and micro-segmentation in a Zero Trust environment. It underscores the importance of a well-defined strategy, user training, and adaptability to changing threat landscapes.

Case Study Three: Cloud-Native Security for a Tech Startup

- *Scenario:* A tech startup building cloud-native applications wanted to prioritize security from the outset to safeguard user data and gain trust in a competitive market.
- *Lessons Learned:* The case study highlights the advantages of integrating security into the development process from the beginning. It emphasizes the use of DevSecOps practices and automation for continuous security monitoring and vulnerability detection.

Case Study Four: AI-Driven Threat Detection for an E-commerce Giant

- *Scenario:* An e-commerce giant implemented AI and machine learning solutions to enhance its threat detection capabilities and protect against evolving cyber threats.
- *Lessons Learned:* This case study illustrates the potential of AI and machine learning in security, particularly for the rapid identification of anomalies and early threat detection. It emphasizes the need for ongoing monitoring and adaptation of AI models to stay ahead of emerging threats.

Case Study Five: Compliance and Data Sovereignty for a Global Corporation

- *Scenario:* A multinational corporation with operations in various regions faced the challenge of complying with diverse data protection regulations and ensuring data sovereignty.
- *Lessons Learned:* This case study underscores the complexity of cross-border data compliance and the importance of selecting cloud providers with a global presence and strong data sovereignty solutions. It also highlights the value of robust data classification and data loss prevention measures.

The case studies offer valuable insights into the challenges and successes of cloud security implementations across various industries, providing valuable lessons for organizations to improve their strategies and practices.

CONCLUSION

This chapter delves into the importance of cloud security in the digital age, highlighting its challenges and opportunities. It discusses the balance between innovation and security, identifying risks, developing robust strategies, and mitigating threats.

The chapter also covers compliance and regulations, navigating complex legal and ethical considerations. It covers best practices for cloud security, including policy and governance, identity and access management, encryption, and data protection. It also discusses emerging technologies like AI and Zero Trust security models.

Cloud security is a dynamic field influenced by technology, regulations, and threats. Organizations must adapt and innovate to stay ahead and protect their digital assets. The journey continues, offering both challenges and opportunities. As organizations embrace cloud technology, they must prioritize security, compliance, and resilience. The next chapter will explore these evolving frontiers and provide insights on how to successfully navigate them.

ABBREVIATIONS

AI - Artificial Intelligence
GDPR - General Data Protection Regulation
HIPAA - Health Insurance Portability and Accountability Act
PCI DSS - Payment Card Industry Data Security Standard
SOX - Sarbanes-Oxley Act
CCPA - California Consumer Privacy Act
DLP - Data Loss Prevention
DevSecOps - Development, Security, and Operations
IAM - Identity and Access Management
SSO - Single Sign-On

REFERENCES

Agrawal, A. V., Magulur, L. P., Priya, S. G., Kaur, A., Singh, G., & Boopathi, S. (2023). Smart Precision Agriculture Using IoT and WSN. In *Handbook of Research on Data Science and Cybersecurity Innovations in Industry 4.0 Technologies* (pp. 524–541). IGI Global. doi:10.4018/978-1-6684-8145-5.ch026

Agrawal, A. V., Pitchai, R., Senthamaraikannan, C., Balaji, N. A., Sajithra, S., & Boopathi, S. (2023). Digital Education System During the COVID-19 Pandemic. In Using Assistive Technology for Inclusive Learning in K-12 Classrooms (pp. 104–126). IGI Global. doi:10.4018/978-1-6684-6424-3.ch005

Agrawal, A. V., Shashibhushan, G., Pradeep, S., Padhi, S. N., Sugumar, D., & Boopathi, S. (2024). Synergizing Artificial Intelligence, 5G, and Cloud Computing for Efficient Energy Conversion Using Agricultural Waste. In Practice, Progress, and Proficiency in Sustainability (pp. 475–497). IGI Global. doi:10.4018/979-8-3693-1186-8.ch026

Al-Issa, Y., Ottom, M. A., Tamrawi, A., & ... (2019). eHealth cloud security challenges: A survey. *Journal of Healthcare Engineering*. PMID:31565209

Anitha, C., Komala, C., Vivekanand, C. V., Lalitha, S., & Boopathi, S. (2023). Artificial Intelligence driven security model for Internet of Medical Things (IoMT). *IEEE Explore*, (pp. 1–7). IEEE.

Arunprasad, R., & Boopathi, S. (2019). Chapter-4 Alternate Refrigerants for Minimization Environmental Impacts: A Review. In Advances In Engineering Technology (p. 75). AkiNik Publications New Delhi.

Awaysheh, F. M., Aladwan, M. N., Alazab, M., Alawadi, S., Cabaleiro, J. C., & Pena, T. F. (2021). Security by design for big data frameworks over cloud computing. *IEEE Transactions on Engineering Management*, 69(6), 3676–3693. doi:10.1109/TEM.2020.3045661

Babu, B. S., Kamalakannan, J., Meenatchi, N., Karthik, S., & Boopathi, S. (2022). Economic impacts and reliability evaluation of battery by adopting Electric Vehicle. *IEEE Explore*, (pp. 1–6). IEEE.

Boopathi, S. (2021). *Pollution monitoring and notification: Water pollution monitoring and notification using intelligent RC boat.*

Boopathi, S. (2023a). Internet of Things-Integrated Remote Patient Monitoring System: Healthcare Application. In *Dynamics of Swarm Intelligence Health Analysis for the Next Generation* (pp. 137–161). IGI Global. doi:10.4018/978-1-6684-6894-4.ch008

Boopathi, S. (2023b). Securing Healthcare Systems Integrated With IoT: Fundamentals, Applications, and Future Trends. In Dynamics of Swarm Intelligence Health Analysis for the Next Generation (pp. 186–209). IGI Global.

Boopathi, S., & Kanike, U. K. (2023). Applications of Artificial Intelligent and Machine Learning Techniques in Image Processing. In *Handbook of Research on Thrust Technologies' Effect on Image Processing* (pp. 151–173). IGI Global. doi:10.4018/978-1-6684-8618-4.ch010

Dotson, C. (2023). *Practical Cloud Security*. O'Reilly Media, Inc.

Durairaj, M., Jayakumar, S., Karpagavalli, V., Maheswari, B. U., Boopathi, S., & ... (2023). Utilization of Digital Tools in the Indian Higher Education System During Health Crises. In *Multidisciplinary Approaches to Organizational Governance During Health Crises* (pp. 1–21). IGI Global. doi:10.4018/978-1-7998-9213-7.ch001

Gozman, D., & Willcocks, L. (2019). The emerging Cloud Dilemma: Balancing innovation with cross-border privacy and outsourcing regulations. *Journal of Business Research*, *97*, 235–256. doi:10.1016/j.jbusres.2018.06.006

Harikaran, M., Boopathi, S., Gokulakannan, S., & Poonguzhali, M. (2023). Study on the Source of E-Waste Management and Disposal Methods. In *Sustainable Approaches and Strategies for E-Waste Management and Utilization* (pp. 39–60). IGI Global. doi:10.4018/978-1-6684-7573-7.ch003

Hema, N., Krishnamoorthy, N., Chavan, S. M., Kumar, N., Sabarimuthu, M., & Boopathi, S. (2023). A Study on an Internet of Things (IoT)-Enabled Smart Solar Grid System. In *Handbook of Research on Deep Learning Techniques for Cloud-Based Industrial IoT* (pp. 290–308). IGI Global. doi:10.4018/978-1-6684-8098-4.ch017

Ingle, R. B., Senthil, T. S., Swathi, S., Muralidharan, N., Mahendran, G., & Boopathi, S. (2023). Sustainability and Optimization of Green and Lean Manufacturing Processes Using Machine Learning Techniques. In IGI Global. doi:10.4018/978-1-6684-8238-4.ch012

Jyoti, A., Shrimali, M., Tiwari, S., & Singh, H. P. (2020). Cloud computing using load balancing and service broker policy for IT service: A taxonomy and survey. *Journal of Ambient Intelligence and Humanized Computing*, *11*(11), 4785–4814. doi:10.100712652-020-01747-z

Karthik, S., Hemalatha, R., Aruna, R., Deivakani, M., Reddy, R. V. K., & Boopathi, S. (2023). Study on Healthcare Security System-Integrated Internet of Things (IoT). In Perspectives and Considerations on the Evolution of Smart Systems (pp. 342–362). IGI Global.

Kavitha, C. R., Varalatchoumy, M., Mithuna, H. R., Bharathi, K., Geethalakshmi, N. M., & Boopathi, S. (2023). Energy Monitoring and Control in the Smart Grid: Integrated Intelligent IoT and ANFIS. In M. Arshad (Ed.), (pp. 290–316). Advances in Bioinformatics and Biomedical Engineering. IGI Global. doi:10.4018/978-1-6684-6577-6.ch014

Koshariya, A. K., Kalaiyarasi, D., Jovith, A. A., Sivakami, T., Hasan, D. S., & Boopathi, S. (2023). AI-Enabled IoT and WSN-Integrated Smart Agriculture System. In *Artificial Intelligence Tools and Technologies for Smart Farming and Agriculture Practices* (pp. 200–218). IGI Global. doi:10.4018/978-1-6684-8516-3.ch011

Koshariya, A. K., Khatoon, S., Marathe, A. M., Suba, G. M., Baral, D., & Boopathi, S. (2023). Agricultural Waste Management Systems Using Artificial Intelligence Techniques. In *AI-Enabled Social Robotics in Human Care Services* (pp. 236–258). IGI Global. doi:10.4018/978-1-6684-8171-4.ch009

Kumar, R., & Goyal, R. (2019). On cloud security requirements, threats, vulnerabilities and countermeasures: A survey. *Computer Science Review, 33*, 1–48. doi:10.1016/j.cosrev.2019.05.002

Kunduru, A. R. (2023). Artificial intelligence usage in cloud application performance improvement. *Central Asian Journal of Mathematical Theory and Computer Sciences, 4*(8), 42–47.

Maguluri, L. P., Ananth, J., Hariram, S., Geetha, C., Bhaskar, A., & Boopathi, S. (2023). Smart Vehicle-Emissions Monitoring System Using Internet of Things (IoT). In Handbook of Research on Safe Disposal Methods of Municipal Solid Wastes for a Sustainable Environment (pp. 191–211). IGI Global.

Maguluri, L. P., Arularasan, A. N., & Boopathi, S. (2023). Assessing Security Concerns for AI-Based Drones in Smart Cities. In R. Kumar, A. B. Abdul Hamid, & N. I. Binti Ya'akub (Eds.), (pp. 27–47). Advances in Computational Intelligence and Robotics. IGI Global. doi:10.4018/978-1-6684-9151-5.ch002

Maheswari, B. U., Imambi, S. S., Hasan, D., Meenakshi, S., Pratheep, V., & Boopathi, S. (2023). Internet of Things and Machine Learning-Integrated Smart Robotics. In Global Perspectives on Robotics and Autonomous Systems: Development and Applications (pp. 240–258). IGI Global. doi:10.4018/978-1-6684-7791-5.ch010

Mohanty, A., Venkateswaran, N., Ranjit, P., Tripathi, M. A., & Boopathi, S. (2023). Innovative Strategy for Profitable Automobile Industries: Working Capital Management. In Handbook of Research on Designing Sustainable Supply Chains to Achieve a Circular Economy (pp. 412–428). IGI Global.

Pramila, P., Amudha, S., Saravanan, T., Sankar, S. R., Poongothai, E., & Boopathi, S. (2023). Design and Development of Robots for Medical Assistance: An Architectural Approach. In Contemporary Applications of Data Fusion for Advanced Healthcare Informatics (pp. 260–282). IGI Global.

Rahamathunnisa, U., Subhashini, P., Aancy, H. M., Meenakshi, S., Boopathi, S., & ... (2023). Solutions for Software Requirement Risks Using Artificial Intelligence Techniques. In *Handbook of Research on Data Science and Cybersecurity Innovations in Industry 4.0 Technologies* (pp. 45–64). IGI Global.

Rahamathunnisa, U., Sudhakar, K., Murugan, T. K., Thivaharan, S., Rajkumar, M., & Boopathi, S. (2023). Cloud Computing Principles for Optimizing Robot Task Offloading Processes. In *AI-Enabled Social Robotics in Human Care Services* (pp. 188–211). IGI Global. doi:10.4018/978-1-6684-8171-4.ch007

Ramudu, K., Mohan, V. M., Jyothirmai, D., Prasad, D., Agrawal, R., & Boopathi, S. (2023). Machine Learning and Artificial Intelligence in Disease Prediction: Applications, Challenges, Limitations, Case Studies, and Future Directions. In Contemporary Applications of Data Fusion for Advanced Healthcare Informatics (pp. 297–318). IGI Global.

Rayhan, R., & Rayhan, S. (2023). *AI and Human Rights: Balancing Innovation and Privacy in the Digital Age.*

Reddy, M. A., Gaurav, A., Ushasukhanya, S., Rao, V. C. S., Bhattacharya, S., & Boopathi, S. (2023). Bio-Medical Wastes Handling Strategies During the COVID-19 Pandemic. In Multidisciplinary Approaches to Organizational Governance During Health Crises (pp. 90–111). IGI Global. doi:10.4018/978-1-7998-9213-7.ch006

Reddy, M. A., Reddy, B. M., Mukund, C., Venneti, K., Preethi, D., & Boopathi, S. (2023). Social Health Protection During the COVID-Pandemic Using IoT. In *The COVID-19 Pandemic and the Digitalization of Diplomacy* (pp. 204–235). IGI Global. doi:10.4018/978-1-7998-8394-4.ch009

R.M., S. P., Bhattacharya, S., Maddikunta, P. K. R., Somayaji, S. R. K., Lakshmanna, K., Kaluri, R., Hussien, A., & Gadekallu, T. R. (2020). Load balancing of energy cloud using wind driven and firefly algorithms in internet of everything. *Journal of Parallel and Distributed Computing, 142*, 16–26. doi:10.1016/j.jpdc.2020.02.010

Sankar, K. M., Booba, B., & Boopathi, S. (2023). Smart Agriculture Irrigation Monitoring System Using Internet of Things. In *Contemporary Developments in Agricultural Cyber-Physical Systems* (pp. 105–121). IGI Global. doi:10.4018/978-1-6684-7879-0.ch006

Satav, S. D., Hasan, D. S., Pitchai, R., Mohanaprakash, T. A., Sultanuddin, S. J., & Boopathi, S. (2024). Next Generation of Internet of Things (NGIoT) in Healthcare Systems. In Practice, Progress, and Proficiency in Sustainability (pp. 307–330). IGI Global. doi:10.4018/979-8-3693-1186-8.ch017

Satav, S. D., & Lamani, D. G, H. K., Kumar, N. M. G., Manikandan, S., & Sampath, B. (2024). Energy and Battery Management in the Era of Cloud Computing. In Practice, Progress, and Proficiency in Sustainability (pp. 141–166). IGI Global. doi:10.4018/979-8-3693-1186-8.ch009

Schneckenberg, D., Benitez, J., Klos, C., Velamuri, V. K., & Spieth, P. (2021). Value creation and appropriation of software vendors: A digital innovation model for cloud computing. *Information & Management*, *58*(4), 103463. doi:10.1016/j.im.2021.103463

Sengeni, D., Padmapriya, G., Imambi, S. S., Suganthi, D., Suri, A., & Boopathi, S. (2023). Biomedical Waste Handling Method Using Artificial Intelligence Techniques. In *Handbook of Research on Safe Disposal Methods of Municipal Solid Wastes for a Sustainable Environment* (pp. 306–323). IGI Global. doi:10.4018/978-1-6684-8117-2.ch022

Shahid, M. A., Islam, N., Alam, M. M., Su'ud, M. M., & Musa, S. (2020). A comprehensive study of load balancing approaches in the cloud computing environment and a novel fault tolerance approach. *IEEE Access : Practical Innovations, Open Solutions*, *8*, 130500–130526. doi:10.1109/ACCESS.2020.3009184

Srinivas, B., Maguluri, L. P., Naidu, K. V., Reddy, L. C. S., Deivakani, M., & Boopathi, S. (2023). Architecture and Framework for Interfacing Cloud-Enabled Robots. In *Handbook of Research on Data Science and Cybersecurity Innovations in Industry 4.0 Technologies* (pp. 542–560). IGI Global. doi:10.4018/978-1-6684-8145-5.ch027

Syamala, M., Komala, C., Pramila, P., Dash, S., Meenakshi, S., & Boopathi, S. (2023). Machine Learning-Integrated IoT-Based Smart Home Energy Management System. In *Handbook of Research on Deep Learning Techniques for Cloud-Based Industrial IoT* (pp. 219–235). IGI Global. doi:10.4018/978-1-6684-8098-4.ch013

Ugandar, R. E., Rahamathunnisa, U., Sajithra, S., Christiana, M. B. V., Palai, B. K., & Boopathi, S. (2023). Hospital Waste Management Using Internet of Things and Deep Learning: Enhanced Efficiency and Sustainability. In M. Arshad (Ed.), (pp. 317–343). Advances in Bioinformatics and Biomedical Engineering. IGI Global. doi:10.4018/978-1-6684-6577-6.ch015

Venkateswaran, N., Kumar, S. S., Diwakar, G., Gnanasangeetha, D., & Boopathi, S. (2023). Synthetic Biology for Waste Water to Energy Conversion: IoT and AI Approaches. In M. Arshad (Ed.), (pp. 360–384). Advances in Bioinformatics and Biomedical Engineering. IGI Global. doi:10.4018/978-1-6684-6577-6.ch017

Venkateswaran, N., Vidhya, K., Ayyannan, M., Chavan, S. M., Sekar, K., & Boopathi, S. (2023). A Study on Smart Energy Management Framework Using Cloud Computing. In 5G, Artificial Intelligence, and Next Generation Internet of Things: Digital Innovation for Green and Sustainable Economies (pp. 189–212). IGI Global. doi:10.4018/978-1-6684-8634-4.ch009

Chapter 9
Data Storage and Transmission Security in the Cloud:
The Artificial Intelligence (AI) Edge

Ankita Nayak
KIIT University, India

Atmika Patnaik
King's College, India

Ipseeta Satpathy
KIIT University, India

B. C. M. Patnaik
KIIT University, India

ABSTRACT

Cloud computing has profoundly changed the face of data management for enterprises, providing increased scalability, ease of access, and cost savings. Nonetheless, this change has highlighted the crucial need for strengthened security measures to protect sensitive data from the ever-changing spectrum of cyber threats. Following the cloud's rise as a storehouse for large datasets, the quest for sophisticated security solutions has gained traction. This motivation has resulted in the incorporation of artificial intelligence (AI) into the cloud security architecture. As cloud storage becomes increasingly popular, organizations are becoming more concerned about data security. Sensitive data is transmitted, ranging from messages and images to financial and health information. As technology advances, there is a growing threat to customer data in the cloud, making greater cloud security more important than ever. This study aims to give a comprehensive insight into the role of AI in data storage and transmission security in the cloud.

DOI: 10.4018/979-8-3693-1431-9.ch009

1. INTRODUCTION

We live in the big data age, with organizations producing, collecting, and storing huge amounts of data on a daily basis, ranging from extremely sensitive business or personal customer data is being replaced with less sensitive data, such as behavioral and analytics for marketing. Aside from the growing amount of data that businesses must be able to collect, handle, and analyze, organizations are embracing cloud services. The traditional network barrier is fast eroding, and security teams are realizing that enterprises must reevaluate existing and past methods of cloud data security. With data and apps no longer living in your data center and more workers working far away from a physical office than ever before, Organizations must figure out how to safeguard data and control access to it as it moves across and through various contexts (Ganne, 2022). The three main pillars of data are Data confidentiality, integrity, and availability. These three broad pillars, sometimes known as the CIA triad, define the basic ideas that constitute the foundation of a robust, successful security infrastructure—or any organization's security program. Any type of attack, vulnerability, or other security issue will almost certainly break one (or more) of these principles. This is why security experts employ this approach to assess possible threats to an organization's data assets. Cloud data security safeguards data stored in the cloud (at rest) or going in and out of the cloud (in motion) from security risks such as unauthorized use, fraud, and manipulation. There is usage of physical security, technical instruments, access management and controls, and organizational regulations. Securing cloud data entails developing ways to safeguard important digital assets and information from potential security breaches, inadvertent errors, and hazards posed by personnel inside an organization. This entails using technological tools, established standards, and operational approaches to protect data confidentiality while allowing authorized access in cloud-based environments. The benefits of cloud computing include a variety of benefits such as the ability to retrieve data from any internet-connected device, lowering the risk of data loss during outages or events, and boosting scalability and agility. At the same time, many organizations are still hesitant to shift sensitive data to the cloud because they are unsure of their security alternatives and how to fulfill legal requirements. (Kumar,2019; Wagh,2020). Cloud security, also known as cloud computing security, is a collection of security precautions designed to protect cloud-based apps, infrastructure, and data. User and device identification, data and resource access control, and data privacy are among the precautions. They also help with regulatory data accuracy. Cloud security is applied in cloud settings to protect a company's data against DDoS attacks, viruses, hackers, and unauthorized access or consumption. There are three main types of cloud environments as mentioned in figure 1 below (Agarwal,2019);

Figure 1. Types of cloud environments
Source – Author's own compilation

Types of Cloud Environments	Public Cloud
	Private Cloud
	Hybrid Cloud

- Public Cloud - Third-party cloud providers that host public cloud services. These services handle full backend administration, removing the need for businesses to build their own cloud infrastructure. Clients often use web browsers to access to these providers' web-based solutions. Maintaining security in public cloud settings requires ensuring safe entrance, maintaining user identities, and validating accesss.
- Private Cloud - Private clouds frequently have stronger security standards than public clouds. This increased security is related to their exclusive attention to certain user groups or people, leveraging the organization's or user's security procedures. The intrinsic isolation of these cloud configurations functions as a precaution against external attacks due to accessibility that is restricted to a single entity.
- Hybrid Cloud - The expanding scalability of public clouds is combined with the better resource management of private clouds in hybrid clouds. These cloud setups connect many settings, including both private and public clouds, allowing for smooth expansion as requirements arise. A well-executed hybrid cloud configuration enables users to browse all of their environments effortlessly via a unified content management system.

The need of strong cloud security cannot be stressed as cloud computing becomes more incorporated into the operations of multiple enterprises. Gartner's forecast of a 23.1% increase in the worldwide public cloud services market during 2021 exemplifies this trend, underlining the growing acceptance of these solutions. While cloud usage is increasing, some IT professionals are still hesitant to fully migrate their data and apps to the cloud. This reluctance stems from worries about security, governance, and compliance, all of which are exacerbated when sensitive data is housed in cloud settings. The concern is about the possible vulnerability of important company information and intellectual property as a result of unintentional disclosures or more sophisticated cyberattacks. To avoid breaches and unauthorized access, critical assets such as client orders, private design blueprints, and financial information require strict cloud protection. Protecting against data breaches and theft is critical not just for maintaining consumer confidence, but also for preserving the intellectual advantages that drive competitiveness. The ability of cloud security measures to strengthen data and precious assets appears as a vital aspect in the route toward cloud integration. It is a critical concern for any organization moving to cloud-based operations. (Tahir et al.,2021). Artificial intelligence (AI) has lately become a hot issue in the news and social media, as technical advances have made AI more powerful and accessible than ever before. AI experts think that unified solutions will substantially influence the cloud security sector. Given the importance of data security, AI may be utilized to alter cloud security and protect data stored in the cloud. MarketsandMarkets predicts that the global AI in cybersecurity market will expand at a CAGR of 23.3% from $8.8 billion in 2020 to $38.2 billion by 2026 (Siriwardhana et al.,2021). According to Statista, the average global expense for a data breach in 2022 will be $4.35 million USD. In terms of cloud breaches, public cloud breaches are more expensive than hybrid cloud breaches. Enterprises with advanced cloud security solutions paid less for data breaches than enterprises with early-stage maturity. This is most likely due to the fact that more advanced security detects and prevents breaches considerably faster than less advanced protection. A well-known German mobile communications subsidiary experienced its second data breach of 2023 in May 2023, when a breach disclosed the PINs, complete names, and phone numbers of over 800 clients, marking the company's ninth data breach since 2018 (Zolfaghari,2022). Organizations are often searching for methods to simplify processes, create more accurate forecasts and insights, and make more informed choices in order to increase income. That is exactly what artificial intelligence claims to achieve. The capacity of AI to replicate the behavior of actual people, preferably a large number of them, is frequently used to streamline corporate decisions and procedures. This simulation is what makes AI "intelligent," and it adds to the numerous ways in which AI is employed in business, notably in data utilization, customer management, and marketing AI is rapidly being used in cloud security because it may help organizations avoid cyberattacks, enhance incident response, and secure sensitive data from unauthorized access. Many organizations and security professionals are looking to AI to help them defend against cyberattacks since AI can analyze data in the cloud and discover trends to detect possible threats, as well as automate security operations like identity verification, access control, and data encryption (Alhayani,2021). AI may also secure data in transit by identifying malicious activity and acting quickly, automating the response process to security issues, and designing stronger security rules. AI may also analyze cloud data to identify possible vulnerabilities, follow down harmful activity, and take relevant action. AI is gaining traction in cloud security due to its enormous potential to transform the cloud security business (Salih,2021). A recent study in Forbes revealed that AI's promise in cloud technology throws a long and fascinating shadow. AI has matured into a faithful companion for those immersed in the cloud world, ushering in a domain of greater efficiency and scalability. It adeptly addresses repetitive or easily categorized chores, increasing our present capacities and promoting improved skills and deliberate choices. Businesses can access a practically endless pool of resources to train AI models, analyze massive datasets, and extract meaningful insights by utilizing the cloud. The scalability of the cloud means that AI applications can manage a wide range of workloads, from small-scale testing to large-scale production deployments, without incurring prohibitive infrastructure expenses. Furthermore, AI is becoming democratized, since it is now available in a variety of organization-ready services. This enables organizations of all sizes to grasp the potential of AI while also leveling the playing field for innovation. For example, accessibility and flexibility enable teams to interact seamlessly across countries, allowing developers to swiftly deploy AI applications without having to worry about underlying infrastructure maintenance (Sayegh,2023). There are several advantages of employing AI in cloud security. AI may assist in identifying risks that people may overlook, as well as providing insights into attacker behaviors. AI may also be used to detect and respond to issues automatically. Azure Sentinel, which is part of the Microsoft Azure cloud suite, is one example of this. This technology enables incident responders to execute security remediation automatically based on the kind of alarm given by a sentinel. This means that the system can detect and correct problems without the need for human interaction. Artificial intelligence (AI) is progressively outsourcing duties to automated technologies as it evolves. This is done to free up the AI's time for more difficult activities or jobs requiring human judgment. This trend has various advantages, including enhanced efficiency and precision. There are, however, certain hazards, such as the possibility of job loss when more and more jobs are transferred to automated systems (Brathwaite,2019).

1.1 The Role of Artificial Intelligence (AI) in Data Loss Prevention (DLP) in the Cloud

Data is the lifeblood of every organization. The adoption of cloud-based Software as a Service (SaaS) platforms, such as Microsoft 365, Google Workspace, and Salesforce, has skyrocketed in recent years. This growth is mostly driven by the need for increased productivity among remote employees and greater team cooperation. As a result, a significant amount of data is stored in the cloud on a regular basis. However, like with traditional hardware-based storage spaces, it is critical to remember that the cloud is not immune to data loss issues. According to HIPAA Journal research, 70%

of firms had data breaches in the public cloud in the previous year. With growing worries about data breaches, cyberattacks, industrial espionage, and the introduction of severe data privacy rules, the use of Data Loss Prevention (DLP) technology has become a critical requirement for modern enterprises. (Hillmann,2019). Data loss may be disastrous for enterprises of any size. Unfortunately, no business is immune to data loss. Every 11 seconds, a company will be the victim of a cyberattack in 2021. Businesses are concerned about more than just external threats. As per to the Verizon 2021 Data Breach Reports Report, insiders were engaged in more than 20% of security breaches. Data loss may have an influence on your company's financial health. The global average cost of a data breach grew from $3.86 million to $4.24 million in 2021, according to the IBM Cost of a Data Breach Report 2021. In addition to financial fines, data loss can result in lost productivity, money, and clients. One of the long-term effects of data loss is that it might ruin your company's brand. As a result, implementing a data loss prevention plan is crucial for protecting corporate data, protecting intellectual property, and remaining in compliance with regulations. DLP solutions ensure that confidential/classified data in your organization is not lost, mistreated, or accessed by unauthorized personnel (Sarker et al.,2021). Data loss prevention (DLP) implies the process of protecting organizations from both data loss and data leakage. Data loss is described as the loss of critical firm data, such as that caused by a ransomware attack. Data loss prevention has to do with protecting data from being transmitted outside the bounds of an organization (Grispos,2019). DLP is an essential tool for companies of all sizes. DLP may help organizations protect their data from a variety of threats and ensure compliance with data security regulations. DLP may be used to secure data in cloud-based apps, databases, and storage systems. DLP is widely used in organizations to safeguard personally identifiable data (PII) and to ensure compliance with every pertinent requirement, in large organizations while achieving visualization of data in Bring Your Own Device (BYOD) environments, secure mobile workforces, and enforcing security and data security on distant cloud systems. The three most common reasons for data leaks are discussed below.;

- Insider threats: A hostile insider or attacker possessing access to a secured user account tries to transport data outside the organization by abusing their privileges.
- Extrusion by attackers: Numerous cyber-attacks target sensitive data. To get access to sensitive data, attackers penetrate the security perimeter using strategies such as phishing, malware, and code injection.
- Unintentional Data Exposure: A lot of data breaches occur as a consequence of employees leaving sensitive data exposed, giving data with open Internet access, or failing to limit access in compliance with organizational standards.

DLP integrated with AI and ML finds business-critical data better and quicker than older systems. Because this DLP is also self-learning, it requires significantly less involvement from IT Teams, allowing them to focus on higher-value activities rather than continually responding to false alarms produced by their DLP solution. DLP systems may use ML to locate and safeguard sensitive data, such as customer PII or PHI, across your cloud apps, APIs, and broader infrastructure. It will start by configuring the DLP system with a few rules so it understands what to look for and how to respond. The DLP's machine learning component then allows the system to learn and probe fresh data, resulting in the automated redaction of sensitive material. Furthermore, machine learning may be applied to user behavior, allowing your DLP system to respond to unsafe or anomalous user behavior by redacting or even preventing users from submitting specific bits of information (Adithya,2022). DLP becomes self-learning with AI. Even when no hard and fast policy has been adopted, it uses past logs, rules, and pattern recognition to detect sensitive data. Furthermore, in the case of an insider attack, AI-driven DLP's user behavior analysis capabilities imply that DLP may prevent a leak or breach in real time while simultaneously assisting end-users in improving their data security understanding (Ge,2022). As data becomes more scattered and hosted in the cloud, data management, and security practices are rapidly developing. AI can analyze regular user behavior and data access patterns to find abnormalities that might signal a data breach or unauthorized access. It may detect atypical login times, locations, and access patterns, assisting in the prevention of data loss due to unauthorized users. DLP systems driven by AI can scan and monitor data at rest, in transit, and in use inside the cloud environment. These systems can identify and block behaviors such as unauthorized data sharing, copying, or downloading. (Laurent,2023). Cloud-based data includes Software as a Service (SaaS) solutions, application hosting, data storage via platforms such as S3, GCP, or Azure, collaboration tools such as Slack, Trello, and Asana, webmail services such as Office 365 and G Suite, and video conferencing tools such as Zoom, Google Meet, and Teams. The difficulty stems from the fact that these cloud services handle large amounts of sensitive data. Employees access this data from a variety of places and devices, both personal and work-related, and it is also shared for the purposes of productivity and cooperation. When attempting to trace the disposition of data and its access by numerous parties, the complexity grows. Consider the following scenario: a single contract exists in 30 duplicates dispersed over 5 unique data sources in 15 locations. This case highlights the need for Data Loss Prevention (DLP) observations and suggestions. These include identifying data sources, detecting possible risks and vulnerabilities, resolving security gaps, prioritizing essential actions, and providing correction alternatives. As the system absorbs insights from inputs and results, the efficacy and precision of these measurements may improve over time. (Stone,2023). The synergy between encryption and AI-driven key management emerges as a strong guardian of sensitive information in the field of data protection, particularly within the complicated landscapes of cloud environments. Encryption, a dependable approach, protects data integrity and secrecy with complex algorithms and encryption keys. However, AI provides a harmonizing conductor for the orchestration of these keys, a delicate endeavor made more difficult by the dynamic nature of cloud data. Within these virtual corridors, AI demonstrates its expertise by assisting in various critical aspects of encryption and key management. Under AI's watchful scrutiny, the cryptic process of key creation transforms into a skill of art and science. AI algorithms, equipped with a grasp of several parameters, generate encryption keys that are naturally resistant to brute-force attacks. Furthermore, AI orchestrates the secure distribution of these keys, ensuring that only those with legal ownership participate in the cryptographic symphony. The concept of key rotation, a paragon of proactive security, finds its beat in the attentive rhythm of AI. AI's automatic hands flawlessly arrange the choreography of timely key movements, an effort to mitigate any breaches. This ensures that the ever-changing symphony of encryption keys stays elusive to malicious attackers (Fowers et al.,2018). AI examines user trends and their ventures into the encrypted domain. If the AI sentry detects an unusual overture - an unauthorized attempt to enter the encrypted realms - it sounds the alert, stopping the would-be intruder in their tracks. The threat of lost or compromised keys looms large in the fabric of data security. In this case, AI serves as a restorer, a digital maestro who uses complex algorithms to revive lost keys from the ashes of forgetfulness or malice. To emphasize its relevance, AI's domain includes compliance and auditing. A scrupulously preserved record of encryption key-related actions is a symbol of commitment to security standards and defence against regulatory audit skepticism.Data can be examined at super-fast rates using AI and machine learning while remaining as accurate as if done by a person. Not to mention error-free results as a result. Managing dispersed and unstructured data is a natural specialization. They need to evaluate as much data as possible to enhance AI. The more information they gather, the more precise and efficient the solution will be. The security staff is frequently required to revise policies and guidelines on a weekly basis, which keeps them on edge and their data at danger. DLP, on the other hand, becomes self-learning thanks to AI. This program detects sensitive data by analysing prior logs, rules, and trends, even when no rigid standards are in place. Furthermore, AI-driven DLP can detect and prevent insider threats in real-time, while simultaneously raising end-user awareness about data security through comprehensive user behaviour analysis (Srikanth,2022).

1.2 AI-Enhanced Behavioral Analysis for Robust Data Storage and Transmission Security in Cloud Environments

Malicious strikes all have one trait: they all behave differently from typical everyday behavior within a system or network. Companies can frequently detect malicious behavior by using signatures that are closely tied to specific sorts of well-known attacks. However, as attackers get more adept, they create new tactics, methods, and procedures (TTPs) that allow them to not only infiltrate weak settings but also move laterally unnoticed. This is where behavioral analysis comes into play. Security experts may now employ behavioral-based tools, algorithms, and AI to establish what the typical behavior of daily users is - and what it is not - with the support of enormous amounts of unfiltered endpoint data. Behavioral analysis may discover current and historical occurrences, trends, and patterns that are outside the bounds of common norms (Zhao,2013). The fast expansion of software and information technology over the last two decades has had a huge impact on the environment we live in and how we interact with it. Engineers have discovered a way to preserve data on how users interact with software, down to how the user moves their mouse. These facts would be useless on their own. However, advancements in analytics capabilities, especially with respect to, have allowed large amounts of user data to be analyzed for findings in recent years. Behavioral analytics is the process of analyzing massive amounts of user data in this manner (Kumari,2020). The basic mechanism in which AI turns out to be a true friend to the cloud is that AI systems commence by learning the typical behaviours of a given cloud environment. They examine data transmission, user interaction, application use, and network traffic trends over time. By doing so, they set a "normal" behaviour baseline for diverse organizations in the cloud ecosystem. After establishing a baseline, AI-powered systems continually monitor ongoing activity. They compare real-time behaviours to the previously learned baseline and mark any departures as anomalies. These anomalies might indicate unauthorized access, data exfiltration, malware activity, or other types of cyber risks. Artificial intelligence-powered behaviour analysis transcends simple rule-based techniques. It uses advanced pattern recognition techniques, such as machine learning algorithms and neural networks, to detect complex and subtle abnormalities that might elude standard security measures. AI systems function in real-time, giving businesses quick insight into possible dangers. Because of this proactive monitoring, attackers have a smaller window of possibility to exploit vulnerabilities. Cloud environments may be extremely dynamic, with fluctuating workloads and infrastructure. AI-powered systems can easily grow to manage massive volumes of data while also adapting to the changing cloud landscape. This versatility is essential for providing constant security coverage (Zhang,2016). Behavioral data is mostly collected through interactions between humans and software

202

or computers. Uploading data to a website or choosing a product on a website are two examples of interactions. These events are kept in databases on a device or, more typically, on corporate servers with date and time stamps in a readily accessible format. The global datasphere will contain approximately 160 zettabytes by 2025 (Hammoud,2020). By analyzing past data connected to data transmission and access in the cloud, AI systems can build baseline behavior patterns. These benchmarks define what constitutes "normal" behavior. As data travels across the cloud environment, AI compares current behavior to these baselines in real-time. When deviations occur, such as odd surges in data transfers or unauthorized access attempts, AI may immediately raise alarms to investigate further (Alipour,2015). As data traverses the complex environment of the cloud, AI compares the current behavior to the set baselines in real time. This attentive monitoring of real-time behaviors versus past standards enables AI to detect departures from expected patterns quickly. These aberrations might appear as odd spikes in data transfers, erratic access attempts, or any other activity that deviates dramatically from the established norms (Pacheco,2018). When such abnormalities are detected, the AI system plays a critical role in generating quick alarms. These alerts are an important technique for alerting security staff to potential dangers or security breaches that require further investigation. AI aids in the timely discovery of security concerns by rapidly raising these alarms, allowing organizations to take proactive actions to control and neutralize possible threats before they grow into severe crises (Rani et.al.,2021). AI can identify irregularities in user behavior that may suggest a security compromise. For example, if a person suddenly begins accessing files that they do not normally access or logs in from an unexpected place, this might indicate a compromised account. AI can detect these irregularities and warn the security team to further probe. Also, we can understand the concept of AI in behavior analysis through an example as in assuming a cloud-based e-commerce platform using AI-powered behavior analysis for security. The system has discovered that the web server receives a continuous stream of HTTP requests from diverse areas during regular operation. It suddenly observes a big rise in requests from a certain IP address in a short period of time, greatly above the normal pace. The AI system might identify this as a potential Distributed Denial of Service (DDoS) assault and take mitigation steps, such as rerouting traffic or applying rate limitation. AI may also assist in more complex circumstances, such as identifying insider threats, in which a legitimate user may be operating maliciously by accessing sensitive data or undertaking unauthorized actions (Muralidhara,2017). As organizations use AI to strengthen their security procedures, it's critical to strike a careful balance between protecting sensitive data and utilizing advanced analytical approaches. The beauty of these systems is their ability to protect user privacy through a sophisticated approach: instead of focusing on individual activities, they emphasize the study of aggregated trends. As a result, AI-powered security systems may detect irregularities and possible risks without interfering with individual users' actions. This method not only reduces the possibility of privacy violations but also conforms to legal frameworks and compliance norms. As a result, organizations may capitalize on AI's capabilities while adhering to their commitment to data privacy and regulatory mandates, ensuring their stakeholders that security is enhanced without jeopardizing individual privacy rights (Turjman,2021). Machine learning algorithms are used by AI-based phishing detection solutions to analyse the content and structure of emails in order to identify probable phishing attempts. These algorithms may recognize trends and abnormalities that suggest a phishing assault by learning from massive volumes of data. AI-based systems may also analyse user behaviour while engaging with emails in order to detect possible phishing assaults. For example, if a user clicks on a suspicious link or inputs personal information in response to a phishing email, AI-based solutions may detect this behaviour and notify security professionals (Moisset,2023). Darktrace, a major cybersecurity startup, uses AI and machine learning to analyse cloud behaviour. Their "Enterprise Immune System" uses artificial intelligence algorithms to understand the typical behaviour of a network, user, or device. It then detects deviations from this baseline, which might indicate possible dangers. Darktrace's AI engine assisted a multinational insurance business in the early detection of a ransomware assault in its cloud infrastructure. Because the AI system detected anomalous patterns of data access and transfer, the security team was able to act before the assault could completely unfold, averting a significant data breach. Another befitting example is Azure Sentinel, Microsoft's cloud-native security information and event management (SIEM) system, which uses AI to identify and respond to attacks. It scans cloud environments for unusual behaviour and patterns across several data sources. A retail firm using Azure Sentinel saw anomalous surges in network traffic emanating from a single IP address in one prominent occurrence. The artificial intelligence-powered system recognized this as a distributed denial-of-service (DDoS) assault and automatically deployed countermeasures to minimize the danger, maintaining uninterrupted service. (Armitage,2022; Ceponis,2021).

1.3 Artificial Intelligence (AI)-Enabled User Authentication Data Transmission and Security: Protecting Cloud Environment

User authentication validates an individual's identity while attempting to access a network or computer resource. It entails approving credentials transferred during network connections, so certifying the authenticity of the user's contact with the system. The authentication procedure guarantees that only authorized users may enter a system, thereby prohibiting unauthorized users from inflicting harm, stealing information, or causing other types of disturbance. Almost all human-to-computer

Figure 2. Main factors used in user authentication
Source – Authors' own compilation

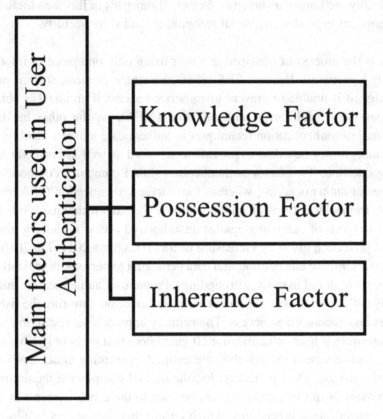

interactions need user authentication, with the exception of circumstances requiring guest or automated logins. It gives users access to networked and internet-connected technologies and services via wired and wireless networks. The three essential factors for user authentication are described below (Chang,2011; Choudhury,2011);

- Knowledge Factor - The knowledge components include all of the information that users must be aware of in order to commence a login procedure and get access to a system. This category includes usernames, IDs, passwords, and personal identification numbers (PINs).
- Possession Factor - All of the items required for users to complete a login are included in the possession criteria. This category includes products such as one-time password tokens, key fobs, mobile apps, and employee identity cards.

- Inherence Factor - Individuals' intrinsic characteristics that demonstrate their identity are known as heredity factors. Biometrics in this area include retina scans, fingerprint scans, facial recognition, and voice security.

SFA is the process of confirming a user using only one piece of information, generally a password. Because SFA relies on a single element, such as password knowledge, it is unable to prevent unauthorized access if an attacker obtains the user's password. Multifactor authentication (MFA), on the other hand, makes use of various authentication techniques to authenticate a user's identity. A user, for instance, it may be asked to provide a password as well as correctly answer a security question. Two-factor authentication (2FA) combines components from two types of authentications, whereas four-factor authentication (4FA) combines elements from all four types of authentications. The latter technique is substantially stronger in terms of defending against unauthorized access because to the higher levels of protection given by increasing factors (Dasgupta,2017; Lal,2016). Large volumes of sensitive and confidential data belonging to persons, organizations, and consumers are stored in noisy surroundings. Proper user authentication guarantees that only authorized users have access to this information, lowering the risk of data breaches and unauthorized access. The primary approach for restricting access to cloud resources is user authentication. It guarantees that users only have access to the data and services to which they are entitled, preventing either inadvertent or purposeful misuse. Data protection legislation and compliance requirements are strict in many businesses and areas. Adherence to these requirements is aided by proper authentication procedures, which ensure that data access is allowed only to authorized personnel (Alizadeh,2016). AI is becoming increasingly important in information security since such technologies are capable of swiftly analysing millions of data sets and identifying a wide range of cyber risks, from virus threats to suspicious behaviour that might lead to a phishing attack. One of the numerous advantages and applications of artificial intelligence is cybersecurity. With the fast growth of cyberattacks and the increasing number of gadgets, artificial intelligence and machine learning can help stay up with cyber criminals by automating threat assessment and response more quickly than traditional software-driven or manual operations (Ciolacu,2018). Behavioral biometrics is one way AI is revolutionizing authentication. To establish a unique user profile, behavioral biometrics analyze trends in human behavior such as typing speed, mouse movement, and touchscreen interactions. To authenticate the user's identity, AI systems may analyze this data in real-time and compare it to the user's known behavior. This method offers an extra degree of protection since it is difficult for attackers to effectively duplicate an individual's distinctive behavior. A further field where AI is making considerable progress in authentication is facial recognition. Deep learning algorithms are used in

AI-powered facial recognition systems to analyze facial traits and produce a biometric template. To authenticate the user's identity, these templates are matched to their recorded face data. Facial recognition is a non-intrusive and convenient verification method that may be used for a variety of purposes, including unlocking cell phones and gaining access to protected facilities (Sharma,2022). Adaptive authentication uses artificial intelligence to continually analyze the risk associated with a user's login attempt based on a variety of criteria such as location, device, time of day, and behavior. The system then modifies the amount of authentication necessary. If a user attempts to log in from an unknown area, for example, the system may request additional authentication procedures. Adaptive authentication is a flexible and adaptive method of authenticating users based on the context of their login attempt, improving security while reducing user friction (Akram,2022). Multi-factor authentication (MFA) Optimization entails employing artificial intelligence (AI) to intelligently adapt the authentication procedure based on the perceived risk of the circumstance. In practice, this implies that when a user tries to access the cloud from a known and trusted device or location, the authentication process may be reduced to only one factor - often a password. This simplified procedure guarantees a pleasant user experience while ensuring security. This optimization contributes to achieving a balance between security and usability. When utilizing trusted devices, users may enjoy a seamless experience while being prompted for further authentication when the system detects possible risks. This dynamic modification improves security while simultaneously adapting to the changing threat landscape. As AI systems learn from patterns and anomalies, their ability to effectively assess risk and alter authentication methods improves over time, resulting in a more intelligent and responsive security solution. (Kavitha,2021). NLP-driven authentication approaches make use of AI's ability to analyze and interpret human language, enabling more complex and context-aware verification procedures. NLP allows systems to comprehend the context of a communication. For example, if a user attempts to access private financial data, the system may request extra authentication elements to validate the user's identity before giving access. It can modify their replies in response to the user's reactions. If the user is hesitant or confused, the system may require additional authentication procedures for verification. (Baclic,2020; Sun,2020).AI is playing a critical role in the development of more secure authentication systems. AI is adding additional levels of security to existing authentication systems through behavioral biometrics, facial recognition, voice recognition, anomaly detection, continuous authentication, and adaptive authentication. These artificial intelligence-powered authentication solutions enable more accuracy, simplicity, and flexibility to new security risks, making them a crucial component of current authentication systems.

CONCLUSION

The future of artificial intelligence in cloud computing is quite intriguing. We are on the cusp of making some significant advances in this field, owing to the rapid advancement of ML technologies and the growing affordability of computer power in cloud computing, which will allow us to handle data quicker and more effectively than ever before. It also assists us in detecting patterns and linkages that might otherwise go undetected. This will have a significant influence on industries such as medical, banking, and logistics. In the realm of medicine, for example, AI is frequently employed in medication research and development to aid in the discovery of novel medicines that will also assist us in better understanding and forecasting human behavior. AI will also help us better understand and predict human behavior. This will help with website and app accessibility, as well as marketing and advertising. Overall, the prospect of AI in cloud computing appears to be bright.

REFERENCES

Adithya, V., Deepak, G., & Santhanavijayan, A. (2022). OntoIntAIC: An Approach for Ontology Integration Using Artificially Intelligent Cloud. In *Advances in Data Computing, Communication and Security: Proceedings of I3CS2021* (pp. 3–13). Springer Nature Singapore. doi:10.1007/978-981-16-8403-6_1

Agrawal, N., & Tapaswi, S. (2019). Defense mechanisms against DDoS attacks in a cloud computing environment: State-of-the-art and research challenges. *IEEE Communications Surveys and Tutorials*, *21*(4), 3769–3795. doi:10.1109/COMST.2019.2934468

Akram, S. V., Joshi, S. K., & Deorari, R. (2022, November). Web Application Based Authentication System. In *2022 International Interdisciplinary Humanitarian Conference for Sustainability (IIHC)* (pp. 1439-1443). IEEE. 10.1109/IIHC55949.2022.10059984

Al-Turjman, F., & Deebak, B. D. (2021). A Proxy-Authorized Public Auditing Scheme for Cyber-Medical Systems Using AI-IoT. *IEEE Transactions on Industrial Informatics*, *18*(8), 5371–5382. doi:10.1109/TII.2021.3126316

Alhayani, B., Mohammed, H. J., Chaloob, I. Z., & Ahmed, J. S. (2021). Effectiveness of artificial intelligence techniques against cyber security risks apply of IT industry. *Materials Today: Proceedings*, 531. doi:10.1016/j.matpr.2021.02.531

Alipour, H., Al-Nashif, Y. B., Satam, P., & Hariri, S. (2015). Wireless anomaly detection based on IEEE 802.11 behavior analysis. *IEEE Transactions on Information Forensics and Security*, *10*(10), 2158–2170. doi:10.1109/TIFS.2015.2433898

Alizadeh, M., Abolfazli, S., Zamani, M., Baharun, S., & Sakurai, K. (2016). Authentication in mobile cloud computing: A survey. *Journal of Network and Computer Applications*, *61*, 59–80. doi:10.1016/j.jnca.2015.10.005

Armitage, J. (2022). *Cloud Native Security Cookbook*. O'Reilly Media, Inc.

Baclic, O., Tunis, M., Young, K., Doan, C., Swerdfeger, H., & Schonfeld, J. (2020). Artificial intelligence in public health: Challenges and opportunities for public health made possible by advances in natural language processing. *Canada Communicable Disease Report*, *46*(6), 161–168. doi:10.14745/ccdr.v46i06a02 PMID:32673380

Brathwaite, S. (2022, August 19). *The state of AI in Cloud Security*. Software Secured. https://www.softwaresecured.com/the-state-of-ai-in-cloud-security/

Čeponis, D. (2021). *Research of machine and deep learning methods application for host-level intrusion detection and classification* [Doctoral dissertation, Vilniaus Gedimino technikos universitetas].

Chang, H., & Choi, E. (2011). User authentication in cloud computing. In *Ubiquitous Computing and Multimedia Applications: Second International Conference*. Springer.

Choudhury, A. J., Kumar, P., Sain, M., Lim, H., & Jae-Lee, H. (2011, December). *A strong user authentication framework for cloud computing. In 2011 IEEE Asia-Pacific Services Computing Conference*. IEEE.

Ciolacu, M., Tehrani, A. F., Binder, L., & Svasta, P. M. (2018, October). Education 4.0-Artificial Intelligence assisted higher education: early recognition system with machine learning to support students' success. In *2018 IEEE 24th International Symposium for Design and Technology in Electronic Packaging(SIITME)* (pp. 23-30). IEEE.

ROI4CIO. (2023). *Darktrace the enterprise immune system*. ROI4CIO. https://roi4cio.com/catalog/en/product/darktrace-the-enterprise-immune-system

Dasgupta, D., Roy, A., & Nag, A. (2017). *Advances in user authentication*. Springer International Publishing. doi:10.1007/978-3-319-58808-7

Fowers, J., Ovtcharov, K., Papamichael, M., Massengill, T., Liu, M., Lo, D., & Burger, D. (2018, June). A configurable cloud-scale DNN processor for real-time AI. In *2018 ACM/IEEE 45th Annual International Symposium on Computer Architecture (ISCA)* (pp. 1-14). IEEE. 10.1109/ISCA.2018.00012

Ganne, A. (2022). Cloud data security methods: Kubernetes vs Docker swarm. *International Research Journal of Modernization in Engineering Technology, 4*(11).

Ge, Z. (2022). Artificial Intelligence and Machine Learning in Data Management. *Future And Fintech, The: Abcdi And Beyond*, 281.

Grispos, G., Glisson, W. B., & Storer, T. (2019). How good is your data? Investigating the quality of data generated during security incident response investigations. *arXiv preprint arXiv:1901.03723*. doi:10.24251/HICSS.2019.859

Hammoud, A., Sami, H., Mourad, A., Otrok, H., Mizouni, R., & Bentahar, J. (2020). AI, blockchain, and vehicular edge computing for smart and secure IoV: Challenges and directions. *IEEE Internet of Things Magazine, 3*(2), 68–73. doi:10.1109/IOTM.0001.1900109

Hillmann, J., & Guenther, E. (2021). Organizational resilience: A valuable construct for management research? *International Journal of Management Reviews, 23*(1), 7–44. doi:10.1111/ijmr.12239

Kavitha, S., Bora, A., Naved, M., Raj, K. B., & Singh, B. R. N. (2021). An internet of things for data security in cloud using artificial intelligence. *International Journal of Grid and Distributed Computing, 14*(1), 1257–1275.

Kumar, G. (2019). A review on data protection of cloud computing security, benefits, risks and suggestions. *United International Journal for Research & Technology, 1*(2), 26–34.

Kumari, A., Gupta, R., Tanwar, S., & Kumar, N. (2020). Blockchain and AI amalgamation for energy cloud management: Challenges, solutions, and future directions. *Journal of Parallel and Distributed Computing, 143*, 148–166. doi:10.1016/j.jpdc.2020.05.004

Lal, N. A., Prasad, S., & Farik, M. (2016). *A review of authentication methods.*

Mishra, S., & Tyagi, A. K. (2022). The role of machine learning techniques in internet of things-based cloud applications. *Artificial intelligence-based internet of things systems*, 105-135.

Moisset, S. (2023, May 25). *How security analysts can use AI in Cybersecurity.* freeCodeCamp.org. https://www.freecodecamp.org/news/how-to-use-artificial-intelligence-in-cybersecurity/#:~:text=AI%2Dbased%20solutions%20can%20also,activity%20and%20alert%20security%20teams

Muralidhara, P. (2017). The evolution of cloud computing security: addressing emerging threats. *International journal of computer science and technology*, *1*(4), 1–33.

Pacheco, J., & Hariri, S. (2018). Anomaly behavior analysis for IoT sensors. *Transactions on Emerging Telecommunications Technologies*, *29*(4), e3188. doi:10.1002/ett.3188

Rani, P., Kavita, Verma, S., Kaur, N., Wozniak, M., Shafi, J., & Ijaz, M. F. (2021). Robust and secure data transmission using artificial intelligence techniques in ad-hoc networks. *Sensors (Basel)*, *22*(1), 251. doi:10.339022010251 PMID:35274628

Sarker, I. H., Kayes, A. S. M., Badsha, S., Alqahtani, H., Watters, P., & Ng, A. (2020). Cybersecurity data science: An overview from machine learning perspective. *Journal of Big Data*, *7*(1), 1–29. doi:10.118640537-020-00318-5

Sayegh, E. (2023, August 23). Artificial Intelligence and clouds: A complex relationship of collaboration and concern. *Forbes*. https://www.forbes.com/sites/emilsayegh/2023/08/23/artificial-intelligence-and-clouds-a-complex-relationship-of-collaboration-and-concern/?sh=7472b5725c19

Sharma, M., & Elmiligi, H. (2022). Behavioral biometrics: Past, present and future. *Recent Advances in Biometrics*, 69.

Siriwardhana, Y., Porambage, P., Liyanage, M., & Ylianttila, M. (2021, June). AI and 6G security: Opportunities and challenges. In *2021 Joint European Conference on Networks and Communications & 6G Summit (EuCNC/6G Summit)* (pp. 616-621). IEEE. 10.1109/EuCNC/6GSummit51104.2021.9482503

Srikanth. (2022, October 14). *Ai preventing next-gen data loss*. Techiexpert. https://www.techiexpert.com/ai-preventing-next-gen-data-loss/

St. Laurent, N. (2023, July 17). *Data loss prevention and the value of Artificial Intelligence*. CISCO. https://blogs.cisco.com/government/data-loss-prevention-and-the-value-of-artificial-intelligence

Stone, M. (2023, January 17). *2023 Cloud Data Loss Prevention (DLP) overview: Concentric*. Concentric AI. https://concentric.ai/a-deep-dive-on-cloud-data-loss-prevention-dlp/

Sun, L., Jiang, X., Ren, H., & Guo, Y. (2020). Edge-cloud computing and artificial intelligence in internet of medical things: Architecture, technology and application. *IEEE Access : Practical Innovations, Open Solutions*, *8*, 101079–101092. doi:10.1109/ACCESS.2020.2997831

Tahir, M., Sardaraz, M., Mehmood, Z., & Muhammad, S. (2021). CryptoGA: A cryptosystem based on genetic algorithm for cloud data security. *Cluster Computing, 24*(2), 739–752. doi:10.100710586-020-03157-4

Wagh, N., Pawar, V., & Kharat, K. (2020). *Educational Cloud Framework—A Literature Review on Finding Better Private Cloud Framework for Educational Hub.* Microservices in Big Data Analytics: Second International, ICETCE 2019, Rajasthan, India.

Zhang, A., Wang, L., Ye, X., & Lin, X. (2016). Light-weight and robust security-aware D2D-assist data transmission protocol for mobile-health systems. *IEEE Transactions on Information Forensics and Security, 12*(3), 662–675. doi:10.1109/TIFS.2016.2631950

Zhao, D., Traore, I., Sayed, B., Lu, W., Saad, S., Ghorbani, A., & Garant, D. (2013). Botnet detection based on traffic behavior analysis and flow intervals. *Computers & Security, 39*, 2-16.

Zolfaghari, B., Yazdinejad, A., Dehghantanha, A., Krzciok, J., & Bibak, K. (2022). The dichotomy of cloud and iot: Cloud-assisted iot from a security perspective. *arXiv preprint arXiv:2207.01590.*

Chapter 10
Privacy and Surveillance in Digital Era:
A Case for India

Vikram Singh

 https://orcid.org/0000-0001-5757-9111
Ch. Devi Lal University, Sirsa, India

Sanyogita Singh
Panjab University, India

ABSTRACT

With a majority of the human population on the internet, online activity has become the order of the day. And that is why the internet is where criminals of every hue and color join forces and innovate in innovative ways. Not all "lands" have laws to deal with cybersecurity and privacy. Criminals across the globe have exploited the gap between technology and laws. The Indian Constitution recognizes privacy as a fundamental right, albeit with certain restrictions. Governments, in the name of providing secure cyberspace, infringe upon the privacy rights of citizens. And surveillance in India is chiefly governed by the Indian Telegraph Act u/s 5, which permits the government and its agencies to surveil provided a qualifying prerequisite preexists. Various surveillance apparatuses have been established by the GoI. Allegedly, the surveillance regime poses a grave threat and a chilling effect on privacy and freedom of expression rights as enshrined in the Indian Constitution. This chapter discusses cybersecurity, privacy, and surveillance regimes in Indian cyberspace.

DOI: 10.4018/979-8-3693-1431-9.ch010

1. INTRODUCTION

As of July 2023, 5.19 billion people (64.6 percent of the world's population) were active internet users, making up more than half of the global population, according to a Statista report. A whopping 4.88 billion of these Internet users make use of social media platforms (Petrosyan, 2023). These numbers suggest that social, political, and economic activities are bound to occur in the cyberspace. With an overwhelming majority of the world's population regularly using the Internet, cyberspace exhibits all the characteristics of Homo sapiens, including participation in unlawful and unethical practices like breach of privacy.

Experts believe that the abrupt withdrawal of ₹500 and ₹1000 banknotes from circulation on November 8, 2016, at midnight, prompted an increase in electronic transactions, which is why cybercrimes have skyrocketed in post-demonetization India (Table 4). Many residents who lacked computer literacy were forced to use electronic means of payment, which exposed cyberquacks (NCRB, 2019). The media began to pay attention to news about cybercrimes and related concerns about invasions of privacy and the electronic surveillance regime in mid-July 2021. This was due to an investigative story on Pegasus Project published by The Wire, which was based on the findings of a global consortium of 17 media groups. *The Wire* published an investigative story on *Pegasus Project* based on the findings of a consortium of 17 media groups spread across the globe (Varadarajan, 2021).

Understanding the cyberspace ecosystem is necessary for securing it. This ecosystem consists of following main components: (1) the internet and telecommunications infrastructure, which is measured by the number of phone and mobile connections, the number of internet users, the amount of e-commerce, and social media users in the nation; (2) the regulatory framework that governs the operations of the cyberspace, such as electronic communications, digital signature certificates, and e-commerce transactions; (3) guaranteeing the safety of cyber-citizens while they carry out their everyday tasks in cyberspace, fostering confidence in the country's cyberinfrastructure, and putting in place an emergency response system to handle cyber-threats; (4) offering a thriving, robust, and resilient cyberspace ecosystem for conducting economic activities; (5) creation of a strong and technologically advanced cyber-legal environment for the purpose of making citizens feel safe, criminals feel scared and uneasy, and governments feel honest and reluctant to spy on their innocent citizens; (6) a well-prepared society and armed forces to defend its territory in any conflict-like situation in the fifth dimension, or cyberwarfare; and (7) most importantly, preparing its society and citizenry for living a peaceful and contented life in the cyberspace by raising digital literacy levels to the point where a sizable portion of the population can work, understand, and produce content for the consumption of others in the cyberspace (Chhibbar, 2020).

The laws and regulations and directives issued (under the laws) by the government to regulate cyberspace comprise the regulatory framework for cyberspace. The twin matters of cyberspace security and digital privacy in India is governed by the Information Technology Act of 2000 and Digital Personal Data Protection Act, 2023. Right to privacy, in general, is protected by Constitution of India as well. The Indian Supreme Court has interpreted the Indian Constitution in a way that makes the right to privacy for citizens fundamental, even though it is subject to certain restrictions. Cyberspace privacy violations are getting more frequent, simpler to carry out, and can have catastrophic consequences. Cyber-surveillance of targeted individuals and large groups by public and corporate organisations is another facet of cyberspace. The Indian Telegraph Act, 1885, u/s. 5(2) and Rule 419(A), notified under this act, govern surveillance in India.

This chapter covers these two closely related aspects of cyberspace, namely, cybersecurity, privacy, and surveillance in the Indian cyberspace. Next section and its subsections are devoted to security concerning Indian cyberspace. Privacy aspects of citizen's rights in cyberspace and relevant law has been discussed Section 3 and cyber-surveillance regime in India has been discussed in Section 4, wherein subsection 4.3 has covered various aspects of Pegasus Project.

2. CYBERSPACE ECOSYSTEM IN INDIA

Looking back, we can see that India's cyberspace began to take shape in 1976 when the National Informatics Centre (NIC) began offering information technology solutions to the government. With the establishment of the NICNET, a wide area network (WAN) by NIC with nodes at each district head office nationwide, in 1987, the Indian cyberspace saw even more growth. NIC used to leverage very small aperture terminal (VSAT) technology to offer email and Internet services during the 1980s and early 1990s. In 1986, the Department of Electronics launched the Education and Research NETwork (ERNET) with funding from the United Nations Development Programme. ERNET supplied University Libraries with Internet and domain services based on both TCP/IP and OSI protocol stacks for approximately ten years. Later, TCP/IP was used for all internet traffic, and OSI was no longer used or supported. After the US government withdrew control over ARPANET in 1989–1990, the Internet quickly expanded outside of the US. Fueled further by the advent of smartphones, availability of cellular mobile phone technology in the latter half of the 20th century, and the sharp decline in Internet data prices in the latter half of the 21st century, the number of Internet users and traffic volumes in India saw an exponential rise. These developments have given rise to the creation of huge Indian cyberspace with the globally largest number of social media users

Table 1. Tele-penetration in India – June 30, 2023 (TRAI, 2023)

Particulars	Wireless	Wired	Total
Telephone subscribers in million (urban)	626.07	27.63	653.70
Telephone subscribers in million (rural)	517.51	2.68	520.19
Total subscription in million	1143.58	30.31	1173.89
Urban tele-density (percent)	127.56%	5.63%	133.19%
Rural tele-density (percent)	57.53%	0.30%	57.83%
Overall tele-density (percent)	82.25%	2.18%	84.43%

and a very big e-Commerce marketplace (Chhibbar, 2020). Following subsection discusses the key components comprising Indian cyberspace ecosystem:

2.1 Cyberspace Infrastructure

The cyberspace infrastructure includes internet penetration in the society in terms of mobile subscribers, internet users, social media users, e-commerce users; and bandwidth, quality, and cost-to-user of the Internet. Table 1 shows the teledensity in rural and urban India in terms of absolute numbers and percentage subscribers.

India has 692 million Internet users, 467 million social media users, and 1170.75 billion (more than 117 crores) mobile subscriber customers as of January 2023 - see Table 2 (DataReportal, 2023). The primary cause of the rise in Internet and social media users may be traced to the shift in enterprises, education, consulting, and socialisation activities—such as alumni meetups, weddings, and consolation meetings—to online platforms following the Covid-19 pandemic's travel limitations.

2.1.1 Cyberspace Regulatory Framework

It consists of legislative artifacts such as cyberlaws and privacy laws, and statutes and regulatory guidelines issued by government for controlling cyberspace. It also encompass the initiatives and strategies adopted by the government to encourage

Table 2. Pan-India internet and social media users (DataReportal, 2023)

Particulars	Jan 2020	Jan 2021	Jan 2023
Mobile subscriptions (million)	1087	1110	1170.75
Internet users (million)	577	624	692
Social media users (million)	370	448	467

public and private investment for development of safe, seamless, and ubiquitous cyber-infrastructure; unbiased and open policies for the distribution of spectrum; opening cyberspace to emerging technologies; creating a system for controlling fake news and illicit cyber-activity; and signing bilateral and multilateral cooperation treaties with other nations.

The extent of security of its cybercitizens and cyber-infrastructure, and readiness and quickness of its cyber-emergency response system define an amicable cyberspace. The creation of cybersecurity strategies, the establishment of a reliable emergency response system, and the provision of cybersecurity training to those in charge of managing, upkeep, and security of vital information infrastructures in the public and commercial sectors—namely, finance, telecommunications, transportation, power, defence, and nuclear—are all necessary to provide a secure ecosystem.

As many as thirty six central organisations are in place in India to protect its cyberspace paraphernalia. In addition, India was one of the first few nations to establish a National Cyber Security Policy, but not much has changed in the field of digital security since the policy's introduction in 2013. The Ministry of Home Affairs, Government of India, outlined the steps to strengthen the nation's cybersecurity in December 2018 in light of the fact that more and more common Indian citizens—read non-techies—are using electronic services for financial transactions since the country saw a demonetization in November 2016. Sensing a little success of 2013 policy and ascension of new challenges like cloud services, use of artificial intelligence in foiling the security measures, and general data protection requirements as per global standards, a National Cybersecurity Strategy 2023 (Draft) has been drafted and circulated to replace the 2013 Cyber Security Policy (Singh & Malik, 2021). Indian cybersecurity comprises the following elements:

- National Security Council of India
- National Information Board
- The Information Technology Act, 2000 amended in 2008
- National Cyber Security Policy, 2013
- National Cyber Security Strategy, 2023 (proposed draft)
- Computer Emergency Response Team – India (CERT-In)
- National Technical Research Organisation (NTRO)
- National Critical Information Infrastructure Protection Centre (NCIIPC)
- Indian Cyber Crime Coordination Centre (I4C)
- IT (Intermediary Guidelines and Digital Media Ethics Code) Rules, 2021
- Information Technology Amendment Rules, 2023
- Digital Personal Data Protection Act, 2023

Table 3. Global cybersecurity index 2020 (GCI-ITU, 2021)

Country	Rank	Score	Country	Rank	Score
United States	1	100	UAE	5	98.06
United Kingdom	2	99.54	Malaysia	5	98.06
Saudi Arabia	2	99.54	Lithuania	6	97.93
Estonia	3	99.48	Japan	7	97.82
South Korea	4	98.52	Canada	8	97.67
Singapore	4	98.52	France	9	97.6
Spain	4	98.52	India	10	97.5
Russian Federation	5	98.06			

2.1.2 Cyber-Economy

The cyber-ecosystem of a country also comprises the economic activities in the related sectors like design, development, manufacturing, export, and import of ICT artifacts and e-commerce infrastructure to name a few. Unsafe cyberspace hinders the growth of economic activities in general (The Centre for Internet and Society, n.d.)

According to (Keelery, 2020), value of the internet economy across India has increased from 125b in FY 2017 to 250b FY 2020 (in billion U.S. dollars). In 2015-16, as much as 5.6 percent of India's gross domestic product was contributed by the Internet economy. In absolute terms, in the year 2020, $537.4 billion was contributed by the Internet economy in the gross domestic product of India. This makes a 16 percent share of the Internet economy in the national GDP-2020. The report in (Sikdar, 2021) further says that half of the Internet economy share came from smartphone apps ($270.9 billion). Phone users working with mobile apps contributed 70% to mobile traffic (Sikdar, 2021).

In the Global Cybersecurity Index 2020 (Table 3), India is placed at 15th position with a score of 97.5 out of 100 and is ranked at position 10.

2.1.3 Cybercrime and Relevant Laws

Like any walk of public life, cyberspace is also marred by the ecosystem of crime and criminals operating in cyberspace. For cyberspace worth being a space, it must have a matching and dynamic legal framework to deal with commercial transactions and crime committed in cyberspace. Bringing the cybercriminals to book is a nightmare for the bricks-and-mortar model of justice delivery (NCRB, 2019; Mehta & Singh, 2012; Mehta & Singh, 2012a).

Table 4. Cybercrimes in India (NCRB, 2022)

Year	Cases Registered	Year	Cases Registered
2005	481	2014	9622
2006	453	2015	11592
2007	556	2016	12317
2008	464	2017	21796
2009	696	2018	27248
2010	1322	2019	44546
2011	2213	2020	50035
2012	3477	2021	52974
2013	5893		

Table 5. Global cybercrime trends (IC3, 2020)

2013 Global Cybercrimes		2016 Global Cybercrimes	
Country	Share	Country	Share
USA	39%	USA	23.96%
UK	8%	China	9.63%
Angola, China, Italy, Turkey, Ukraine	3% each	Brazil	5.84%
India, Bangladesh, Brazil, Israel, Holland	2% each	India	5.11%

2.1.4 Cyber-Literacy

Cyber-literacy involves imparting cognitive and technical skills for effective use of internet resources through cyber-infrastructure and computer & internet education. In 2021, India had a rank of 73 out of 120 countries for internet literacy (Basuroy, 2022). It is thus essential to focus on digital awareness and education. For a cyber-ecosystem to thrive it must relate itself to the masses. It requires that a common citizen is literate in cyberspace activities. Further, for self-sustaining cyberspace, a country also needs to invest in higher education and research funding in cyber-technologies. Mass cyber-awareness programmes and large-scale training programmes for service staff, law enforcement workforce, and judiciary are also required (Mehta & Singh, 2013; Shah, 2016). The main components of cyber-literacy include the following:

Working in cyberspace: It requires basic technical knowledge for accessing cyberspace through tools like web browsers, emails clients, social networking apps, citizen/customer service portals of governments and banks, e-commerce portals, etc. In India, around 30m (3 crores) people were trained under *Pradhan Mantri Gramin Digital Saksharta Abhiyan* – a GoI digital literacy programme over a period of three years (2018-2020). Of this, 12.6m people were trained in basic digital literacy in the FY 2020-21 alone (Statista Research Department, 2021).

Understanding cyberspace: Understanding the modus operandi of cyberspace helps appreciate the appropriate online behaviour, net etiquettes, honey traps, and common dos and don'ts while surfing and working in various domains of cyberspace. It also helps an individual in understanding the terms of use of internet & services and verification of genuineness of the internet content.

Creating cyberspace content: This comprises using tools to design, develop and distribute/upload the text, hypertext, images, videos, RSS feeds, and blogs on the Internet. Creating and uploading the active Internet content transforms an Internet consumer into participating netizen.

2.1.5 Cyberwarfare

For many, cyberwarfare is no longer restricted to fiction books and sci-fi movies. In the future, wars shall be fought in the fifth dimension namely cyberspace, apart from four traditional warfare dimensions – land, sea, air, and space. A sound and safe cyber-ecosystem require vibrant cyber diplomacy and foreign policy and preemption capabilities in the cyber warfare domain. Further, it is implicit that all the components comprising the cyberspace ecosystem grow harmoniously thereby meaning that technological developments in cyberspace; awareness, education, and research in cyberspace technologies; economic and commercial activities in cyberspace; cyber laws and cybersecurity policies and infrastructure; etc. all keep pace with each other, lest skewed cyberspace may result.

2.2 Regulatory Mechanisms in Indian Cyberspace

Primarily, the Indian cyberspace is regulated by the Information Technology Act, 2000 with its latest amendments affected in 2008 – almost thirteen years back at the time of writing of this chapter. Thirteen years is quite a long time when developments in the information technology field are considered. Quite a few technologies like cloud computing and storage, social computing, big data analytics, and blockchain technologies have sprung up in the meantime. New technologies have provided several new avenues and modi-operandi to cybercriminals. Various players in cyberspace are resorting to highly sophisticated ways to snoop on targets for varied purposes (Sarmah et al., 2017; Shailesh et al., 2015).

Table 6. Punitive provisions of Information Technology Act [IT Act 2000, n.d.)

Cyber Offence/Cybercrime Description	Relevant Section	Nature of Offence	Penalty/Punishment/ Compensation up to
Damage to computer and communication system	43	Civil offence	₹1 crore
Failure to protect data	43A	Civil offence	₹5 crore
Failure to report to Authority	44A	Civil offence	₹15 lac/instance
Failure to file periodic return	44B	Civil offence	₹5k/day
Failure to maintain record	44C	Civil offence	₹10k/day
Contravention not specified in ITAA2008	45	Civil offence	₹25k
Tampering with computer source documents	65	Cognizable Bailable	3 year jail term OR ₹20 lac fine OR both
Failure to comply with the orders of controller	68	Non cognizable Bailable	2 year jail term OR ₹1 lac fine OR both
Failure to assist the agency	69	Cognizable nonbailable	7 year jail term AND fine
Failure to block public access when so directed	69A	Cognizable nonbailable	7 year jail term AND fine
Failure to decrypt data for law enforcing agency	69B	Cognizable bailable	3 year jail term AND fine
Unauthorized access to protected system	70	Cognizable nonbailable	10 year jail term AND fine
Offensive or false messages	66A	Cognizable bailable	3 year jail term AND fine
Receiving stolen computer	66B	Cognizable bailable	3 year jail term OR ₹1 lac fine OR both
Identity theft	66C	Cognizable bailable	3 year jail term AND ₹1 lac fine
Cheating by personation	66D	Cognizable bailable	3 year jail term AND ₹1 lac fine
Violation of privacy	66E	Cognizable bailable	3 year jail term OR ₹2 lac fine OR both
Cyberterrorism	66F	Cognizable nonbailable	Life term
Obscenity in electronic format	67	Cognizable bailable nonbailable (after 1st conviction)	3 year jail term AND ₹5 lac fine (1st conviction) 5 year jail term AND ₹10 lac fine (after 1st conviction)
Pornography in electronic format	67A	Cognizable and bailable (nonbailable after 1st conviction)	5 year jail term AND ₹10 lac fine (1st conviction) 7 year jail term AND ₹10 lac Fine (after 1st conviction)
Pedophilia in electronic format	67B	Cognizable bailable (nonbailable after 1st conviction)	5 year jail term AND ₹10 lac fine (1st conviction) 7 year jail term AND ₹10 lac fine (after 1st conviction)

Although the IT Act 2000 and its subsequent amendment in 2008, are attempted at bridging the gap of proper national cyber laws in India, it could not come up to the expectations of the dynamically changing turf of Indian cyberspace. With the world of cybercrime becoming murkier by the day exponential growth of social media in the second decade of the 21st Century, the present provisions of Indian cyber law seem wanting in teeth and expanse (Sawaneh et al., 2021). Further, the false sense of anonymity in cyberspace lends quite a good number of unsuspecting and innocuous internet users to the net of cybercriminals. Major punitive provisions provided in the ITA Act 2008 to administer and govern cyberspace are presented in Table 6:

In relation to the corporate operations, techno-legal directives including cyber forensics and cybersecurity diligence of the Companies Act of 2013 also are applied in addition to IT Act. The Companies (Management and Administration) Rules, 2014 drafted and notified under the ambit of the Companies Act 2013 have prescribed the guidelines regarding companies' cybersecurity obligations, lest the onus lies on upon the company top-level management (Kaur & Ramkumar, 2022).

3. PRIVACY IN INDIAN CYBERSPACE

Information and communication technologies in cyberspace affect human privacy in very different ways that were previously not even possible. An individual's privacy may be encroached upon in more ways than one and digital devices have only added teeth and expanse to such incursions upon personal privacy (Schwartz, 1999). Modern smartphone devices are all potential surveillance devices with several apps having user permissions to access phonebooks, microphones, cameras, location, images, audio, and videos files stored on the device (Lindsay, 2014; Ardhapurkar et al., 2010).

Further, with ever-increasing social and economic interactions taking place online, individuals share their personal information while using various internet services and particularly so while surfing social media networks. The personal information so shared include name, email, birthday, vocation, hometown, workplace and home addresses, real-time locations, interests, status, relationships, photos, videos, etc. Millions of smartphone users of free mobile apps run at a risk of their personal information being sold and misused by the promoters of free apps. In lands with no Data Protection Laws/Rules, there is no legal remedy in case of misuse of personal information by these apps. In the situation elucidated above, the importance of data and privacy protection gains importance (Khan, 2013).

Table 7. Data protection laws - 194 Jurisdictions (UNCTD, n.d.)

Status of Data Protection Law	Number of Countries	% of Countries
Countries having Data Protection Legislation in place	137	71%
Countries having Draft Data Protection Legislation	18	9%
Countries having no Data Protection Law	29	15%
Countries providing no data	10	5%

3.1 Privacy Laws in India

In India, two cases, decided by its Supreme Court, have cast doubts on its citizens' Right to Privacy. In both the cases, namely, M.P. Sharma v. Satish Chandra of 1954 and Kharak Singh v. State of Uttar Pradesh of 1962, the apex court had held that privacy was not a fundamental right. These two decisions were pronounced by eight-judge and six-judge benches, respectively. But, in 2017, a nine-judge constitutional bench of the Supreme Court of India, in Puttaswamy v. Union of India, has ruled that the right to privacy is a fundamental right, albeit, it is not absolute.

Thereafter, independent analysts have held informational privacy as one of the facets of privacy rights. Threats to the breach of information privacy may come from state as well as non-state actors. This warrants that Union Govt. place a personal information protection regime to safeguard the informational privacy of its citizens.

3.2 Privacy Invasion in Digital Age

The incursion on someone's privacy could happen in one of the following two ways (DeVries, 2003):

(a) Intruding the personal privacy (breech of autonomy): This involves intrusion upon an individual's seclusion by way of snooping, recording, or listening to her/his private activities; or trespassing into an individual's private property. Concrete instances of this kind of intrusion include photographing someone in a try-room, call recording, hacking someone's account on a bank server or an email server.

(b) Misuse of private information: This kind of breach involves disclosing an individual's private information, such as medical history or sexual orientation, without permission. Very often, there is an overlap in two types of privacy invasion, and sometimes occurrence of one kind of privacy breach leads to another kind of breach as well.

Breach of personal information may have far-reaching repercussions on an individual's life. For instance, our personal information like customer names, Aadhaar number (India's national personal id), addresses, income and expenditure details, call details, internet access details, travel details, purchase preferences, music and entertainment choices, credit score, and credit history, study loans, driving records, educational certificates, marital status, etc. are not stored on devices within our confines and control (DeVries, 2003).

Another dimension of informational privacy is someone's medical and health-related information, wherein its breach might lead to life-shattering experiences, for example, disclosure of someone being HIV positive can ruin her/his social life and can even affect the professional life and workplace. Personal information databases maintained by banks, NBFCs, Govt. agencies like UIDAI/Aadhaar pose problems in the realm of digital information privacy (Singh & Malik, 2021).

Search, watch, and seizure of someone's digital property and personal information is quite different from that of physical property. Digital information may be searched, copied, and (mis)used even without the owners being aware of it. Once the unauthorized control of digital resources is taken, existing digital information may be changed/manipulated and new incriminating material may be planted. Further, searching and removing a "banned" book or a copy of a periodical from circulation is difficult in comparison to tracking (and taking down) the digital content on the Internet (Schwartz, 1999; (Schwartz, 1999a)).

In the Bhima-Koregaon case of 2018, the digital forensic report by a US-based cyber- forensic lab "Arsenal Consulting" has claimed that the computer of one of the co-accused Ms. Rona Wilson was hacked, and as many as 22 computer files were planted days after the January 2018 violence. These files have been cited as evidence by Maharashtra police and the National Investigating Agency (NIA) of India (Schwartz, 1999b).

Data mining and big data analytics can be used by state authorities to profile marginalized sections of society to draft welfare schemes or to snoop them to preempt any impending uprising. China is using its "Police Cloud" to keep track of its religious and ethnic minorities. Social media companies have more access to users' personal information than the user herself/himself (Benwal, 2021).

3.3 Privacy in Digital India

Privacy concerns in the digital age could be attributed to state and non-state actors, both. In the name of *all-important* national security, security agencies of the state profile their citizens based on their digital life. Profiling a whole lot of public segments through a *bricks-and-mortar* model may be impractical, whereas, digital profiling techniques are faster and less resource-intensive. Accordingly, states indulge in citizen profiling in the name of (and for the purpose of) national security. Of lately, the capabilities of non-state actors to process and (mis)use has increased dramatically. For instance, Uber knows where we visit frequently. In case, we use Google online maps, then Google knows we stopped for a roadside tea or a breakfast (Network of Chinese Human Rights Defenders, 2018).

Although, specific personal data and information protection law has not been promulgated in India as yet (July 31, 2021), yet sections 43, 66(E) and 72 specify the penalty and punishment for violation of privacy. Section 43 of the IT Act, although not directly addressing the privacy issue, provides for payments of compensation up to ₹1 crore for downloading, copying, extracting, destroying, deleting, or altering any data or information that may cause a wrongful loss or wrongful gain to a person.

Section 66E addresses, albeit limited to images of the private area of a person, the issue of *punishment for violation of privacy* in the digital space. Anybody who intentionally, and without her/his consent, captures, publishes, or transmits the images of her/his private area is liable to be punished with a jail term of up to three years or a fine up to ₹2 lac, or both. Section 72 also specifies the *"penalty for breach of confidentiality and privacy"*. A person who discloses to other person(s) "any electronic record, book, register, correspondence, information, document or other material without the consent of the person concerned" in a manner not otherwise allowed in IT Act, shall invite punishment of a jail term up to two years, or a fine up to ₹1 lac or both. Next subsection (3.4) discusses the Digital Personal Data Protection Act 2023 - another stepping stone in the privacy debate in Indian cyberspace in somewhat more details.

3.4 Digital Personal Data Protection Act 2023

Both, to protect the right of individuals to protect their personal data and recognise the need to process such personal data for governance purposes, on August 11, 2023, the Indian government announced the passage of the Digital Personal Data Protection Act, 2023, which, in contrast to the European GDPR, places a strong emphasis on consent as the main legal justification for processing personal data. The following requirements must be met: consent must be "freely given," "specific," "informed," "unconditional," and shown by a "clear affirmative action." However, the Act gives the federal government the authority to inform specific Data Fiduciaries—any organisation or person that chooses the objectives and methods for processing personal data—of certain exemptions from specific requirements. One such need is "notice for consent." In the case of these entities, the duty to obtain free and informed permission will still be in effect. However, it may be claimed that a Data Principal (a person whose data is being processed) will not be able to grant informed consent if there is no requirement to provide notification for consent (Mathias, 2023).

However, questions are raised regarding the government's exemptions, which would undermine the act's intended purpose. In certain circumstances, the rights of the data principal and the duties of the data fiduciaries (apart from data security) do not apply. These consist of (i) crime prevention and investigation, and (ii) the upholding of legal rights or claims. Certain activities may be exempted by the central government from the Bill's application through notification. These consist of (i) processing by government organisations for the sake of state security and public order, and (ii) gathering data for research, archiving, or statistical purposes (Nagrajan et al., 2023).

The Act also leaves open the possibility of harm from the handling of personal data. Financial losses, identity theft, reputational damage, prejudice, and illogical surveillance and profiling could all occur as a result of processing personal data. The Data Principal also lacks the ability to receive data in an interoperable format or the right to restrict the release of personal data via the internet, in contrast to entities of a similar nature in several jurisdictions (Nagrajan et al., 2023).

The passing of DPDP Act 2023 has had two effects on RTI Act 2005. The RTI Act is explicitly prohibited from allowing a third party to get an individual's personal information, even though it has improved an individual's access to personal information kept by the controllers and data fiduciaries. The DPDP Act requires reporting of specific misuses of personally identifiable information about individuals that has been digitally stored, but it makes no mention of potential harm to Data Principal. However, it does provide for the imposition of penalties in the event that its prohibitions are violated. The legislation does not address compensation or insurance coverage for injury caused to Data Principal. Additionally, this Act offers no safeguards against state overreach for people's private information (Nagrajan et al., 2023).

4. CYBER-SURVEILLANCE IN INDIA

Beginning in the second decade of the 21st century, the government agencies in India have introduced a wide array of cyber-surveillance measures, marking a shift from targeted surveillance through traditional means to mass surveillance through digital means. Surveillance, for the purpose of the present discussion, may be classified in the following two ways: (i) government and private surveillance, and (ii) targeted and mass surveillance. In this section, governments' targeted and mass cyber-surveillance apparatus in general and the Indian Union in particular, have been discussed (The Centre for Internet and Society, n.d.).

Reasonable expectation of privacy to protect human dignity has been acknowledged and incorporated to varying extents in the constitutional frameworks of democracies across the globe. But, since the writing of constitutions and the digital revolution are not temporally synchronized, states' security agencies don't apply the same standard to cyberspace searches as are usually applied to the search of physical evidence. In the hyped national security environment all over the world, efforts of digital tuning of legislative frameworks are not paying due attention to digital privacy concerns (DeVries, 2003).

In India, the vast powers of the Union and Provincial governments to snoop on its citizens stem from the Indian Telegraph Act, 1885, and the Information Technology Act, 2000. While the former law was promulgated in the colonial era itself, the latter too has reflections of pre-independence laws. To add to brawl are the state acts like MCOCA, permitting the state government to intercept communications.

4.1 Targeted and Mass Surveillance

Targeted surveillance is a form of scrutiny aimed at a specific individual or an organization of interest upon the existence of a prior suspicion. In most jurisdictions including India, there is a concept of lawful interception under certain circumstances. Lawful targeted surveillance is allowed in Indian jurisdiction under Telegraph Act, MCOCA[1], and UAPA[2].

Mass surveillance encompasses an entire or a major part of a population or an ethnic group to monitor their social, economic, political, or even religious interactions. This kind of surveillance is often carried out by agencies on the part of provincial and federal governments. United States' NSA's project PRISM belonged to this category. The legality of mass surveillance projects is decided by the law of the land, but as a rule of thumb, mass surveillance is an indicator of a totalitarian regime. Mass surveillance is often linked to compromised dignity and privacy of citizens, limited political and civil rights, as also to national security, terrorism, and social unrest. The remainder of this section discusses the various surveillance regimes in India.

U/s 5 of the Indian Telegraph Act, 1885, the governments – Union as well as State - are empowered to take possession of any *telegraph*[3] or intercept any *telegraphic communication*[4] in the matters of public emergency, public safety, national security, sovereignty and integrity, friendly relations with foreign states, and to pre-empt an offence. The law, however, pre-requires the Officials of the Ministry of Home Affairs to follow the procedure laid down in the law[5]. In India, although telephone tapping is considered a serious invasion of an individual's privacy and the right to privacy has been upheld as a fundamental right[6]. All in all, citizens' privacy right in India is not absolute but is subject to certain restrictions laid down by its apex court.

Under section 14 of MCOCA, interception of wire, electronic, or oral communications are permitted by the prior approval of competent authority, and the intercepted artifacts are admissible evidence in the court of law. Such permissions are allowed only to investigating officers of the rank of Superintendent of Police and further subject to rigorous prerequisites.

Also, UAPA has been alleged to interfere with a person's privacy in an arbitrary and unlawful manner. "Personal Knowledge" of the investigating officer without any written validation whatsoever from the judiciary suffices for searches, seizures, and arrests. UAPA also empowers the officers to intercept the accused person's communications without any independent prior approval or monitoring.

4.1.1 Lawful Interception and Monitoring

Installation of *Lawful Interception* mechanism is a prerequisite for every licensed telecommunication network and internet service provider. LIM is a secret mass cyber- surveillance system deployed and operated by the Centre for Development of Telematics (C- DOT). This mechanism allows the GoI agencies to intercept voice and video calls, text and multimedia messages, internet traffic, subscriber's particulars, call history, recharge and payment history, emails, browsing history, and other such user activities of Indian users. The LIM mechanism is deployed at the gateways of desired ISP(s) and its capabilities bypass the ISPs. Of late, as a licensing requirement, telcos in India have to deploy LIM on their own to enable the GoI to "lawfully intercept" the user traffic (The Centre for Internet and Society, n.d.; Xynou & Hickok, n.d.).

LIM is carried out u/s 5(2) of the Indian Telegraph Act, 1885, read with rule 419(A) of Indian Telegraph (Amendment) Rules of 2007, notified under this Act. Further, on January 2, 2014, the Department of Telecommunication, GoI has issued Standard Operating Procedures (SOPs) for lawful interception of communications in the country (The Centre for Internet and Society, n.d.; Xynou & Hickok, n.d.).

4.1.2 National Intelligence Grid (NATGRID)

NATGRID was established in 2009 in the aftermath of the Mumbai terror attacks of 2008. NATGRID has access to real-time data collected by 21 different organizations including banks, insurance companies, railways, immigration, telcos, and income tax department. NATGRID shares its information with 11 central agencies which include the Research and Analysis Wing (RAW), Intelligence Bureau (IB), National Investigation Agency (NIA), Central Bureau of Investigation (CBI), and Narcotics Control Bureau (NCB), and Enforcement Directorate (ED) among others. NATGRID is a tool, and not an agency, that helps security agencies to find and locate terror suspects by using data sets pooled by 21 organizations mentioned above. NATGRID has been criticized on the two charges – usurping of privacy in the name of national security and efficacy in achieving its stated goal of preempting terror, for it does not share information with states' agencies (The Centre for Internet and Society, n.d.; Xynou & Hickok, n.d.).

4.1.3 Centralised Monitoring System (CMS)

CMS is a centralized mechanism of intercepting telecommunications bypassing the telecom operators to screen all kinds of traffic including messages, voice calls, and internet usage. Software running at CMS server(s) is supposed to sniff the telecom signals to classify them into genuine communication and otherwise. Intricacies of traffic analysis algorithms have become very sophisticated with the incorporation of classification techniques empowered by data mining, big data analytics, machine learning, and deep learning. Fig. 1 and Fig. 2 below show monitoring mechanisms in the pre-CMS and post- CMS era, respectively (The Centre for Internet and Society, n.d.; Xynou & Hickok, n.d.; Litton, 2015).

Figure 1. Indian surveillance regime in pre-CMS era
(Nagrajan et al., 2023)

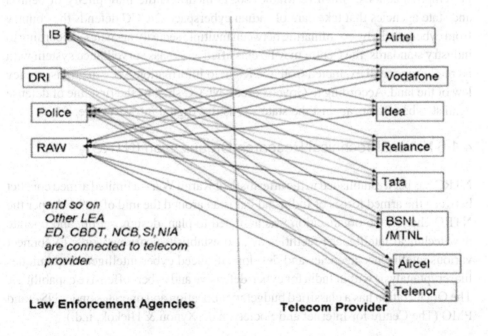

4.1.4 Network Traffic Analysis (NETRA)

NETRA is an Indian Government software system developed for interception and analysis of internet traffic filtered using a pre-defined but dynamic logic. The system has been designed and developed by the Centre for Artificial Intelligence and Robotics (CAIR), a Defence Research and Development Organisation (DRDO) laboratory, and is used by the IB and RAW, India's internal and external security outfits, respectively. Modus operandi wise, NETRA is different from the CMS. NETRA watches everything the target users do online, whereas the CMS taps the communication network. NETRA can monitor the text contents of your emails, Facebook chats, and blogs using keyword-based filters (The Centre for Internet and Society, n.d.; Xynou & Hickok, n.d.; Joshi & Das, 2015).

4.1.5 National Cyber Coordination Centre (NCCC)

The National Cyber Coordination Centre (NCCC), an MHA entity, is a multiagency entity capable of performing assessing the cyber-threats in real-time. This Centre generates reports whereupon law enforcement agencies can take proactive and pre-emptive actions. Singh & Malik (2021) mentions the multiplicity of central and state agencies that take care of Indian cyberspace. NCCC defends the country from cyberattacks by coordinating between multiple security agencies. According to industry standards, the Centre may be classified as a mass surveillance system with its modus operandi exempted from the Right to Information Act – the transparency law of the land. According to Govt. sources, NCCC shall be the first line of defense against cyber threats against the state's sensitive digital infrastructure.

4.1.6 National Technical Research Organization (NTRO)

NTRO has been established in the aftermath of Kargil War – a limited armed conflict between the armed forces of India and Pakistan around the mid of 1999. As per the NTRO charter, the organization was assigned to plan, design, set up, and operate new technical intelligence facilities as also establish secure networks to connect various intelligence agencies and develop advanced cyber-intelligence techniques like cryptanalysis within India for cyber-defensive and cyber- offensive capabilities. The Organization has a classified budgetary allocation and operates under NSA and PMO (The Centre for Internet and Society, n.d.; Xynou & Hickok, n.d.).

Figure 2. Indian surveillance regime in post-CMS era
(Xynou & Hickok, n.d.)

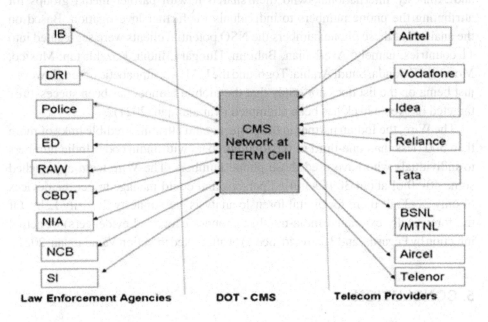

| Law Enforcement Agencies | DOT - CMS | Telecom Providers |

4.2 The Pegasus Row

The world got to know of iOS exploitation by Pegasus[7] in August 2016 when Ahmed Mansoor, an Arab human rights activist received a text message having a hyperlink to secretive information about torture in UAE prisons. Investigation of the hyperlink by the Canada-based Citizen Lab confirmed it as social engineering spyware. The investigation attributed the spyware to the NSO Group and the spyware code contained entries relevant to Apple's iOS7 released in 2013.

In India, people heard the name of Pegasus in 2019 when *Whatsapp* notified that its communications might have been compromised by the Pegasus spyware during a 12-day time window stretching from April 29, 2019 to May 10, 2019). Another controversy involving Pegasus started on July 18, 2021 when *The Wire* broke a story on *The Pegasus Project* - a collaborative investigation involving more than 80 journalists belonging to 17 media groups based in 10 countries spread over Europe, the Americas, Middle-East and South Asia. The project has been coordinated by the *Forbidden Stories* of France. Cyber-forensics tech-support was lent by Amnesty International's Security Lab and the results were peer- reviewed by Canada-based *Citizen Labs* (Varadarajan, 2021).

The data (about 50000 phone numbers) were accessed by the Forbidden Stories and Amnesty International, who then shared it with partner media groups for attributing the phone numbers to individuals for further investigation. Based on the analysis of these phone numbers the NSO potential clients were segregated into 11 countries, namely, Azerbaijan, Bahrain, Hungary, India, Kazakhstan, Mexico, Morocco, Rwanda, Saudi Arabia, Togo, and the UAE – in alphabetic order. However, just being on the list does not imply that the mobile number has been successfully targeted or even a hack has been attempted (Varadarajan, 2021).

The Wire, the Indian partner in the project could attribute credible links of more than 300 (less than one-third of the total numbers with India code) India numbers to individuals who have used those phone numbers. The Wire team approached some 40-50 of about 300 identified persons and could manage to get the devices of only 21-22 of them for digital forensic analysis ate Amnesty Security Labs. Of the forensically examined India-number phones, 7 retained evidence(s) of actual infection by Pegasus, and 3 had evidence(s) of attempted infection Varadarajan, 2021).

5. CONCLUSION

Security was a primary consideration in the conception, design, and evolution of the Internet. It began as a communication network and developed into a platform for exchanging resources and data. Back then, the main goal was to build a strong and resilient communication network that would not collapse completely in the event of partial damage. And, with the global cyberspace almost half the size of the global human population (and ever-increasing), cyberspace inherits all the traits of human society – crime inclusive. India is rapidly turning into a digital nation in all spheres of public life, including banking, education, entertainment, military, and NBFCs. As a result, privacy breaches, surveillance, and cybercrimes are increasing in both terms - absolute and relative numbers. Moreover, the security of Indian cyberspace has become a topic of public discussion, as most people use digital technologies for daily chores and they have to part with their personal details (Aadhaar card) for almost all govt. schemes.

In absence of any specific cybersecurity law in India, the Information Technology Act, 2000, a dismally inadequate legislation in this respect, has to be invoked among other traditional provisions. The principal aim of the Information Technology Act and its 2008 amendment, which added digital signatures, was to facilitate e-commerce and related payment concerns. Furthermore, in the meantime, a number of novel information technologies have advanced from research to implementation, including big data analytics, machine learning, deep learning, internet of things, cloud computing, and cloud storage. The IT Act is not simply aware of these developments.

Accordingly, to come at par with technological developments and to bridge the gaps between technology adoption and the corresponding legal framework, and reassure the individuals and organisations operating in the cyberspace, the Information Technology Act needs to be amended and a separate special cybersecurity law dealing with different facets of the Indian cyberspace also needs to be promulgated.

With the IoT becoming mainline, internet-enabled devices have become ubiquitous, in homes and at workplaces. Internet-enabled appliances and other devices are assigned IP addresses so that they could be operated and controlled remotely, for example, while driving home you can issue voice commands to your car to switch on the air conditioner(s) of your home so that you will find your home cool when you arrive, or you can open the main entrance to the house without alighting your car. An individual's privacy may be encroached upon in more ways than one. But, at the same time, these capabilities add to cyber-threats and possibly incursions in your at-home privacy.

Promulgation of the Indian DPDP Act, 2023 is an effort towards addressing the issue of safeguarding individuals' digital privacy and personal data. It gives people more control over their data by introducing strict data protection regulations. The act requires data localization for sensitive personal information and places onus on data controllers and processors to guarantee data privacy and security. Along with strong penalties for non-compliance, it also creates a Data Protection Authority to monitor adherence to the act and enforce it. In India, where the digital landscape is expanding rapidly, the DPDP Act is a major step towards preserving digital privacy. However, to what extent does the Act achieves its objectives, will become evident in the times to come.

IoT and digital devices like smart phones have the potential to act as lethal surveillance devices, and particularly so, with several apps having user permissions to access the content of the devices and I/O devices to receive and transmit the data using the smartphone. And, with the focus shifted to government surveillance in wake of Pegasus Project telephone data leaks, it is high time the government's projects with the potential to surveil its masses are debated and questioned. Pegasus leaks themselves need to be probed at an appropriate level and truth must prevail so that the citizenry is reassured about their right to privacy, the robustness of India cyber-infrastructure, and the security and safety of their digital assets including devices, data, and software.

REFERENCES

Ardhapurkar, S., Srivastava, T., Sharma, S., Chaurasiya, V., & Vaish, A. (2010). Privacy and Data Protection in Cyberspace in Indian Environment. *International Journal of Engineering Science and Technology*, 2(5), 942–951.

Basuroy, T. (2022, October 14). *Cybercrime in India - Statistics & Facts 2021*. Statista. https://www.statista.com/statistics/1097071/india-number-of-cyber-crimes-by-leading-state/

Benwal, N. (2021, February 11). Bhima-Koregaon Case: Key Evidence Was Planted? *The Free Press Journal*. https://epaper.freepressjournal.in/2990683/Free-Press-Mumbai-Epaper-Edition/11-Feb-2021

Chhibbar, A. (2020). *Navigating the Indian Cyberspace Maze - Guide for Policymakers*. KW Publishers Pvt. Ltd.

DataReportal. (2023, September 25). *Digital 2023 India*. Data Reportal. https://datareportal.com/reports/digital-2023-india

DeVries, W. T. (2003). Protecting Privacy in the Digital Age. *Berkeley Technology Law Journal*, *18*(1), 283–311.

GCI-ITU. (2021). *Global Cybersecurity Index 2020*. ITU. https://www.itu.int/dms_pub/itu-d/opb/str/D-STR-GCI.01-2021-PDF-E.pdf

Government of India. (n.d.). *Information Technology Act 2000 Amended in 2008*. Ministry of Electronics and Information Technology, Government of India. https://www.meity.gov.in/writereaddata/files/it_amendment_act2008%20%281%29_0.pdf

IC3 (Internet Crime Complaint Centre). (2020). *Internet Crime Report 2020*. IC3. https://www.ic3.gov/Media/PDF/AnnualReport/2020_IC3Report.pdf

Joshi, M., & Das, P. (2015). *India's Intelligence Agencies: In Need of Reform and Oversight*, Issue Brief #98. Observer Research Foundation. https://www.orfonline.org/wp-content/uploads/2015/07/IssueBrief_98.pdf

Kaur, J., & Ramkumar, K. R. (2022). The Recent Trends in Cyber Security: A Review. *Journal of King Saud University. Computer and Information Sciences*, *34*(8), 5766–5781. doi:10.1016/j.jksuci.2021.01.018

Keelery, S. (2020, October 16). *Internet Economy Value India: 2016-2020*. Statista. https://www.statista.com/statistics/792053/india-value-of-internet-economy/

KhanR. (2013). *Cyber Privacy Issues in India*. SSRN. doi:10.2139/ssrn.2357266

Lindsay, D. (2014). The Right to Be Forgotten - European Data Protection Law. In Emerging Challenges in Privacy Law: Comparative Perspectives (pp. 290-293). Cambridge University Press.

Litton, A. (2015). The State of Surveillance in India: The Central Monitoring System's Chilling Effect on Self-Expression. *Washington University Global Studies Law Review, 14*(4), 799-822. https://openscholarship.wustl.edu/cgi/viewcontent.cgi?article=1556&context=law_globalstudies

Mathias, S. (2023, August 22). *Indian Parliament Passes Digital Personal Data Protection Act*. Kochhar & Co. Legal Update. https://www.huntonprivacyblog.com/2023/08/22/india-passes-digital-personal-data-protection-act/

Mehta, S., & Singh, V. (2012). Internet Usage and Cyber-Victimization in Indian Society. *Academic Discourse, 1*(2), 124–131.

Mehta, S., & Singh, V. (2012a). Combating the Cybercrime: Practices in Indian Society. *International Journal of Computing and Business Research, 3*(3), 1–10.

Mehta, S., & Singh, V. (2013). A Study of Awareness about Cyberlaws in the Indian Society. *International Journal of Computing and Business Research, 4*(1), 124–131.

Nagrajan, R., Kumar, A., Kartik, J. C. S., Gupta, S., Kakarya, D., Raghuvanshi, P., & Mathur, S. (2023). *Decoding the Digital Personal Data Protection Act, 2023*. KPMG. https://assets.kpmg.com/content/dam/kpmg/in/pdf/2023/08/decoding-the-digital-personal-data-protection-act-2023.pdf

National Crimes Record Bureau. (2022). *Crime in India 2021*. NCRB. https://ncrb.gov.in/en/Crime-in-India-2021

Network of Chinese Human Rights Defenders. (2018, July 16). (submitted to). [The Committee on the Elimination of Racial Discrimination.]. *Joint Civil Society Report*.

Petrosyan, A. (2023, September 22). Worldwide Digital Population 2023. Statista Report. https://www.statista.com/statistics/617136/digital-population-worldwide/

Rathore, M. (2023, July 10). *Amount of Trained Beneficiaries in Digital Literacy in India FY 2018-2022*. Statista Report. https://www.statista.com/statistics/1196927/india-trained-be neficiaries-in-digital-literacy-scheme/

Sarmah, A., Sarmah, R., & Baruah, A. J. (2017). A Brief Study on Cyber Crime and Cyber Laws of India. *International Research Journal of Engineering and Technology*, *4*(6), 1633–1641.

Sawaneh, I. A., Kamara, F. K., & Kamara, A. (2021). Cybersecurity: A Key Challenge to the Information Age in Sierra Leone. *Asian Journal of Interdisciplinary Research*, *4*(1), 35–46. doi:10.34256/ajir2114

Schwartz, P. M. (1999). Internet Privacy and the State. *Connecticut Law Review*, *815*. https://escholarship.org/uc/item/37x3z12g

Schwartz, P. M. (1999a). Internet Privacy and the State. *Connecticut Law Review*, *815*. https://escholarship.org/uc/item/37x3z12g

Schwartz, P. M. (1999b). Privacy and Democracy in Cyberspace. *Vanderbilt Law Review*, *52*, 1609–1701. https://escholarship.org/uc/item/2fq3v1mj

Shah, J. (2016). A Study of Awareness About Cyber Laws for Indian Youth. *International Journal of Trend in Scientific Research and Development*, *1*(1), 10–16. doi:10.31142/ijtsrd54

Sikdar, A. (2021, March 10). The Economic Impact of Internet in India. Economic Update. *Times of India*. https://timesofindia.indiatimes.com/blogs/economic-update/th e-economic-impact-of-internet-in-india/

Singh, V., & Malik, V. (2021). Indian Cybersecurity Turf: A 2020 Position Paper. *Journal of Network Security*, *9*(1), 42–47.

The Centre for Internet and Society. (n.d.). *India's Surveillance State – Communications Surveillance in India*. CIS. https://cis-india.org/internet-governance/blog/security-surv eillance-and-data-sharing.pdf

The Centre for Internet and Society. (n.d.). *State of Cyber Security and Surveillance in India - A Review of the Legal Landscape*. CIS. https://cis-india.org/internet-governance/blog/state-of-cyber-security-and-surveillance-in-india.pdf

TRAI (Telecom Regulatory Authority of India). (2023, August 24). *Highlights of Telecom Subscription Data as on 30th June, 2023*. Press Release No. 27/2023. TRAI. https://www.trai.gov.in/sites/default/files/PR_No.77of2023.pdf

UNCTD. (n.d.). *Data Protection and Privacy Legislation Worldwide.* The United Nations Conference on Trade and Development. https://unctad.org/page/data-protection-and-privacy-legislation-worldwide

Varadarajan, S. (2021, July 30). Revealed: How the Wire and its Partners Cracked the Pegasus Project and What it Means for India. *The Wire.* https://thewire.in/media/revealed-how-the-wire-partners-cracked-pegasus-project-implications-india

Xynou, M., & Hickok, E. (n.d.). *Security, Surveillance and Data Sharing Schemes and Bodies in India.* Centre for Internet and Society, India. https://cis-india.org/internet-governance/blog/security-surveillance-and-data-sharing.pdf

ENDNOTES

[1] Maharashtra Control of Organised Crime Act, 1999 (MCOCA) was firstly promulgated as an ordinance and subsequently ratified by the Maharashtra state legislature. The Bill became the law with the assent of the President of India under Article 245 of Indian Constitution that applies to subjects in concurrent list.

[2] Unlawful Activities (Prevention) Act, 1967 (UAPA) is aimed at preempting the happening of unlawful activities directed against the integrity and sovereignty of Indian state.

[3] The amended Telegraph Act defines the term 'telegraph' as: "*any appliance, instrument, material or apparatus used or capable of use for transmission or reception of signs, signals, writing, images and sounds or intelligence of any nature by wire, visual or other electro-magnetic emissions, Radio waves or Hertzian waves, galvanic, electric or magnetic means.*" In digital age, taking possession of the telegraph translates in to taking possession of communication and computing devices used to affect wired or wireless communications. This includes mobile phone, smart phones, tablets, notepads, laptops, personal computers, etc.

[4] Telegraphic communications include the use of wired and wireless telegraphy, telephones, teletype, radio communications and digital data communications. And, the instant law does not define the term "interception", therefore, the popular dictionary meaning of the word is adopted, i.e. an act of listening in and recording communications, intended for another party, for the purpose of intelligence or counterintelligence.

[5] In a 1996 decision in People's Union for Civil Liberties v. Union of India & Anr, the Supreme Court of India bench comprising Justices Kuldip Singh and Saghir Ahmad has stated that *"The first step under Section 5(2) of the Telegraph Act is the occurrence or happening of any public emergency or the existence of a public safety interest. Thereafter, the competent and concerned authority under section 5(2) of the Telegraph Act is authorized to pass an order of interception after recording its satisfaction that it is mandatory or expedient so to do in the interest of:*

i. Sovereignty and integrity of India.

ii. Security of the State.

iii. Friendly relations with foreign states.

iv. Public order.

v. Preventing incitement or inducement to the commission of an offence.

In the instant case, the Supreme Court of India has termed the telephone tapping a serious invasion into individual's privacy, but allowed the lawful interception has been allowed under certain circumstances u/s 5 of the Indian Telegraph Act, 1885.

[6] In the Puttaswamy v. Union of India case-decision delivered on August 24, 2017, a nine-judge constitutional bench of the Supreme Court of India has held the right to privacy as a fundamental right protected under Part III, Article 21 of the Indian Constitution.

[7] Pegasus is a spyware developed by an Israeli cybersecurity firm NSO Group. As per the group's claims, the Pegasus is licensed only to Government organisations (intelligence agencies, law enforcement agencies, and militaries) vetted by Israeli Defence Ministry, to combat terror and crime. The software suit compromises and surveilles on the targeted devices running Windows, MacOS, Android, and iOS operating systems.

Chapter 11
A Model for Trust Decision, Data Analysis, and Evaluation to Identify Quality Web Services

Shobhana Kashyap
National Institute of Technology, Jalandhar, India

Avtar Singh
iD https://orcid.org/0000-0001-7526-6813
National Institute of Technology, Jalandhar, India

ABSTRACT

Cloud computing has emerged as a powerful paradigm for delivering web services, and includes scalability, flexibility, and cost efficiency. Due to functional overlap and diversity, web services form a major challenge for selecting adequate services to develop user-provider trust. To address the issue, this study presented a machine learning based trusted model to assist users in selecting trustworthy web services. In the initial stage, using K-Means clustering method the services are selected based on three clusters such as high, medium, and low trust. Next, the trust score is generated by evaluating performance parameters to identify the best services. Experiments conducted with QWS datasets demonstrate that the proposed approach efficiently predicts adequate services with a minimum error rate and high accuracy gain. This technique achieves a 99.32%, 99.36% and 99.48% accuracy rates for the low, medium, and high trust prediction, respectively. The result shows that it is more effective than existing approaches and builds a strong trust relation between users and providers.

DOI: 10.4018/979-8-3693-1431-9.ch011

1. INTRODUCTION

Cloud computing has sparked a great deal of interest from both industry and academia since it was proposed (Z. Li et al., 2017). The National Institute of Standards and Technology (NIST) (Mell & Grance, 2011) says that, this computing provides lots of services to the users, including PlatformAsAService (PaaS), InfrastructureAsAService (IaaS), and SoftwareAsAService (SaaS) (G. Kaur & Bala, 2021; Sahi, 2015). Examples include Amazon Web Services (AWS) (Hormozi et al., 2012; Shyam & Manvi, 2016), Microsoft Azure (Nawrocki et al., 2021), Google Cloud Platform (GCP) (Liu et al., 2017; Mehmood et al., 2018), and many more. These services offer on-demand access to computing resources, such as databases, storage, and virtual machines (VMs), as well as higher-level services such as analytics, machine learning, and software applications (Abdullah et al., 2020; G. Kaur & Bala, 2021; O. Sharma & Saini, 2016). There are several options for selecting a single service to complete a specific task. For example, if an individual wants to store their data and asks for a storage service, there are multiple options available. Choosing one of the best storage services among many is, however, a time-consuming and tedious task (Rahimi et al., 2021).

One of the services in cloud computing is web service (WS), which refers to a cloud-based service that can be accessed over the internet using standard web protocols such as Hypertext Transfer Protocol (HTTP) (Padhy et al., 2011). The selection of the best cloud service is an important factor in establishing trust between the user and the provider (Whaiduzzaman et al., 2014). It also has a massive impact on the success and productivity of the business. Trust in the cloud refers to the belief and confidence that a cloud user (CU) has in the ability of a cloud service provider (CSP) to securely and effectively store, process, and manages sensitive data and applications. It covers various aspects, including data privacy, security, reliability, and compliance with regulatory standards.

A high level of trust is essential for customers to adopt cloud services and for CSPs to build and maintain a loyal customer base (Gupta et al., 2013). It is a key element in the achievement of cloud computing and can affect the adoption, utilization, and overall satisfaction of customers with cloud services (W. Li et al., 2021). According to research (Hasnain et al., 2022), a trustworthy WS has low response time (RT) instance values and high throughput (TP) instance values. In contrast to this, the disparity between the promised instance values and the original values acquired by users indicates untrusted services (Hasnain et al., 2020). But the previous studies found that high TP and low RT values can be indicators of a trusted WS, but they do not guarantee trustworthiness. A service may have high TP and low RT values but still have vulnerabilities or lack adequate security measures, making it untrusted. Additionally, even if a service provides guaranteed instance values, these values may not match the original values achieved by users due to various factors such as network conditions, server capacity, and the complexity of the requested operation.

Classifying cloud services as trusted or untrusted depends on several factors, including the security measures used by the service provider, the reputation of the provider, and the level of control the user has over their data and applications. Trustworthiness in WSs is a complex issue that involves a combination of factors, including security measures, reputation, compliance, user control, and performance. The values for RT and TP should be considered along with other factors when evaluating the trustworthiness of a WS.

When examining past research, it was observed that the preponderance of studies paying attention only on web service selection (WSS) without addressing customer-provider trust. In addition, classifying services based on QWS traits and determining whether services fall under the categories of trustworthy or untrusted is a challenging experience. The precise prediction of possible system performance-enhancing services is also a research hurdle. These are the gaps that motivate us to propose a solution to these issues. The current research solves the problem of selecting the optimal service. The first approach makes the group of different categories of trust based on quality attributes. A new set of data is generated, and a novel predictive model is then proposed. To check the performance of the model, the research compares the novel technique with the existing one. A trust score formula is applied to give rank to the most optimal service. This trusted model helps to select efficient services.

The following contributions are made in this paper:

- The paper addresses the challenge of categorizing services as trusted or untrusted by employing a clustering method that evaluates the value of each instance.
- The paper provides an extensive analysis of the quality metrics attained by users and providers in the area of web services.
- A hybrid approach called Supervised Ensemble-Based Prediction (SupEbP) that empowers users in selecting trustworthy web services.
- The innovative predictive method introduced in this study is thoroughly compared with existing methods, allowing for the identification of superior performance measure classifiers.
- By employing a trust score mechanism, this study successfully resolves the selection of the best Web Service Subset (WSS), ensuring optimal decision-making.

The remainder of the work is discussed as follows: the relevant literature about the existing trust is included in Section 2 of this research. Section 3 outlines the paper's organization. Section 3 describes the problem statement and formulation of

Figure 1. Structure of the paper

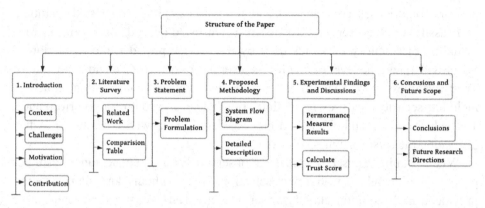

the research. Section 4 is a detailed description of the proposed methodology; Section 5 describes the experimental findings and discussion; and Section 6 summarizes the proposed study and discusses its implications for future research. Fig. 1 depicts the general organization of the paper.

2. LITERATURE SURVEY

This section discusses the importance of trust in selecting WSs in cloud environments. Based on the discussions, the requirements for a qualified belief assessment approach are given; these standards are used to evaluate all existing technologies using a standard set of criteria.

Numerous businesses are currently shifting to the cloud due to its extensive range of services. And CUs are growing more reliant on these services, while cloud suppliers are doing their best to provide the finest service possible to their clients, which is a vital job. Previous research has shown the importance of trust for both CUs and CSP. This is one method for improving both sides' performances. As a result, trust evaluation and prediction are viable answers to this problem. Many service life cycle stages, including service selection (Ding et al., 2014; Somu et al., 2018)service composition (Somu, Gauthama, et al., 2020; Yasmina, 2022), and service recommendation (Gao et al., 2020; Su et al., 2017; Wang et al., 2019a) play a crucial role in establishing trust between the provider and the recipient. In the preponderance of these studies, it is considered that the attributes of service values are known. Even so, user, time, location, etc. all affect a service's QoS value. Hence, QoS prediction is crucial to service lifecycles.

Reviewing the literature has shown that there are several distinct attempts to encourage the automation of a few aspects of the WSS process. The majority of researchers agree that some parts of this process can be taken over by software agents. The most important difference is in the criteria that the agents use to choose who to appoint. Some researchers use semantics to determine whether a WS is relevant to the current task (De Moor & Van Den Heuvel, 2004), while others focus on the quality of the WSs [4]. But a lot of researchers have come to realize that trust and reputation are important for the success of a system built with the chosen WSs [6].

The study (Hasnain et al., 2020) presents a method to rank WSs based on TP and RT using a trust prediction and confusion matrix. According to (S. K. Sharma et al., 2016) job opportunities and trust are the two most essential variables affecting cloud computing adoption. The research (Saoud et al., 2016) conducted a trust evaluation of online services using fuzzy-based credibility, and they highlighted the limits of those trust-based WSS methodologies to facilitate utilized end-user ratings. Researchers are also concerned about ambiguity and discrimination, which influenced end-user evaluations for online services. To address the ambiguity and distortions in end-user evaluations of online services, a fuzzy-based methodology was presented. Several tests were conducted to assess the recommended trust approach. The projected approach enhanced trust feature and resilience, according to the

Table 1. Comparison between different trusts based web service selection techniques

References	Problem	Technique	Solution	Dataset/Platform	Limitation
(Z. Li et al., 2017)	Trusting cloud services is harder due to the open environment and monolithic management structure.	Methodology for evaluating the credibility of services considering multiple factors	Identify the fraudulent ratings and dynamic enhancement of the credibility evaluation	Net logo platform	Work is limited to simulation tools. No experimental work is implemented on real cloud applications.
(Mohanty et al., 2010)	Rapidly adding new WSs to a dynamic company environment might degrade service quality and customer satisfaction.	This study used well-known classification algorithms to predict WS quality using quality criteria.	This research can categorize a new WS into one of four model-based classifications.	QWS Dataset	NA
(Wang et al., 2019b)	While choosing cloud services, consumers must consider QoS diversity and complexity.	The CSTEM model is proposed.	The model appears to protect entities and improves user experience and communication efficiency.	Myeclipse platform integrated with CloudSim simulation package	By incorporating additional trust dynamic updating elements of cloud services assessment, the CSTEM could be enhanced. The real cloud prototype system is missing.

continued on following page

243

Table 1. Continued

References	Problem	Technique	Solution	Dataset/Platform	Limitation
(Somu et al., 2018)	Researchers in service-oriented contexts concern about the trustworthiness of assessment data because objective and subjective evaluation data affect service selection model accuracy.	The HBFFOA model is proposed.	The proposed method finds reliable CSPs.	WS-DREAM Dataset	NA
(Hasnain et al., 2020)	Depending on the assessment criteria, ranking WSs is a difficult task.	Ranking online services according to TP and RT using a proposed trust prediction and decision table.	Predicting trustworthy and untrustworthy customers when invoking a WS has optimized selection in a group of similar online services.	WS-Dream dataset	The proposed model only measures confidentiality and reliability of WSs. Security of WSs can't be found.
(Hasnain et al., 2022)	Accurate prediction is important for selection of WSs.	Proposed identifying WSs using trust scores from the categorization method.	Solve the problem of selection of WSs using ranking mechanism.	WS-Dream dataset	Work is limited to Classification techniques regression techniques will be added in future.
(Somu, R, et al., 2020)	The determination of service rating according to QoS is an NP-Complete issue.	Improved Binary Gravitational Search Strategy (IBGSS) technique is proposed.	The paper provides solution for choosing an appropriate CSP from the few available possibilities.	WS-Dream dataset	NA
(Ding et al., 2014)	Cloud service evaluation is expensive and time-consuming; it's not feasible to evaluate all vendors' trustworthiness for each client.	Developed a new service selection method that incorporates missing value prediction and multi-attribute dependability.	Assess trustworthiness by meeting consumer expectations.	QoS Dataset	Work is limited to static approach.
(Gao et al., 2020)	As the number of services is enormous and growing quickly, it's necessary to establish a user's eligibility.	Proposed a context-aware NCF model and fuzzy clustering technique.	The CNCF model finds latent characteristics in past QoS data and cluster features.	WS-Dream dataset	Time series forecasting and deep learning concepts will be added in future.
Proposed Method	Selection of optimal service among various is a tedious task. It lacks the trust relationship between client and service provider.	Categorize the trusted and untrusted services using the clustering method. And then predict the category of the service that is reliable to the user.	Helps to determine the best service which leads to an increase in the performance and efficiency of the organization.	QWS Dataset	Work is limited to WSB framework. The model only worked for QWS attributes.

results. The study (Sherchan et al., 2011) offers a Hidden Markov Model (HMM) based trust prediction model for WSs. Using a dynamic training pool, the proposed model employs a dynamic training approach that integrates temporal sensitivity. The idea of a continually updated training pool allows the system to assimilate the most recent data-based knowledge. The study also covers the development of the suggested model and algorithm, as well as its application to real-world data and assessment. The study (Su et al., 2017)suggests a trust-aware technique for accurate customized QoS prediction. Researchers discover a group of comparable services by aggregating them and estimate the QoS of active users by combining the QoS data of credible similar consumers with that of similar services. The current research is focused on the selection process therefore, Table 1 represents the comparison among the previous and proposed research for WSS to build trust.

3. PROBLEM STATEMENT

Cloud computing is capable to provide multiple services for a single application. The most difficult aspect of this computing is picking the appropriate service depending on the user's needs. This process helps to resolve the trust issues while user chooses the services for their system. This section discusses the existing system to determine the problem formulation and Fig. 2 depicts the general architecture of cloud computing trusted model.

3.1 Problem Formulation

The optimal selection of cloud WSs for building trust whenever it takes input data from the services offered by CSPs. The research considers a single CU denoted by {U1} and multiple CSPs' named as {S1, S2, S3,…, Sn}.There are various questionnaires originated from the user side to service provider regarding service selection. *Can a user Trust their service?* Which service is efficient, reliable, and optimal for their organization? Multiple servers who provide services denoted by {WS1, WS2, WS3, …,WSn} each of them assures the user about their services. It is challenging for the user to choose the best one based on the trust factor. Therefore, the current research introduced a reliable model that returns the solution to the problem.

Figure 2. General architecture of trusted model

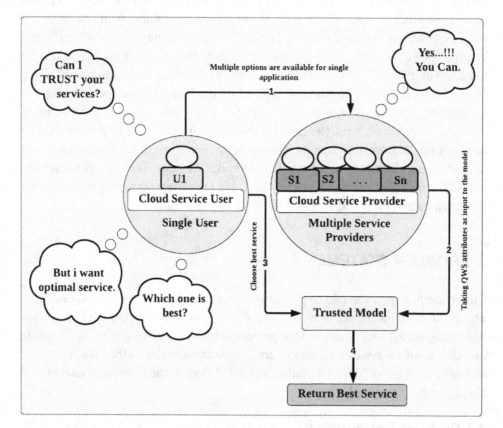

4. PROPOSED METHODOLOGY

This section describes the proposed technique along with the process that involves trust prediction of WS clients. The subsections define the proposed strategy which will be discussed in further detail.

4.1 Dataset Collection

The experiment performed on two WSs datasets collected from the zenodo website, generated by (Al-Masri & Mahmoud, 2008), and whose URL links are presented in Table 2. The QWS1 dataset comprises 365 WSs, while the QWS2 dataset has 2,507 WSs with their QWS measures using the WSB architecture.

Each instance in this record shows a WS and the nine QWS measures that relate to it. The first nine components are QWS measurements that have been evaluated over six days using several WS benchmarking tools. The QWS values are the arithmetic

Table 2. URL link of web services

S. No.	Web service name	Link
1.	QWS1	https://zenodo.org/record/3557012#.Y-DHZ3ZBxPZ
2.	QWS2	https://zenodo.org/record/3557008#.Y-DHr3ZBxPa

Table 3. Dataset Description

ID	Attribute Name	Description	Unit
F1	Availability	Percentage of successful requests	(in %)
F2	Best Practices	The extent to which a Web service follows	(in %)
F3	Compliance	The percentage of a WSDL document that adheres to the WSDL standard	(in %)
F4	Documentation	Measure of documentation (i.e. description tags) in WSDL	(in %)
F5	Latency	Time taken for the server to process a given request	(in ms)
F6	Reliability	The proportion of error messages to total messages	(in %)
F7	Response Time	The amount of time takes to submit a request and then get a response to that request	(in ms)
F8	Success ability	Number of response / number of request messages	(in %)
F9	Throughput	The number of responses to request messages	(invokes/second)
F10	Services Name	Name of the Web service	NR
F11	WSDL Address	Location of the Web Service Definition Language (WSDL) file on the Web	NR

*NR=Not Required

mean of the values measured during the specified time period. The last two options provide the service name and WSDL document reference. The description of the dataset can be shown in Table 3.

4.2 Data Preprocessing

The data collection phase is followed by data preparation for data analysis or machine learning efforts. It refers to the processes and procedures used to cleanse, modify, and prepare raw data for further analysis. Typically, the preparation of data comprises the following steps. Data cleaning entails finding and addressing missing or inaccurate numbers, outliers, and discrepancies in the data. The transformation of the data includes transforming data from one format to another, such as translating category variables to numeric variables or scaling variables to a common range. Data reduction is the process of lowering the data's complexity by deleting duplicate or superfluous elements or through sampling. The data integration process involves merging data from numerous sources and addressing any inconsistencies or disputes. Data discretization is the process of categorizing continuous variables into discrete groups. Normalization of data entails scaling the data to a common range to avoid some variables from overwhelming the analysis across all variables.

For data preparation, the current study employs the data normalization approach, the formula for which is presented in Equation 1. The primary objective of data normalization is to bring all of the features or variables to the same scale and limit the impact of characteristics with big values, which can sometimes control the learning algorithm or analysis. Normalizing the data guarantees that each feature contributes an equal amount to the analysis or machine learning model. The method guarantees that the data are of high quality, consistent, and appropriate for further analysis, simulation, or visualization. There are many normalization strategies used in data preprocessing, however, min-max normalization is employed in this research. This method normalizes the data from 0 to 1 and equation 1 is presented for min-max normalization.

$$Normalizaion = \frac{Attribute_{value} - Min\_value_{attribute}}{Max\_value_{attribute} - Min_{value attribute}} \tag{1}$$

4.3 Categorization of Trust Value

The experimental data consist of two distinct datasets. In the first sample group, the rankings of the services are classified as platinum, gold, silver, and bronze. It is absolutely uncomplicated to forecast the online service's ranking. The second data contains simply WS quality characteristics. Hence, it is difficult to forecast the classes of WSs based on trust, which complicates the selection process. This research employs clustering as a solution to the challenge of ranking WSs.

K-means clustering learning technique is used to group data points into a predetermined number of clusters based on their similarity. It is a common approach for grouping data, and its implementation is quite straightforward. Below is the K-means clustering algorithm's step for categorizing types of services (High Trust, Medium Trust, and Low Trust) are discussed.

K-Means Clustering Algorithm
Input: Features= {F1, F2, F3,..., F9}
Output: Generate Target Class.
Split the data into 3 clusters {HT, MT, LT} //Comment: Number of clusters (NoC)
START
STEP1 Select the features
Choose the NoC {K=3} into which data is splitting i.e.{ HT, MT,LT}
STEP 2 Initialize Centroids
Randomly choose K data points as cluster centroids.
STEP 3 Assign data points to the closest centroid:
Calculate the centroid-data point distance,
then
Distribute data points to the nearest centroid.

STEP 4 Find each cluster's mean

then

Upgrade cluster centroid.

STEP 5 Reiterate steps 3 and 4 until convergence is reached:

Rebind data points to the closest centroid

and

Update the centroids until the assignment of data points to clusters does not change or the centroids stop moving.

STEP 6 Analyze the findings and decide the best number of clusters depending on the data and the issue domain.

End

4.4 Classification Approaches

In this section the classification approaches that are using for experimental work are discussed. First this study used existing methods then a novel technique is developed. Accurate prediction of trusted and untrusted services is a big challenge (Hasnain et al., 2022; Sherchan et al., 2011; Su et al., 2017). Thus, efficient machine learning models are needed for a particular dataset; the Table 4 discussed and compared different machine learning techniques with their pros and cons.

Table 4. Pros and cons of different classification approaches

References	Model Name	Pros	Cons
(Akinwunmi & Olajubu, 2015; Khan & Gupta, 2020; Shyam & Manvi, 2016; Wan & Gao, 2016)	Bayesian Network	• Capabilities to include past information. • Manage unpredictable and partial information. • Availability and explain ability.	• Model and its predictions challenging to understand. • Inaccuracies in the data that might affect the accuracy of the predictions. • Problems in upgrading the model.
(Ebadifard & Babamir, 2021; Flores et al., 2018; Ibrahim & Saleh, 2020; Mehmood et al., 2018; Prakash et al., 2020; Thottakkara et al., 2016; Wan & Gao, 2016)	Naïve Bayes	• Computationally efficient method for classifying vast volumes of data. • Handle a high number of features and variables, making it an excellent option for text classification applications with multiple variables.	• All indicators are independent of one another, which is not always the scenario. This leads to a loss of precision and accuracy. • It is sensitive to the quality of the training data; if the data is biased or includes mistakes, the algorithm's performance may deteriorate.

continued on following page

Table 4. Continued

References	Model Name	Pros	Cons
(Kashyap & Singh, 2022; Pal et al., 2022; Zhang et al., 2018)	Logistic Regression	• Simple to apply and explain, it is popular choice for both learners and specialists. • Support a high number of attributes and factors, making it an excellent option for classification jobs involving several variables. • The results are interpretable, making it simple to explain how each parameter leads to the final classification choice.	• In real-world applications, the assumption that connection between characteristics and target variable is linear may not always true. This might result in a loss of precision and accuracy. • Not perform well when dealing with classification problems that are exceedingly complicated or non-linear.
(Cao et al., 2018; 0_BASE_ Analysis of Job Failure and Prediction Model for Cloud Computing Using Machine Learning _ Enhanced Reader.Pdf, 2022; K. Kaur et al., 2022; Kececi et al., 2020; Mahmoud, 2022; Wan & Gao, 2016)	Random Forest	• It is a robust algorithm capable of handling difficult and nonlinear classification jobs. • This technique is efficient and insensitive to outliers and missing data. • It offers interpretable outcomes, making it simple to understand.	• This algorithm is computationally costly and demand substantial processing resources for huge datasets or complicated models. • The algorithm is not performing well when working with extremely skewed or missing value datasets.
(Aljulayfi & Djemame, 2021; Amekraz & Hadi, 2022; Flores et al., 2018; Kaneda & Mineno, 2016; K. Kaur et al., 2022; Liu et al., 2017; Mehmood et al., 2018; Mohanty et al., 2010)	Support Vector Machine	• It is a strong algorithm that can manage difficult and quasi categorization problems. • Handle a huge number of features, making it an excellent option for classification jobs involving a big number of variables. • Both sequentially and non-linearly distinct data may be effectively handled using SVM. • Even when working with tiny or noisy datasets, SVM performs well in terms of generalization.	• SVM is computationally demanding and substantial processing resources for big datasets or complicated models. • Sensitive to the selection of kernel function, and selecting the incorrect kernel might result in poor performance. • The lengthy training period of SVM makes it unsuitable for datasets with a high number of examples. • SVM is susceptible to the quality of the training data; if the data is biased or includes mistakes, the algorithm's performance may decrease.
(Model et al., 2019) (Atef et al., 2022)	AdaBoost	• It is potent linear classifier capable of handling challenging classification jobs. • It is insensitive to the selection of class label and is compatible with all classifier types. • Handle datasets with a high number of features, making it an excellent option for classification jobs involving several variables. • Even when dealing with noisy or unbalanced datasets, AdaBoost may deliver high classification results.	• It is susceptible to the reliability of the training examples; if the data is skewed or includes mistakes, the algorithm's performance may decrease. • It over fit the training data if the method employs an excessive number of poor classifiers. • AdaBoost may be computationally costly, particularly when huge datasets or complicated models are involved.

continued on following page

250

Table 4. Continued

References	Model Name	Pros	Cons
(Behera & Nayak, 2020)(Okafor et al., 2022)(Shu et al., 2021)	Neural Network	• It is very strong classification algorithms capable of handling difficult classification jobs. • It learns complicated, non-linear correlations between input data, making them suited for applications in which feature interactions are not straightforward or clear. • Text, photos, and audio are examples of data types. • Give a high degree of precision in classification tasks, especially those requiring high precision.	• It is computationally costly, particularly when working with huge datasets or intricate models. • If the model is too complicated or the training set is too small, neural networks may over fit the training data. • Interpreting neural networks may be challenging, especially when working with big or sophisticated models. • Neural networks need a considerable quantity of training data to attain high performance, which makes them unsuitable for jobs with little or poor-quality training data.
(Atef et al., 2022; Chen et al., 2022; Time, 2022; Vahora & Chauhan, 2019; Yan et al., 2022)	Deep Learning	• It is very effective and capable of handling complicated categorization jobs. • Automatically discover hierarchical representations of input data, making it suited for jobs where the connections between characteristics are neither straightforward nor simple. • Used to a vast array of inputs, including text, pictures, and audio. • Deliver high accuracy in classification jobs, especially those requiring great precision.	• Computationally intensive, particularly when working with huge datasets or complicated models. • If the model is very complicated or the training set is too small, it over fit the training data. • Difficult to read, this makes it challenging to comprehend how the model makes judgments. • Takes a huge quantity of training data to achieve acceptable performance, which makes it unsuitable for problems with little or low-quality training data.

4.5 Cross Validation

Cross-validation (CV) is an important machine-learning approach to assess the accuracy and consistency of a model. It is a useful approach for choosing the best machine learning model. Researchers in the field of ML often use k-fold CVs rather than other types. But picking the k value selection at random reduces the performance of algorithms and is difficult to use. Previous literature shows that many learning methods vary in k and model validation performance. So, it is essential to the ideal value of k in the k-fold CV.

The study reveals how the effectiveness of machine learning algorithms changes when the validation values of k = 5, k = 10, and k = 15 are varied. The dataset is trained with various classifiers and uses each k number to predict whether a user selects a trustworthy service or not. Further it also concludes that a well-selected value for k results in more precision.

4.6 Performance Measures

In general, data cleansing and preprocessing serve to generate new data. This information is then used in predictive models to generate probabilities as outputs. But the issue is how the effectiveness of the model is measured. To solve this problem there are some performance parameters available like confusion matrix, accuracy, precision, recall etc. The section discusses these parameters that are used for checking the effectiveness of the algorithm.

Confusion matrix: A confusion matrix is a table used to assess the performance of an algorithm for machine learning. In supervised learning, it is often used to assess the accuracy of a classification model. This matrix summarizes the number of accurate and inaccurate predictions produced by the model. It is built by comparing the anticipated labels of a model to the actual labels of the data. Typically, the confusion matrix is shown as a four-column table, with each cell representing a potential combination of expected and actual labels. The following are the four cells of the confusion matrix:

True positives (TP): A positive (or target) class was successfully predicted by the model.
False positives (FP): The model predicted a positive class wrongly.
True negatives (TN): The model accurately predicted a non-target class (or negative class).
False negatives (FN): The model predicted a negative class wrongly.

These are used to evaluate the efficacy of a machine-learning model.

Accuracy: From all the classes (positive and negative), how many of them we have predicted correctly. Accuracy should be high as possible. To compute accuracy from this confusion matrix, the total of true positives and true negatives must be divided by the sum of all four values.

$$Accuracy = \frac{True_{Positive} + True_{Negative}}{True_{Positive} + True_{Negative} + False_{Positive} + False_{Negative}} \tag{2}$$

Precision: The equation 3 stated by saying how many of the expected positive classes are actually positive. Maximum precision should be achieved.

$$Precision = \frac{True_{Positive}}{True_{Positive} + False_{Positive}} \tag{3}$$

Recall: The equation 4 can be clarified by stating, for all favourable classes, how many of them are accurately predicted. Maximum recall should be preserved.

$$Recall = \frac{True_{Positive}}{True_{Positive} + False_{Negative}} \tag{4}$$

F-Measure/F1-Score: Comparing two models with poor precision but high recall or vice versa are complicated. As a result, researchers employ F-Score to compare them. F-score measures both Recall and Precision simultaneously. It substitutes Harmonic Mean for Arithmetic Mean by treating extreme values more strongly.

$$F - Measure = \frac{2*Recall*Precision}{Recall + Precision} \tag{5}$$

4.7 Proposed Trust Prediction Algorithm

The section discussed the novel technique that describes the selection of optimal service based on trustworthy model named as M_{best}. To achieve the best model the ensemble technique is used along with the following steps discussed in Algorithm 2.

Algorithm 2

Input: Dataset {QWS1 and QWS2}

Output: Find Best Model {M_{best}}

START

Step1: Initialize Dataset.

Step 2 Date Preprocessing

Using Algorithm 1 {K-means Clustering}

Return Categorization of Trust Classes {HT,MT,LT}

Generation of New dataset { $QWS1_{new}$ and $QWS2_{new}$}

Step 3 Apply k-Fold Cross Validation method {where, k=5,10,15}

Step 4 Compute existing classification models {M1,M2,M3,...,Mn}

Step 5 Evaluate Accuracy using equation {2} for all models

{Acc_{m1}, $Acc_{m2,}$ Acc_{m3},..., Acc_{m8}}

Find the maximum accuracy Acc_{max} of two models=max(Acc_{m1}, $Acc_{m2,}$ Acc_{m3},..., Acc_{m8})

Return (Acc_{max1} and Acc_{max2})

Step 6 Generate a new model M_{best}

By Aggregating the models based on Acc_{max1} and Acc_{max2}

Step 7 Evaluate accuracy using equation {2} for new model i.e. Acc_{mbest}

Table 5. Performance measure comparisons

Dataset	Model	K-Fold	Accuracy	Precision	Recall	F-Score
QWS Dataset 1	Bayesian Network	5	94.23%	0.942	0.942	0.942
		10	94.51%	0.945	0.945	0.944
		15	**94.78%**	0.948	0.948	0.947
	Naïve Bayes	**5**	**94.78%**	0.948	0.948	0.947
		10	94.51%	0.952	0.948	0.949
		15	**94.78%**	0.949	0.945	0.946
	Logistic Regression	5	90.38%	0.904	0.904	0.901
		10	**91.48%**	0.915	0.915	0.913
		15	90.66%	0.907	0.907	0.904
	Random Forest	**5**	**96.43%**	0.965	0.964	0.964
		10	**96.43%**	0.965	0.964	0.964
		15	96.15%	0.962	0.962	0.961
	Support Vector Machine	5	98.08%	0.981	0.981	0.98
		10	98.08%	0.981	0.981	0.98
		15	**98.35%**	0.984	0.984	0.983
	AdaBoost	5	96.98%	0.97	0.97	0.97
		10	**98.35%**	0.984	0.984	0.983
		15	97.80%	0.978	0.978	0.978
	Neural Network	**5**	**97.53%**	0.976	0.975	0.972
		10	**97.53%**	0.976	0.975	0.972
		15	97.25%	0.974	0.973	0.972
	Deep Learning	5	95.60%	0.961	0.956	0.957
		10	95.05%	0.957	0.951	0.952
		15	**95.88%**	0.963	0.959	0.96
	Proposed Method	5	98.78%	0.988	0.988	0.987
		10	**98.99%**	0.989	0.989	0.988
		15	98.32%	0.984	0.984	0.982

continued on following page

Table 5. Continued

Dataset	Model	K-Fold	Accuracy	Precision	Recall	F-Score
QWS Dataset 2	Bayesian Network	5	95.13%	0.952	0.951	0.952
		10	**95.33%**	0.954	0.953	0.954
		15	95.29%	0.954	0.953	0.953
	Naïve Bayes	5	93.62%	0.94	0.936	0.937
		10	**93.70%**	0.941	0.937	0.938
		15	93.66%	0.941	0.937	0.937
	Logistic Regression	5	**94.85%**	0.95	0.949	0.948
		10	94.85%	0.949	0.949	0.948
		15	94.34%	0.943	0.943	0.943
	AdaBoost	5	97.85%	0.978	0.978	0.978
		10	**98.17%**	0.982	0.982	0.982
		15	98.09%	0.981	0.981	0.981
	Support Vector Machine	5	**98.01%**	0.98	0.98	0.98
		10	97.81%	0.978	0.978	0.978
		15	97.97%	0.98	0.98	0.98
	Random Forest	5	92.48%	0.925	0.925	0.925
		10	92.56%	0.926	0.926	0.926
		15	**92.60%**	0.926	0.926	0.926
	Neural Network	5	96.89%	0.97	0.969	0.969
		10	96.81%	0.97	0.968	0.968
		15	**96.93%**	0.971	0.969	0.97
	Deep Learning	5	92.63%	0.928	0.928	0.927
		10	**92.85%**	0.929	0.93	0.929
		15	92.67%	0.928	0.927	0.926
	Proposed Method	5	98.48%	0.985	0.985	0.985
		10	98.56%	0.986	0.986	0.986
		15	**98.60%**	0.986	0.986	0.986

Step 8 Compare Acc_{mbest} with all models $\{Acc_{m1}, Acc_{m2}, Acc_{m3}, \cdots, Acc_{m8}\}$
Step 9 Return
End

4.8 Trust Score Estimation

The objective of designing the model is to build a relationship between user and provider. Therefore, in the next stage of proposed method trust score is calculated. Highest value of the trust score indicates the reliability and optimality of the services whereas lowest score give the less reliable services. Previous investigation shows that there is no single method for quantifying WS quality because different indicators can have different values for multiple services. A potential approach for evaluating the Quality of Web Services (QWS) involves calculating a weighted score by considering a set of relevant criteria. For example, one can create a weighted average of the following measures: RT, availability, reliability, TP, security, performance, etc. Next, the weighting of each statistic is based on its relative value, with a larger weighting indicating greater importance. Then, a score is calculated for each measure based on its performance, with higher scores indicating better performance. Multiplying each metric score by its weight, adding up the results, then dividing by the total weight yields a weighted average score that measures online service quality as a whole.

The current work use Trust Score prediction given in the equation 6 below indicated the correct categorization of trustworthy instances originating from WS invocations, and then we compute the rank of each WS based on the classification results:

$$TrustScore = \frac{True_{Positive}}{True_{Positive} + False_{Positive} + True_{Negative} + False_{Negative}} \tag{6}$$

5. EXPERIMENTAL FINDINGS AND DISCUSSIONS

This section discusses WS categorization and experimental findings of the proposed method. In QWS dataset 1, a variety of services have previously been ranked in terms of quality attributes. Therefore, getting an accurate assessment of trust in this scenario was not challenging. However, with the second dataset, the ranking was not done before. Thus, the KNN clustering algorithm was employed to classify the trust level. It divided trust into three categories, of which the first category includes high trust which holds services that provide good quality attributes and values. The second category, named medium trust, includes services that partially satisfy user needs. And the third category is Low Trust which holds services with poor metric values.

When this method is employed to evaluate qws1, 246 cases of high trust, 113 of medium trust and 5 of low trust are analysed. Similar method evaluated on qws2 and finds 1411 high trust, 596 medium trusts, and 500 low trust instances are examined. These two newly generated data are applied as inputs to various classification algorithms. According to the paper's findings, the following nine algorithms selected for the evaluation named as Random Forest (RF), Naive Bayes (NB), Bayesians Network (BN), Logistic Regression (LR), Support Vector Machine (SVM), AdaBoost (AB), Neural Network (NN), Deep Learning (DL), and Proposed Method (PM). The outcomes of several machine-learning methods and their corresponding parameter values are shown in Table 5. It also includes other parameters such as precision, recall, and f-score for the various methods.

Afterward, k-fold cross-validation is used in order to identify the best model. Different values of k = {5, 10, 15} are used for model building and assigned for model validation. For qws1, both BN and NB algorithms achieved a maximum accuracy value of 94.78% when k=15 and k= {5, 10} respectively. Compared with both of these algorithms LR attains a low value i.e. 91.48% when k=10. But RF obtains highest value i.e. 96.43% when k = {5, 10}. Next SVM and AB both reached highest accuracy of 98.35% when k=15 and k=10 respectively. Compared with both NN gets 1% less value i.e. 97.53% when k= {5, 10}. Next, DL accomplish value of 95.88% which is highest than BN, NB, and LR but lower than RF, SVM, AB, and NN.

In case of qws2, both BN and NB algorithms achieved a maximum accuracy value of 95.33% and 93.70% respectively when k= 10. Compared with both of these algorithms LR attains 94.85% when k= {5, 10} which is lower than BN and highest than NB. But AB and SVM both obtains highest value i.e. 98.17% and 98.01% respectively when k = 10. RF obtained lowest accuracy value i.e. 92.60% when k=15. NN gets 96.93% when k= 15. Next, DL accomplish value of 92.85% when k=10.From the Table 5, the study conclude that in both datasets the proposed technique achieved highest value among all existing algorithms.

Fig. 3 shows the accuracy plot of different classification algorithms. The diagram conclude that proposed method achieves the maximum values of 98.99% at 10-fold, 98.78% at 5-fold, and 98.32% at 15-fold for QWS dataset 1. From Fig. 4 depicts that QWS dataset 2 achieves the highest accuracy percentile values at 98.60% 15-fold, 98.56% 10-fold, and 98.48% 5-fold in case of proposed method.

The previous literature study provided valuable suggestions for choosing trustworthy providers. However, there are some drawbacks highlighted by the researcher and the research gaps are discussed below. When choosing a WS, it's important to consider quality web attributes of the application to ensure that user can trust the provider. To make decision for CU the calculation of trust using prediction

Figure 3. Accuracy comparisons QWS dataset 1

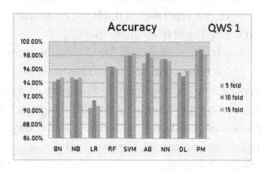

Figure 4. Accuracy comparisons QWS dataset 2

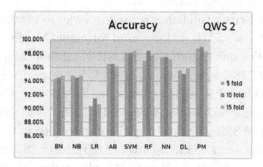

and ranking mechanism are considered. But still there are other factors such as security, reputation etc are available.

- Reviews related to product where user should read customer reviews and check ratings to get an idea of the service provider's reputation.
- The information includes provider's security measures, such as SSL encryption and data backups. It is necessary for provider having a clear privacy policy that explains how they will use and protect your data.
- The transparency of the company required for open and honest about their practices.
- Consider the provider's experience and track record in the industry. Look for information on the provider's support services, such as customer service and technical support.

These factors help a user to find a WS provider that provides trust based on reliable and secure services.

6. CONCLUSION AND FUTURE SCOPE

In cloud computing, quality features play an essential role for selection of WSs to maximize the performance. Designing a trust model for predicting reliable services without assigning any rank is a very complex task. For selection of WS, it's important to consider quality web attributes of the application to ensure that user can trust the provider. To solve these challenges, a novel technique for WSS is proposed using the feedback for quality attributes instances from WSs users. In the initial step, the dataset is partitioned into different classes of trust using K-means method. The partition enhances the scoring factors in the prediction of WSs. Next, the result evaluation is based on a comparison of various classifications with the proposed methods. Hence, the proposed technique outperforms the existing technique based on the performance measures. Apart from calculating trust from prediction and ranking mechanisms, there are other factors to help a CU make an informed decision. Future advancements in the field involve incorporating security factors such as encrypted data and privacy policies to support trust mechanism between consumers and suppliers. Implementing these advanced technologies will be essential in enhancing trust-building efforts.

REFERENCES

Abdullah, L., Li, H., Al-Jamali, S., Al-Badwi, A., & Ruan, C. (2020). Predicting Multi-Attribute Host Resource Utilization Using Support Vector Regression Technique. *IEEE Access : Practical Innovations, Open Solutions*, 8, 66048–66067. doi:10.1109/ACCESS.2020.2984056

Akinwunmi, A. O., & Olajubu, E. A. (2015). Trust : A Requirement for Cloud Technology Adoption. *(IJACSA). International Journal of Advanced Computer Science and Applications*, 6(8), 112–118.

Al-Masri, E., & Mahmoud, Q. H. (2008). Investigating web services on the world wide web. *Proceeding of the 17th International Conference on World Wide Web 2008, WWW'08*, (pp. 795–804). ACM. 10.1145/1367497.1367605

Aljulayfi, A., & Djemame, K. (2021). *A Machine Learning based Context-aware Prediction Framework for Edge Computing Environments. Closer*, (pp. 143–150). ScitePress. doi:10.5220/0010379001430150

Amekraz, Z., & Hadi, M. Y. (2022). CANFIS: A Chaos Adaptive Neural Fuzzy Inference System for Workload Prediction in the Cloud. *IEEE Access : Practical Innovations, Open Solutions*, 10, 49808–49828. doi:10.1109/ACCESS.2022.3174061

Atef, S., Ismail, N., & Eltawil, A. B. (2022). A new fuzzy logic based approach for optimal household appliance scheduling based on electricity price and load consumption prediction. *Advances in Building Energy Research*, *16*(2), 262–280. doi:10.1080/17512549.2021.1873183

Behera, M. K., & Nayak, N. (2020). A comparative study on short-term PV power forecasting using decomposition based optimized extreme learning machine algorithm. *Engineering Science and Technology, an International Journal*, *23*(1), 156–167. doi:10.1016/j.jestch.2019.03.006

Cao, R., Yu, Z., Marbach, T., Li, J., Wang, G., & Liu, X. (2018). Load Prediction for Data Centers Based on Database Service. *Proceedings - International Computer Software and Applications Conference*, *1*(August), (pp. 728–737). IEEE. 10.1109/COMPSAC.2018.00109

Chen, L., Zhang, W., & Ye, H. (2022). Accurate workload prediction for edge data centers: Savitzky-Golay filter, CNN and BiLSTM with attention mechanism. *Applied Intelligence*, *52*(11), 13027–13042. doi:10.100710489-021-03110-x

De Moor, A., & Van Den Heuvel, W. J. (2004). Web service selection in virtual communities. *Proceedings of the Hawaii International Conference on System Sciences*, (pp. 3105–3114). IEEE. 10.1109/HICSS.2004.1265468

Ding, S., Xia, C. Y., Le Zhou, K., Yang, S. L., & Shang, J. S. (2014). Decision Support for Personalized Cloud Service Selection through Multi-Attribute Trustworthiness Evaluation. *PLoS One*, *9*(6), e97762. doi:10.1371/journal.pone.0097762 PMID:24972237

Ebadifard, F., & Babamir, S. M. (2021). Autonomic task scheduling algorithm for dynamic workloads through a load balancing technique for the cloud-computing environment. *Cluster Computing*, *24*(2), 1075–1101. doi:10.100710586-020-03177-0

Flores, A. C., Icoy, R. I., Pena, C. F., & Gorro, K. D. (2018). An evaluation of SVM and naive bayes with SMOTE on sentiment analysis data set. *ICEAST 2018 - 4th International Conference on Engineering, Applied Sciences and Technology: Exploring Innovative Solutions for Smart Society*, (pp. 1–4). IEEE. 10.1109/ICEAST.2018.8434401

Gao, H., Xu, Y., Yin, Y., Zhang, W., Li, R., & Wang, X. (2020). Context-Aware QoS Prediction with Neural Collaborative Filtering for Internet-of-Things Services. *IEEE Internet of Things Journal*, *7*(5), 4532–4542. doi:10.1109/JIOT.2019.2956827

Gupta, P., Goyal, M. K., & Kumar, P. (2013). Trust and reliability based load balancing algorithm for cloud IaaS. *Proceedings of the 2013 3rd IEEE International Advance Computing Conference, IACC 2013* (pp. 65–69). IEEE. 10.1109/IAdCC.2013.6514196

Hasnain, M., Ghani, I., Pasha, M. F., & Jeong, S. R. (2022). Machine Learning Methods for Trust- based Selection of Web Services. *KSII Transactions on Internet and Information Systems, 16*(1), 38–59.

Hasnain, M., Pasha, M. F., Ghani, I., Imran, M., Alzahrani, M. Y., & Budiarto, R. (2020). Evaluating Trust Prediction and Confusion Matrix Measures for Web Services Ranking. *IEEE Access : Practical Innovations, Open Solutions, 8*, 90847–90861. doi:10.1109/ACCESS.2020.2994222

Hormozi, E., Hormozi, H., Akbari, M. K., & Javan, M. S. (2012). Using of machine learning into cloud environment (a survey): Managing and scheduling of resources in cloud systems. *Proceedings - 2012 7th International Conference on P2P, Parallel, Grid, Cloud and Internet Computing, 3PGCIC 2012.* IEEE. 10.1109/3PGCIC.2012.69

Ibrahim, L. M., & Saleh, I. A. (2020). A solution of loading balance in cloud computing using optimization of Bat swarm Algorithm. *Journal of Engineering Science and Technology, 15*(3), 2062–2076.

Ibrahim, L. M., & Saleh, I. A. (2022). BASE_Analysis of Job Failure and Prediction Model for Cloud Computing Using Machine Learning _ Enhanced Reader.pdf. *Sensors, 22.* doi:10.3390/s22052035

Kaneda, Y., & Mineno, H. (2016). Sliding window-based support vector regression for predicting micrometeorological data. *Expert Systems with Applications, 59*, 217–225. doi:10.1016/j.eswa.2016.04.012

Kashyap, S., & Singh, A. (2022). An Ensemble-Based Method for Predicting Facebook Check-ins. *Soft Computing: Theories and Applications*, (pp. 263–285). Springer. doi:10.1007/978-981-16-1740-9_23

Kaur, G., & Bala, A. (2021). OPSA: an optimized prediction based scheduling approach for scientific applications in cloud environment. In Cluster Computing (Vol. 24, Issue 3, pp. 1955–1974). doi:10.100710586-021-03232-4

Kaur, K., Garg, S., Aujla, G. S., Kumar, N., & Zomaya, A. Y. (2022). A Multi-Objective Optimization Scheme for Job Scheduling in Sustainable Cloud Data Centers. *IEEE Transactions on Cloud Computing, 10*(1), 172–186. doi:10.1109/TCC.2019.2950002

Kececi, A., Yildirak, A., Ozyazici, K., Ayluctarhan, G., Agbulut, O., & Zincir, I. (2020). Implementation of machine learning algorithms for gait recognition. *Engineering Science and Technology, an International Journal, 23*(4), 931–937. doi:10.1016/j.jestch.2020.01.005

Khan, F. M., & Gupta, R. (2020). ARIMA and NAR based prediction model for time series analysis of COVID-19 cases in India. *Journal of Safety Science and Resilience, 1*(1), 12–18. doi:10.1016/j.jnlssr.2020.06.007

Li, W., Wu, J., Cao, J., Chen, N., Zhang, Q., & Buyya, R. (2021). Blockchain-based trust management in cloud computing systems: a taxonomy, review and future directions. In Journal of Cloud Computing, 10(1). doi:10.118613677-021-00247-5

Li, Z., Liao, L., Leung, H., Li, B., & Li, C. (2017). Evaluating the credibility of cloud services. *Computers & Electrical Engineering, 58*, 161–175. doi:10.1016/j.compeleceng.2016.05.014

Liu, C., Liu, C., Shang, Y., Chen, S., Cheng, B., & Chen, J. (2017). An adaptive prediction approach based on workload pattern discrimination in the cloud. *Journal of Network and Computer Applications, 80*(December 2016), 35–44. doi:10.1016/j.jnca.2016.12.017

Mahmoud, Q. H. (2022). Analysis of Job Failure and Prediction Model for Cloud Computing Using Machine Learning. *Sensors, 22*.

Mehmood, T., Latif, S., & Malik, S. (2018). Prediction of Cloud Computing Resource Utilization. *2018 15th International Conference on Smart Cities: Improving Quality of Life Using ICT and IoT, HONET-ICT 2018*, (pp. 38–42). IEEE. 10.1109/HONET.2018.8551339

Mell, P., & Grance, T. (2011). *The NIST Definition of Cloud Computing Recommendations of the National Institute of Standards and Technology*. National Institute of Standards and Technology Special Publication. doi:10.6028/NIST.SP.800-145

Model, A., Users, M., Wang, H., Yang, Z., & Shi, Y. (2019). Next Location Prediction Based on an Adaboost-Markov Model of Mobile Users. *Sensors 2019, 19*(1475), 1–19. doi:10.3390/s19061475

Mohanty, R., Ravi, V., & Patra, M. R. (2010). Web-services classification using intelligent techniques. *Expert Systems with Applications, 37*(7), 5484–5490. doi:10.1016/j.eswa.2010.02.063

Nawrocki, P., Osypanka, P., Nawrocki, P., & Osypanka, P. (2021). Cloud Resource Demand Prediction using Machine Learning in the Context of QoS Parameters. *Journal of Grid Computing, 19*(2), 1–20. doi:10.1007/s10723-021-09561-3

Okafor, C. E., Okafor, E. J., & Ikebudu, K. O. (2022). Evaluation of machine learning methods in predicting optimum tensile strength of microwave post-cured composite tailored for weight-sensitive applications. *Engineering Science and Technology, an International Journal, 25*, 100985. doi:10.1016/j.jestch.2021.04.004

Padhy, R. P., Ratra, M. R., & Satapathy, S. C. (2011). Cloud Computing : Security Issues and Research Challenges. *IRACST - International Journal of Computer Science and Information Technology & Security (IJCSITS), 1*(2), 136–146.

Pal, A., Das, G., Hanheide, M., Candea Leite, A., & From, P. J. (2022). An Agricultural Event Prediction Framework towards Anticipatory Scheduling of Robot Fleets: General Concepts and Case Studies. In Agronomy, 12(6). doi:10.3390/agronomy12061299

Prakash, K. B., Imambi, S. S., Ismail, M., Kumar, T. P., & Pawan, Y. V. R. N. (2020). Analysis, prediction and evaluation of COVID-19 datasets. *International Journal of Emerging Trends in Engineering Research, 8*(5), 2199–2204. doi:10.30534/ijeter/2020/117852020

Rahimi, M., Navimipour, N. J., Hosseinzadeh, M., Moattar, M. H., & Darwesh, A. (2021). *Toward the efficient service selection approaches in cloud computing.* Emerald. doi:10.1108/K-02-2021-0129

Sahi, S. K. (2015). A Review on Workload Prediction of Cloud Services. *International Journal of Computer Applications, 109*(9), 975–8887.

Saoud, Z., Faci, N., Maamar, Z., & Benslimane, D. (2016). A fuzzy-based credibility model to assess Web services trust under uncertainty. *Journal of Systems and Software, 122*, 496–506. doi:10.1016/j.jss.2015.09.040

Sharma, O., & Saini, H. (2016). VM Consolidation for Cloud Data Center Using Median Based Threshold Approach. *Procedia Computer Science, 89*, 27–33. doi:10.1016/j.procs.2016.06.005

Sharma, S. K., Al-Badi, A. H., Govindaluri, S. M., & Al-Kharusi, M. H. (2016). Predicting motivators of cloud computing adoption: A developing country perspective. *Computers in Human Behavior, 62*, 61–69. doi:10.1016/j.chb.2016.03.073

Sherchan, W., Nepal, S., & Bouguettaya, A. (2011). A trust prediction model for service web. *Proc. 10th IEEE Int. Conf. on Trust, Security and Privacy in Computing and Communications, TrustCom 2011, 8th IEEE Int. Conf. on Embedded Software and Systems, ICESS 2011, 6th Int. Conf. on FCST 2011*, (pp. 258–265). IEEE. 10.1109/TrustCom.2011.35

Shu, W., Zeng, F., Ling, Z., Liu, J., Lu, T., & Chen, G. (2021). Resource Demand Prediction of Cloud Workloads Using an Attention-based GRU Model. *Proceedings - 2021 17th International Conference on Mobility, Sensing and Networking, MSN 2021*, (pp. 428–437). IEEE. 10.1109/MSN53354.2021.00071

Shyam, G. K., & Manvi, S. S. (2016). Virtual resource prediction in cloud environment: A Bayesian approach. *Journal of Network and Computer Applications*, 65, 144–154. doi:10.1016/j.jnca.2016.03.002

Somu, N., R, G. R. M., Kirthivasan, K., & S, S. S. V. (2018). A trust centric optimal service ranking approach for cloud service selection. *Future Generation Computer Systems*, 86, 234–252. doi:10.1016/j.future.2018.04.033

Somu, N., R, G. R. M., Kaveri, A., & K, A. R. (2020). IBGSS : An Improved Binary Gravitational Search Algorithm based search strategy for QoS and ranking prediction in cloud environments. *Applied Soft Computing*, 88, 105945. doi:10.1016/j.asoc.2019.105945

Su, K., Xiao, B., Liu, B., Zhang, H., & Zhang, Z. (2017). TAP: A personalized trust-aware QoS prediction approach for web service recommendation. *Knowledge-Based Systems*, 115, 55–65. doi:10.1016/j.knosys.2016.09.033

Thottakkara, P., Ozrazgat-Baslanti, T., Hupf, B. B., Rashidi, P., Pardalos, P., Momcilovic, P., & Bihorac, A. (2016). Application of machine learning techniques to high-dimensional clinical data to forecast postoperative complications. *PLoS One*, 11(5), 1–19. doi:10.1371/journal.pone.0155705 PMID:27232332

Vahora, S. A., & Chauhan, N. C. (2019). Deep neural network model for group activity recognition using contextual relationship. *Engineering Science and Technology, an International Journal*, 22(1), 47–54. doi:10.1016/j.jestch.2018.08.010

Wan, Y., & Gao, Q. (2016). An Ensemble Sentiment Classification System of Twitter Data for Airline Services Analysis. *Proceedings - 15th IEEE International Conference on Data Mining Workshop, ICDMW 2015*. IEEE. 10.1109/ICDMW.2015.7

Wang, Y., Wen, J., Wang, X., Tao, B., & Zhou, W. (2019a). A cloud service trust evaluation model based on combining weights and gray correlation analysis. *Security and Communication Networks*, 2019, 1–11. doi:10.1155/2019/2437062

Wang, Y., Wen, J., Wang, X., Tao, B., & Zhou, W. (2019b). A Cloud Service Trust Evaluation Model Based on Combining Weights and Gray Correlation Analysis. *Security and Communication Networks, 2019*, 2019. doi:10.1155/2019/2437062

Whaiduzzaman, M., Haque, M. N., Rejaul Karim Chowdhury, M., & Gani, A. (2014). A study on strategic provisioning of cloud computing services. In *Scientific World Journal* (Vol. 2014). Hindawi Publishing Corporation. doi:10.1155/2014/894362

Yan, J., Rui, L. L., Yang, Y., Chen, S., & Chen, X. (2022). Resource Scheduling Algorithms for Burst Network Flow in Edge Computing. *Lecture Notes in Electrical Engineering, 808 LNEE*. Springer. doi:10.1007/978-981-16-6554-7_173

Yasmina, R. Z. (2022). *Web service selection and composition based on uncertain quality of service*. Wiley. doi:10.1002/cpe.6531

Zhang, J., Li, W., Zhang, J., Xie, N., Zhang, X., Yue, K., & Kumar, D. (2018). Machine Learning Based Resource Allocation of Cloud Computing in Auction. *CMC, 56*(1), 123–135. doi:10.3970/cmc.2018.03728

Compilation of References

Ibrahim, L. M., & Saleh, I. A. (2022). BASE_Analysis of Job Failure and Prediction Model for Cloud Computing Using Machine Learning _ Enhanced Reader.pdf. *Sensors, 22.* doi:10.3390/s22052035

Abdiansah, A., & Wardoyo, R. (2015). Time complexity analysis of support vector machines (SVM) in LibSVM. *International Journal of Computer Applications, 128*(3), 28–34. doi:10.5120/ijca2015906480

Abdullah, L., Li, H., Al-Jamali, S., Al-Badwi, A., & Ruan, C. (2020). Predicting Multi-Attribute Host Resource Utilization Using Support Vector Regression Technique. *IEEE Access : Practical Innovations, Open Solutions, 8,* 66048–66067. doi:10.1109/ACCESS.2020.2984056

Abubakar, A. I., Chiroma, H., Muaz, S. A., & Ila, L. B. (2015). A review of the advances in cyber security benchmark datasets for evaluating data-driven based intrusion detection systems. *Procedia Computer Science, 62,* 221–227. doi:10.1016/j.procs.2015.08.443

Achar, S. (2022). *Adopting Artificial Intelligence and Deep learning techniques in cloud computing.* Research Gate. https://www.researchgate.net/profile/Sandesh-Achar/publication/366205412_Adopting_Artificial_Intelligence_and_Deep_Learning_Techniques_in_Cloud_Computing_for_Operational_Efficiency/links/6397a7df11e9f00cda3de394/Adopting-Artificial-Intelligence-and-Deep-Learning-Techniques-in-Cloud-Computing-for-Operational-Efficiency.pdf

Achar, S. (2021). An Overview of Environmental Scalability and Security in Hybrid Cloud Infrastructure Designs. *Asia Pacific Journal of Energy and Environment, 8*(2), 39–46. doi:10.18034/apjee.v8i2.650

Achar, S. (2022). Adopting artificial intelligence and deep learning techniques in cloud computing for operational efficiency. *International Journal of Information and Communication Engineering, 16*(12), 567–572.

Adhikari, M., Koley, S., & Arab, J. (2017). Cloud Computing: A Multi-workflow Scheduling Algorithm with Dynamic Reusability. *Arabian Journal for Science and Engineering, 43*(2), 645–660. doi:10.100713369-017-2739-0

Adithya, V., Deepak, G., & Santhanavijayan, A. (2022). OntoIntAIC: An Approach for Ontology Integration Using Artificially Intelligent Cloud. In *Advances in Data Computing, Communication and Security: Proceedings of I3CS2021* (pp. 3–13). Springer Nature Singapore. doi:10.1007/978-981-16-8403-6_1

Agrawal, A. V., Pitchai, R., Senthamaraikannan, C., Balaji, N. A., Sajithra, S., & Boopathi, S. (2023). Digital Education System During the COVID-19 Pandemic. In Using Assistive Technology for Inclusive Learning in K-12 Classrooms (pp. 104–126). IGI Global. doi:10.4018/978-1-6684-6424-3.ch005

Agrawal, A. V., Shashibhushan, G., Pradeep, S., Padhi, S. N., Sugumar, D., & Boopathi, S. (2024). Synergizing Artificial Intelligence, 5G, and Cloud Computing for Efficient Energy Conversion Using Agricultural Waste. In Practice, Progress, and Proficiency in Sustainability (pp. 475–497). IGI Global. doi:10.4018/979-8-3693-1186-8.ch026

Agrawal, A. V., Magulur, L. P., Priya, S. G., Kaur, A., Singh, G., & Boopathi, S. (2023). Smart Precision Agriculture Using IoT and WSN. In *Handbook of Research on Data Science and Cybersecurity Innovations in Industry 4.0 Technologies* (pp. 524–541). IGI Global. doi:10.4018/978-1-6684-8145-5.ch026

Agrawal, N., & Tapaswi, S. (2019). Defense mechanisms against DDoS attacks in a cloud computing environment: State-of-the-art and research challenges. *IEEE Communications Surveys and Tutorials*, *21*(4), 3769–3795. doi:10.1109/COMST.2019.2934468

Ajeh, D., Ellman, J., & Keogh, S. (2014). A cost modelling system for cloud computing. *In 2014 14th International Conference on Computational Science and Its Applications,* (pp. 74-84). IEEE.

Akinwunmi, A. O., & Olajubu, E. A. (2015). Trust : A Requirement for Cloud Technology Adoption. *(IJACSA). International Journal of Advanced Computer Science and Applications*, *6*(8), 112–118.

Akram, S. V., Joshi, S. K., & Deorari, R. (2022, November). Web Application Based Authentication System. In *2022 International Interdisciplinary Humanitarian Conference for Sustainability (IIHC)* (pp. 1439-1443). IEEE. 10.1109/IIHC55949.2022.10059984

Alarifi, A., Dubey, K., Amoon, M., Altameem, T., Abd El-Samie, F. E., Altameem, A., & Nasr, A. A. (2020). Energy efficient hybrid framework for green cloud computing. *IEEE Access : Practical Innovations, Open Solutions*, *8*, 115356–115369. doi:10.1109/ACCESS.2020.3002184

Aldhyani, T. H., & Alkahtani, H. (2022). Artificial Intelligence Algorithm-Based Economic Denial of Sustainability Attack Detection Systems: Cloud Computing Environments. *Sensors (Basel)*, *22*(13), 4685. doi:10.339022134685 PMID:35808184

Alghofaili, Y., Albattah, A., Alrajeh, N., Rassam, M. A., & Al-Rimy, B. A. S. (2021). Secure cloud infrastructure: A survey on issues, current solutions, and open challenges. *Applied Sciences (Basel, Switzerland)*, *11*(19), 9005. doi:10.3390/app11199005

Alhayani, B., Mohammed, H. J., Chaloob, I. Z., & Ahmed, J. S. (2021). Effectiveness of artificial intelligence techniques against cyber security risks apply of IT industry. *Materials Today: Proceedings*, 531. doi:10.1016/j.matpr.2021.02.531

Ali, A. (2017). Unsupervised feature learning and automatic modulation classification using deep learning. *Physical Communication, 25*(1).

Alipour, H., Al-Nashif, Y. B., Satam, P., & Hariri, S. (2015). Wireless anomaly detection based on IEEE 802.11 behavior analysis. *IEEE Transactions on Information Forensics and Security, 10*(10), 2158–2170. doi:10.1109/TIFS.2015.2433898

Al-Issa, Y., Ottom, M. A., Tamrawi, A., & ... (2019). eHealth cloud security challenges: A survey. *Journal of Healthcare Engineering*, 2019. PMID:31565209

Alizadeh, M., Abolfazli, S., Zamani, M., Baharun, S., & Sakurai, K. (2016). Authentication in mobile cloud computing: A survey. *Journal of Network and Computer Applications, 61*, 59–80. doi:10.1016/j.jnca.2015.10.005

Aljulayfi, A., & Djemame, K. (2021). *A Machine Learning based Context-aware Prediction Framework for Edge Computing Environments. Closer*, (pp. 143–150). ScitePress. doi:10.5220/0010379001430150

Al-Masri, E., & Mahmoud, Q. H. (2008). Investigating web services on the world wide web. *Proceeding of the 17th International Conference on World Wide Web 2008, WWW'08*, (pp. 795–804). ACM. 10.1145/1367497.1367605

Al-Turjman, F., & Deebak, B. D. (2021). A Proxy-Authorized Public Auditing Scheme for Cyber-Medical Systems Using AI-IoT. *IEEE Transactions on Industrial Informatics, 18*(8), 5371–5382. doi:10.1109/TII.2021.3126316

Alzoubi, K., Aljawarneh, N. M., Alsafadi, Y., Al-Radaideh, A. T., & Altahat, S. (2020). Role of Cloud Computing in Service Quality, Information Quality & Low Costs: An Empirical Study on Jordanian Customs. *International Journal of Academic Research in Business & Social Sciences, 10*(6), 522–532. doi:10.6007/IJARBSS/v10-i6/7330

Amekraz, Z., & Hadi, M. Y. (2022). CANFIS: A Chaos Adaptive Neural Fuzzy Inference System for Workload Prediction in the Cloud. *IEEE Access : Practical Innovations, Open Solutions, 10*, 49808–49828. doi:10.1109/ACCESS.2022.3174061

Anitha, C., Komala, C., Vivekanand, C. V., Lalitha, S., & Boopathi, S. (2023). Artificial Intelligence driven security model for Internet of Medical Things (IoMT). *IEEE Explore*, (pp. 1–7). IEEE.

Anitha, C., Komala, C., Vivekanand, C. V., Lalitha, S., & Boopathi, S. (2023). Artificial Intelligence driven security model for Internet of Medical Things (IoMT). *IEEE Explore*, 1–7.

Ansari, M. F., Dash, B., Sharma, P., & Yathiraju, N. (2022). The Impact and Limitations of Artificial Intelligence in Cybersecurity: A Literature Review. *International Journal of Advanced Research in Computer and Communication Engineering, 11*(9). doi:10.17148/IJARCCE.2022.11912

Apruzzese, G., Laskov, P., Montes de Oca, E., Mallouli, W., Brdalo Rapa, L., Grammatopoulos, A. V., & Di Franco, F. (2023). The role of machine learning in cybersecurity. *Digital Threats : Research and Practice*, *4*(1), 1–38. doi:10.1145/3545574

Ardhapurkar, S., Srivastava, T., Sharma, S., Chaurasiya, V., & Vaish, A. (2010). Privacy and Data Protection in Cyberspace in Indian Environment. *International Journal of Engineering Science and Technology*, *2*(5), 942–951.

Armitage, J. (2022). *Cloud Native Security Cookbook*. O'Reilly Media, Inc.

Arunprasad, R., & Boopathi, S. (2019). Chapter-4 Alternate Refrigerants for Minimization Environmental Impacts: A Review. In Advances In Engineering Technology (p. 75). AkiNik Publications New Delhi.

Asharaf, Z., Ganne, A., & Mazher, N. (2023). *Artificial Intelligence in Cloud Computing Security*. Research Gate.

Atef, S., Ismail, N., & Eltawil, A. B. (2022). A new fuzzy logic based approach for optimal household appliance scheduling based on electricity price and load consumption prediction. *Advances in Building Energy Research*, *16*(2), 262–280. doi:10.1080/17512549.2021.1873183

Awaysheh, F. M., Aladwan, M. N., Alazab, M., Alawadi, S., Cabaleiro, J. C., & Pena, T. F. (2021). Security by design for big data frameworks over cloud computing. *IEEE Transactions on Engineering Management*, *69*(6), 3676–3693. doi:10.1109/TEM.2020.3045661

Babu, B. S., Kamalakannan, J., Meenatchi, N., Karthik, S., & Boopathi, S. (2022). Economic impacts and reliability evaluation of battery by adopting Electric Vehicle. *IEEE Explore*, (pp. 1–6). IEEE.

Baclic, O., Tunis, M., Young, K., Doan, C., Swerdfeger, H., & Schonfeld, J. (2020). Artificial intelligence in public health: Challenges and opportunities for public health made possible by advances in natural language processing. *Canada Communicable Disease Report*, *46*(6), 161–168. doi:10.14745/ccdr.v46i06a02 PMID:32673380

Basuroy, T. (2022, October 14). *Cybercrime in India - Statistics & Facts 2021*. Statista. https://www.statista.com/statistics/1097071/india-number-of-cyber-crimes-by-leading-state/

Behera, M. K., & Nayak, N. (2020). A comparative study on short-term PV power forecasting using decomposition based optimized extreme learning machine algorithm. *Engineering Science and Technology, an International Journal*, *23*(1), 156–167. doi:10.1016/j.jestch.2019.03.006

Benwal, N. (2021, February 11). Bhima-Koregaon Case: Key Evidence Was Planted? *The Free Press Journal*. https://epaper.freepressjournal.in/2990683/Free-Press-Mumbai-Epaper-Edition/11-Feb-2021

Berman, D. S., Buczak, A. L., Chavis, J. S., & Corbett, C. L. (2019). A survey of deep learning methods for cyber security. *Information (Basel)*, *10*(4), 122. doi:10.3390/info10040122

Bhajantri, L. B., & Mujawar, T. (2019). A survey of cloud computing security challenges, issues and their countermeasures. *2019 Third International Conference on I-SMAC (IoT in Social, Mobile, Analytics and Cloud)(I-SMAC)*, (pp. 376–380). ACM. 10.1109/I-SMAC47947.2019.9032545

Bitter, C., Elizondo, D. A., & Watson, T. (2010, July). Application of artificial neural networks and related techniques to intrusion detection. In *The 2010 International Joint Conference on Neural Networks (IJCNN)* (pp. 1-8). IEEE. 10.1109/IJCNN.2010.5596532

Boopathi, S. (2021). *Pollution monitoring and notification: Water pollution monitoring and notification using intelligent RC boat.*

Boopathi, S. (2023). Deep Learning Techniques Applied for Automatic Sentence Generation. In Promoting Diversity, Equity, and Inclusion in Language Learning Environments (pp. 255–273). IGI Global. doi:10.4018/978-1-6684-3632-5.ch016

Boopathi, S. (2023b). Securing Healthcare Systems Integrated With IoT: Fundamentals, Applications, and Future Trends. In Dynamics of Swarm Intelligence Health Analysis for the Next Generation (pp. 186–209). IGI Global.

Boopathi, S. (2023a). Internet of Things-Integrated Remote Patient Monitoring System: Healthcare Application. In *Dynamics of Swarm Intelligence Health Analysis for the Next Generation* (pp. 137–161). IGI Global. doi:10.4018/978-1-6684-6894-4.ch008

Boopathi, S., & Kanike, U. K. (2023). Applications of Artificial Intelligent and Machine Learning Techniques in Image Processing. In *Handbook of Research on Thrust Technologies' Effect on Image Processing* (pp. 151–173). IGI Global. doi:10.4018/978-1-6684-8618-4.ch010

Brathwaite, S. (2022, August 19). *The state of AI in Cloud Security.* Software Secured. https://www.softwaresecured.com/the-state-of-ai-in-cloud-security/

Bresniker, K. (2019). Grand Challenge. *Computer, 52*(12). https://ieeexplore.ieee.org/abstract/document/8909930

Brezany, P., Ludescher, T., & Feilhauer, T. (2017). Cloud-dew computing support for automatic data analysis in life sciences. *In 2017 40th International Convention on Information and Communication Technology, Electronics and Microelectronics (MIPRO),* (pp. 365-370). IEEE.

Buczak, A. L., & Guven, E. (2015). A survey of data mining and machine learning methods for cyber security intrusion detection. *IEEE Communications Surveys and Tutorials, 18*(2), 1153–1176. doi:10.1109/COMST.2015.2494502

Burda, D., & Teutenberg, F. (2015). Understanding Service Quality and System Quality Success Factors in Cloud Archiving From an End-User Perspective. *Information Systems Management, 32*(4), 266–284. doi:10.1080/10580530.2015.1079998

Butt, U. A., Mehmood, M., Syed, B. H. S., Amin, R., Shaukat, M. W., Raza, S. M., Suh, D. Y., & Piran, M. J. (2020). A review of machine learning algorithms for cloud computing security. *Electronics (Basel), 9*(9), 1379. doi:10.3390/electronics9091379

Calderon, R. (2019). *The benefits of artificial intelligence in cybersecurity.*

Cao, R., Yu, Z., Marbach, T., Li, J., Wang, G., & Liu, X. (2018). Load Prediction for Data Centers Based on Database Service. *Proceedings - International Computer Software and Applications Conference, 1*(August), (pp. 728–737). IEEE. 10.1109/COMPSAC.2018.00109

Čeponis, D. (2021). *Research of machine and deep learning methods application for host-level intrusion detection and classification* [Doctoral dissertation, Vilniaus Gedimino technikos universitetas].

Chang, H., & Choi, E. (2011). User authentication in cloud computing. In *Ubiquitous Computing and Multimedia Applications: Second International Conference.* Springer.

Chen, L., Zhang, W., & Ye, H. (2022). Accurate workload prediction for edge data centers: Savitzky-Golay filter, CNN and BiLSTM with attention mechanism. *Applied Intelligence, 52*(11), 13027–13042. doi:10.100710489-021-03110-x

Chhibbar, A. (2020). *Navigating the Indian Cyberspace Maze - Guide for Policymakers.* KW Publishers Pvt. Ltd.

Chinnaiah, M. R., & Niranjan, N. (2018, January). Fault tolerant software systems using software configurations for cloud computing. *Journal of Cloud Computing (Heidelberg, Germany), 7*(1), 3. doi:10.118613677-018-0104-9

Choudhury, A. J., Kumar, P., Sain, M., Lim, H., & Jae-Lee, H. (2011, December). *A strong user authentication framework for cloud computing. In 2011 IEEE Asia-Pacific Services Computing Conference.* IEEE.

Ciolacu, M., Tehrani, A. F., Binder, L., & Svasta, P. M. (2018, October). Education 4.0-Artificial Intelligence assisted higher education: early recognition system with machine learning to support students' success. In *2018 IEEE 24th International Symposium for Design and Technology in Electronic Packaging(SIITME)* (pp. 23-30). IEEE.

Cloud, I., Miyaho, N., Suzuki, S., Tokyo, Y. (2014). Study of a backup service concept using secure distributed networks. *IEICE Communication society-global newsletter, 38*(3), 2

Coro. (2022). *The Biggest Cyber Security Threats.* Coro. https://go.coro.net/cyberthreats2022

Daabseha, T. K. I. K., Raqqada, R. A., Albayaydahb, H. S., Alqarallahb, R. E., Alhtibata, A., Alzbouna, E., & Aldamena, H. K. (2023). Linking between cloud computing and productivity: The mediating role of information integration. *International Journal of Data and Network Science, 7,* 1–8.

Dang, L. M., Piran, M. J., Han, D., Min, K., & Moon, H. (2019). A survey on internet of things and cloud computing for healthcare. *Electronics (Basel), 8*(7), 768. doi:10.3390/electronics8070768

Dasgupta, D., Roy, A., & Nag, A. (2017). *Advances in user authentication.* Springer International Publishing. doi:10.1007/978-3-319-58808-7

DataReportal. (2023, September 25). *Digital 2023 India*. Data Reportal. https://datareportal.com/reports/digital-2023-india

Dave, D., Meruliya, N., Gajjar, T. D., Ghoda, G. T., Parekh, D. H., & Sridaran, R. (2018). Cloud security issues and challenges. In *Big Data Analytics: Proceedings of CSI 2015*, (pp. 499-514). Springer Singapore. 10.1007/978-981-10-6620-7_48

De Moor, A., & Van Den Heuvel, W. J. (2004). Web service selection in virtual communities. *Proceedings of the Hawaii International Conference on System Sciences,* (pp. 3105–3114). IEEE. 10.1109/HICSS.2004.1265468

DeVries, W. T. (2003). Protecting Privacy in the Digital Age. *Berkeley Technology Law Journal, 18*(1), 283–311.

Dhanya, D., Kumar, S. S., Thilagavathy, A., Prasad, D., & Boopathi, S. (2023). Data Analytics and Artificial Intelligence in the Circular Economy: Case Studies. In Intelligent Engineering Applications and Applied Sciences for Sustainability (pp. 40–58). IGI Global.

Dilek, S., Cakır, H., & Aydın, M. (2015, January). Applications of Artificial Intelligence Techniques to Combating Cyber Crimes: A Review. *International Journal of Artificial Intelligence & Applications, 6*(1), 21–39. doi:10.5121/ijaia.2015.6102

Ding, S., Xia, C. Y., Le Zhou, K., Yang, S. L., & Shang, J. S. (2014). Decision Support for Personalized Cloud Service Selection through Multi-Attribute Trustworthiness Evaluation. *PLoS One, 9*(6), e97762. doi:10.1371/journal.pone.0097762 PMID:24972237

Dotson, C. (2023). *Practical Cloud Security*. O'Reilly Media, Inc.

Durairaj, M., Jayakumar, S., Karpagavalli, V., Maheswari, B. U., Boopathi, S., & ... (2023). Utilization of Digital Tools in the Indian Higher Education System During Health Crises. In *Multidisciplinary Approaches to Organizational Governance During Health Crises* (pp. 1–21). IGI Global. doi:10.4018/978-1-7998-9213-7.ch001

Ebadifard, F., & Babamir, S. M. (2021). Autonomic task scheduling algorithm for dynamic workloads through a load balancing technique for the cloud-computing environment. *Cluster Computing, 24*(2), 1075–1101. doi:10.100710586-020-03177-0

El Haloui, M., & Kriouile, A. (2017). A Decision-Support Model Enabling a Proactive Vision of Cloud Computing Adoption. *Proc. of the 2nd International Conference of Cloud Computing Technologies and Applications–CloudTech*, (pp. 24-26). IEEE.

Fang, X., Koceja, N., Zhan, J., Dozier, G., & Dipankar, D. (2012). An artificial immune system for phishing detection. *Evolutionary Computation (CEC)*. IEEE. 10.1109/CEC.2012.6256518

Fernandes, D. A. B., Soares, L. F. B., Gomes, J. V., Freire, M. M., & Inácio, P. R. M. (2014). Security issues in cloud environments: A survey. *International Journal of Information Security, 13*(2), 113–170. doi:10.100710207-013-0208-7

Flores, A. C., Icoy, R. I., Pena, C. F., & Gorro, K. D. (2018). An evaluation of SVM and naive bayes with SMOTE on sentiment analysis data set. *ICEAST 2018 - 4th International Conference on Engineering, Applied Sciences and Technology: Exploring Innovative Solutions for Smart Society*, (pp. 1–4). IEEE. 10.1109/ICEAST.2018.8434401

Fowers, J., Ovtcharov, K., Papamichael, M., Massengill, T., Liu, M., Lo, D., & Burger, D. (2018, June). A configurable cloud-scale DNN processor for real-time AI. In *2018 ACM/IEEE 45th Annual International Symposium on Computer Architecture (ISCA)* (pp. 1-14). IEEE. 10.1109/ISCA.2018.00012

Ganne, A. (2022). Cloud data security methods: Kubernetes vs Docker swarm. *International Research Journal of Modernization in Engineering Technology, 4*(11).

Gao, H., Xu, Y., Yin, Y., Zhang, W., Li, R., & Wang, X. (2020). Context-Aware QoS Prediction with Neural Collaborative Filtering for Internet-of-Things Services. *IEEE Internet of Things Journal, 7*(5), 4532–4542. doi:10.1109/JIOT.2019.2956827

Gasmi, H., Bouras, A., & Laval, J. (2018). LSTM recurrent neural networks for cybersecurity named entity recognition. *ICSEA, 11*, 2018.

GCI-ITU. (2021). *Global Cybersecurity Index 2020*. ITU. https://www.itu.int/dms_pub/itu-d/opb/str/D-STR-GCI.01-2021-PDF-E.pdf

Ge, Z. (2022). Artificial Intelligence and Machine Learning in Data Management. *Future And Fintech, The: Abcdi And Beyond*, 281.

Ge, C., Liu, Z., Xia, J., & Fang, L. (2019). Revocable identity-based broadcast proxy re-encryption for data sharing in clouds. *IEEE Transactions on Dependable and Secure Computing, 18*(3), 1214–1226. doi:10.1109/TDSC.2019.2899300

George, A. S., & Sagayarajan, S. (2023). Securing Cloud Application Infrastructure: Understanding the Penetration Testing Challenges of IaaS, PaaS, and SaaS Environments. *Partners Universal International Research Journal, 2*(1), 24–34.

Ghanem, K., Aparicio-Navarro, F. J., Kyriakopoulos, K. G., Lambotharan, S., & Chambers, J. A. (2017, December). Support vector machine for network intrusion and cyber-attack detection. In 2017 sensor signal processing for defence conference (SSPD) (pp. 1-5). IEEE. doi:10.1109/SSPD.2017.8233268

Gnanaprakasam, C., Vankara, J., Sastry, A. S., Prajval, V., Gireesh, N., & Boopathi, S. (2023). Long-Range and Low-Power Automated Soil Irrigation System Using Internet of Things: An Experimental Study. In Contemporary Developments in Agricultural Cyber-Physical Systems (pp. 87–104). IGI Global.

Goodfellow, I., Pouget-Abadie, J., Mirza, M., Xu, B., Warde-Farley, D., Ozair, S., & Bengio, Y. (2014). Generative adversarial nets. *Advances in Neural Information Processing Systems, 27*.

Government of India. (n.d.). *Information Technology Act 2000 Amended in 2008.* Ministry of Electronics and Information Technology, Government of India. https://www.meity.gov.in/writereaddata/files/it_amendment_act2008%20%281%29_0.pdf

Gozman, D., & Willcocks, L. (2019). The emerging Cloud Dilemma: Balancing innovation with cross-border privacy and outsourcing regulations. *Journal of Business Research, 97,* 235–256. doi:10.1016/j.jbusres.2018.06.006

Greeshmanth, R. C., & Shah, M. A. (2023). Novel secure data protection scheme using Martino homomorphic encryption. *Journal of Cloud Computing (Heidelberg, Germany), 12*(1), 47. doi:10.118613677-023-00425-7

Grispos, G., Glisson, W. B., & Storer, T. (2019). How good is your data? Investigating the quality of data generated during security incident response investigations. *arXiv preprint arXiv:1901.03723.* doi:10.24251/HICSS.2019.859

Grusho, A., Zabezhailo, M., Zatsarinnyi, A., & Piskovskii, V. (2017). On some artificial intelligence methods and technologies for cloud-computing protection. *Mathematical Linguistics, 51*(2), 62–74.

Guarino, A. (2013, June). Autonomous intelligent agents in cyber offence. In *2013 5th International Conference on Cyber Conflict (CYCON 2013)* (pp. 1-12). IEEE.

Gulmezoglu, B., Eisenbarth, T., & Sunar, B. (2017). Cache-based application detection in the cloud using machine learning. In *Proceedings of the 2017 ACM on Asia Conference on Computer and Communications Security,* (pp. 288-300). ACM. 10.1145/3052973.3053036

Guo, H., Zhang, Z., Xu, J., An, N., & Lan, X. (2018). Accountable proxy re-encryption for secure data sharing. *IEEE Transactions on Dependable and Secure Computing, 18*(1), 145–159. doi:10.1109/TDSC.2018.2877601

Gupta, P., Goyal, M. K., & Kumar, P. (2013). Trust and reliability based load balancing algorithm for cloud IaaS. *Proceedings of the 2013 3rd IEEE International Advance Computing Conference, IACC 2013* (pp. 65–69). IEEE. 10.1109/IAdCC.2013.6514196

Gutierrez, J. N. P., & Lee, K. (2020). An Attack-based Filtering Scheme for Slow Rate Denial-of-Service Attack Detection in Cloud Environment. *J. Multim. Inf. Syst., 7*(2), 125–136. doi:10.33851/JMIS.2020.7.2.125

Hai, T., Zhou, J., Lu, Y., Jawawi, D., Wang, D., Onyema, E. M., & Biamba, C. (2023). Enhanced security using multiple paths routine scheme in cloud-MANETs. *Journal of Cloud Computing (Heidelberg, Germany), 12*(1), 68. doi:10.118613677-023-00443-5

Halabi, T., & Bellaiche, M. (2017, April). Towards quantification and evaluation of security of cloud service providers. *J. Inf. Secur. Appl., 33,* 55–65. doi:10.1016/j.jisa.2017.01.007

Halabi, T., & Bellaiche, M. (2018, June). A broker-based framework for standardization and management of cloud security-SLAs. *Computers & Security, 75,* 59–71. doi:10.1016/j.cose.2018.01.019

Hammoud, A., Sami, H., Mourad, A., Otrok, H., Mizouni, R., & Bentahar, J. (2020). AI, blockchain, and vehicular edge computing for smart and secure IoV: Challenges and directions. *IEEE Internet of Things Magazine*, *3*(2), 68–73. doi:10.1109/IOTM.0001.1900109

Harikaran, M., Boopathi, S., Gokulakannan, S., & Poonguzhali, M. (2023). Study on the Source of E-Waste Management and Disposal Methods. In *Sustainable Approaches and Strategies for E-Waste Management and Utilization* (pp. 39–60). IGI Global. doi:10.4018/978-1-6684-7573-7.ch003

Harvard Press. (n.d.). *Privacy Preserving Machine Learning.* Harvard Press.

Hasnain, M., Ghani, I., Pasha, M. F., & Jeong, S. R. (2022). Machine Learning Methods for Trust- based Selection of Web Services. *KSII Transactions on Internet and Information Systems*, *16*(1), 38–59.

Hasnain, M., Pasha, M. F., Ghani, I., Imran, M., Alzahrani, M. Y., & Budiarto, R. (2020). Evaluating Trust Prediction and Confusion Matrix Measures for Web Services Ranking. *IEEE Access : Practical Innovations, Open Solutions*, *8*, 90847–90861. doi:10.1109/ACCESS.2020.2994222

Hassan, H., Nasir, M., Herry, M., Khairudin, N., & Adon, I. (2017). Factors influencing cloud computing adoption in small and medium enterprises. *Journal of Information and Communication Technology*, *16*(1), 21–41. doi:10.32890/jict2017.16.1.8216

He, Z., Zhang, T., & Lee, R. B. (2017). Machine learning based DDoS attack detection from source side in cloud. In *2017 IEEE 4th International Conference on Cyber Security and Cloud Computing (CSCloud)*, (pp. 114-120). IEEE. 10.1109/CSCloud.2017.58

Heilig, L., & Voß, S. (2014). A scientometric analysis of cloud computing literature. *IEEE Transactions on Cloud Computing*, *2*(3), 266–278. doi:10.1109/TCC.2014.2321168

Hema, N., Krishnamoorthy, N., Chavan, S. M., Kumar, N., Sabarimuthu, M., & Boopathi, S. (2023). A Study on an Internet of Things (IoT)-Enabled Smart Solar Grid System. In *Handbook of Research on Deep Learning Techniques for Cloud-Based Industrial IoT* (pp. 290–308). IGI Global. doi:10.4018/978-1-6684-8098-4.ch017

Hesamifard, E., Takabi, H., Ghasemi, M., & Jones, C. (2017). Privacy-preserving machine learning in cloud. In *Proceedings of the 2017 on cloud computing security workshop*, (pp. 39-43). ACM. 10.1145/3140649.3140655

Hewa, T., Braeken, A., Liyanage, M., & Ylianttila, M. (2022). Fog computing and blockchain-based security service architecture for 5g industrial iot-enabled cloud manufacturing. *IEEE Transactions on Industrial Informatics*, *18*(10), 7174–7185. doi:10.1109/TII.2022.3140792

Hillmann, J., & Guenther, E. (2021). Organizational resilience: A valuable construct for management research? *International Journal of Management Reviews*, *23*(1), 7–44. doi:10.1111/ijmr.12239

Hoang, X. D., & Nguyen, Q. C. (2018). Botnet detection based on machine learning techniques using DNS query data. *Future Internet*, *10*(5), 43. doi:10.3390/fi10050043

Hormozi, E., Hormozi, H., Akbari, M. K., & Javan, M. S. (2012). Using of machine learning into cloud environment (a survey): Managing and scheduling of resources in cloud systems. *Proceedings - 2012 7th International Conference on P2P, Parallel, Grid, Cloud and Internet Computing, 3PGCIC 2012.* IEEE. 10.1109/3PGCIC.2012.69

Huang, Q., Yang, Y., & Fu, J. (2018). Secure data group sharing and dissemination with attribute and time conditions in the public cloud. *IEEE Transactions on Services Computing, 14*(4), 1013–1025. doi:10.1109/TSC.2018.2850344

Hwang, K., Shi, Y., & Bai, X. (2014). Scale-out vs. scale-up techniques for cloud performance and productivity. *In 2014 IEEE 6th International Conference on Cloud Computing Technology and Science,* (pp. 763-768). IEEE.

Hyungsoo, J., Yongsu, P., Chi-Won, S., & Sooyong, K. (2017). Parity-based personal data recovery service in cloud. *Cluster Computing, 20*(3), 2655–2668. doi:10.100710586-017-0805-8

Ibrahim, L. M., & Saleh, I. A. (2020). A solution of loading balance in cloud computing using optimization of Bat swarm Algorithm. *Journal of Engineering Science and Technology, 15*(3), 2062–2076.

IC3 (Internet Crime Complaint Centre). (2020). *Internet Crime Report 2020.* IC3. https://www.ic3.gov/Media/PDF/AnnualReport/2020_IC3Report.pdf

Ingle, R. B., Senthil, T. S., Swathi, S., Muralidharan, N., Mahendran, G., & Boopathi, S. (2023). Sustainability and Optimization of Green and Lean Manufacturing Processes Using Machine Learning Techniques. IGI Global. doi:10.4018/978-1-6684-8238-4.ch012

Isharufe, W., Jaafar, F., & Butakov, S. (2020). Study of security issues in platform-as-a-service (paas) cloud model. *2020 International Conference on Electrical, Communication, and Computer Engineering (ICECCE),* (pp. 1–6). IEEE. 10.1109/ICECCE49384.2020.9179414

Jaatun, M.G., Lambrinoudakis, C., Rong, C. (2017). Special issue on security in cloud computing. *J Cloud Comp, 17.*

Jena, M., Das, U., & Das, M. (2022). A Pragmatic Analysis of Security Concerns in Cloud, Fog, and Edge Environment. In Predictive Data Security using AI: Insights and Issues of Blockchain, IoT, and DevOps. Springer Nature Singapore.

Joshi, M., & Das, P. (2015). *India's Intelligence Agencies: In Need of Reform and Oversight,* Issue Brief #98. Observer Research Foundation. https://www.orfonline.org/wp-content/uploads/2015/07/IssueBrief_98.pdf

Jyoti, A., Shrimali, M., Tiwari, S., & Singh, H. P. (2020). Cloud computing using load balancing and service broker policy for IT service: A taxonomy and survey. *Journal of Ambient Intelligence and Humanized Computing, 11*(11), 4785–4814. doi:10.100712652-020-01747-z

Kaneda, Y., & Mineno, H. (2016). Sliding window-based support vector regression for predicting micrometeorological data. *Expert Systems with Applications, 59,* 217–225. doi:10.1016/j.eswa.2016.04.012

Kang, M. J., & Kang, J. W. (2016). Intrusion detection system using deep neural network for in-vehicle network security. *PLoS One, 11*(6), e0155781. doi:10.1371/journal.pone.0155781 PMID:27271802

Karthik, S., Hemalatha, R., Aruna, R., Deivakani, M., Reddy, R. V. K., & Boopathi, S. (2023). Study on Healthcare Security System-Integrated Internet of Things (IoT). In Perspectives and Considerations on the Evolution of Smart Systems (pp. 342–362). IGI Global.

Kashyap, S., & Singh, A. (2022). An Ensemble-Based Method for Predicting Facebook Check-ins. *Soft Computing: Theories and Applications*, (pp. 263–285). Springer. doi:10.1007/978-981-16-1740-9_23

Kaur, G., & Bala, A. (2021). OPSA: an optimized prediction based scheduling approach for scientific applications in cloud environment. In Cluster Computing (Vol. 24, Issue 3, pp. 1955–1974). doi:10.100710586-021-03232-4

Kaur, J., & Ramkumar, K. R. (2022). The Recent Trends in Cyber Security: A Review. *Journal of King Saud University. Computer and Information Sciences, 34*(8), 5766–5781. doi:10.1016/j.jksuci.2021.01.018

Kaur, K., Garg, S., Aujla, G. S., Kumar, N., & Zomaya, A. Y. (2022). A Multi-Objective Optimization Scheme for Job Scheduling in Sustainable Cloud Data Centers. *IEEE Transactions on Cloud Computing, 10*(1), 172–186. doi:10.1109/TCC.2019.2950002

Kavitha, C. R., Varalatchoumy, M., Mithuna, H. R., Bharathi, K., Geethalakshmi, N. M., & Boopathi, S. (2023). Energy Monitoring and Control in the Smart Grid: Integrated Intelligent IoT and ANFIS. In M. Arshad (Ed.), (pp. 290–316). Advances in Bioinformatics and Biomedical Engineering. IGI Global. doi:10.4018/978-1-6684-6577-6.ch014

Kavitha, S., Bora, A., Naved, M., Raj, K. B., & Singh, B. R. N. (2021). An internet of things for data security in cloud using artificial intelligence. *International Journal of Grid and Distributed Computing, 14*(1), 1257–1275.

Kececi, A., Yildirak, A., Ozyazici, K., Ayluctarhan, G., Agbulut, O., & Zincir, I. (2020). Implementation of machine learning algorithms for gait recognition. *Engineering Science and Technology, an International Journal, 23*(4), 931–937. doi:10.1016/j.jestch.2020.01.005

Keelery, S. (2020, October 16). *Internet Economy Value India: 2016-2020*. Statista. https://www.statista.com/statistics/792053/india-value-of-internet-economy/

Khan, S., Al-Mogren, A. S., & AlAjmi, M. F. (2015). Using cloud computing to improve network operations and management. *In 2015 5th National Symposium on Information Technology: Towards New Smart World (NSITNSW)*, (pp. 1-6). IEEE.

Khan, F. M., & Gupta, R. (2020). ARIMA and NAR based prediction model for time series analysis of COVID-19 cases in India. *Journal of Safety Science and Resilience, 1*(1), 12–18. doi:10.1016/j.jnlssr.2020.06.007

Khan, N., & Al-Yasiri, A. (2016). Identifying cloud security threats to strengthen cloud computing adoption framework. *Procedia Computer Science, 94*, 485–490. doi:10.1016/j.procs.2016.08.075

KhanR. (2013). *Cyber Privacy Issues in India*. SSRN. doi:10.2139/ssrn.2357266

Khashan, O. A. (2020). Hybrid lightweight proxy re-encryption scheme for secure fog-to-things environment. *IEEE Access : Practical Innovations, Open Solutions, 8*, 66878–66887. doi:10.1109/ACCESS.2020.2984317

Kim, J., Kim, J., Thu, H. L. T., & Kim, H. (2016, February). Long short term memory recurrent neural network classifier for intrusion detection. In 2016 international conference on platform technology and service (PlatCon) (pp. 1-5). IEEE. doi:10.1109/PlatCon.2016.7456805

Koley, S., & Ghosh, S. (2015). Cloud Computing with CDroid OS based on fujitsu Server for Mobile Technology. *Bilingual International Conference on Information Technology: Yesterday, Today, and Tomorrow*. Research Gate.

Koley, S., Ghosh, S. (2014). CDroid in Fujitsu Server for Mobile Cloud. *Data Analytics and Business Intelligence: Emerging Paradigms, 80*.

Koley, S., & Acharjya, P. P. (2022). *Prevalence of Multi-Agent System Consensus in Cloud Computing*. Multi Agent Systems. doi:10.1007/978-981-19-0493-6_4

Koley, S., Acharjya, P. P., Keshari, P., & Mandal, K. K. (2022). *Predictive Analysis of Biomass with Green Mobile Cloud Computing for Environment Sustainability. Green Mobile Cloud Computing*. Springer. doi:10.1007/978-3-031-08038-8_12

Koley, S., & Ghosh, S. (2014). Cloud Computing with CDroid OS based on Fujitsu Server for Mobile Technology. *SKIT Research Journal., 4*(2), 1–6.

Koley, S., & Jain, R. (2015). Advanced Technique for best use of CDroid OS for Mobile Cloud and Sharing. *Bilingual International Conference on Information Technology: Yesterday, Today, and Tomorrow*. SSRN. 10.2139srn.2873585

Koley, S., & Singh, N. (2014). Cdroid: Used In Fujitsu Server For Mobile Cloud. *SSRN, 2*, 1–14. doi:10.2139srn.2873457

Koshariya, A. K., Kalaiyarasi, D., Jovith, A. A., Sivakami, T., Hasan, D. S., & Boopathi, S. (2023). AI-Enabled IoT and WSN-Integrated Smart Agriculture System. In *Artificial Intelligence Tools and Technologies for Smart Farming and Agriculture Practices* (pp. 200–218). IGI Global. doi:10.4018/978-1-6684-8516-3.ch011

Koshariya, A. K., Khatoon, S., Marathe, A. M., Suba, G. M., Baral, D., & Boopathi, S. (2023). Agricultural Waste Management Systems Using Artificial Intelligence Techniques. In *AI-Enabled Social Robotics in Human Care Services* (pp. 236–258). IGI Global. doi:10.4018/978-1-6684-8171-4.ch009

Kumar, R., Lal, S. P., & Sharma, A. (2016). Detecting denial of service attacks in the cloud. Proc. *IEEE 14th Int. Conf. Dependable, Autonomic Secure Comput., 14th Int. Conf. Pervas. Intell. Comput*. IEEE. 10.1109/DASC-PICom-DataCom-CyberSciTec.2016.70

Kumar, G. (2019). A review on data protection of cloud computing security, benefits, risks and suggestions. *United International Journal for Research & Technology*, *1*(2), 26–34.

Kumari, A., Gupta, R., Tanwar, S., & Kumar, N. (2020). Blockchain and AI amalgamation for energy cloud management: Challenges, solutions, and future directions. *Journal of Parallel and Distributed Computing*, *143*, 148–166. doi:10.1016/j.jpdc.2020.05.004

Kumar, P. R., Meenakshi, S., Shalini, S., Devi, S. R., & Boopathi, S. (2023). Soil Quality Prediction in Context Learning Approaches Using Deep Learning and Blockchain for Smart Agriculture. In R. Kumar, A. B. Abdul Hamid, & N. I. Binti Ya'akub (Eds.), (pp. 1–26). Advances in Computational Intelligence and Robotics. IGI Global. doi:10.4018/978-1-6684-9151-5.ch001

Kumar, P., & Alphonse, P. J. A. (2018, April). Attribute based encryption in cloud computing: A survey, gap analysis, and future directions. *Journal of Network and Computer Applications*, *108*, 37–52. doi:10.1016/j.jnca.2018.02.009

Kumar, R., & Goyal, R. (2019). On cloud security requirements, threats, vulnerabilities and countermeasures: A survey. *Computer Science Review*, *33*, 1–48. doi:10.1016/j.cosrev.2019.05.002

Kunduru, A. R. (2023). Artificial intelligence usage in cloud application performance improvement. *Central Asian Journal of Mathematical Theory and Computer Sciences*, *4*(8), 42–47.

Kwame, O.-B. O. A., Xia, Q., Sifah, E. B., Christian, N. A. C., Xia, H., & Gao, J. (2022). A Proxy Re-Encryption Approach to Secure Data Sharing in the Internet of Things Based on Blockchain. *IEEE Vol*, *16*(1), 2164–5188.

Lal, N. A., Prasad, S., & Farik, M. (2016). *A review of authentication methods*.

Lal, P., & Bharadwaj, S. S. (2015). Assessing the performance of cloud-based customer relationship management systems. *Skyline Business Journal*, *11*(1), 89–101.

Leo, O., Thomas, A., & Hussain, S. (2023). *Uses of Artificial Intelligence Techniques in Cyber security: A Narrative Overview*. IEEE.

Li, W., Wu, J., Cao, J., Chen, N., Zhang, Q., & Buyya, R. (2021). Blockchain-based trust management in cloud computing systems: a taxonomy, review and future directions. In Journal of Cloud Computing, 10(1). doi:10.118613677-021-00247-5

Licklider, J. C. R. Britannica, The Editors of Encyclopaedia. *Encyclopedia Britannica*, https://www.britannica.com/biography/J-C-R-Licklider [Accessed 01 June 2023].

Li, J. H. (2018). Cyber security meets artificial intelligence: A survey. *Frontiers of Information Technology & Electronic Engineering*, *19*(12), 1462–1474. doi:10.1631/FITEE.1800573

Li, J., Wang, S., Li, Y., Wang, H., Wang, H., Wang, H., Chen, J., & You, Z. (2019). An Efficient Attribute-Based Encryption Scheme With Policy Update and File Update in Cloud Computing. *IEEE Transactions on Industrial Informatics, 15*(2), 1919–4770. doi:10.1109/TII.2019.2931156

Li, K. (2017). Quantitative modeling and analytical calculation of elasticity in cloud computing. *IEEE Transactions on Cloud Computing, 8*(4), 1135–1148. doi:10.1109/TCC.2017.2665549

Lindsay, D. (2014). The Right to Be Forgotten - European Data Protection Law. In Emerging Challenges in Privacy Law: Comparative Perspectives (pp. 290-293). Cambridge University Press.

Linguistics, M. (2017). Trust issues that create threats for cyber-attacks in cloud computing. Proc. *IEEE 17th Int. Conf. Parallel Distrib. Syst.* (pp. 900–905). IEEE. 10.1109/ICPADS.2011.156

Litton, A. (2015). The State of Surveillance in India: The Central Monitoring System's Chilling Effect on Self-Expression. *Washington University Global Studies Law Review, 14*(4), 799-822. https://openscholarship.wustl.edu/cgi/viewcontent.cgi?article=1556&context=law_globalstudies

Liu, C., Liu, C., Shang, Y., Chen, S., Cheng, B., & Chen, J. (2017). An adaptive prediction approach based on workload pattern discrimination in the cloud. *Journal of Network and Computer Applications, 80*(December 2016), 35–44. doi:10.1016/j.jnca.2016.12.017

Li, Z., Liao, L., Leung, H., Li, B., & Li, C. (2017). Evaluating the credibility of cloud services. *Computers & Electrical Engineering, 58*, 161–175. doi:10.1016/j.compeleceng.2016.05.014

Maguluri, L. P., Ananth, J., Hariram, S., Geetha, C., Bhaskar, A., & Boopathi, S. (2023). Smart Vehicle-Emissions Monitoring System Using Internet of Things (IoT). In Handbook of Research on Safe Disposal Methods of Municipal Solid Wastes for a Sustainable Environment (pp. 191–211). IGI Global.

Maguluri, L. P., Arularasan, A. N., & Boopathi, S. (2023). Assessing Security Concerns for AI-Based Drones in Smart Cities. In R. Kumar, A. B. Abdul Hamid, & N. I. Binti Ya'akub (Eds.), (pp. 27–47). Advances in Computational Intelligence and Robotics. IGI Global. doi:10.4018/978-1-6684-9151-5.ch002

Mahan, F., Rozehkhani, S. M., & Pedrycz, W. (2021). A novel resource productivity based on granular neural network in cloud computing. *Complexity, 2021*, 2021. doi:10.1155/2021/5556378

Maheswari, B. U., Imambi, S. S., Hasan, D., Meenakshi, S., Pratheep, V., & Boopathi, S. (2023). Internet of Things and Machine Learning-Integrated Smart Robotics. In Global Perspectives on Robotics and Autonomous Systems: Development and Applications (pp. 240–258). IGI Global. doi:10.4018/978-1-6684-7791-5.ch010

Mahmoud, Q. H. (2022). Analysis of Job Failure and Prediction Model for Cloud Computing Using Machine Learning. *Sensors, 22*.

Markets and Markets. (2019). *AI in cybersecurity market*. Markets and Markets www.marketsandmarkets.com

Martínez Torres, J., Iglesias Comesaña, C., & García-Nieto, P. J. (2019). Machine learning techniques applied to cybersecurity. *International Journal of Machine Learning and Cybernetics*, *10*(10), 2823–2836. doi:10.100713042-018-00906-1

Mathias, S. (2023, August 22). *Indian Parliament Passes Digital Personal Data Protection Act*. Kochhar & Co. Legal Update. https://www.huntonprivacyblog.com/2023/08/22/india-passes-digital-personal-data-protection-act/

McDaniel, P., Launchbury, J., Martin, B., Wang, C., & Kautz, H. (2020). *Artificial intelligence and cyber security: opportunities and challenges technical workshop summary report.* Networking & Information Technology Research And Development Subcommittee And The Machine Learning & Artificial Intelligence Subcommittee Of The National Science & Technology Council.

Mehmood, T., Latif, S., & Malik, S. (2018). Prediction of Cloud Computing Resource Utilization. *2018 15th International Conference on Smart Cities: Improving Quality of Life Using ICT and IoT, HONET-ICT 2018*, (pp. 38–42). IEEE. 10.1109/HONET.2018.8551339

Mehta, S., & Singh, V. (2012). Internet Usage and Cyber-Victimization in Indian Society. *Academic Discourse*, *1*(2), 124–131.

Mehta, S., & Singh, V. (2012a). Combating the Cybercrime: Practices in Indian Society. *International Journal of Computing and Business Research*, *3*(3), 1–10.

Mehta, S., & Singh, V. (2013). A Study of Awareness about Cyberlaws in the Indian Society. *International Journal of Computing and Business Research*, *4*(1), 124–131.

Mell, P., & Grance, T. (2011). *The NIST Definition of Cloud Computing Recommendations of the National Institute of Standards and Technology*. National Institute of Standards and Technology Special Publication. doi:10.6028/NIST.SP.800-145

Mishra, S., & Tyagi, A. K. (2022). The role of machine learning techniques in internet of things-based cloud applications. *Artificial intelligence-based internet of things systems*, 105-135.

Mittal, H., Tripathi, A. K., Pandey, A. C., Venu, P., Menon, V. G., & Pal, R. (2022). A novel fuzzy clustering-based method for human activity recognition in cloud-based industrial IoT environment. *Wireless Networks*, *8*, 1–3. doi:10.100711276-022-03011-y

Model, A., Users, M., Wang, H., Yang, Z., & Shi, Y. (2019). Next Location Prediction Based on an Adaboost-Markov Model of Mobile Users. *Sensors 2019*, *19*(1475), 1–19. doi:10.3390/s19061475

Mohanty, A., Venkateswaran, N., Ranjit, P., Tripathi, M. A., & Boopathi, S. (2023). Innovative Strategy for Profitable Automobile Industries: Working Capital Management. In Handbook of Research on Designing Sustainable Supply Chains to Achieve a Circular Economy (pp. 412–428). IGI Global.

Mohanty, R., Ravi, V., & Patra, M. R. (2010). Web-services classification using intelligent techniques. *Expert Systems with Applications*, *37*(7), 5484–5490. doi:10.1016/j.eswa.2010.02.063

Moisset, S. (2023, May 25). *How security analysts can use AI in Cybersecurity.* freeCodeCamp.org. https://www.freecodecamp.org/news/how-to-use-artificial-intelligence-in-cybersecurity/#:~:text=AI%2Dbased%20solutions%20can%20also,activity%20and%20alert%20security%20teams

Moreno-Vozmediano, R., Montero, R. S., Huedo, E., & Llorente, I. M. (2019). Efficient resource provisioning for elastic cloud services based on machine learning techniques. *Journal of Cloud Computing (Heidelberg, Germany), 8*(1), 1–18. doi:10.118613677-019-0128-9

Morgan, S. (2022, January 19). *2022 Cybersecurity Almanac: 100 Facts, Figures, Predictions And Statistics.* Cybersecurity Ventures. https://cybersecurityventures.com/cybersecurity-almanac-2022/

Mueller, H., Gogouvitis, S. V., Seitz, A., & Bruegge, B. (2017). Seamless computing for industrial systems spanning cloud and edge. *In 2017 International Conference on High Performance Computing & Simulation (HPCS),* (pp. 209-216). IEEE. 10.1109/HPCS.2017.40

Mukhopadhyay, B., Bose, R., & Roy, S. (2020). A novel approach to load balancing and cloud computing security using SSL in IaaS environment. *International Journal (Toronto, Ont.), 9*(2).

Muralidhara, P. (2017). The evolution of cloud computing security: addressing emerging threats. *International journal of computer science and technology, 1*(4), 1–33.

Muralidhara, P. (2017). The Evolution Of Cloud Computing Security: Addressing Emerging Threats. *International Journal Of Computer Science And Technology, 1*(4), 1–33.

Nagrajan, R., Kumar, A., Kartik, J. C. S., Gupta, S., Kakarya, D., Raghuvanshi, P., & Mathur, S. (2023). *Decoding the Digital Personal Data Protection Act, 2023.* KPMG. https://assets.kpmg.com/content/dam/kpmg/in/pdf/2023/08/decoding-the-digital-personal-data-protection-act-2023.pdf

Nassif, B., Talib, M. A., Nasir, Q., Albadani, H., & Dakalbab, F. M. (2021). Machine Learning for Cloud Security: A Systematic Review. *IEEE Access : Practical Innovations, Open Solutions, 9,* 20717–20735. doi:10.1109/ACCESS.2021.3054129

National Crimes Record Bureau. (2022). *Crime in India 2021.* NCRB. https://ncrb.gov.in/en/Crime-in-India-2021

Nawrocki, P., Osypanka, P., Nawrocki, P., & Osypanka, P. (2021). Cloud Resource Demand Prediction using Machine Learning in the Context of QoS Parameters. *Journal of Grid Computing, 19*(2), 1–20. doi:10.1007/s10723-021-09561-3

Nenvani, G., & Gupta, H. (2016). A survey on attack detection on cloud using supervised learning techniques. In *2016 Symposium on Colossal Data Analysis and Networking (CDAN),* (pp. 1-5). IEEE. 10.1109/CDAN.2016.7570872

Network of Chinese Human Rights Defenders. (2018, July 16). (submitted to). [The Committee on the Elimination of Racial Discrimination.]. *Joint Civil Society Report.*

Okafor, C. E., Okafor, E. J., & Ikebudu, K. O. (2022). Evaluation of machine learning methods in predicting optimum tensile strength of microwave post-cured composite tailored for weight-sensitive applications. *Engineering Science and Technology, an International Journal, 25,* 100985. doi:10.1016/j.jestch.2021.04.004

Ostroukh, A. V., & Salniy, A. G. (2015). Research of Performance Linux Kernel File Systems. *International Journal of Advanced Studies, 5*(2), 12–17. doi:10.12731/2227-930X-2015-2-2

Pacheco, J., & Hariri, S. (2018). Anomaly behavior analysis for IoT sensors. *Transactions on Emerging Telecommunications Technologies, 29*(4), e3188. doi:10.1002/ett.3188

Padhy, R. P., Ratra, M. R., & Satapathy, S. C. (2011). Cloud Computing : Security Issues and Research Challenges. *IRACST - International Journal of Computer Science and Information Technology & Security (IJCSITS), 1*(2), 136–146.

Padron, J. M., & Ojeda-Castro, A. (2017). Cyberwarfare: Artificial intelligence in the frontlines of combat. *International Journal of Information Research and Review, 4*(6), 4208–4212.

Pal, A., Das, G., Hanheide, M., Candea Leite, A., & From, P. J. (2022). An Agricultural Event Prediction Framework towards Anticipatory Scheduling of Robot Fleets: General Concepts and Case Studies. In Agronomy, 12(6). doi:10.3390/agronomy12061299

Pallaprolu, S. C., Sankineni, R., Thevar, M., Karabatis, G., & Wang, J. (2017, June). Zero-day attack identification in streaming data using semantics and Spark. In *2017 IEEE International Congress on Big Data (BigData Congress)* (pp. 121-128). IEEE. 10.1109/BigDataCongress.2017.25

Pandey, U., Rajput, M., & Singh, R. (2023). Role of Machine Learning in Resource Usages and Security Challenges for Cloud Computing: Survey. In *2023 International Conference on Artificial Intelligence and Smart Communication (AISC),* (pp. 525-530). IEEE. 10.1109/AISC56616.2023.10085687

Parameswarappa, P., Shah, T., & Lanke, G. R. (2023). A Machine Learning-Based Approach for Anomaly Detection for Secure Cloud Computing Environments. In *2023 International Conference on Intelligent Data Communication Technologies and Internet of Things (IDCIoT),* (pp. 931-940). IEEE. 10.1109/IDCIoT56793.2023.10053518

Parast, F. K., Sindhav, C., Nikam, S., Yekta, H. I., Kent, K. B., & Hakak, S. (2022). Cloud computing security: A survey of service-based models. *Computers & Security, 114,* 102580. doi:10.1016/j.cose.2021.102580

Patel, A., Taghavi, M., Bakhtiyari, K., & Jr, J. (2012). An Intrusion Detection And Prevention System In Cloud Computing: A Systematic Review. *Journal of Network and Computer Applications, 36*(1), 25–41. doi:10.1016/j.jnca.2012.08.007

Patil, P. (2016). Artificial intelligence in cyber security. *International Journal of research computer application and robotics.*

Pavithra, B. (2023). Cloud Security Analysis using Machine Learning Algorithms. In *2023 Second International Conference on Augmented Intelligence and Sustainable Systems (ICAISS)*, (pp. 704-708). IEEE. 10.1109/ICAISS58487.2023.10250594

Petrosyan, A. (2023, September 22). Worldwide Digital Population 2023. Statista Report. https://www.statista.com/statistics/617136/digital-population-worldwide/

Pirro, G., Talia, D., Trunfio, P., Missier, P., & Goble, C. (2008). *ERGOT: Combining DHTs and SONs for Semantic-Based Service Discovery on the Grid.* (CoreGRID Technical Report Number TR-0177). CoreGRID.

Prakash, K. B., Imambi, S. S., Ismail, M., Kumar, T. P., & Pawan, Y. V. R. N. (2020). Analysis, prediction and evaluation of COVID-19 datasets. *International Journal of Emerging Trends in Engineering Research*, 8(5), 2199–2204. doi:10.30534/ijeter/2020/117852020

Pramila, P., Amudha, S., Saravanan, T., Sankar, S. R., Poongothai, E., & Boopathi, S. (2023). Design and Development of Robots for Medical Assistance: An Architectural Approach. In Contemporary Applications of Data Fusion for Advanced Healthcare Informatics (pp. 260–282). IGI Global.

Rahamathunnisa, U., Subhashini, P., Aancy, H. M., Meenakshi, S., Boopathi, S., & ... (2023). Solutions for Software Requirement Risks Using Artificial Intelligence Techniques. In *Handbook of Research on Data Science and Cybersecurity Innovations in Industry 4.0 Technologies* (pp. 45–64). IGI Global.

Rahamathunnisa, U., Sudhakar, K., Murugan, T. K., Thivaharan, S., Rajkumar, M., & Boopathi, S. (2023). Cloud Computing Principles for Optimizing Robot Task Offloading Processes. In *AI-Enabled Social Robotics in Human Care Services* (pp. 188–211). IGI Global. doi:10.4018/978-1-6684-8171-4.ch007

Raheja, S., & Munjal, G. (2021). Classification of Microsoft office vulnerabilities: a step ahead for secure software development. *Bio-inspired Neurocomputing*, (pp. 381-402).

Raheja, S., Munjal, G., Jangra, J., & Garg, R. (2021). Rule-Based Approach for Botnet Behavior Analysis. *Intelligent Data Analytics for Terror Threat Prediction: Architectures, Methodologies, Techniques and Applications*, (pp. 161-179).

Rahimi, M., Navimipour, N. J., Hosseinzadeh, M., Moattar, M. H., & Darwesh, A. (2021). *Toward the efficient service selection approaches in cloud computing.* Emerald. doi:10.1108/K-02-2021-0129

Ramanpreet, K. (2023). Artificial intelligence for cybersecurity: Literature review and future research directions. *Information Fusion, 97,* 101804. doi:10.1016/j.inffus.2023.101804

Ramudu, K., Mohan, V. M., Jyothirmai, D., Prasad, D., Agrawal, R., & Boopathi, S. (2023). Machine Learning and Artificial Intelligence in Disease Prediction: Applications, Challenges, Limitations, Case Studies, and Future Directions. In Contemporary Applications of Data Fusion for Advanced Healthcare Informatics (pp. 297–318). IGI Global.

Rani, P., Kavita, Verma, S., Kaur, N., Wozniak, M., Shafi, J., & Ijaz, M. F. (2021). Robust and secure data transmission using artificial intelligence techniques in ad-hoc networks. *Sensors (Basel)*, *22*(1), 251. doi:10.339022010251 PMID:35274628

Rathore, M. (2023, July 10). *Amount of Trained Beneficiaries in Digital Literacy in India FY 2018-2022*. Statista Report. https://www.statista.com/statistics/1196927/india-trained-beneficiaries-in-digital-literacy-scheme/

Rawai, N. M., Fathi, M. S., Abedi, M., & Rambat, S. (2013). Cloud computing for green construction management, *Third International Conference on Intelligent System Design and Engineering Applications*, (pp. 432-435). IEEE.

Rayhan, R., & Rayhan, S. (2023). *AI and Human Rights: Balancing Innovation and Privacy in the Digital Age*. DOI.

Reddy, M. A., Gaurav, A., Ushasukhanya, S., Rao, V. C. S., Bhattacharya, S., & Boopathi, S. (2023). Bio-Medical Wastes Handling Strategies During the COVID-19 Pandemic. In Multidisciplinary Approaches to Organizational Governance During Health Crises (pp. 90–111). IGI Global. doi:10.4018/978-1-7998-9213-7.ch006

Reddy, M. A., Reddy, B. M., Mukund, C., Venneti, K., Preethi, D., & Boopathi, S. (2023). Social Health Protection During the COVID-Pandemic Using IoT. In *The COVID-19 Pandemic and the Digitalization of Diplomacy* (pp. 204–235). IGI Global. doi:10.4018/978-1-7998-8394-4.ch009

Rigdon, E. E., Sarstedt, M., & Ringle, C. M. (2017). On comparing results from CB-SEM and PLS-SEM: Five perspectives and five recommendations. *Marketing: ZFP–Journal of Research and Management*, *39*(3), 4–16.

RM, S. P., Bhattacharya, S., Maddikunta, P. K. R., Somayaji, S. R. K., Lakshmanna, K., Kaluri, R., Hussien, A., & Gadekallu, T. R. (2020). Load balancing of energy cloud using wind driven and firefly algorithms in internet of everything. *Journal of Parallel and Distributed Computing*, *142*, 16–26. doi:10.1016/j.jpdc.2020.02.010

ROI4CIO. (2023). *Darktrace the enterprise immune system*. ROI4CIO. https://roi4cio.com/catalog/en/product/darktrace-the-enterprise-immune-system

Saha, M., Sengupta, A., & Das, A. (2020). *Cyber Threats in Artificial Intelligence*.

Sahi, S. K. (2015). A Review on Workload Prediction of Cloud Services. *International Journal of Computer Applications*, *109*(9), 975–8887.

Saini, D. K., Kumar, K., & Gupta, P. (2022). Security issues in IoT and cloud computing service models with suggested solutions. *Security and Communication Networks*, *2022*, 2022. doi:10.1155/2022/4943225

Salman, T., Bhamare, D., Erbad, A., Jain, R., & Samaka, M. (2017). Machine learning for anomaly detection and categorization in multi-cloud environments. In *2017 IEEE 4th international conference on cyber security and cloud computing (CSCloud)*, (pp. 97-103). IEEE. 10.1109/CSCloud.2017.15

Samuel, P., Jayashree, K., Babu, R., & Vijay, K. (2023). Artificial Intelligence, Machine Learning, and IoT Architecture to Support Smart Governance. In K. Saini, A. Mummoorthy, R. Chandrika, & N. Gowri Ganesh (Eds.), *AI, IoT, and Blockchain Breakthroughs in E-Governance* (pp. 95–113). IGI Global. doi:10.4018/978-1-6684-7697-0.ch007

Sankar, K. M., Booba, B., & Boopathi, S. (2023). Smart Agriculture Irrigation Monitoring System Using Internet of Things. In *Contemporary Developments in Agricultural Cyber-Physical Systems* (pp. 105–121). IGI Global. doi:10.4018/978-1-6684-7879-0.ch006

Saoud, Z., Faci, N., Maamar, Z., & Benslimane, D. (2016). A fuzzy-based credibility model to assess Web services trust under uncertainty. *Journal of Systems and Software*, *122*, 496–506. doi:10.1016/j.jss.2015.09.040

Sarirete, A., Balfagih, Z., Brahimi, T., Lytras, M. D., & Visvizi, A. (2022). Artificial intelligence and machine learning research: Towards digital transformation at a global scale. *Journal of Ambient Intelligence and Humanized Computing*, *13*(7), 3319–3321. doi:10.100712652-021-03168-y

Sarker, I. H., Kayes, A. S. M., Badsha, S., Alqahtani, H., Watters, P., & Ng, A. (2020). Cybersecurity data science: An overview from machine learning perspective. *Journal of Big Data*, *7*(1), 1–29. doi:10.118640537-020-00318-5

Sarmah, A., Sarmah, R., & Baruah, A. J. (2017). A Brief Study on Cyber Crime and Cyber Laws of India. *International Research Journal of Engineering and Technology*, *4*(6), 1633–1641.

Satav, S. D., & Lamani, D. G, H. K., Kumar, N. M. G., Manikandan, S., & Sampath, B. (2024). Energy and Battery Management in the Era of Cloud Computing. In Practice, Progress, and Proficiency in Sustainability (pp. 141–166). IGI Global. doi:10.4018/979-8-3693-1186-8.ch009

Satav, S. D., Hasan, D. S., Pitchai, R., Mohanaprakash, T. A., Sultanuddin, S. J., & Boopathi, S. (2024). Next Generation of Internet of Things (NGIoT) in Healthcare Systems. In Practice, Progress, and Proficiency in Sustainability (pp. 307–330). IGI Global. doi:10.4018/979-8-3693-1186-8.ch017

Sawaneh, I. A., Kamara, F. K., & Kamara, A. (2021). Cybersecurity: A Key Challenge to the Information Age in Sierra Leone. *Asian Journal of Interdisciplinary Research*, *4*(1), 35–46. doi:10.34256/ajir2114

Saxena, A., Asbe, C., & Vashishth, T. (2023). Leveraging a Novel Machine Learning Approach to Forecast Income and Immigration Dynamics. *Multidisciplinary Science Journal*, *5*. . doi:10.31893/multiscience.2023ss0202

Sayegh, E. (2023, August 23). Artificial Intelligence and clouds: A complex relationship of collaboration and concern. *Forbes*. https://www.forbes.com/sites/emilsayegh/2023/08/23/artificial-intelligence-and-clouds-a-complex-relationship-of-collaboration-and-concern/?sh=7472b5725c19

Schneckenberg, D., Benitez, J., Klos, C., Velamuri, V. K., & Spieth, P. (2021). Value creation and appropriation of software vendors: A digital innovation model for cloud computing. *Information & Management*, *58*(4), 103463. doi:10.1016/j.im.2021.103463

Schwartz, P. M. (1999). Internet Privacy and the State. *Connecticut Law Review, 815*. https://escholarship.org/uc/item/37x3z12g

Schwartz, P. M. (1999b). Privacy and Democracy in Cyberspace. *Vanderbilt Law Review, 52*, 1609–1701. https://escholarship.org/uc/item/2fq3v1mj

Selvarajan, S., Srivastava, G., Khadidos, A. O., Khadidos, A. O., Baza, M., Alshehri, A., & Lin, J. C.-W. (2023). An artificial intelligence lightweight blockchain security model for security and privacy in IIoT systems. *Journal of Cloud Computing (Heidelberg, Germany), 12*(1), 38. doi:10.118613677-023-00412-y PMID:36937654

Sengeni, D., Padmapriya, G., Imambi, S. S., Suganthi, D., Suri, A., & Boopathi, S. (2023). Biomedical Waste Handling Method Using Artificial Intelligence Techniques. In *Handbook of Research on Safe Disposal Methods of Municipal Solid Wastes for a Sustainable Environment* (pp. 306–323). IGI Global. doi:10.4018/978-1-6684-8117-2.ch022

Shahid, M. A., Islam, N., Alam, M. M., Su'ud, M. M., & Musa, S. (2020). A comprehensive study of load balancing approaches in the cloud computing environment and a novel fault tolerance approach. *IEEE Access : Practical Innovations, Open Solutions, 8*, 130500–130526. doi:10.1109/ACCESS.2020.3009184

Shah, J. (2016). A Study of Awareness About Cyber Laws for Indian Youth. *International Journal of Trend in Scientific Research and Development, 1*(1), 10–16. doi:10.31142/ijtsrd54

Shakeabubakor, A. A., Sundararajan, E., & Hamdan, A. R. (2015). Cloud computing services and applications to improve productivity of university researchers. *International Journal of Information and Electronics Engineering, 5*(2), 153. doi:10.7763/IJIEE.2015.V5.521

Sharma, M., & Elmiligi, H. (2022). Behavioral biometrics: Past, present and future. *Recent Advances in Biometrics, 69*.

Sharma, V., Verma, V., & Sharma, A. (2019). Detection of DDoS attacks using machine learning in cloud computing. In *Advanced Informatics for Computing Research: Third International Conference, ICAICR 2019,* (pp. 260-273). Springer Singapore. 10.1007/978-981-15-0111-1_24

Sharma, O., & Saini, H. (2016). VM Consolidation for Cloud Data Center Using Median Based Threshold Approach. *Procedia Computer Science, 89*, 27–33. doi:10.1016/j.procs.2016.06.005

Sharma, S. K., Al-Badi, A. H., Govindaluri, S. M., & Al-Kharusi, M. H. (2016). Predicting motivators of cloud computing adoption: A developing country perspective. *Computers in Human Behavior, 62*, 61–69. doi:10.1016/j.chb.2016.03.073

Sheet, M. F., & Saeed, M. J. (2022). Behavioral Features of Users as a Security Solution in Cloud Computing. In *2022 8th International Conference on Contemporary Information Technology and Mathematics (ICCITM),* (pp. 25-29). IEEE. 10.1109/ICCITM56309.2022.10031680

Sherchan, W., Nepal, S., & Bouguettaya, A. (2011). A trust prediction model for service web. *Proc. 10th IEEE Int. Conf. on Trust, Security and Privacy in Computing and Communications, TrustCom 2011, 8th IEEE Int. Conf. on Embedded Software and Systems, ICESS 2011, 6th Int. Conf. on FCST 2011*, (pp. 258–265). IEEE. 10.1109/TrustCom.2011.35

Shu, W., Zeng, F., Ling, Z., Liu, J., Lu, T., & Chen, G. (2021). Resource Demand Prediction of Cloud Workloads Using an Attention-based GRU Model. *Proceedings - 2021 17th International Conference on Mobility, Sensing and Networking, MSN 2021*, (pp. 428–437). IEEE. 10.1109/MSN53354.2021.00071

Shyam, G. K., & Manvi, S. S. (2016). Virtual resource prediction in cloud environment: A Bayesian approach. *Journal of Network and Computer Applications, 65*, 144–154. doi:10.1016/j.jnca.2016.03.002

Sikdar, A. (2021, March 10). The Economic Impact of Internet in India. Economic Update. *Times of India*. https://timesofindia.indiatimes.com/blogs/economic-update/the-economic-impact-of-internet-in-india/

Singh, V., & Malik, V. (2021). Indian Cybersecurity Turf: A 2020 Position Paper. *Journal of Network Security, 9*(1), 42–47.

Siriwardhana, Y., Porambage, P., Liyanage, M., & Ylianttila, M. (2021, June). AI and 6G security: Opportunities and challenges. In *2021 Joint European Conference on Networks and Communications & 6G Summit (EuCNC/6G Summit)* (pp. 616-621). IEEE. 10.1109/EuCNC/6GSummit51104.2021.9482503

Somu, N., R, G. R. M., Kaveri, A., & K, A. R. (2020). IBGSS : An Improved Binary Gravitational Search Algorithm based search strategy for QoS and ranking prediction in cloud environments. *Applied Soft Computing, 88*, 105945. doi:10.1016/j.asoc.2019.105945

Somu, N., R, G. R. M., Kirthivasan, K., & S, S. S. V. (2018). A trust centric optimal service ranking approach for cloud service selection. *Future Generation Computer Systems, 86*, 234–252. doi:10.1016/j.future.2018.04.033

Sowinski, D. (2023). *Cloud security in the era of artificial intelligence*. Security Intelligence. https://securityintelligence.com/posts/cloud-security-in-the-era-of-artificial-intelligence/

Srikanth. (2022, October 14). *Ai preventing next-gen data loss*. Techiexpert. https://www.techiexpert.com/ai-preventing-next-gen-data-loss/

Srinivas, B., Maguluri, L. P., Naidu, K. V., Reddy, L. C. S., Deivakani, M., & Boopathi, S. (2023). Architecture and Framework for Interfacing Cloud-Enabled Robots. In *Handbook of Research on Data Science and Cybersecurity Innovations in Industry 4.0 Technologies* (pp. 542–560). IGI Global. doi:10.4018/978-1-6684-8145-5.ch027

St. Laurent, N. (2023, July 17). *Data loss prevention and the value of Artificial Intelligence*. CISCO. https://blogs.cisco.com/government/data-loss-prevention-and-the-value-of-artificial-intelligence

Stone, M. (2023, January 17). *2023 Cloud Data Loss Prevention (DLP) overview: Concentric.* Concentric AI. https://concentric.ai/a-deep-dive-on-cloud-data-loss-prevention-dlp/

Subramanian, E. K., & Tamilselvan, L. (2019). A focus on future cloud: Machine learning-based cloud security. *Service Oriented Computing and Applications, 13*(no. 3), 237–249. doi:10.100711761-019-00270-0

Sudha, V., & Akiladevi, R. (2022). An integrated IoT blockchain security technique based on decentralized applications. Internet of Everything: Smart Sensing Technologies, 123-143.

Suganya, M., & Sasipraba, T. (2023). Stochastic Gradient Descent long short-term memory based secure encryption algorithm for cloud data storage and retrieval in cloud computing environment. *Journal of Cloud Computing (Heidelberg, Germany), 12*(1), 74. doi:10.118613677-023-00442-6

Su, K., Xiao, B., Liu, B., Zhang, H., & Zhang, Z. (2017). TAP: A personalized trust-aware QoS prediction approach for web service recommendation. *Knowledge-Based Systems, 115*, 55–65. doi:10.1016/j.knosys.2016.09.033

Sun, L., Jiang, X., Ren, H., & Guo, Y. (2020). Edge-cloud computing and artificial intelligence in internet of medical things: Architecture, technology and application. *IEEE Access : Practical Innovations, Open Solutions, 8*, 101079–101092. doi:10.1109/ACCESS.2020.2997831

Sun, Y., Susilo, W., Zhang, F., & Fu, A. (2018). CCA-secure revocable identity-based encryption with ciphertext evolution in the cloud. *IEEE Access : Practical Innovations, Open Solutions, 6*, 56977–56983. doi:10.1109/ACCESS.2018.2873019

Syamala, M., Komala, C., Pramila, P., Dash, S., Meenakshi, S., & Boopathi, S. (2023). Machine Learning-Integrated IoT-Based Smart Home Energy Management System. In *Handbook of Research on Deep Learning Techniques for Cloud-Based Industrial IoT* (pp. 219–235). IGI Global. doi:10.4018/978-1-6684-8098-4.ch013

Taddeo, M., McCutcheon, T., & Floridi, L. (2019). Trusting artificial intelligence in cybersecurity is a double-edged sword. *Nature Machine Intelligence, 1*(12), 557–560. doi:10.103842256-019-0109-1

Tahir, M., Sardaraz, M., Mehmood, Z., & Muhammad, S. (2021). CryptoGA: A cryptosystem based on genetic algorithm for cloud data security. *Cluster Computing, 24*(2), 739–752. doi:10.100710586-020-03157-4

Tasneem, S., Gupta, K. D., Roy, A., & Dasgupta, D. (2022, December). Generative Adversarial Networks (GAN) for Cyber Security: Challenges and Opportunities. In *Proceedings of the 2022 IEEE Symposium Series on Computational Intelligence*, (pp. 4-7). IEEE.

Teh, S. K., Ho, S. B., Chan, G. Y., & Tan, C. H. (2016). A framework for cloud computing use to enhance job productivity. *In 2016 IEEE Symposium on Computer Applications & Industrial Electronics (ISCAIE)*, (pp. 73-78). IEEE. 10.1109/ISCAIE.2016.7575040

The Centre for Internet and Society. (n.d.). *India's Surveillance State – Communications Surveillance in India*. CIS. https://cis-india.org/internet-governance/blog/security-surveillance-and-data-sharing.pdf

The Centre for Internet and Society. (n.d.). *State of Cyber Security and Surveillance in India - A Review of the Legal Landscape*. CIS. https://cis-india.org/internet-governance/blog/state-of-cyber-security-and-surveillance-in-india.pdf

Thottakkara, P., Ozrazgat-Baslanti, T., Hupf, B. B., Rashidi, P., Pardalos, P., Momcilovic, P., & Bihorac, A. (2016). Application of machine learning techniques to high-dimensional clinical data to forecast postoperative complications. *PLoS One*, *11*(5), 1–19. doi:10.1371/journal.pone.0155705 PMID:27232332

TRAI (Telecom Regulatory Authority of India). (2023, August 24). *Highlights of Telecom Subscription Data as on 30th June, 2023*. Press Release No. 27/2023. TRAI. https://www.trai.gov.in/sites/default/files/PR_No.77of2023.pdf

Tyugu, E. (2011, June). Artificial intelligence in cyber defense. In *2011 3rd International conference on cyber conflict* (pp. 1-11). IEEE.

Ugandar, R. E., Rahamathunnisa, U., Sajithra, S., Christiana, M. B. V., Palai, B. K., & Boopathi, S. (2023). Hospital Waste Management Using Internet of Things and Deep Learning: Enhanced Efficiency and Sustainability. In M. Arshad (Ed.), (pp. 317–343). Advances in Bioinformatics and Biomedical Engineering. IGI Global. doi:10.4018/978-1-6684-6577-6.ch015

UNCTD. (n.d.). *Data Protection and Privacy Legislation Worldwide*. The United Nations Conference on Trade and Development. https://unctad.org/page/data-protection-and-privacy-legislation-worldwide

Vahora, S. A., & Chauhan, N. C. (2019). Deep neural network model for group activity recognition using contextual relationship. *Engineering Science and Technology, an International Journal*, *22*(1), 47–54. doi:10.1016/j.jestch.2018.08.010

Varadarajan, S. (2021, July 30). Revealed: How the Wire and its Partners Cracked the Pegasus Project and What it Means for India. *The Wire*. https://thewire.in/media/revealed-how-the-wire-partners-cracked-pegasus-project-implications-india

Vashishth, T. K., Kumar, B., Sharma, V., Chaudhary, S., Kumar, S., & Sharma, K. K. (2023). The Evolution of AI and Its Transformative Effects on Computing: A Comparative Analysis. In B. Mishra (Ed.), *Intelligent Engineering Applications and Applied Sciences for Sustainability* (pp. 425–442). IGI Global., doi:10.4018/979-8-3693-0044-2.ch022

Vashishth, T. K., Sharma, V., Chaudhary, S., Panwar, R., Sharma, S., & Kumar, P. (2023). Advanced Technologies and AI-Enabled IoT Applications in High-Tech Agriculture. In A. Khang (Ed.), *Handbook of Research on AI-Equipped IoT Applications in High-Tech Agriculture* (pp. 155–166). IGI Global., doi:10.4018/978-1-6684-9231-4.ch008

Vashishth, T. K., & Vikas, B. (2023). *Exploring the Role of Computer Vision in Human Emotion Recognition: A Systematic Review and Meta-Analysis. 2023 Second International Conference on Augmented Intelligence and Sustainable Systems (ICAISS)*, Trichy, India. 10.1109/ICAISS58487.2023.10250614

Veeranjaneyulu, R., Boopathi, S., Narasimharao, J., Gupta, K. K., Reddy, R. V. K., & Ambika, R. (2023). Identification of Heart Diseases using Novel Machine Learning Method. *IEEE- Explore*, 1–6.

Venkateswaran, N., Vidhya, K., Ayyannan, M., Chavan, S. M., Sekar, K., & Boopathi, S. (2023). A Study on Smart Energy Management Framework Using Cloud Computing. In 5G, Artificial Intelligence, and Next Generation Internet of Things: Digital Innovation for Green and Sustainable Economies (pp. 189–212). IGI Global. doi:10.4018/978-1-6684-8634-4.ch009

Venkateswaran, N., Kumar, S. S., Diwakar, G., Gnanasangeetha, D., & Boopathi, S. (2023). Synthetic Biology for Waste Water to Energy Conversion: IoT and AI Approaches. In M. Arshad (Ed.), (pp. 360–384). Advances in Bioinformatics and Biomedical Engineering. IGI Global. doi:10.4018/978-1-6684-6577-6.ch017

Wagh, N., Pawar, V., & Kharat, K. (2020). *Educational Cloud Framework—A Literature Review on Finding Better Private Cloud Framework for Educational Hub.* Microservices in Big Data Analytics: Second International, ICETCE 2019, Rajasthan, India.

Wan, Y., & Gao, Q. (2016). An Ensemble Sentiment Classification System of Twitter Data for Airline Services Analysis. *Proceedings - 15th IEEE International Conference on Data Mining Workshop, ICDMW 2015*. IEEE. 10.1109/ICDMW.2015.7

Wang, S., Jia, S., & Zhang, Y. (2019). Verifiable and multi-keyword searchable attribute-based encryption scheme for cloud storage. *IEEE Access : Practical Innovations, Open Solutions*, 7, 50136–50147. doi:10.1109/ACCESS.2019.2910828

Wang, Y., Wen, J., Wang, X., Tao, B., & Zhou, W. (2019a). A cloud service trust evaluation model based on combining weights and gray correlation analysis. *Security and Communication Networks*, 2019, 1–11. doi:10.1155/2019/2437062

Whaiduzzaman, M., Haque, M. N., Rejaul Karim Chowdhury, M., & Gani, A. (2014). A study on strategic provisioning of cloud computing services. In *Scientific World Journal* (Vol. 2014). Hindawi Publishing Corporation. doi:10.1155/2014/894362

Williams, D. R., & Tang, Y. (2013). Impact of office productivity cloud computing on energy consumption and greenhousegas emissions. *Environmental Science & Technology*, 47(9), 4333–4340. doi:10.1021/es3041362 PMID:23548097

Wiranda, N., & Sadikin, F. (2021). Machine Learning for Security and Security for Machine Learning: A Literature Review. In *2021 4th International Conference on Information and Communications Technology (ICOIACT)*, (pp. 197-202). IEEE. 10.1109/ICOIACT53268.2021.9563985

Wirkuttis, N., & Klein, H. (2017). Artificial intelligence in cybersecurity. *Cyber, Intelligence, and Security*, 1(1), 103–119.

Wu, Y., Wu, L., & Cai, H. (2023). Cloud-edge data encryption in the internet of vehicles using Zeckendorf representation. *Journal of Cloud Computing (Heidelberg, Germany), 12*(1), 39. doi:10.118613677-023-00417-7

Xin, Y., Kong, L., Liu, Z., Chen, Y., Li, Y., Zhu, H., Gao, M., Hou, H., & Wang, C. (2018). Machine learning and deep learning methods for cybersecurity. *IEEE Access : Practical Innovations, Open Solutions, 6*, 35365–35381. doi:10.1109/ACCESS.2018.2836950

Xynou, M., & Hickok, E. (n.d.). *Security, Surveillance and Data Sharing Schemes and Bodies in India*. Centre for Internet and Society, India. https://cis-india.org/internet-governance/blog/security-surveillance-and-data-sharing.pdf

Yadav, T., & Rao, A. M. (2015). Technical aspects of cyber kill chain. In Security in Computing and Communications: Third International Symposium, SSCC 2015. Springer International Publishing.

Yan, J., Rui, L. L., Yang, Y., Chen, S., & Chen, X. (2022). Resource Scheduling Algorithms for Burst Network Flow in Edge Computing. *Lecture Notes in Electrical Engineering, 808 LNEE*. Springer. doi:10.1007/978-981-16-6554-7_173

Yasmina, R. Z. (2022). *Web service selection and composition based on uncertain quality of service*. Wiley. doi:10.1002/cpe.6531

Zahoman, LWu, LKe, JQu, WWang, WWang, H. (2019). Accountable Outsourcing Location-Based Services With Privacy Preservation. *IEEE Access Vol, 7*, 2169–3536.

Zeng, P., & Choo, K.-K. R. (2018). A New Kind of Conditional Proxy Re-Encryption for Secure Cloud Storage. *IEEE Access : Practical Innovations, Open Solutions, 6*, 2169–3536. doi:10.1109/ACCESS.2018.2879479

Zhang, A., Wang, L., Ye, X., & Lin, X. (2016). Light-weight and robust security-aware D2D-assist data transmission protocol for mobile-health systems. *IEEE Transactions on Information Forensics and Security, 12*(3), 662–675. doi:10.1109/TIFS.2016.2631950

Zhang, J., Li, W., Zhang, J., Xie, N., Zhang, X., Yue, K., & Kumar, D. (2018). Machine Learning Based Resource Allocation of Cloud Computing in Auction. *CMC, 56*(1), 123–135. doi:10.3970/cmc.2018.03728

Zhao, D., Traore, I., Sayed, B., Lu, W., Saad, S., Ghorbani, A., & Garant, D. (2013). Botnet detection based on traffic behavior analysis and flow intervals. *Computers & Security, 39*, 2-16.

Zolfaghari, B., Yazdinejad, A., Dehghantanha, A., Krzciok, J., & Bibak, K. (2022). The dichotomy of cloud and iot: Cloud-assisted iot from a security perspective. *arXiv preprint arXiv:2207.01590*.

About the Contributors

Sachin Chaudhary completed his Graduation from MJPRU, and Post Graduation from AKTU, Moradabad, U.P. Currently Pursuing his Ph.D. in Computer Science and Engineering from Govt. Recognized University. Presently, he is working as an Assistant Professor in the Department of Computer Science and Applications, IIMT University, Meerut, U.P, India. He has been awarded as Excellence in teaching award 2019. He is the reviewer member of some reputed journals. He has published several book chapters and research papers of national and international reputed journals.

Eugene Berna I is currently working as an Assistant Professor in the Department of Artificial Intelligence and Machine Learning, Bannari Amman Institute of Technology, Sathyamangalam. She completed her M.E in Computer Science and Engineering from Dhanalakshmi Srinivasan Engineering College, Anna University. She is pursuing her PhD from Anna University in Information and Communication Engineering and presently working in Machine Learning, Natural Language Processing and Deep Learning Projects. She has teaching experience of more than 10 years.

J. Jeyalakshmi has received B.Tech degree in Information Technology from Kamaraj College of Engineering and Technology affiliated to Anna University, Chennai, India in 2005, and M.Tech degree from Sathyabama University, Chennai, India in 2009. She has obtained Ph.D from Anna University, Chennai, India. She has published in several International Journals and Conferences. Her areas of interest include Data Analysis, Social Media Analysis.She is presently working as a Senior Assistant Professor at Department of Computer Science and Engineering, Amrita School of Computing, Amrita Vishwa Vidhyapeetham, Chennai, India.

Vijay K. is working as Assistant Professor (SG) in the department of Computer Science and Engineering, Rajalakshmi Engineering College, Chennai, Tamilnadu, India. He is B.Tech., M.E., graduate and pursuing PhD in Anna University, Chennai in the area of Cloud Computing. Having 16+ years of experience in teaching. Received the award, "Active Participation Youth", under CSI Service Award at the CSI

Annual Convention 2016. He was awarded with "Inspire Faculty Partnership Level award" in 2017 (Bronze Level) by Infosys. He is a life time member of Computer Society of India, IEI-India. He received Best Faculty Award many times. Presented/ published more than 30+ papers in various Conferences and Journals. His areas of interest include Cloud Computing, Image Processing, IOT and Machine Learning.

Shobhana Kashyap is a Research Scholar in Department of CSE in Dr. B. R. Ambedkar National Institute of Technology, Jalandhar Punjab, India since 2019. She has completed her master's from Thapar University, Patiala India. Her current research is concerned with Machine Learning and Cloud Computing. She has two year teaching experience and written papers for national and international conferences.

Santanu Koley earned his doctorate in philosophy (PhD) from CSJM University in Kanpur, Uttar Pradesh, India in 2013, and he is currently employed as a professor in the department of computer science and engineering at Haldia Institute of Technology in Haldia, West Bengal, India. In addition to sixteen years of teaching experience, he has more than fourteen years of research experience from several AICTE-approved engineering colleges across India. Dr. Koley has published more than 30 research papers in journals and conferences from throughout the nation and the world. The areas of cloud computing, digital image processing, artificial intelligence, and machine learning are where he is currently concentrating his research efforts.

Bhupendra Kumar completed his Graduation and Post Graduation from Chaudhary Charan Singh University, Meerut, U.P. and Ph.D. in Computer Science and Engineering from Mewar University, Hapur. Presently, he is working as a Professor in the Department of Computer Science and Applications, IIMT University, Meerut, U.P. He has been a huge teaching experience of 19 years. He is the reviewer member of some reputed journals. He has published several book chapters and research papers of national and international reputed journals.

Manoj Kumar obtained his Ph.D. Computer Science from The Northcap University, Gurugram. He did his B. Tech in computer science from Kurukshetra University. He obtained M. Sc. (Information Security and Forensics) degree from ITB, Dublin in and M. Tech from ITM University. Mr. Kumar has 9.5+ years of experience in research and academics. He published over 29 publications in reputed journals and conferences. He published 2 books and 5 patents with his team. Presently, Mr. Kumar is working on the post of assistant professor (SG), (SoCS) in university of petroleum and energy studies, Dehradun. He is a member of various professional bodies and reviewed for many reputed journals. He is Editorial Board Member in The

International Arab Journal of Information Technology (IAJIT), Jordon and Journal of Computer Science Research, Singapore. He is recognized as Quarterly Franklin Member (QFM) by London Journal Press from March 2019 onwards and Bentham Ambassador (India) on behalf of Bentham Science Publisher. He delivered various key speech and talks in national and international forums. He got best researcher award 2020 from ScenceFather research community.

Rajneesh Panwar Graduated and Post Graduated in Mathematics and Computer Application from Ch. Charan Singh University, Meerut (U.P.) and received his M. Tech. in Computer Science from Shobhit University, Meerut. Presently, he is working as an Assistant Professor in the School of Computer Science and Application IIMT University, Meerut, U.P. He qualifies GATE 2021 and UGC-NET June 2020 and December 2020. He has published several book chapters and research papers of national and international repute.

B.C.M. Patnaik is a Professor at KIIT University for Economics and Finance. Specialise in Rural development, Developmental Economics, Behavioral Economics and Micro-Finance.

S. Gnanavel is currently working as an Associate Professor in the department of Computing Technologies at SRM Institute of Science and Technology, Kattankulathur, Chennai, India. He Received the B.Tech (IT), M.E (CSE) and Ph.D. degree from Anna University Chennai, India. He has over 14 years of teaching and research experience. He works in the area of Multimedia transmission on Wireless Networks, Internet of Things and cloud security. His current research interests are in Machine Leaning, cyber security and cloud computing. He is a life time member of MISTE, ACM and MIANG. He published many papers in international refereed journals and conferences. He is serving as a reviewer for many journals and conferences.

Ipseeta Satpathy is a senior professor at KIIT University. Specializes in Psychology, Behavioral Science, and Organisational Behaviour.

Kewal Krishan Sharma is a professor in computer sc. in IIMT University, Meerut, U.P, India. He did his Ph.D. in computer network with this he has MCA, MBA and Law degree also. He did variously certification courses also. He has an overall experience of around 33 year in academic, business and industry. He wrote a number of research papers and books.

Vikas Sharma completed his Graduation and Post Graduation from Chaudhary Charan Singh University, Meerut, U.P. Currently Pursuing his Ph.D. in Computer

Science and Engineering from Govt. Recognized University. Presently, he is working as an Assistant Professor in the Department of Computer Science and Applications, IIMT University, Meerut, U.P. He has been awarded as Excellence in teaching award 2019. He is the reviewer member of some reputed journals. He has published several book chapters and research papers of national and international reputed journals.

Avtar Singh is working as an Assistant Professor in Department of CSE in Dr. B. R. Ambedkar National Institute of Technology, Jalandhar Punjab, India. He received the B.Tech and M.Tech degree in Computer Science Engineering from the Electro Technical University, Saint Petersburg Russia (LETI) in 1999 and 2001 respectively. In 2001, he served more than 5 years in IT industry Bangalore and leading educational institutions in year 2006. His research areas of interests include Cloud Computing, Internet of Things (IoT), Parallel and Distributed Computing and Machine Learning. He is a member of IEEE and ACM organization. He has written number of papers for national and international journals, conferences and one patent. He is currently guiding 4 research scholars at Ph.D. levels and three master's students. He has published extensively in these areas and has supervised 10 Master's students. He has organized five STC events.

Tarun Kumar Vashishth is an active academician and researcher in the field of computer science with 21 years of experience. He earned Ph.D. Mathematics degree specialized in Operations Research; served several academic positions such as HoD, Dy. Director, Academic Coordinator, Member Secretary of Department Research Committee, Assistant Center superintendent and Head Examiner in university examinations. He is involved in academic development and scholarly activities. He is member of International Association of Engineers, The Society of Digital Information and Wireless Communications, Global Professors Welfare Association, International Association of Academic plus Corporate (IAAC), Computer Science Teachers Association and Internet Society. His research interest includes Cloud Computing, Artificial Intelligence, Machine Learning and Operations Research; published more than 20 research articles with 1 book and 10 book chapters in edited books. He is contributing as member of editorial and reviewers boards in conferences and various computer journals published by CRC Press, Taylor and Francis, Springer, IGI global and other universities.

Index

A

Accountable Proxy Re-encryption 147-150, 162
Adversarial Attacks 56, 100, 108, 126
AI and Machine Learning 10, 35, 164-165, 182, 187, 201, 204
Anomaly Detection 36, 54-55, 95-96, 102, 106, 108, 110, 114, 118, 121, 123, 125, 131, 135, 207, 209
Artificial Intelligence (AI) 34-35, 45, 51-55, 85-86, 90, 92, 95, 97, 100, 102, 111-113, 115-116, 122, 124, 126, 128, 194, 197-198, 207

B

Backup 1, 7, 25-26, 28, 59-60, 63, 65-76, 78-80, 183, 186
base64 encoding 147-148, 153-154, 162

C

Central repository 59
CI/CD 1, 23-25, 32
Cloud Computing 1-4, 28-32, 35-38, 41, 43-44, 56-57, 59-64, 72, 77-78, 80-86, 89, 96, 108-112, 114, 123, 126, 145, 149, 162, 164-171, 173-174, 189-190, 192-196, 208-211, 220, 232, 239-240, 243, 245, 259, 261-263, 265
Cloud Security 1-7, 9, 11, 14, 19, 27-28, 30, 34, 37-38, 52-58, 81, 85-86, 88-92, 95-97, 99-103, 105-111, 113-114,
119-126, 164, 173-174, 178-184, 186-189, 191, 194-198, 209
cloud service providers 2, 4-7, 57, 75, 78, 114, 166, 168, 173, 181, 239
cloud services 3, 5-6, 9-10, 16, 23, 39, 41, 51-52, 59-60, 63, 67, 110, 166-167, 169-170, 172, 174, 180, 195-196, 200, 217, 239-241, 262-263
Compliance 2-9, 11-12, 14, 21-23, 27, 66, 100, 106, 121, 123-124, 165, 167, 169-170, 172, 174, 176-188, 196, 199, 201, 204, 206, 240-241
cyber security 47, 57, 109-110, 127-128, 131-133, 141, 143-146, 208, 217, 234, 236
Cyber Threats 35, 71, 85-87, 113, 126, 140, 142, 145, 186-187, 194, 230
Cyberthreats 34-35, 144

D

Data Encryption 6, 15, 21, 26, 49, 84, 123, 174, 197
Data loss prevention 14, 16, 104, 183, 185, 187-188, 194, 198-200, 211
Data Protection and Privacy 122, 124, 165, 180, 237
Data Security 1-2, 8, 14-15, 23, 32, 37, 63, 69, 81, 122, 148, 166, 172, 174, 181, 188, 194-195, 197, 199-201, 210, 212, 226
data sharing 147-148, 150-151, 161-162, 200, 237
Data Storage 8, 26, 60, 63, 67, 75, 83, 164,

166-167, 194, 200, 202
Deep Learning 29-30, 32, 37, 40, 44, 101, 109, 116-118, 126, 137, 139-140, 143, 146, 190, 193, 206, 209, 229, 232, 257
DevSecOps 1, 177, 187-188
Digital Age 31, 113, 164-167, 175, 187, 192, 223-224, 234, 237
Digital Personal Data Protection Act 215, 217, 225, 235
Disaster Recovery 2, 7, 25-28, 32, 64, 67, 72-73, 166, 179
DRaaS 27, 32

E

ethical concerns 102, 165

G

GDPR 8, 14, 21, 32, 100, 106, 108, 124, 180, 188, 225

H

High Security Distribution and Rake Technology 65-66
HIPAA 8, 14, 21, 32, 100, 180, 186, 188, 198

I

IaaS 1-5, 29-30, 32, 41, 89, 167, 240, 261
IaC 1, 24-25, 32
Identity Management 11, 85
IDPS 7, 17, 19, 32, 45-46, 131-132, 134, 137
Information Technology Act 2000 234
Innovation 2-4, 29, 31-32, 35, 79, 164-172, 175-178, 187, 190, 192-193, 198
Internet of Things (IoT) 11, 30, 62, 87, 106, 112, 129, 190-191
Intrusion Detection 7, 17, 19, 32, 45, 47, 52, 54, 91, 94, 131, 135-136, 139, 143-145, 179, 183, 185, 209

L

Linux Box 71-72

M

Machine Learning (ML) 34-35, 55, 85-86, 88, 90, 92, 95, 97, 100, 102, 112-113, 115-116, 124, 126, 134
MFA 6, 12-13, 32, 183, 185, 206-207

N

NACLs 18, 32
Natural Language Processing (NLP) 98, 112, 116, 122
Neural Networks 46, 89, 116-118, 138-139, 143-144, 202

P

PaaS 1-2, 4-5, 29, 32, 41, 168, 240
Parity cloud 67-68
Parity Cloud Service 67-68
passive cyber attacks 147
PCI DSS 8, 14, 21, 32, 181, 188
predictive model 241
Privacy 8, 29, 31, 35, 51, 54, 56, 62, 67, 72, 74-76, 83, 100, 102, 105, 108, 114, 122-124, 126, 149, 163, 165-166, 168, 170, 172, 179-182, 188, 190, 192, 195, 199, 203-204, 213-216, 222-228, 232-238, 240, 258-259, 264
Proxy Re-Encryption (PRE) technique 147, 149

R

RAID 26, 32
RBAC 6, 12-13, 16, 22, 32, 113, 183, 185
Resilience 1, 25, 166, 188, 210, 243, 262
Risk Assessment 120-121, 164-165, 178-179

S

SIEM 19-20, 22, 33, 179, 204
SOC 2 8, 21, 33
SSO 12-13, 33, 183, 185, 188
Surveillance 133, 213-215, 222, 226-233, 235-237

T

Threat Detection 2, 11, 20, 34, 55, 90, 93, 96, 105, 107, 113-115, 125, 132, 136, 142, 187
Threat hunting 107
Threat Intelligence 40, 95, 98-99, 102-104, 121
Threat Landscape 2, 9, 11, 28, 86-87, 90-91, 94, 96, 101, 121, 177, 180, 207
trust 10, 35, 57, 67, 79, 87, 109, 140-141, 147, 150, 161, 164, 174-175, 177, 186-188, 239-243, 245-246, 248, 253, 256-259, 261-265

W

WAF 18, 33

Z

Zero Trust Security 10, 164, 177, 186, 188

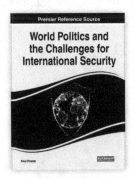

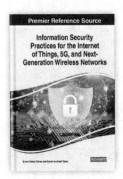
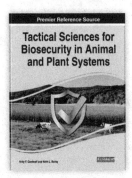

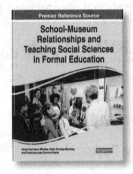
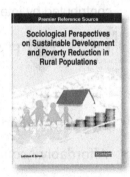

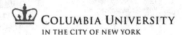

Printed in the United States
by Baker & Taylor Publisher Services

Printed in the United States
by Baker & Taylor Publisher Services